The Look of Things

UNC | COLLEGE OF ARTS AND SCIENCES
Germanic and Slavic Languages and Literatures

From 1949 to 2004, UNC Press and the UNC Department of Germanic & Slavic Languages and Literatures published the UNC Studies in the Germanic Languages and Literatures series. Monographs, anthologies, and critical editions in the series covered an array of topics including medieval and modern literature, theater, linguistics, philology, onomastics, and the history of ideas. Through the generous support of the National Endowment for the Humanities and the Andrew W. Mellon Foundation, books in the series have been reissued in new paperback and open access digital editions. For a complete list of books visit www.uncpress.org.

The Look of Things
Poetry and Vision around 1900

CARSTEN STRATHAUSEN

UNC Studies in the Germanic Languages and Literatures
Number 126

Copyright © 2003

This work is licensed under a Creative Commons CC BY-NC-ND license. To view a copy of the license, visit http://creativecommons.org/licenses.

Suggested citation: Strathausen, Carsten. *The Look of Things: Poetry and Vision around 1900*. Chapel Hill: University of North Carolina Press, 2003. DOI: https://doi.org/10.5149/9780807863237_Strathausen

Library of Congress Cataloging-in-Publication Data

Names: Strathausen, Carsten.
Title: The look of things : poetry and vision around 1900 / by Carsten Strathausen.
Other titles: University of North Carolina studies in the Germanic languages and literatures ; no. 126.
Description: Chapel Hill : University of North Carolina Press, [2003] Series: University of North Carolina Studies in the Germanic Languages and Literatures. | Includes bibliographical references and index.
Identifiers: LCCN 2002152317 | ISBN 978-1-4696-1516-5 (pbk: alk paper) | ISBN 978-1-4696-5845-2 (ebook)
Subjects: German poetry — 20th century — History and criticism. | German poetry — 19th century — History and criticism. | Rilke, Rainer Maria, 1875-1926 — Criticism and interpretation. | Hofmannsthal, Hugo von, 1874-1929 — Criticism and interpretation. | George, Stefan Anton, 1868-1933 — Criticism and interpretation. | Aestheticism (Literature).
Classification: LCC PT551.S77 2003 | DDC 831/.91209 — dc21

To Valerie and Clara

CONTENTS

Acknowledgments *xi*
Introduction *1*

Part I
1. The Speaking Gaze of Modernity *35*
2. Intuition and Language *73*

Excursus
Methods of Reading *107*

Part II
3. Aestheticism, Romanticism, and the Body of Language *137*
4. Hofmannsthal and the Voice of Language *146*
5. Rilke's Stereoscopic Vision *190*
6. Other as Same: The Politics of the George Circle *237*

Notes *275*
Works Cited *297*
Index *311*

ILLUSTRATIONS

1. Title page of the first edition of *Der Teppich des Lebens* by Stefan George, 1900 *15*
2. Editorial commentary on the first edition of *Der Teppich des Lebens* by Stefan George, 1900 *16*
3. Two poems from the first edition of *Der Teppich des Lebens* by Stefan George, 1900 *17*
4. Photo of the train accident at the Gare Montparnasse in Paris in October 1895 *36*
5. Auguste Rodin, *The Gates of Hell*, 1880–1917 *214*
6. Auguste Rodin, *The Gates of Hell*, 1880–1917, detail *215*
7. Paul Cézanne, *Still Life with Curtain and Flowered Pitcher*, ca. 1899 *217*
8. Table of contents of the first publication of the *Blätter für die Kunst*, October 1892 *249*
9. Photograph of Stefan George by Theodor Hilsdorf, ca. 1928 *251*

ACKNOWLEDGMENTS

I am indebted to many of my colleagues and friends who have supported me during the many years that I worked on this project. First and foremost, many thanks to Roger Cook for his congenial support throughout my junior years at the University of Missouri as well as for his good humor and endless patience when working with me on early drafts of this book. Peter Gilgen, Noah Heringman, Brad Prager, and Nancy West all provided detailed and extremely helpful commentaries on single chapters of the manuscript. Bill Kerwin, Karen Piper, and Jeff Williams always gave me good advice and kept my spirits up during the final stages of the project, as did the entire crowd at Teller's (you know who you are!). Ulrich Baer and Neil H. Donahue offered valuable suggestions for revision of the final manuscript. This book would never have seen the light of day without the tireless efforts of Jonathan Hess, series editor for the University of North Carolina Studies in the Germanic Languages and Literatures, who always found the time to answer my questions and helped me along at every stage of the publication process. Adam Gori did an excellent job copyediting the final version of the manuscript, correcting numerous stylistic and syntactical errors. Many thanks also to the various institutions that granted me permission to reprint photos and illustrations, in particular to Ute Oelmann from the Stefan George-Archiv in Stuttgart. Both the University of Missouri Research Board and the Research Council provided financial support for this project. Finally, I want to express my gratitude to Kenneth S. Calhoon. The most inspiring thinker I have known, Ken guided me through my dissertation years at the University of Oregon and helped me to get on track for an academic job. This book is dedicated to my wife, Valerie Kaussen, and our daughter, Clara, with all my love.

THE LOOK OF THINGS

Introduction

> Epistemology is true as long as it recognizes the inadequacy of its own approach and lets itself be propelled forward by the impossibility of the task itself. It becomes untrue by pretending it is successful.
> —Adorno, *Zur Metakritik der Erkenntnistheorie* 33[1]

Question and Answer, or Aesthetics Revisited

This study examines the relationship between poetry, philosophy, and the visual media around 1900. More specifically, it focuses on questions of aesthetic mediation in the poetic works of Hugo von Hofmannsthal, Rainer Maria Rilke, and Stefan George. The question of mediation, of course, is central not only to German Aestheticist poetry, but also to literary scholarship and philosophical inquiries in general, which, as Jean-François Lyotard has recently argued, is characterized by its condemnation of all possible answers in favor of ever new and unanswerable questions.[2] If a question can be answered, Lyotard caricatures the philosophical position, it was either not adequately formulated or merely a technical question, meaning that it should not have been asked at all.

Unlike Lyotard, I am inclined to take the issue more seriously. Since the investigation into the essence of things and the concomitant notion of absolute truth is, by definition, located beyond the dichotomy of question and answer, it follows that a true question cannot be answered, or, put differently: its answer would be superfluous, because it would already be inherent within the question itself. "[I]n philosophy," Theodor W. Adorno remarks, "any authentic question almost always in a certain way includes its answer" (Sondern in Philosophie schließt stets fast die authentische Frage in gewisser Weise ihre Antwort ein) (*Negative Dialektik* 71).[3] Adorno's cautious formulation ("almost," "in a certain way") betrays a critical distance toward the metaphysical history of this kind of thinking, which he sees exemplified in Martin Heidegger's ontology. Yet Heidegger is certainly not its only proponent, as Walter Benjamin's opening remarks in the *Origin of German Tragic Drama* may serve to illustrate. Writing before his serious engagement with and commitment to Marxism, he argues that the unity of truth is "out of" or "beyond all question" (*außer Frage*), as he puts it, since otherwise one would necessarily become trapped in an infinite regress of question and answer: "For if the integral unity in the essence of truth were open to question, then the question would have to be: how far is the answer to the question already given in any conceivable reply which truth might give to questions. And the answer to this question would necessarily provoke the same question again, so that the unity of truth would defy all questioning" (Wäre nämlich die integrale Einheit im Wesen der Wahrheit erfragbar, so müßte die Frage lauten, inwiefern auf sie die Antwort selbst schon gegeben sei in jeder denkbaren Antwort, mit der Wahrheit Fragen entspräche. Und wieder müßte vor der Antwort auf diese Frage die gleiche sich wiederholen, dergestalt, daß die Einheit der Frage jeder Fragestellung entginge) (*Ursprung; Gesammelte Schriften* I/1: 210).[4]

To a certain degree, Benjamin accepts the epistemological dilemma constitutive of philosophical thought, whose eternal quest for primordial meaning cannot succeed lest it were to lose its reason for being, and thus, paradoxically, its proper meaning. An answer found signifies truth lost, which is why Lyotard's mockery of the entire philosophical tradition sells the real issue short. At stake is less the paradoxical (or tautological) nature of human thought, but the question of how to come to terms with it. This problem of presentation (*Darstellung*) is crucial to the history of philosophy, and both its formulation and its aesthetic "solution" take on a peculiar shape in modernist poetry around 1900. *The Look of Things* focuses on precisely this shape in works by Hofmannsthal, Rilke, and George. I realize, of course, that my topic may seem questionable to those readers for whom the poetic search for truth and beauty epitomizes the very ideological perils of bourgeois Aestheticism.[5] Why, indeed, should contemporary scholarship be interested in what traditionally has been dismissed as a decadent and conservative, if not openly reactionary, aesthetic paradigm?

To answer this question, we must recall how recent scholarship has sought to salvage the aesthetic, namely by expanding its traditional scope from the realm of high art to that of popular and mass culture. By means of this shift, the relevance of cultural artifacts could be reasserted without recourse to outmoded and ideologically suspect notions such as authorship, subjectivity, or truth. To the contrary, aesthetic criticism became synonymous with designing a critical apparatus with which to analyze contemporary society and culture as the overdetermined result of economic, political, and ideological factors. One of the earliest and most sophisticated proponents of this approach, Fredric Jameson, argued in 1979 "that we must rethink the opposition high culture/mass culture in such a way that the emphasis on evaluation to which it has traditionally given rise . . . is replaced by a genuinely historical and dialectical approach to these phenomena. Such an approach demands that we read high and mass culture as objectively related and dialectically interdependent phenomena, as twin and inseparable forms of the fission of aesthetic production under capitalism" (*Signatures* 14). Whereas Jameson still argues with reference to particular works of art (films, novels, painting, etc.), the rise of cultural studies during the 1980s and 1990s precipitated the inclusion of everyday phenomena such as sports events, TV shows, and political campaigns into the debate.

While I am sympathetic to this expansion of critical inquiry to the realm of popular culture—a move that bridges the gap between academia and other social institutions and thus enables an overall critique of contemporary Western culture—I also recognize the potential loss of an aesthetic perspective and the insights it yields. For once traditional aesthetic categories are cut off from the specific art-objects and the ideal realm to which they originally referred and instead are projected onto a wide variety of cultural phenomena, they cannot but undergo a crucial transformation that fundamentally alters their analytical value and critical potential. If everything in today's culture can be subjected to a critique that vehemently rejects the very ideal of aesthetic autonomy, then the difference between art and reality, the aesthetic and the sociopolitical realm becomes completely blurred, if not effaced. This loss of distinctions, however, impedes and ultimately disables our inquiry into the various modes of mediation and representation that shape society. Rilke's famous thing-poems are simply not the same as the mundane, everyday objects they describe, but instead enable us to reflect upon and critique the difference between words and things. Art mediates reality, and it is precisely in and through this process of mediation that a social or cultural critique becomes possible at all.

It follows that the current trend toward obliterating the cultural divide between high and low art, or, more drastically, between aesthetics and politics, is highly ambivalent: Empowering and debilitating at the same time, it allows critics to expand their traditionally limited purview and to engage contemporary culture with a clear sense of social responsibility and purpose in mind, while, at the same time, exposing this discourse to the danger of itself falling prey to the very commercialization it seeks to critique (the various fashion trends in today's academic market being only one symptom among many). In order to maintain its analytical potential, the realm of the aesthetic certainly must respond to, yet also remain different from, that of economics, politics, or ethics so as to enable the very possibility of their critique. This is precisely why the later Adorno insisted on the paradoxical definition of the work of art as both autonomous and a *fait social*, meaning that art must be conceptualized as both independent from and contingent upon the social world. Any effort to hypostatize one of the two poles is to lose the crucial tension between them, a loss that literally results in the collapse not only of the aesthetic realm and the very notion of the work of art, but also of the critical discourse that refers to it.[6]

To side with Adorno against academic populism (understood in the sense of discussing popular culture in a vernacular or popular language in order to be received by as large an audience as possible) is not to subscribe uncritically to his mandarin elitism nor is it to endorse his misguided denunciation of jazz and other forms of popular entertainment as the epitome of the culture industry, which are, therefore, unworthy of intellectual criticism. As Andreas Huyssen has argued, Adorno himself was quite aware of the interdependency between modernism and mass culture in spite of the fact that he failed to examine the overall effect and emancipatory potential of this relationship by means of a comprehensive study of popular art.[7] In other words, Adorno's polemics against mass culture should not obscure the fact that his aesthetic theory nonetheless remains pertinent and offers an important venue of critique even in the context of postmodern culture. One of the major achievements of Fredric Jameson is to have continued Adorno's project precisely along these lines. Jameson's incisive analysis of Hollywood blockbuster movies as well as his discussion of postmodern art clearly shows the degree to which these artifacts are significant in their own right and can serve to illuminate the very mode of production they seek to obscure.

The lesson to be learned from Adorno, then, concerns the peculiar kind of personal investment that links literary and cultural critics to the subject matter they scrutinize. I am not referring to the traditional notion that one must like or enjoy art in order to criticize it, but that one must approach art with a particular purpose and interest in mind, namely that of using it as a vantage point from which to gain critical perspective. Whatever the primary focus of the investigation — be it the realm of popular culture or that of high modernist art — the goal of the critic must be to unveil the underlying tension between ideology and its critique, between the utopian promise inherent in art and the frustration it suffers once called upon to realize itself. In Jameson's words, even cultural critics investigating popular art must seek to unveil the "cultural revolution" (*Political Unconscious* 95) that underlies and inadvertently reconfigures capitalist society such that "the works of mass culture cannot be ideological without at one and the same time being implicitly or explicitly Utopian as well" (*Signatures* 29). It is precisely this tension that I propose to reexamine in this study on modernist poetry and its relation to visual perception around 1900.

Hence, the major reason for writing a book on German high literary modernism is not to claim that some aesthetic objects are simply more suited for this kind of critical engagement than others. Although Aestheticist poetry does indeed reflect and comment upon the relationship between art and life, word and world, this metareflexivity is not enough to grant these works some exceptional status, if only for the reason that this view all too easily leads back to the essentializing perspective on art, beauty, and truth that conservative critics have advocated for decades. Nor is it sufficient to argue that the utopian dimension of modernism has become shortchanged and almost forgotten in much of recent scholarship about postmodernity, which I think is true, but hardly constitutes a unique case in cultural history. Yet it is equally obvious that one cannot discuss the contemporary dystopian affect of postmodern culture without reference to and analysis of the modern paradigm it allegedly supersedes, and this conjunction certainly provides some justification for my own revisiting of modernist poetry.

In the end, however, this return to the works of German Aestheticism and their recognition as cultural artifacts still worthy of intellectual analysis cannot be justified outside of my actual engagement with them. This statement implies that critics cannot but invest particular works of art with the power to speak "truthfully" about the world or to facilitate insights that could not be attained otherwise. Without this investment and the belief that there is something out there to be discovered in and through aesthetic discourse, critics are left with only two options: either to return to a simplistic Marxist determinism based on the base-superstructure model or to embrace the postmodern loss of critical distance altogether, which, from the very beginning, undermines any attempt to engage postmodernism or to conceive of viable alternatives to the depthlessness and lack of historicity in contemporary culture. Hence, cultural criticism must retain some notion of "relative autonomy" with reference to the cultural sphere lest it loses the theoretical-methodological ground on which to base its own critique. Regardless of one's evaluative position vis-à-vis the postmodern paradigm, the crucial point is that both advocates and adversaries cannot but reflect upon and thus "objectify" cultural artifacts in order to examine retroactively the contradictory forces that influenced both their own insights and the cultural realm they inhabit. The critical engagement of this necessity is both a distinguishing characteristic of high literary modernism and a central concern of this book.

If the critic needs to account for and recuperate her own subjective investment into cultural objects during the course of her critique, then questions of methodology become primary. Particularly in his earlier work, Jameson reflects productively upon how to bridge the gap between the aesthetic surface (the text or film under investigation) and the underlying "mode of production" he aims to comprehend in all its complexity.[8] For Jameson, this complexity spells out history as such, and the cultural object is crucial in this regard since "history is inaccessible to us except in textual form, or in other words, ... it can be approached only by way of prior (re)textualization" (*Political Unconscious* 82) — which is to say that the work of art is not simply an ideological symptom or the mere effect of the economic base, as orthodox Marxism would have us believe, but has always already reconfigured and thus altered the situation to which it responds. Hence, the subject in question is both the cause and the effect of its own critique. The strength of Jameson's readings lies precisely in his reluctance to dissolve this paradox. Instead, he recognizes it as the only means to gain access to what cannot be referred to or seized otherwise than through the mode of its mediation.

Unlike Jameson's, however, my analysis of German poetry around 1900 is more concerned with exploring this process of mediation than with the discovery of what lurks behind it. Since I discuss my own methodology at length in the excursus entitled "Methods of Reading," suffice it to say here that notions such as aesthetic mediation and self-reflexivity are central to my argument. This, however, is not to endorse the Baudrillardian notion of hyperreality, according to which there is no world behind words and no referent behind signs. One need not deny that books can burn and bodies matter in order to pursue the question of how the turn of the century tried to come to terms with notions such as materiality, truth, or subjectivity in the first place. Instead, what ensues from this shift of emphasis are readings less interested in *judging* high modernism's views on the social function of art — for such judgments are themselves subject to historical change — than in raising *questions* about how and why Aestheticism emerged at that particular point in time and what lessons might be learned from studying its cultural artifacts today. Hence, I want to know what aesthetic strategies German poets mobilized around 1900 in order to resist both the epistemological power of philosophy on the one hand and the increasing cultural appeal of photography and film on the other. Why does Edmund Husserl assume that it is possible to translate the essence of things into the prose of the concept? How are words and things related in his eyes or in those of his contemporaries? And how do these questions of representation shape the pervasive "language-crisis" that allegedly haunted the aesthetic, philosophical, and scientific discourse about subjectivity at the time?

Particularly the last question points to the pivotal role of language in Aestheticist poetry and thus highlights a fundamental methodological dilemma in studies of aesthetic mediation around 1900. For literary criticism *implicitly* relies upon and thus presupposes the very representational function of language modernist poetry *explicitly* sets out to critique. This contradiction is, of course, as vexing as it is ultimately inevitable, but its critical engagement is nonetheless essential for the discursive strategies that sustain high literary modernism. Since philosophical discourse increasingly acknowledged this predicament in the course of its own history, my reading of Aestheticist poetry must come to terms with this history as well. Particularly since the end of the eighteenth century, philosophy began to shift emphasis from ideas to words and thus recognized the constitutive function of language for the question of meaning or truth. For most contemporary thinkers, the "linguistic turn" in modern philosophy was one "for the better," as W. V. Quine argues, for it led to the "abandonment of the goal of a first philosophy prior to natural science" (*Theories and Things* 67). According to Quine, "language is a social art" (*Word and Object* ix) and hence severed from the ideal realm of primordial truth to which it lays claim. There is no transcendental point of view, no position that remains completely unaffected by its object of study or the epistemological framework supporting it. "Truth is immanent, and there is no higher. We must speak from within a theory, albeit any of various" (*Theories and Things* 21f.), Quine concludes.

Using Quine's terminology, one might say that Jameson must speak from within a Marxist theoretical framework insofar as he insists on economics as the ultimately determining instance and asserts that one "does not have to argue the reality of history: necessity . . . does that for us" (*Political Unconscious* 82). Jameson, therefore, conceives of the political perspective "as the absolute horizon of all reading and all interpretation" (*Political Unconscious* 17), and much of today's cultural studies is indeed based on the same premise. The integrity of their and Jameson's analysis notwithstanding, my own study of the *Look of Things* around 1900 relies more strongly on the hermeneutic tradition that spans from Schleiermacher and German Romanticism up to Hans-Georg Gadamer, Martin Heidegger, Giorgio Agamben, and Gianni Vattimo. Indeed, twentieth-century hermeneutics regards language as that which cannot not be presupposed in philosophical or aesthetic discourse and thus insists on the primacy of language much like Jameson insists on the primacy of history for the reading of literary texts. Needless to say, these two notions are not mutually exclusive but rather inform and supplement each other, since history sediments into language, as Adorno argued in response to Heidegger's "Jargon of Authenticity." In the excursus, I discuss the relationship between Adorno and Heidegger at length. Here, I would like to hint briefly at Heidegger's own lifelong "journey toward language" in order to outline the basic premise of the hermeneutic preoccupation with language.

In a lengthy footnote that, in my eyes, represents the dislocated center of his reflections on Heidegger, Jacques Derrida reveals the unquestionable foundation of Heidegger's philosophical inquiry in the affirmative gesture — the "Zusage" — of language. According to Derrida, the fact that "there is" language is "an affirmation anterior to any question and more proper to thought than any question" (*Of Spirit* 131). Which is to say that the "linguistic turn" of philosophy does not necessarily abort the search for the primordial ground of thinking or the thing itself, as Quine suggests. Rather, it simply redefines the playing field of modern thought. In a crucial reversal, the goal now becomes to "make language itself speak," since "the being of language," Heidegger suggests, might also be understood as "the language of being" (Das Wesen der Sprache: Die Sprache des Wesens) (*Unterwegs zur Sprache* 181). Heidegger's word game implies that Being as such is revealed in and through language. The word that lets language speak itself simultaneously voices the essence of Being. Once language finds its proper voice, things will express themselves in their own language since words and things are inextricably intertwined: "The thing itself," the Italian philosopher Giorgio Agamben recently concluded, "is not a thing: it is the very sayability, the very openness at issue in language, which, in language, we always presuppose and forget, perhaps because it is at bottom its own oblivion and abandonment" (*Potentialities* 35).

It is one of the central theses of this book that the philosophical effort to voice the potentiality of language to speak itself is located at the heart of the so-called "language-crisis" and German high literary modernism around 1900. My goal is not simply to demonstrate the imaginative play with language that traditionally has been associated with both Aestheticist poetry and deconstructive criticism, but to reexamine its utopian aspirations as a direct response to particular sociohistorical circumstances. Hence, I critically engage the tradition of the hermeneutic inquiry into language in order to review the linguistic turn in philosophy as it is reflected in and modified by Aestheticist poetry. I argue that modernist poetry both inherits and demolishes the philosophical search for absolute truth. On the one hand, truth is said to reside exclusively within language, while, on the other hand, the realm of language is being expanded to comprise an entire universe of its own. Language no longer merely describes the world, but literally situates it as such. Although this elevation and the concomitant reification of poetic language to the very ground level of Being aims to dehistoricize language, it simultaneously cannot but highlight the epistemological and social crisis it seeks to solve. This dilemma is responsible for the highly ambivalent relationship between art and life around 1900. Aestheticism objectifies language and thus liberates it from its traditional role of representation. Words are being stripped bare of their historical meaning in order to serve as purified building blocks with which to recreate an uncontaminated world and a new reality. This purification, however, can only be achieved in and through a gesture of radical annihilation aimed toward established values and norms, traditional linguistic means of signification, and, ultimately, reality itself, which is regarded as the inferior opposite to art and the nascent world it allegedly carries within.

Given this belief in the evocative power of language, I think it is misleading to refer to a pervasive "language-crisis" around 1900, as I argue in the first part of the book. One of the most popular catchwords in scholarly discussions of German modernism, the "language-crisis" promotes a predominately negative and limited perspective on modernist poetry as inherently decadent or irrational. In order to contextualize and contest this perspective, the first two chapters situate the aestheticization of reality around 1900 in a broader historical and philosophical context. I ask which cultural developments made it plausible or feasible for artists and intellectuals at the time to regard poetry as the privileged medium that determines the look of things. Simply put, I contest that there ever really was a "language-crisis." Instead, there existed a much more profound and universal crisis in perception and representation that affected language as well as the visual media at the time. In support of my claim, I provide a historical survey regarding different philosophical theories of vision and language from the Renaissance to the arrival of film, discussing texts that range from Galileo and Berkeley to Husserl and Bergson. My goal is to trace the two major "scopic regimes" of modernity: the Cartesian model of a disembodied eye, typified in the camera obscura and photography on the one hand, and a physiological model of corporal vision evident in Baroque culture and nineteenth-century modernism on the other.

The conflict between these two paradigms reached its zenith around 1900, meaning that the turn of the century witnessed a clash between the objective and subjective models of vision. This clash led to serious doubts about the accuracy of visual perception and modern science, a doubt that haunted all media and forms of representation at the time. Contrary to language, however, film and photography were able to redeem themselves in the eyes of a mass audience as a cultural novelty seemingly unconcerned with the truthful representation of reality. Language, on the other hand, still appeared to be at the center of the epistemological "crisis," and modernist poetry came to be regarded as the major symptom for the modern dilemma of representation. I want to emphasize, however, that the poetry of Hofmannsthal, Rilke, and George does not simply reflect the period's lost faith in the representational power of language to gain access to either truth or external reality. Rather, language around 1900 ceased to function as a dependable means of signification because it was being charged with the impossible task of unveiling its own essence and the world it carries within. The goal of Aestheticism was to render present the mode of representation itself in order to reveal the secret of life allegedly hidden within or behind linguistic structures — which is to say that the traditional perspective on the "language-crisis" obscures a more positive and constructive vision of modernism's attempt to objectify and reempower language.

Obviously, Aestheticism's idealization of poetry appears problematic and even dangerous given the rise of twentieth-century totalitarianism, which also sought to abolish the tension between art and reality by subjecting the latter to the former. However, the often reductionist comparison of Aestheticism and Nazism overlooks the fact that many of the best poems around 1900 labor to keep that tension intact in spite of their explicit exhortation to the contrary. In other words, there is still something to be learned from this period's (over)investment in the aesthetic, and the widespread belief to the contrary rests upon several interrelated misconceptions about the nature of Aestheticism. Since I have already discussed the problematic aspects of the so-called "language-crisis," let me continue with some clarifying remarks on the *l'art pour l'art* movement around 1900. Scholars' reference to the "autonomy of art" is troublesome not only in the Marxist sense that this concept owes its very existence to the socioeconomic structure it disavows. More important, it often suggests a total disinterest in real life that fundamentally skews the true objectives of many of its advocates. For modernism's strong emphasis on the complex interplay of autonomous aesthetic particles is certainly directed against the existing status quo, but not against social life as such, which, on the contrary, it seeks to rejuvenate. Art is declared autonomous in order to provide an autonomous viewpoint from which to criticize and overcome the alienation in modern society. The goal is not to eternally separate the two, but to allow one to adapt to and ultimately inhabit the utopian space opened by the other.

To acknowledge the underlying sociopolitical aspirations of German Aestheticism is not to disregard its escapist tendencies or its reactionary potential. On the contrary, it means that the eventual failure of high literary modernism to change society can only properly be evaluated on the basis of its utopian claims. Without taking the latter seriously, one is bound to misunderstand the enigmatic self-referentiality of modernist poetry as a mere wordplay or a kind of negative inversion of the Romantic longing for the Absolute. The entire *l'art pour l'art* movement thus appears as the decadent exploration of aesthetic autonomy bereft of the sociopolitical dimension that actually informed it. In the eyes of Aestheticism, however, the investigation of language functions as the prerequisite for a radical critique of modern culture, meaning that the withdrawal from everyday life into the poetic realm of pure language signifies, on a different level, a decisive turn toward the sociopolitical reality it seems to disavow. Language is thus understood both as the symptom of and the remedy for the pervasive sense of social and cultural alienation around 1900.

This leads me to a second point, namely that Aestheticism must not simply be equated with early German Romanticism or German Idealism. As I argue at length in the fourth chapter, Aestheticism is an imploded version of Romanticism. It does not project its aesthetic visions outward into an infinite world of eternal becoming, nor does it seek refuge in the poetic imagination of the reader. Instead, modernist poetry claims to be completely self-authenticating and thus autonomous from all external forces. At the same time, however, Aestheticism cannot entirely free itself from the scientific heritage of the nineteenth century that resists all forms of metaphysical speculation and demands positive proof for everything it sees. In order to legitimate its alleged insights into "life," poetry around 1900 focuses on the materiality of language. It looks upon words as things in their own right. Writing a poem becomes synonymous with building a world, not only in the hermeneutic sense of producing meaning, but also in the material sense of constructing a visual object in space.

Aestheticism's emphasis on both vision and materiality is crucial because it proves that German high literary modernism is not simply opposed to modern science or popular culture, but also shaped by it, which is my third argument. Adorno, for one, astutely recognized this interdependency as the symptom of a pervasive sociohistorical crisis at the beginning of the twentieth century: "Both [modernist art and mass culture] bear the scar of capitalism, both contain elements of change.... Both are torn halves of freedom, to which however, they do not add up" (Beide [moderne Kunst und Massenkultur] tragen die Wundmale des Kapitalismus, beide enthalten Elemente der Veränderung ... beide sind die auseinandergerissenen Hälften der ganzen Freiheit, die doch aus ihnen nicht sich zusammenaddieren läßt) (Adorno, qtd. in Benjamin, *Gesammelte Schriften* I/3: 1003). In spite of their rhetoric, the poetic works of Rilke, Hofmannsthal, and George indeed reflect the various ties connecting high and low art that contemporary scholarship today is so eager to demonstrate. Hofmannsthal, for example, was fascinated by the new medium of film and wrote several film scripts himself, while Rilke took a lively interest in the development of new technologies as well as the fashion trends at the time.[9]

Indeed, Aestheticism acknowledges and visualizes the cultural shift from words to images and the concomitant importance of "seeing" as a form of knowledge in the twentieth century. Poetry around 1900 focuses on the visible *Gestalt* of language as a means to compete aesthetically with the increasing popularity and "reality effect" of photographic images. Modernist poetry self-reflectively celebrates its own words as both transparent signs and material entities, meaning that words and things become inextricably intertwined. This aesthetic self-referentiality accounts for the enigmatic nature of Aestheticism. It asks the reader to accept the visible appearance of mere letters on the page as incontestable evidence for the primordial materiality of language. As a printed medium, poetry cannot but acquire a "face" of its own. In the eyes of Aestheticism, this means that the text functions as a mediator between word and image. It is both something to look at and something that informs and guides our vision. Hence, poetic language around 1900 does more than just describe or picture the physical experience of looking, as is commonly held by secondary critics. Rather, modernist poetry claims to enable a more profound kind of perception that grants intuitive insights into the very texture of the natural world. Aestheticism tries to shape the look of things in and through poetic language.

In the last two chapters, I address the implications of Aestheticism's attempt to merge language and vision in light of more recent discussions regarding the relationship between literary texts and mass media. If language indeed possesses a "face" in the twofold sense of the term as that which sees and is being seen, this also means that language cannot simply be replaced by visual imagery. Put differently, it means that the very opposition between text and image, between literature and the new media is ill conceived because the two are essentially interdependent and presuppose each other. I shall, indeed, argue this thesis throughout the book. At present, however, I would like to redeem my earlier premise that one cannot adequately discuss Aestheticist poetry without engaging it directly by means of a close reading.

Of Circles and Riddles

Let me turn to the introductory poem of Stefan George's collection *Der Teppich des Lebens* (1900) to examine the formal and methodological consequences that result once modernist poetry rejects the "shackles of referentiality," as Rilke put it.

Der Teppich

Hier schlingen menschen mit gewächsen tieren
Sich fremd zum bund umrahmt von seidner franze
Und blaue sicheln weisse sterne zieren
Und queren sie in dem erstarrten tanze.

Und kahle linien ziehn in reich-gestickten
Und teil um teil ist wirr und gegenwendig
Und keiner ahnt das rätsel der verstrickten. .
Da eines abends wird das werk lebendig.

Da regen schauernd sich die toten äste
Die wesen eng von strich und kreis umspannet
Und treten klar vor die geknüpften quäste
Die lösung bringend über die ihr sannet!

Sie ist nach willen nicht: ist nicht für jede
Gewohnte stunde: ist kein schatz der gilde.
Sie wird den vielen nie und nie durch rede
Sie wird den seltnen selten im gebilde.

(*Werke* I: 190)

The Tapestry

Here men are oddly meshed with beasts and plants
Which silken fringes frame to harmonies,
Cerulean crescents in arrested dance
Are scored and trimmed with silver galaxies.

The arabesque is crossed with barren lines,
The single parts are tangled and at strife,

Figure 1. Title page of the first edition of Der Teppich des Lebens *by Stefan George, 1900. Courtesy of the Stefan George-Archiv, Stuttgart.*

And the enigma of the snared remains
Until, one night, the fabric leaps to life.

The patterned boughs begin to stir and veer,
The creatures locked in arc and square come out
Before the knotted tassels, limned and clear,
And bring the answer that dissolves your doubt.

It is not at your beck, is not for each
Accustomed day, and not what guilds could share,

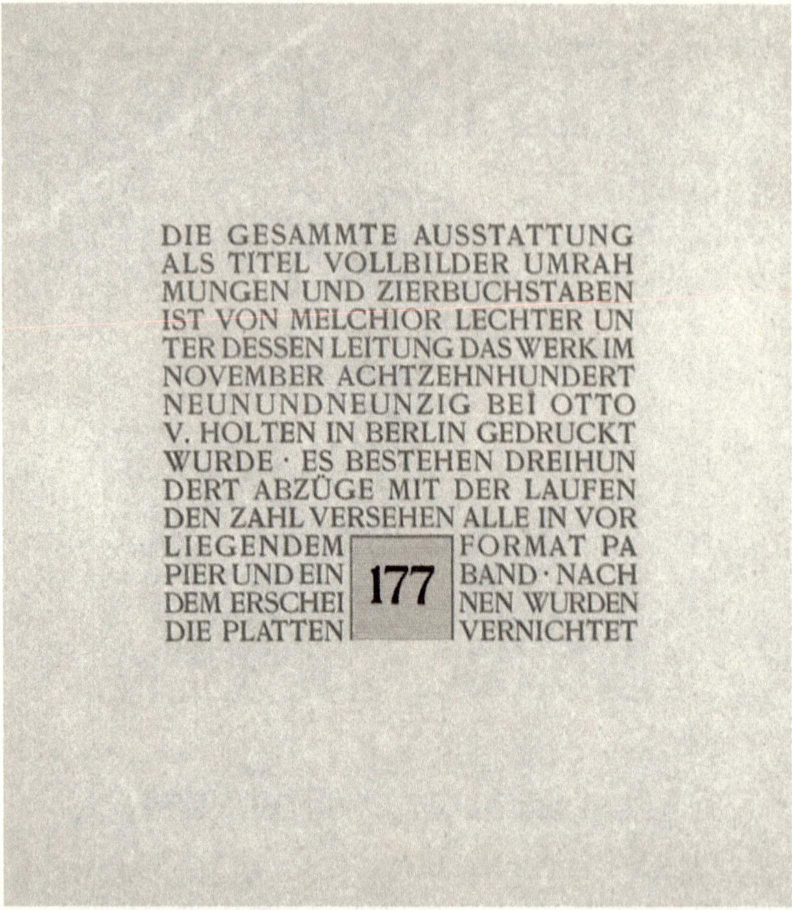

> DIE GESAMMTE AUSSTATTUNG
> ALS TITEL VOLLBILDER UMRAH
> MUNGEN UND ZIERBUCHSTABEN
> IST VON MELCHIOR LECHTER UN
> TER DESSEN LEITUNG DAS WERK IM
> NOVEMBER ACHTZEHNHUNDERT
> NEUNUNDNEUNZIG BEI OTTO
> V. HOLTEN IN BERLIN GEDRUCKT
> WURDE · ES BESTEHEN DREIHUN
> DERT ABZÜGE MIT DER LAUFEN
> DEN ZAHL VERSEHEN ALLE IN VOR
> LIEGENDEM FORMAT PA
> PIER UND EIN **177** BAND · NACH
> DEM ERSCHEI NEN WURDEN
> DIE PLATTEN VERNICHTET

Figure 2. Editorial commentary on the first edition of Der Teppich des Lebens *by Stefan George, 1900. Courtesy of the Stefan George-Archiv, Stuttgart.*

> And never for the many, nor through speech
> It comes incarnate rarely to the rare.
>
> (*The Works of Stefan George* 185)

The self-referentiality of the poem—the interdependency of word and thing, sign and object—is emphasized from its very beginning, for the demonstrative "Hier" refers as much to the verses that follow as to the carpet they describe. Similarly, the "wesen eng von strich und kreis umspannet" are meant to evoke the arabesque patterns of the carpet, yet also allude to the strange

Figure 3. Two poems from the first edition of Der Teppich des Lebens *by Stefan George, 1900. Courtesy of the Stefan George-Archiv, Stuttgart.*

geometrical shapes we have learned to identify as letters and words—literally the q's, d's, b's, and p's in words like "queren," "lebendig," and "gebilde." Etymologically speaking, the word "text" (from the Latin *textus*) refers to the fabric or composition of written language. During the eighteenth century, the arabesque, much like Egyptian hieroglyphs, was itself considered to be a form of writing, a correspondence that further elucidates the self-reflexive structure of George's poem.

The reader is invited to visualize the confusing disarray of the carpet's arabesque patterns in the form of the poem's own language, particularly in light of George's idiosyncratic form of writing, which visualizes and emphasizes the obscure strangeness of written words. The St-G print-type, developed by Melchior Lechter, shows no capitalization except at the beginning of the line, hardly uses any punctuation, and replaces commas with dots at medium height of the line. The innovative *Gestalt* of George's language—its mere appearance in the form of writing—serves to authenticate the actual presence of the object it depicts. Both realms, the surface of the carpet and that of the paper displaying the poem, are intertwined: one cannot become alive or meaningful without the other. The words refer to the carpet, which refers back to the words—a self-contained circle of two complementary beings consumed in the "rigid dance" of presence and absence, nonsense and meaning.

The carpet, however, is "the carpet of life," whose obscure chaos it represents. The being-together of humans, animals, and plants interlaced with the moon and the stars above unites heaven and earth, immanence and transcendence. Heidegger's "Geviert" comes to mind—the interrelated coexistence of mortals and gods, earth and world—as well as Hofmannsthal's life-philosophical insight regarding the interconnectedness of life: "Through us Being weaves its tremendous web" ([D]urch uns hindurch webt das Sein sein ungeheures Gewebe) ("Nachlass," *RA; GW* 3: 379). Hence, the reader must distinguish between three different levels on which the poem operates, the first being the verses themselves, the second the pattern of the carpet they describe, and the last the mysterious realm of life to which the carpet alludes. All three levels are literally and visually presented in the shape of words such that any reference to either of these realms immediately echoes on the others as well. For example, the beginning of the poem emphasizes the strangeness and intricacy of the carpet's pattern, which appears to be both self-absorbed and impenetrable to the gaze of the beholder. The poem mirrors this design by means of a continuous string of words that stretches over the first four lines. Most of these words are not separated by the syntactically required conjunctions and commas, creating an amalgamation of figures and sounds that cannot but evoke the "strange," "rigid," and "convoluted" pattern of the carpet.

A look at the first edition of *Der Teppich des Lebens* from 1900 corroborates this reading. The collection includes three parts with twenty-four poems each, and every poem consists of four stanzas with four verses to each stanza. This rigid and highly regulated structure points to the interconnectedness of the poems themselves and endows them with a kind of material presence. They are not only part of the larger collection, but literally constitute the book as a whole. The poems are the architectural inside, the inner skeleton of an outer shell that is commonly called a book. George's *Teppich des Lebens*, in other words, must be conceived as a living entity. The rich ornamentation and different colors that embellished the first limited edition of only 300 copies was meant to visualize the life both contained within and called forth by the poems (see illustrations).[10] As in medieval manuscripts, George's letters merge with the surrounding space, and his words literally find their place between other objects, such as the two candelabras on the title page, or they form a square whose surface resembles the carpet described in the title poem. George's "work" is alive, but it is also caught or contained within a formal structure that does not allow for actual movement in space.

This aesthetic confinement and its possible transcendence are the central theme of George's "Teppich." The end of the second stanza introduces a sudden change within the "work" understood as both the carpet and the poem. They are said to come alive, and this transformation is presented as an internal movement from intricacy to clarity that "brings the solution that you have sought." Ironically, this line is the most puzzling of the entire poem, since it blatantly contradicts the previous stanza. Not only did "we" not seek an answer, but we are told that literally "nobody" is even aware of there being a riddle to begin with: "Und keiner ahnt das rätsel der verstrickten." It follows that the coming alive of the work must be understood as an autonomous, self-initiating process that retrospectively creates the very riddle to which it provides a solution. It is only after the enlivening of movement (and the movement of life) within the work that we become aware of having pondered an answer to the riddle it allegedly poses. This paradox is constitutive of George's poem. The solution sought by the "you" (i.e., the readers of George's poem and/or the beholder of the carpet) is to unveil the secret of life during the act of reading since the carpet is said to become alive in the very words describing it. The poem, however, much like the arabesque pattern of the carpet, infinitely recoils from such interpretative efforts, which immediately become ensnared in the loop of endless referral from signifier to signified, from words to patterns and patterns to words. And yet, apart from this playfulness, the poem nonetheless triumphantly declares to have given us the solution we sought.

Given this dynamic interplay of revelation and concealment, promise and revocation at work in the poem, readers face a fundamental choice: they can either consider the promise unkept, the circle empty, and the poem mere humbug—there is no solution, there are only words—or they can accept this play itself as the solution sought and found. For the latter is said to materialize in a particular movement of the arabesque, a "stepping out of" and away from the surface within which it had hitherto been arrested. The solution literally steps into being. It is said to take shape in the transition from the "Hier" to the "Da" (Freud's "Fort-Da" comes to mind) that connects the first and the second half of the poem. The "answer we sought" requires this process of distancing to become alive, since it is constituted by the space that both detaches it from and binds it to the object it has left behind. The nature of this space harbors the solution to the riddle of life.

What kind of space is it? Not a geographical space, at least not in the sense that it would become manifest within the structure of the work itself. The formal composition of the poem does not reflect any change whatsoever between the second and the third stanza. Everything remains constant throughout, starting with the four equal stanzas of four lines each, the regular pentameter and the alternating rhyme. The many anaphers and the redundant sentence structures further highlight the formal stasis of the poem from beginning to end. The space in question seems of a temporal nature. It is suddenly "there one evening" and is characterized by a kind of movement that is merely stipulated without being represented at all. It is a literal nonspace, a space simultaneously opened and closed by the repetition of the verses proclaiming it. It does not emerge because of a rupture, but, on the contrary, because of a lack of rupture. It originates in and through the monotony and redundancy of the words following one another, and it is this redundancy that endows the poem with its incantatory quality. The solution is the work of magic. It designates the very moment at which the carpet and the poem acquire a meaning for "us" that cannot be named without immediately being lost. This meaning materializes in a space that is both present and absent, revealed and concealed in the movement of poetic language activated during the process of reading.

Heidegger revered this dynamic process of revelation and concealment as characteristic of the work of art (i.e., his notion of "aletheia" in his lectures on Parmeneides and Heraklit). Indeed, some of his later reflections on language appear to have been written with George's poem in mind, although he never explicitly refers to it. In his essays *On the Way to Language*, for example,

Heidegger refers to the textual "Geflecht" whose movements the thinker has to follow. Stepping into language and guided by it, the poet is able to call forth what otherwise would remain invisible: "What looks like a confused tangle becomes untangled when we see it in the light of the way-making movement, and resolves into the release brought about by the way-making movement disclosed in Saying. That movement delivers Saying to speech.... The way-making of Saying into spoken language is the delivering bond that binds by appropriating. Language, thus delivered into its own freedom, can be concerned solely with itself" (*Way to Language* 131) (Was wie ein wirres Geflecht aussieht, löst sich, aus der Bewëgung erblickt, in das Befreiende, das die in der Sage ereignete Be-wëgung erbringt. Sie entbindet die Sage zum Sprechen.... Die Bewëgung der Sage zur Sprache ist das entbindende Band, das verbindet, indem es er-eignet. Also in ihr eigenes Freies entbunden, kann die Sprache sich einzig um sich selbst bekümmern) (*Unterwegs zur Sprache* 262). Heidegger's reflections on and in language skirt the ineffable threshold separating word and thing. "Saying," for Heidegger, "means: showing, making apparent" (Sagen heißt: Zeigen, Erscheinen lassen) (*UzS* 214); it is a "saying which, in showing, lets beings appear in their 'it is'" (die Sage, die zeigend Seiendes in sein *es ist* erscheinen läßt) (*UzS* 237). Things reveal themselves in and through speech, calling them into the open. Outside of language, there is neither something nor nothing, neither presence nor absence. We literally cannot say what remains outside of language — a tautology, to be sure, but one that emphasizes the circuity of Heidegger's own reflections, which he himself explicitly endorsed. If things step into being and are only within the realm of language (i.e., "Language is the house of Being" [Sprache ist das Haus des Seins] ["Brief" 313]), then thought cannot avoid performing the circular movement outlined above. Since there is no Archimedean point of view outside of language, the issue is not to escape the hermeneutic circle, Heidegger argues in *Sein und Zeit*, but "to enter it adequately and in a meaningful way" (*Sein und Zeit* 153).[11] Once one moves within this circle, however, the apparent chaos of being subsides. Life becomes both sayable and visible and gains a meaning of its own.

Heidegger's journey through language describes philosophically what George asserts poetically: the truth of life cannot be wrested from its constitutive relationship with language and presented as if it were an autonomous, tangible object in the material world. Rather, it remains interwoven with the language from which it emerges. The "solution" gains meaning (i.e., "steps" into being as what it is) only within the movement away from the object toward the word that calls it. This movement is the signifying game of language that also sustains the poem as a whole. The "solution" consists in the existence of discourse: it is but the very words that announce it. The poem keeps its promise of revealing the truth precisely by refusing to speak of anything but the ability of language itself to speak.

"Die Sprache verspricht (sich)," Paul de Man would argue later with reference to Rousseau (*Allegories of Reading* 277), and it is the nature of this promise that constitutes the enigma of art. George's poem claims to become alive because the meaning and being of life is always already inherent in the very language it speaks. The truth about "stepping out" of life's chaos is to step back into language. The poem thus relocates the relationship between linguistic sign and material referent within the interior of the sign itself where it figures as the movement of presence and absence, signifier and signified. Truth (about the carpet, the poem, about life) materializes only after the reader understands that there is no-thing beyond language: "Without the word no thing can be" (Kein Ding sei, wo das Wort gebricht), George ends his famous poem "Ein Wort" from 1928. The reader must finally regard language itself to be the truth both the poem and the carpet promised to reveal. Language is Being, Being is meaning, meaning is language. The circle closes.

The readers of George's poem, however, must determine whether they are in or out. A difficult decision, it may account for the highly polarized debate about the "quality" of modernist poetry now and then. George's poem, for one, does not tolerate any ambiguity on this point since the solution shall forever remain concealed from the many and revealed only to the chosen few — a stipulation that repeats the familiar gesture of inclusion and exclusion constitutive of the George circle. The reader either believes in the promise of art and accepts George as its prophet or she does not. At issue, in other words, is the paradoxical "enigmaticalness" (*Rätselcharakter*) of art (Adorno), that is, the "enigma that art itself is," as Heidegger puts it ("Der Ursprung des Kunstwerkes"; *Holzwege* 67). Art promises a solution it cannot provide yet claims to keep nonetheless by virtue of the promise as such: "Whether the promise is a deception — that constitutes the enigma" (Ob die Verheißung Täuschung ist, das ist das Rätsel), Adorno murmurs (*Ästhetische Theorie* 193), since "to solve the enigma is equal to determining the reason for its insolubility" ([d]as Rätsel lösen ist soviel wie den Grund seiner Unlösbarkeit angeben) (*ÄT* 185). Adorno, of course, endorsed the promise of art only to the degree that it remained conscious of its own unreality, meaning that any attempt to realize the utopian visions of modernism in the empirical world necessarily gives rise to their undoing. With reference to George's "The Carpet," for example, Adorno argued that the aestheticist stance of the George circle as well as George's poetic technique merely served to obfuscate the emptiness of the secret they allegedly harbor. Since "the stated secret itself does not exist" ("George und Hofmannsthal" 199), Adorno ultimately concludes: "The more empty the secret, the more important the stance of its keeper becomes" (Je leerer das Geheimnis, um so mehr bedarf sein Wahrer der Haltung) ("George und Hofmannsthal" 200).

By contrast, I believe that Adorno's own rigid stance concerning the allegedly lacking quality and self-serving nature of German Aestheticism at times forecloses the more balanced and open approach he later outlined in his *Aesthetic Theory*. Adorno's often problematic (mis)readings of Heidegger are the philosophical counterpart to his own difficulties in finding a balanced, that is, appreciative, yet also critical approach to modernist poetry around 1900. The problem is that scholars cannot simply rely upon the already established and seemingly objective terminological apparatus of literary analysis since modernist poetry consciously refuses to be relegated to an object of study in the academic sense. It is based upon the exact opposite premise, namely the enigmatic and infinite potential for meaning inherent in language that can never be fully "grasped" either literally or figuratively. And yet, critics cannot simply relinquish their external perspective and lose themselves in the textual universe, as Heidegger all too often does. Aestheticism's faith in the magical power of language hence gives rise to the crucial methodological question of how best to approach the enigmatic character of these texts, from the inside or the outside of their own hermeneutic "circle"?

The only possible "solution" for this predicament consists in the self-reflexivity of literary criticism envisioned in both Heidegger's and Adorno's approach. At their best, they practice a kind of reading that reflects upon its own technique as a means to respond to the poetic technique it seeks to comprehend. Without this self-reflexivity, the scholarly search for truth necessarily gets lost in a poetic universe that claims to provide the primordial ground for the very notion of truth as such. Therefore, both my theoretical interests and my perspective on poetry are informed by Adorno's and Heidegger's reflections on modern art, and one of the goals of this book is to stage a more productive encounter between the two philosophers than is apparent in most studies. Given my focus on the interpretation of Aestheticist poetry, this encounter will have to take place with reference to their various commentaries on literary texts. Overall, I believe that Adorno tends to be too suspicious and Heidegger too gullible vis-à-vis the poetic ideals of Aestheticism. For the political dimension of modernist poetry resides not exclusively in the works themselves, as both philosophers imply at times, but materializes within the particular cultural practices and ideological frameworks to which they are subjected.

These various contexts within which a work is situated are created and activated in the course of reading, meaning that critics must learn to accept that, to some degree, they inevitably shape the truth they claim to perceive in the text. Literary criticism inheres within reading and unfolds during the process. This ideal of a critical discourse taking shape in and through the process of its application remains the only meaningful approach to providing an adequate critique of high literary modernism. Ultimately, no doubt, it is doomed to fail, but this failure will prove more productive than the apparent success of an "objective" critique. The academic fear of losing critical distance and being seduced by the object of study is itself based upon the scientific (and ideologically suspect) premise that distance alone guarantees a certain sense of objectivity, whereas close contact contaminates the results of the entire investigation. By contrast, I believe this kind of contamination to be inevitable: the critics's own language is always already tainted by the very problem Aestheticism seeks to address, and my primary cause for concern lies in the scholarly call for a method allegedly able to avoid this "affliction" altogether.

This concern was shared by most writers around 1900 who sought to undermine the entire scientific model of question and answer, hypothesis and verification/falsification. Similar to the messianic ideals alive in Benjamin's pre-Marxist texts, truth, by definition, was sensed to be "out of question" (außer Frage) (*Ursprung; GS* I/1: 210) precisely because it was claimed to inhere within the language that asked for it. The excursus of this book will take a closer look at what exactly this means by examining these methodological concerns in the context of the contemporary debate on (post)hermeneutic studies and deconstruction. In short, I argue that the critic must both be seduced by the text and resist it at the same time. To get *at* the text, in other words, is to get *into* the text and then move toward the boundaries that sustain it. Staying with the metaphor of the (hermeneutic) circle, the goal of a successful reading would be to remain neither inside nor outside, but to approach and finally tarry on its perimeter in an effort to investigate the borderline that both separates and unites text and world, meaning and materiality.

Such a reading differs from what is commonly called the deconstructive model in that it regards the material presence of language not simply as a subversive force forever undermining the work of art. Rather, it is constitutive of art in a positive and genuinely *con*-structive rather than *de*-structive sense. Aestheticism projects forth a more positive vision of language than deconstruction or nonhermeneutic methods of reading have given it credit for so far. Similar to George's poem that keeps its promise to solve the riddle of life by providing insights into the reasons why it cannot be solved, Aestheticism in general identifies itself with the gesture of renunciation as a means of finding itself. Although it carries its own undoing within, modernist poetry accepts and builds upon this self-negation as a basis for a new, utopian reconstruction of an aestheticized world. Emphasizing the visual dimension of the "solution" it proclaims, George's poem "The Carpet" is exemplary in this regard: "Sie wird den vielen nie und nie durch rede / Sie wird den seltnen selten im gebilde." The last line specifies the particular kind of language meant to speak and be spoken: it is neither the idle talk of the masses (Heidegger's "Gerede" of the "man") nor the everyday discourse against which the *Blätter für die Kunst* rage. It is, rather, the formed language of a particular aesthetic "discipline" in the twofold meaning of the word, the skillful mastery of the poetic genre. The riddle of life is thus solved in the "Gestalt" of poetry by means of the enigmatic look it bestows upon and reveals within language.

The constructive and critical potential of this Aestheticist stance is as important for cultural modernity as the real danger of it being reabsorbed into the very reification it sought to escape. In saying this, one need not be apologetic for the latent and often manifest collaboration of the George-circle and its members with ultraconservative and totalitarian forces during the first half of the twentieth century. But one also cannot identify high literary modernism solely with its dangerous political implications while ignoring or rendering suspect its utopian promise of liberation. In doing so, critics such as Georg Lukács have divested the aesthetic realm of an inherent ambivalence that founds its credibility and its sense of truth.

The Look of Things

My comparative reading of works by Hofmannsthal, Rilke, and George in the second part of the book literally spells out this ambivalence at work within Aestheticism's peculiar perspective on language. Recognized as the major poets of their time, their work yields insight into the attempt of high literary culture to protect itself against the fundamental social and cultural changes that characterize the period around 1900. If indeed "all neo-Romantic words are last ones," as Adorno claims ("George und Hofmannsthal" 235), one might regard the poetic effort to "speak the things" as the final and most desperate defense of high modernism to use words rather than pictures to render the modern world intelligible and whole. The distinct emphasis on the figurative power of language around 1900 can thus be read both as a concession to and a rejection of the scopic nature of modernity.

The title of this book tries to capture this interdependency of language and vision. The "look of things" is a central theme in German Aestheticism, where it resonates within a complex network of interrelated social and philosophical topics at the time. It not only refers to the—possibly deceptive—visual appearance of external objects, but also evokes the power of everything to look back at us once we have learned to look at it. According to Heidegger, this reciprocal gaze and its relationship to language distinguished the premodern world: "Saying was in itself the allowing to appear of that which the saying ones saw because it had already looked at them" ("Words"; *Way to Language* 139) (Das Sagen war in sich das Erscheinenlassen dessen, was die Sagenden erblickten, weil es sie zuvor schon angeblickt hatte) ("Das Wort"; *Unterwegs zur Sprache* 219). The turn of the century is trying to rediscover this lost language. It struggles to express a way of looking at things that saves them from the mere functionality and use-value to which they have been relegated in the modern era. Rilke's work is exemplary in revitalizing this allegedly lost relationship between vision, language, and the world. For him, the poet must literally "speak" a different vision of life into existence. The ninth Duino elegy emphasizes how all things in life are endowed with a soul of their own—what Rilke elsewhere refers to as a "thing-soul" (*Dingseele*) ("Puppen"; *Werke* VI: 1073)—that becomes alive in the gaze of the beholder, but dies in a "Tun ohne Bild." The latter denounces human negligence as it overlooks the essence of things and thus violates not only their nature, but ours as well.

For Rilke, to see is to be seen in return. All things, common use objects and works of art alike, not only are known to us, but "know us as well," as Rilke states in a letter to a friend (Rilke, *Briefe aus Muzot* 335f.). Things look back at us once we have learned to look at them, enabling a mutual recognition process that gives way to human self-awareness: "denn da ist keine Stelle, / die dich nicht sieht. Du mußt dein Leben ändern" (I: 557). Rilke's famous poem "Archaïscher Torso Apollos" from the *New Poems* is paradigmatic in that it evokes the comprehensive power of a returned gaze rarely engendered, but nonetheless inherent in all things. In his "Erlebnis" (1913), to provide another example, Rilke describes a mythical experience he attributes to the "other side of nature." Once the artist is able to enter this "uninterrupted realm" of pure being, he becomes one with a nature that looks back at him: "A flower that grew next to him and *whose blue gaze* he had known several times before *now touched him* from a more spiritual distance, but with such an impenetrable meaning as if nothing could be hidden anymore" (Eine Vinca, die in seiner Nähe stand, und *deren blauem Blick* er wohl auch sonst zuweilen begegnet war, *berührte ihn* jetzt aus geistigerem Abstand, aber mit so unerschöpflicher Bedeutung, als ob nun nichts mehr zu verbergen sei) ("Erlebnis"; VI: 1037ff.; my emphasis). In the purified realm of poetic perception, the gaze again achieves a tactile quality that physically connects and thus merges subject and object into the "Weltinnenraum." Rilke's oxymoron evokes a form of immanent transcendence or subjective objectivity that posits the identity of nonidentities without, however, eradicating their difference. Rather, these paradoxes are (dis)solved in the reciprocal gaze that not only captures the essence of life, but is life itself:

Siehe, ich lebe. Woraus? Weder Kindheit noch Zukunft
werden weniger. . . . Überzähliges Dasein
entspringt mir im Herzen.

(*Werke* I: 720)

Look, I am alive. How is it done? Neither my childhood
nor my future grows less. . . . More life than I can hold
springs up in my heart.[12]

What survives in Rilke's poetic vision is the eternal fullness of Being summoned forth by a speaking gaze that joins together past and future, subject and object, all within the linguistic parameters of a life well looked at: "Siehe, ich lebe."

Rilke's attempt to engender a different kind of vision that truly captures the look of things is central to modernist poetry and art around 1900. The *New Poems,* for example, reflect the strong influence of Cézanne's paintings, about which critics said "that every brushstroke has its own perspective... its own point of view" (Köhnen 86). Similarly, Rodin's often fragmentary sculptures are usually assembled from a variety of different parts, each representing a distinct point of view—which is to say that art and aesthetics at the turn of the century call upon the reciprocity of the gaze in order to replace the superficiality of scientific knowledge with the deeper truth silently spoken by the things themselves. If "being and the world can only be justified as an aesthetic phenomenon," as Nietzsche claimed in his *Birth of Tragedy* from 1871 ("Die Geburt der Tragödie"; *Werke* I: 40), then the artist's ability to register the look of things is modernity's last hope for cultural renewal. The often evoked myth about the inspirational, divine origin of Rilke's poetic work clearly characterizes him as the embodiment of Nietzsche's ideal artist, the poet, whom he characterized as a subject-less aesthetic force transformed into the "pure, clear eye of the sun" ("Die Geburt der Tragödie" 43).

This metaphor is ubiquitous around 1900 and once again emphasizes the intertwinement of language and vision. Praised as the one who first gave the world the very *Gestalt* it needed to appear, Stefan George is likened by his disciple Wolters to a divine presence whose gaze gives life: the eye of the poet "looks at what appears, yet that which is looked upon actually creates the gaze" (Es schaut das erscheinende an, aber das angeschaute erzeugt erst den Blick. Alles was ist, wurde so als besonderes sein, als Gestalt) (Wolters 145f.). The entire world is said to gain shape in and through this poetic gaze. It is literally contained within George's circle since his poetry is the *Gestalt* of being and his eye is "the only eye of the world" (145). Similarly, Hofmannsthal's early work centers on the power of the poetic *Augenblick* to restore the mythical "pre-existence" of unalienated life characterized by the look of things. His texts, paradoxically, seek to describe "something that looks at us out of all things with an expression beyond all words" ([E]twas das aus den Dingen uns mit Liebesblick anschaut, mit einem Ausdruck über allen Worten) (*RA; GW* III: 387).[13] Life, for Hofmannsthal, must be mastered visually, both in the sense of the physical sensation of seeing images and by expressing them metaphorically in the literary realm: "I am a poet because I experience things visually" (Ich bin ein Dichter, weil ich bildlich erlebe), he claimed ("Nachlass"; *RA* III: 382).

In short, German modernist poetry claims to perceive the voice of a pure and unalienated language still alive within the look of things. Given the importance of this motif throughout the modern era, it is hardly surprising to find the idyllic scenario of the "seen seer" also among the most popular in twentieth-century philosophy. Besides Husserl and Bergson, whose work will be discussed in detail in the second chapter of this book, one might also point to Benjamin, for whom the return of the gaze defines the auratic experience of nature and art: "To perceive the aura of an object we look at means to invest it with the ability to look at us in return" (Die Aura einer Erscheinung erfahren, heißt, sie mit dem Vermögen belehnen, den Blick aufzuschlagen) ("Motifs"; *Illuminations* 188). For Sartre, Lacan, and Merleau-Ponty, the "Other's look" decenters human vision and subverts its inherent power structure: no longer the sole bearer of the look, the subject becomes the object of a gaze that relegates it to the periphery of a visual network it does not control.[14] Heidegger, too, regarded the return of the gaze as indicative of a different kind of being in the world that, like Greek antiquity, still regarded inanimate objects as subjects in their own right, partaking of the spirit of life: "Being looked at by beings, integrated into their openness and thus sustained by it, moved back and forth within his oppositions and distinguished by his own discord: this is the essence of man during the time of the great Greeks" (Vom Seienden angeschaut, in dessen Offenes einbezogen und einbehalten und so von ihm getragen, in seinen Gegensätzen umgetrieben und von seinem Zwiespalt gezeichnet sein: das ist das Wesen des Menschen in der großen griechischen Zeit) ("Die Zeit des Weltbildes"; *Holzwege* 91). For Heidegger, this "discord" (*Zwiespalt* or *Riß*) by no means signifies an alienation among self and world. On the contrary, it structures a harmonious being-together as nonidentical entities commanding each other's presence: "The conflict is not a rift [*Riß*] as a mere cleft is ripped open; rather, it is the intimacy with which opponents belong to each other" (*Poetry* 63) (Der Streit ist kein Riß als das Aufreißen einer bloßen Kluft, sondern der Streit ist die Innigkeit des Sichzugehörens der Streitenden) ("Der Ursprung des Kunstwerkes" 51). Adorno, finally, links the motif back to the enigmatic nature of works of art, which he identifies as their gaze "looking back at the beholder" (*Ästhetische Theorie* 185).

The Look of Things examines the mythical experience of this reciprocal gaze and the story it tells. As a literary topos around 1900, the look of things is a symptom of an unfulfilled longing at the heart of modernity that still seeks to establish an immediate, unalienated, and nonsignifying contact among every-thing in the world. And yet, although evoked as the image of a quasi-mythical sense that transcends language and reveals the primordial bond between subject and object, self and other, the "look of things" bespeaks deception nonetheless. For the double genitive operating underneath has always already undermined the presence of meaning and opened up another scene of signification that, once again, opposes appearance and essence, surface and depth, reality and representation. Aestheticism's central metaphor of visual immediacy immediately deconstructs itself and remains trapped in the prisonhouse of language from which it had hoped to escape.

The best poems at the time, however, reflect that knowledge, too. They lament their inevitable failure to realize their utopian visions, yet simultaneously celebrate this failure as their ultimate success. For it is only by failing to re-present the things themselves that language can provide the primordial ground for their very being. In other words, the magical power of language to call forth the presence of things hinges upon its mimetic weakness and its proper self-destruction. Only a nonfunctional language can function as the basis for the rejuvenation of life. This paradox regarding the relationship of Being and language causes critics to focus on either the negative (Adorno) or the positive (Heidegger) aspects of modernist poetry, when, in fact, both facets are inextricably intertwined. The strength of Aestheticism consists in exploring this paradox, that is, the simultaneity of success and failure, meaning and nonsense inherent in language. In order to authenticate its (lost) insight into things, poetry around 1900 not only focuses on the *Gestalt* of language, but often leaves a tangible imprint of this self-reflective process that materializes in the form of punctuation signs (ellipses, colons, periods, etc.). My readings will show that these signs bear significantly upon the inherent meaning-potential of the poem, without, however, making sense in and of themselves. Rather, they indicate the precise moment at which language "matters" and finds its own means of expression beyond the epistemological divide of signifier and signified, question and answer. To read these signs is to look into the face of language.

Or so it seems—at least if one is willing to be duped by the mere "look of things" instead of examining the discursive strategies that sustain it. Given its practical impossibility, the philosophical and aesthetic efforts to present the embodiment of meaning might be compared to the astounding tricks of professional magicians aiming to convince us of their ability to transform magical language and a gesture of their hand into the fluttering dove it releases. And indeed, around 1900, mysteries abound: all things, you see, have eyes of their own while language is said to speak itself, and signs are identified with material objects, much like cinema's empty screen is somehow believed to magically present the things it depicts. Of course we all know better, but, as Christian Metz points out, the "credulous person is . . . still seated beneath the incredulous one, or in his heart, it is he who continues to believe, who disavows what he knows" (*The Imaginary Signifier* 72). This suspension of disbelief is the operative paradigm of the culture around 1900, epitomized by the anecdote about the credulous spectator witnessing the birth of cinema in 1895 who, nonetheless, had good reasons to remain gullible vis-à-vis the cultural and scientific novelties of the time, as I argue in the following chapter. Yet there are reasons to maintain such a naivete even today, since whoever plainly calls a playful illusion by its name somewhat identifies himself both as an enlightened philistine and a kind of "spoil-sport with whom one does not want to have anything to do," as Hans-Georg Gadamer once phrased it.[15] Indeed, the point is not just to denounce poetic magic by pounding one's fist on the table as a crude means to insist on the indisputable matter of fact. As with all magicians, the pleasure for the spellbound spectator (or reader) lies in witnessing the process as such while trying to figure out how they did it. Such is the goal of this book, a critical look at a time period obsessed with the nature and interdependency of words, images, and things.

PART I

1 The Speaking Gaze of Modernity

> Sometimes, I think what we are lacking is not learned prose,
> but learned poetry.
> —Niklas Luhmann[1]

The Breakthrough of Modern Media

Let me begin with a look. A look, that is, at a particular photograph. Dated October 1895, it depicts an almost intact locomotive that smashed through the glass facade of the Gare Montparnasse in Paris and crashed onto the street below. A rather curious event, the accident prompted headlines in the daily newspaper *Le Figaro*, according to which the train was running at full throttle when it arrived at the station. Unable to activate the brakes, the engineer had jumped from the locomotive, leaving the train to lunge beyond the end of the tracks and onto the street. Eyewitnesses recalled "an unbearable sound, similar to an explosion, which suddenly occurred. Part of the [station's] facade wall was pushed forward and a locomotive, emerging from out of the hole, fell onto the 'Place de Rennes,' in the midst of a crowd of horrified pedestrians," killing one woman instantly (*Le Figaro*, 23 Oct. 1895).

The connection between this accident and the emergence of film becomes obvious if one remembers Lumière's first public presentation of *L'Arrivée d'un train à la Ciotat* only a couple of months later in Paris. Lumière's film, showing a train slowly approaching the camera, is generally regarded as the literal arrival of motion pictures.[2] Rumors have it that during its first showing, the spectators dodged aside for fear of being run over by the train. The accuracy of this anecdote has been subjected to doubt ever since, as the spectator's terror seems inconsistent with both their overall level of education and their familiarity with photography in particular.[3] The relevance of the anecdote, according to most critics, lies in the way it emphasizes the absolute novelty of film aesthetics, particularly the unprecedented power of the cinematic apparatus to represent reality. It also, one might add, speaks to the

Figure 4. Photo of the train accident at the Gare Montparnasse in Paris in October 1895. ND/Roger-Viollet.

often desperate search of historiography to identify the "real" and proper beginning of particular developments, to capture the presence of its original moment of departure.[4]

Nonetheless, the aesthetic rupture caused by the violent "breakthrough" of motion pictures is strikingly exemplified by the actual train accident at the Gare Montparnasse. The latter lends new credibility to the anxious fantasy of the "incredulous spectator," for it proves, in the most literal sense imaginable, that Lumière's vision was far from fictional after all. The "real" locomotive smashing through the facade of Gare Montparnasse — its violent penetration through the flat surface that delineates the interior space to which the train belongs — signifies the violent and disastrous intrusion of aesthetic representation into reality that nineteenth-century bourgeois aesthetics had declared intolerable since it would destroy the educational and cathartic essence of art. The "false" story about the frightened reaction of Lumière's audience somewhat authenticates the physical violence inherent in modern means of representation. Read in conjunction with each other, the "images" of Lumière's train and the wrecked locomotive at Gare Montparnasse are symptomatic of an aesthetic and technological revolution that literally shattered the closed *intérieur* of autonomous art into pieces, burying the "incredulous spectator" underneath the rubble it left behind. "Media define what is real," media theorist Friedrich Kittler claims; "they are always already beyond aesthetics" (*Grammophon, Film, Typewriter* 10).

Kittler's point is aptly illustrated by the fact that most descriptions and information regarding the surreal sight of the accident at Gare Montparnasse were from the very beginning drawn from the photograph rather than the actual scene itself. *Le Figaro,* for example, provided a drawing of the curious sight at Gare Montparnasse, claiming that it was "very exact, because this drawing does not rely on some fashionable inspiration, but is done after a splendid photograph, a true masterpiece" (*Le Figaro,* 24 Oct. 1895). This belief in the authenticity of photography and its "message without a code" (Barthes) again attests to the aforementioned invasion of modern representation into the real. It is also reminiscent of the widespread and publically voiced fear that the former might actually define or even begin to replace the latter. Such anxieties had already dominated nineteenth-century discourse on photography and later echoed throughout the history of film criticism.[5] In 1911, for example, Anton Guilio Bragaglia defined the movie camera as a machine less concerned with the mimesis of visual reality than with its independent production,[6] and Siegfried Kracauer argued in 1927 that the photographic image rearranged fragmented parts of reality into a new whole, thus replacing reality with its own representation.[7]

All of these concerns serve as an important reminder that today's worries about "the liquidation of the real" (Jean Baudrillard) in a fully simulated and hyperreal society are as old as the invention of photography itself. In fact, they are even older than that. The debate concerning the rivalry between representation and reality refers back at least to the printing press and the increasing competition between "book experience" and "world experience," as Hans Blumenberg argues. The Renaissance's attempt to "read the book of nature" already presupposed the successful transformation of things into signs. The latter are seen as the sine qua non for a meaningful experience of being in the world, and the twentieth-century discussion regarding the influence of modern media upon our perception of reality simply revisits the tedious and seemingly endless debate of what it means to represent objects through the use of signs. For every sign, be it iconic, linguistic, symbolic, or other, must supplant the referent and usurp its place. The sign is a fetish. It cannot but disclose the absence of what it claims to render present. Inevitably, the process of signification has always already lost the primordial contact with things it seeks to establish: "*Spricht* die Seele, so spricht, ach, die *Seele* schon nicht mehr," Schiller had already lamented, and Lacan's more recent definition of the real as that which cannot be symbolized merely restates the same issue.

My excuse for recapitulating the basics of semiotic theory lies in the danger of losing sight of them when discussing modernist culture at the turn of the century. Given the proliferation of distinct forms of representation around 1900, critics now and then have been prone to exaggerate the differences between them in a way that neglected their shared ground of signification. For the difference between traditional aesthetics and modern media is not absolute, but refers instead to different "ways of worldmaking," to use Nelson Goodman's terminology. My overall claim is that there has been too much emphasis in recent academic discussion on the domain of the visual over and against the verbal, of the media over and against traditional art. As a consequence, modernist poetry becomes identified with a conventional, culturally obsolete, and, most important, inherently conservative aesthetics vis-à-vis the radically avant-gardist role played by the visual media around

1900. The problem is not to advance these distinctions as such, but to polarize them in such a way that they appear to be factual rather than fictitious, necessary rather than arbitrary.

In order to counterbalance this impression, this chapter emphasizes the discursive foundation that gives rise to the entire debate in the first place. In spite of their "more than real" appearance, the magical power of modern media to "define" reality (Friedrich Kittler) remains precisely that: an arbitrary definition dependent upon the discourse network that determines the epistemological parameters of what we are able or willing to see. The field of the visible is not simply given as such, but subject to profound changes depending upon a variety of interrelated sociopolitical, economic, and cultural forces. The history of film and media criticism—what has aptly been called "cinema's third machine" (Sabine Hake)—reveals the degree to which every time period literally writes its own theory of the modern media. Trying to understand film, early discourse on film in the 1910s and 1920s shaped the meaning of the moving pictures it claimed merely to describe: "[T]heorists analyzed the mechanisms by which film was constituted as a cultural and artistic practice and, on the basis of its formal characteristics, tried to articulate the relationship between narrative, representation, and visual pleasure," claims Hake (Hake x). If the combined pictures of Lumière's train and the fateful accident at Gare Montparnasse can be said to illustrate the destruction of traditional bourgeois art, they are assigned this meaning primarily through the plethora of metaphorical descriptions portraying both train and cinema as icons of the technological and scientific achievements of the nineteenth century.[8] Both have been invented and circumscribed within this discursive field of modernity. Indeed, the breakthrough of film remains one of the favorite metaphors of twentieth-century art and aesthetic theory, from Kurt Pinthus and René Margritte to Walter Benjamin, Theodor W. Adorno, and beyond.[9]

This chapter presents an overview of the history of modern perception in order to situate the media competition around 1900 within a broader context regarding the "nature" of linguistic representation and its relation to the visual. My overall goal is to put into perspective Kittler's stark and one-sided juxtaposition of traditional aesthetics and modern media. I want to begin with a brief look at the famous "Kino-Debatte" between 1909 and 1929. As Anton Kaes has shown, the early discussion about the rise and status of cinema as art entailed a series of ideological distinctions such as high (elitist) versus low (popular) art or the emancipatory versus the impoverishing power of aesthetic experience. Much of the polemics surrounding these distinctions, however, was driven by particular socioeconomic interests completely unrelated to aesthetic concerns. Given its broad popular appeal, cinema not only threatened to undermine the traditional distinction between art and entertainment, which was still of crucial importance to the bourgeois middle class in order to uphold its own self-image of refined taste and higher education. More important, film threatened to expose the economic basis of all art, including literature: "Cinema functioned as a kind of catalyst in the quarrel about the commodification of art" (Kaes, "Kino-Debatte" 13; my translation). Cinema laid to rest the bourgeois notion of autonomous art not primarily in an aesthetic sense, but in an economic one. Although the two aspects cannot easily be disentangled, one should be mindful of the often biased and self-interested perspective of many cultural critics and writers lamenting the demise of language around 1900. Exploiting bourgeois anxieties and raising the specter of a brainless and illiterate world of images, their comments also served the function to increase public awareness about the economic plight of writers.

In this sense, the popular sentiment of the famous "language-crisis" around 1900 is the "product" of a much broader cultural shift from word to image that upset the social status quo and threatened the livelihood of those dealing in words, so to speak. At the same time, it testifies to the social ambitions of others trying to break free from previous market constraints by embracing mass culture. At the turn of the century, reference to the "language-crisis" is both fashionable and lucrative, and this is one of the reasons why it ought to be applied prudently. Indeed, I regard the term itself as a misnomer. It promotes a predominately negative and limited perspective on modernist literature and implies that there was a crisis with regard to language, but not with regard to the media, a crisis in the arts, but not in the sciences. That view, however, fundamentally distorts the picture. For neither is the crisis of language unique for this particular time period (the history of philosophy particularly after the eighteenth century testifies to that, and Romantic poetry already objectifies language and thus prefigures a "language-crisis"), nor does the crisis around 1900 apply exclusively to language. On the contrary, the entire nineteenth century was haunted by an overall ambiguity of "meaning," since positivism had to come to terms with the self-contradictory tendencies of empirical research. The "language-crisis" must not be seen as the cause of this epistemological dilemma, but merely represents one of its many symptoms.

In support of this claim, the remainder of this chapter will focus on nineteenth-century science and philosophy and advance two interrelated theses. First, I argue that the epistemological distinction between vision and language became increasingly unstable since physiological research during the nineteenth century proved the arbitrary nature of perception and its interdependency with language. From a scientific perspective, there was absolutely no reason to trust images any more than words. My second argument contends that the ensuing need to interpret every-thing affected all means of representation, including the modern media. Film "defines" reality, to be sure, yet one must keep in mind that this reality itself had become too fragmented to make immediate sense of anymore, and this is why it was in need of a definition in the first place. At the turn of the century, the question of what exactly constitutes reality had become a matter of debate, because all things were seen in a constant state of flux. Film certainly was the most adequate aesthetic expression of this phenomenon, but this does not mean that the medium remained unaffected by the profound ambiguities at the heart of modernity. Cinema is symptomatic of a real crisis of representation for which it can only offer an imaginary solution in the form of projected images on the screen.

By contrast, Kittler's rigid distinction between traditional aesthetics and modern media not only presupposes a stable frame of reference that had ceased to exist or had become dissolved within what Henri Bergson called the "élan vital" of life itself. Kittler also prioritizes a particular cultural divide during a time period that increasingly undermined and questioned such categorical distinctions. And finally, he regards the rise of modern media as more or less responsible for the pervasive epistemological crisis around 1900, and this leads him to exaggerate their influence upon art and science alike. For Kittler, modern technology and media are primary for the development of cultural modernity, whereas I would claim they are enveloped in a dialectical process in which they function simultaneously as both symptoms and causes. The media are constitutive of and constituted by the modern industrialization of space and time, at the center of which looms the dilemma regarding the nature of reality and representation around 1900 that affects language as well as other media. The latter, however, were able to redeem themselves in the eyes of mass audiences as a cultural novelty whereas language was not. Intellectuals at the time simply singled out and focused on language as the center of the crisis because it had fallen prey to its own philosophical history and its entanglement with objective knowledge. Throughout the modern era, it had helped to voice promises it was unable to keep, meaning that a broad epistemological crisis was immediately reconfigured and understood as a "language-crisis."

And indeed, once faced with the media's spectacular power of mimetic representation, modernist poetry seemed outdated and hence prompted to question its own right to exist. However, if one situates the deliberate self-referentiality of modernist poetry within the larger context of the self-destructive tendencies haunting nineteenth-century positivism, the traditional emphasis of the nihilistic, "corpse"-like (Barthes, *Writing Degree Zero* 5ff.), "negative" (Eric B. Williams 72, 77), and "decadent" (Wolfdietrich Rasch) nature of high modernism must be reevaluated. The media competition also had an emancipatory effect on modernism since it helped liberate poetry from the "shackles of representation," as Rilke put it. Which is to say that those who took an earnest interest in the "crisis" of language apart from its popularized appeal and seriously began investigating the nature of verbal representation were soon to focus on its constructive potential. For the "language-crisis" allowed literary modernism to explore the materiality of language and its constitutive role for the visual presentation of things. Aestheticism, in other words, is not any more "negative" or "decadent" than German Romanticism, and the actual difference — up and beyond such catchwords — between these two periods will be discussed at length in the third chapter.

The Art of Reading the Book of Nature

The search for a reliable foundation on which to ground objective knowledge characterizes the modern era since the Renaissance. Once the hierarchically ordered structure of medieval society had broken down and been replaced by humanist ideals, the overall goal became to establish an original worldview based not on antiquated tradition and scholastic arguments, but on individual studies and self-guided reason. This new perspective focused on the scientific ideal of the immediate observation of nature. Looking at things themselves rather than examining and comparing antiquated scriptures, Galileo, the founder of modern physics, is able to read the universe like the medieval scholar studied an old manuscript, for "this grand book, the universe, . . . is written in the language of mathematics, and its characters are triangles, circles, and other geometric figures without which it is humanly impossible to understand a single word of it; without these, one wanders in a dark labyrinth" (Galileo 328).

Galileo's idealized concept of reading remains operative throughout the history of modern science and philosophy. According to Hans Blumenberg, the metaphor of the "book of nature" was alien to Greek philosophy and gained currency only in the sociohistorical context of a popular reaction against the medieval emphasis on sacred scriptures. As the increasingly influential, yet illiterate class of urban laymen sought to gain access to divine truths, they were forced to look beyond the universe of written texts and turn toward nature instead. This search for a total coincidence between meaning and matter both inspires and haunts modern science. On the one hand, it allowed thinkers to presuppose and identify the presence of meaning as always already given within nature itself. Renaissance scholars, for example, turned toward hieroglyphs and emblematic forms of writing in the vain hope to find traces of a historical "thing-writing" encrypted therein (Assmann 242), and much of nineteenth-century empiricism was built upon the same premise.

On the other hand, however, truth proper remained forever out of reach since it inevitably got caught in the web of signification surrounding it. In spite of the seemingly egalitarian nature of the new Galilean perspective on things, the book of nature "cannot be read by everyone," Blumenberg contends (77), since the "emerging science of the modern age has its own rhetoric" (Blumenberg 68). Whatever sign system is believed to hold the secrets of nature, be it mathematical symbols or philosophical concepts, the observer still needed to be initiated into the art of reading before he was able to truly "see" anything at all. Moreover, although Galileo's general goal was to decipher the code of nature solely on the basis of simple observation, there always remained the necessity to translate one's insights into some kind of language in order to authenticate the result. This need to translate or represent truth continuously threatened to expose the contingency of all scientific knowledge. The problem is that truth is held to be self-evident when in fact it only emerges within a particular context or a specific frame of reference. Although the scientific objective insists on the paragon of things making themselves known in their own language, this can only be revealed through the various structures of representation that undermine it.

Throughout the rise of modern science, this dilemma was simply "solved" by presupposing the possibility of merging vision and language into a harmonious, self-effacing system of signification. Modernity, in other words, is predicated upon the ideal notion of a "speaking gaze" able to read the book of nature. The term is Foucault's. In his discussion of medical perception around 1800, he introduces the scientific ideal of a speaking gaze as the central premise in clinical discourse during the age of empiricism. This gaze, Foucault maintains, is full of language, a true, unalienated language not its own, but spoken by the object it perceives. In the empiricist's view, matter carries its own language within. The clinical eye not only sees the object, but also reads it, lighting up its essence: "The paradoxical ability to *hear a language* as soon as it *perceives a spectacle*" (*Birth of the Clinic* 108) allows the medical gaze around 1800 to bring to light "the syntax of the language spoken by things themselves in an original silence" (*Birth* 109).

According to Foucault, the notion of the speaking gaze represented "no more than a brief period of euphoria" around 1800 (*Birth* 117). By contrast, this chapter argues that the ideal of a total equilibrium between vision and language remains operative throughout the modern history of scientific and philosophical discourse. This is not to deny some epistemological changes or "breaks," such as Foucault himself diagnosed in his other writings. But these ruptures do not fundamentally alter the modern belief in a self-evident truth written into the heart of matter. The historical changes concern less this ideal itself than the ways in which it is being discussed, acknowledged, or disavowed in scientific discourse.

Foucault's own analysis of the speaking gaze around 1800 provides a case in point. He argues that the clinical gaze marks the transition from a purely rational to an empirical science, or, to use Foucault's terminology, from the classical to the modern episteme. Whereas the former had primarily been interested in the geometrical distribution of all objects in space, the latter attempts to simply read the visible structure of an individual object. Nonetheless, the central task of positivist research still lies in determining the universal syntax of a scientific discourse whose authenticity is beyond question. Although the nature of this discourse has changed, its actual goal has not. For Galileo or Descartes, the "natural" language promising objective insights was mathematics and geometry. For nineteenth-century scholars, however, this natural language had become identified with an ideal or pure language underlying everyday speech. According to this view, one is able to express the inherent truth of things not because God has written the grandiose book of nature—for we forever fail to comprehend His language—but because the absolute grammar informing everyday speech guarantees meaning, if only we are "initiated into true speech" and learn to understand its constitutive syntax. As Foucault put it: "One now sees the visible only because one knows the language; things are offered to him who has penetrated the closed world of words, and if these words communicate with things, it is because they obey a rule that is intrinsic to their grammar" (*Birth* 115). For nineteenth-century positivism, this initiation into a pure, nonrhetorical language seems possible, and with it "a moment of balance between speech and spectacle. A precarious balance, for it rests on a formidable postulate: that all that is *visible* is *expressible*, and that it is *wholly visible* because it is *wholly expressible*" (*Birth* 115).

This idealized balance between language and vision is constitutive of the modern project at large and moves into the center of philosophical and aesthetic discourse around 1900. Foucault's metaphor of the "speaking gaze" conjuring the nonmetaphorical realm of language and being—of being *as* language—is echoed, for example, in Husserl's poignant summary of the phenomenological enterprise, according to which "the entire art consists in letting the seeing eye speak" (*Idee der Phänomenologie* 62). This similarity is hardly surprising, given that the Western tradition has continuously regarded visual perception as the privileged means of access to the real world. Sight provides a bridge between the interior realm of the mind and the exterior realm of matter: to see is to know. However, since theories regarding the "nature" of vision and its relationship to knowledge must be analyzed via the linguistic structure of their interrelating discourses, the history of vision is intertwined with that of language. Discourse defines vision, and words construct images. "Perception does not exist," Derrida provocatively states in his discussion of Husserl (Derrida, *Speech and Phenomena* 45). This is not to deny that visual perception really takes place and that we actually "see" images, but to insist that any attempt to simply say what we see inevitably becomes entangled in the arduous process of translating data from one medium to the other, from vision to language.

Of course it remains legitimate to distinguish between different kinds of representation, for example words and images, and to elaborate upon the intrinsic characteristics of each. According to Lessing's *Laokoon*, for example, language operates in time through the trail of signification. It defers meaning. The image, by contrast, is bound to space and identifies meaning, renders it present momentarily. However, although Lessing's perspective regarding the classical opposition between word and image seems self-evident, his observations are nonetheless based upon a comprehensive set of unquestioned norms and idealized concepts, as W. J. T. Mitchell has demonstrated.[10] Most art historians today agree about the essentially mixed "nature" of media, arguing that there is not and never was a "pure" form of representation. Perception, and vision in particular, has a history that must be studied by reference to the various discourses constituting it, as Benjamin, Foucault, Merleau-Ponty, and others have done—which is to say that "sight cannot be divorced from the discourses that we use to interpret both what and how we have seen," as another critic phrases it (Burnett 31). The nineteenth-century belief in the "innocent eye" is based on a "myth" since "seeing is never just registering" (Gombrich 116, 298), the art historian E. H. Gombrich contends. Instead, seeing requires the active interpretation and reshaping of raw information into a coherent image. Critics' references to the "nature" of words or images are either convenient labels for the highly complex nexus existing between them or are indicative of certain value judgments (such as mass vs. elitist culture) informing the entire discussion as such. Given the normative basis of any attempt to discover the nature of perception, it is hardly surprising to find huge discrepancies with regard to how different epochs and individual artists conceptualized and evaluated the word-image relationship. As W. J. T. Mitchell points out, the scale ranges from the naive equation of iconic forms of representation with reality itself all the way to denouncing images precisely for their attempted imitation of a reality they necessarily fail to apprehend. The discrepancy between these views attests to the seemingly trivial insight that neither images nor words ever measure up to the real thing each signifies, and that language and vision cannot entirely be separated from each other.

This is to say that the basic problem of "media transposition," which according to Kittler specifically characterizes the discourse network around 1900 (*Discourse Networks* 265), is central to the ocularcentrism of Western philosophy in general. The overall goal throughout was to sustain the integrity of visual perception within language, to communicate the natural clarity of images via the artificial blurriness of words, while at the same time trying not to lose touch with the immediate sensual experience that was said to distinguish vision. And yet there always remained an irreducible linguistic element that undermined the seemingly truthful account of vision. As David Michael Levin put it, "[T]he accounts of vision that figure in philosophical discourse more often than not seem to be not so much faithful phenomenological descriptions or objectively accurate empirical descriptions but, rather, ideal models with a distinctively normative rhetorical function" (*Sites of Vision* 8). In philosophical discourse on sensory perception, language thus emerges as both the enabler and inhibitor of visual truth. On the one hand, it literally allows us to come to terms with intuitive insights that otherwise would remain ineffable and essentially foreign to those who do not experience them. Yet, on the other hand, it is also responsible for the distortion and falsification of vision, whose sensual immediacy gets lost within the symbolic universe of arbitrary signs. Vision, properly speaking, takes place neither within the text nor outside of it. Perceptual intuition is born and dies in discourse, and the truth about vision comes alive only within the very language that ostracizes it.

And yet, modern philosophical and scientific writings on perception desperately seek to reconcile both poles, trying to capture sight in and through language and to (ad)dress their insights in a word. The philosophical and scientific dream of a "speaking gaze" conjures a language that does not signify, but coincides with the things themselves. It envisions an authentic moment that captures meaning beyond the flow of time without succumbing to a mere illustration of the world as it appears to be. More than an image, yet less than a word, the speaking gaze lives in that impossible space in between—Rilke's "Zwischenräume der Zeit"—where immediate knowledge and instantaneous meaning is imagined to materialize in the form of a purified sign unbound by the laws of signification. The ideal itself seems caught in a "dialectics at a standstill," one might say, a metaphor that, for Walter Benjamin, defines the nature of "true images" inherent in language ("Passagenwerk"; *Gesammelte Schriften* V/1: 577; N 2a, 3). It is crucial to remember that the "dialectical image," for Benjamin, does not refer to actual pictures (i.e., painting, photography, film), but is meant entirely metaphorically: "Only dialectical images are true (i.e., not archaic) images; and the place, where one encounters them, is language" (Nur dialektische Bilder sind echte [d.h.: nicht archaische] Bilder; und der Ort, an dem man sie antrifft, ist die Sprache) (*GS* V/1: 577; N 2a, 3). Benjamin's idiosyncratic version of the speaking gaze able to "express the linguistic essence of things" ("Sprache"; GS II/1: 142) would expose, in the flash of a moment, the commodification and reification at the heart of capitalist society and open a gateway toward a different, more authentic world buried underneath.

In short, the speaking gaze of modernity does not translate vision into language, but identifies one in and through the other. As such, it epitomizes the ultimate goal of hermeneutics because it signifies a kind of epiphany that transcends the realm of signification. However, since the speaking gaze defines an ideal art of reading that cannot be redeemed in any particular instance, this discrepancy will sooner or later have to be addressed and somehow "solved" if the ideal itself is to be sustained. This is exactly what happens during the course of the nineteenth century, which increasingly acknowledged and tried to account for the interdependency of language and vision. The rise of physiological research and experimental studies began to ascertain the complexity of our visual apparatus. Scientists discovered that what we see is both predetermined by our biological makeup and informed by culturally acquired codes that are, at least to some degree, arbitrary. Once the subjective dimension of visual perception had become recognized, it was no longer possible to believe in the objective, pregiven congruence of matter and meaning written into the book of nature since empirical observation might disclose the world not as it is, but as it appears to us given our physiological and cultural limitations. The newly discovered facts about vision thus necessitated new models of explanation. However, I argue that these explanations, too, remained caught in the same aporias that prompted them, and that much of nineteenth-century scientific discourse both inherits and perpetuates modernity's dilemma regarding the allegedly ideal nature of visual perception.

Nineteenth-Century Theories of Vision

Martin Jay has argued that the modern era from its very beginning was characterized by a variety of competing "scopic regimes." The most influential among these were the normative model of monocular perspectivalism discovered during the Renaissance and typified by the camera obscura and its modern successor in the form of photography on the one hand, and the Baroque prototype of modernism that first emphasized the corporal and erratic nature of vision on the other hand. During the Renaissance and the age of rationalism, the former clearly triumphed over the latter in the realms of science, philosophy, and art. With the rise of British empiricism in the eighteenth century, however, the conflict between the objective and subjective model of vision became ever more pronounced. British philosophers opened up an epistemological gap between the perceiving subject and the perceived world of objects. Given the subjective foundation of scientific observation, the very notion of objective knowledge represented "an immense puzzle" for the eighteenth century, as Edmund Husserl contends (*Krisis* 91): "What a paradox! Nothing could cripple the peculiar force of the rapidly growing and, in their own accomplishments, unassailable exact sciences or the belief in their truth. And yet, as soon as one took into account that they are the accomplishments of the consciousness of knowing subjects, their self-evidence and clarity were transformed into incomprehensible absurdity" (*Krisis* 92).[11]

The disembodied eye of consciousness favored by Descartes increasingly had to come to terms with the subjective and physiological constraints that literally shaped the visual field of the human eye. In fact, recent critics have pointed out that this conflict is already latent in Descartes's own treatise on optics and visual perception.[12] The rise of positivism finally brings about a full-blown perceptual crisis that affects science, culture, and philosophy alike. The gap between the normative ideal of disembodied vision and the multitude of subjective viewpoints emanating from the human body cannot be bridged anymore. The end of the nineteenth century witnessed the culmination of the smoldering conflict between the two basic, yet opposed, models of vision developed in the modern era: one objective and the guarantor of scientific truth, the other subjective and untrustworthy.

Obviously, the debate about the subjective versus the objective understanding of vision stands in close proximity to the Kantian dilemma regarding the a priori categories of the human mind. Contrary to Kant, however, the nineteenth-century discussion is no longer confined to the realm of speculative metaphysics, but takes place in the context of modern science. Most of the advocators of visual subjectivism were scientists who relied on empirical facts rather than philosophical arguments. Yet, ironically, their own research helped to undermine the very ideal of an objective understanding of the world they sought to uphold. A primary example for the self-destructive tendencies of empiricism are the psychological studies of human attention undertaken by Wilhelm Wundt in the 1870s and 1880s. According to Jonathan Crary, Wundt was able to prove that the attentive observation of an object resulted from the simultaneous repression of other stimuli that might distract the mind—which is to say that "[a]ttention always contained within itself the condition for its own disintegration.... Attention and distraction were not two essentially different states but existed on a single continuum" (Crary, "Unbinding Vision" 50f.). If attention was not simply a preestablished norm structuring human consciousness, but instead was constituted upon an arbitrary process governed by "an indeterminate set of variables" (Crary, "Unbinding Vision" 51), it follows that the positivist notion of a "speaking gaze" reading the essence of things is exposed as an idealist construction at odds with the facts of vision. To perceive the world in a certain way simply means to focus attention on particular characteristics while excluding others. Any attempt to see things for what they are is subject to their active reconstruction by the attentive observer. Empiricism thus undermined its own premise regarding the ability to observe and analyze objectively the material world beyond the realm of human consciousness.

Once physiological research had scientifically proven the subjectivity of human feelings and the unreliability of our senses, it became increasingly difficult to suture the positivist worldview in the face of these facts. Following the groundbreaking work of Johannes Müller, Hermann von Helmholtz, to cite another example, was able to prove that the content of human perception is independent from its external cause. According to Helmholtz, the human eye functions like a camera obscura, except that we perceive visual images regardless of the specific nature of the stimulus that affects the eye, be it light from the outside or physical pressure exerted on the eyeball with a finger. Rather, the nerves connected to the visual apparatus necessarily and without fail relate any external input in terms of visual images: "Physiological studies now teach that the more fundamental differences [among the senses] are completely independent of the kind of external agent by which the sensations are excited," Helmholtz argued ("The Facts of Perception" 370).

This, in turn, meant that the same external stimulus produces different sensations on our body: the same light rays that our eyes perceive as visual images are experienced as heat once they hit the surface of our skin, simply because the affected nerves are programmed to translate or interpret these stimuli according to the laws of the organ to which they are connected. It follows that there are no immediate or motivated connections between outside reality and internal sensation. Helmholtz emphasized that we cannot deduce from the content of our perceptions the specific nature of the external stimuli that caused the sensation to appear. Rather, these connections are arbitrary and have to be learned or established through experience alone because our perceptions function as mere signs and not as mimetic images of the outside world. There is, however, according to Helmholtz, a correlation between the structures of the real world and the internal processes governing our perceptual apparatus, a kind of parallel that allows us to formulate concepts or laws of human perceptions linked to the outside: "The excitations of the nerves in the brain and the ideas in our consciousness can be considered images of processes in the external world insofar as the former parallel the latter, that is, insofar as they represent the similarity of objects by a similarity of signs and thus represent a lawful order by a lawful order" ("Recent Progress" 186). In other words, while there is no inherent connection between single elements of the external and internal world, there is a parallel between the structural makeup and the internal laws governing both systems: "If the same kinds of things in the world of experience are indicated by the same signs, then the lawful succession of equal effects from equal causes will be related to a similar regular succession in the realm of our sensations" ("Facts" 372).

This structural parallel is the sine qua non of visual perception. According to Helmholtz, it allows us to make meaningful inferences from one system to the other, which in turn gives rise to the laws governing either: "What we can attain ... is knowledge of lawful order in the realm of reality, since this can actually be presented in the sign system of our sense impressions" ("Facts" 388). Helmholtz thus explicitly refuted the "nativistic" theory of perception in favor of his own "empirical" theory. Whereas the former stipulates a direct correspondence between each sign and its referent, the latter relocates this correspondence on a purely structural level such that changes in the external world give rise to different perceptions within. "Learning to see" hence means to create a consistent system of signs that interprets incoming stimuli according to certain empirical laws that enable us to infer hypotheses about the external world. These beliefs in turn are subject to empirical verification or falsification through physical action or moving about in space.

The one philosopher whom Helmholtz hardly ever fails to mention in his essays on visual perception is Kant, in particular his *Critique of Pure Reason* and its reflections on the transcendental status of time and space. Helmholtz agrees with Kant in regarding space as an a priori form of intuition. By force of the analogy that he draws in his own theory between internal sign system and outside world, Helmholtz is forced to recognize the law of causality as "a transcendental law, a law which is given a priori" ("Facts" 390), for, "if we give it up, we give up all claim to be able to think about these or any other matters" ("Facts" 405). Contrary to Kant, however, Helmholtz regards the axioms or geometrical laws that structure space not as transcendental, but as conventional, since they are "based upon a large number of random experiences" ("Facts" 407). It is with the help of these conventional laws of geometry and space that "the correspondence between the psychic and physical equivalence of spatial magnitudes" can be established ("Facts" 407).[13]

The reason for Helmholtz's deliberate and rather detailed discussion of Kant lies in his effort to acknowledge the irrefutable validity of Kant's doctrine of the *Ding an sich* without, however, conceding that we have no means at all to understand or analyze the external world since this would frustrate his own ambitions as an empirical scientist. Yet if the laws of geometry originate with experience, Helmholtz is justified in using visual perception as a means to gain access, if not to the *Ding an sich,* then at least to the structural laws governing real spatial relations as outlined above. This, in turn, allows Helmholtz to explore different reasons other than the Kantian laws of human consciousness to be held accountable for our limited understanding of the outside world. For Helmholtz, the major force inhibiting knowledge is nothing but language, and it is precisely this reductionist effort to find a culprit for the larger epistemological crisis haunting the nineteenth century that leads to the emergence of a "language-crisis" around 1900. Faced with a true dilemma in scientific research, Helmholtz scapegoats language as that which stands in the way of scientific progress and cultural renewal. To be sure, the difference between vision and language does not lie in their empirical nature, for both are arbitrary sign systems based upon a series of experiments that in the course of time have become completely naturalized and hence function as "unconscious inferences." Rather, what separates language and vision concerns the way in which information is being processed. Helmholtz contrasts the lengthy descriptions of objects via words with the comprehensive immediacy provided by sensory intuition: "Language is much too poor for the exact description of the many sense impressions which even a single object, especially one of somewhat irregular or complicated form, affords the eye and the hand. To describe such impressions in words, moreover, would be an enormously lengthy, time-consuming occupation" ("The Origin and Interpretation of Our Sense Impressions"; *Selected Writings* 503).

Helmholtz regards language as a secondary sign-system derived retrospectively from the visual and tactile experiences which themselves form primary or original sign-systems. From his early lectures to his late works, Helmholtz continues to uphold the view that sensible impressions are at least equal, if not superior to language as far as knowledge is concerned.[14] Moreover, since "our senses speak to us in language which can express far more delicate distinctions and richer varieties than can be conveyed by words" ("Progress" 222), Helmholtz maintains that it requires the eye and sensitivity of an artist to "understand" and "know" the external world beyond the realm of language. Art functions as a training manual for consciously experiencing and interpreting our immediate physical sensations in order to gain a more meaningful and broader access to reality than language alone can provide. Hence, art is not the "other" of science, but its proper vocation: "The true scientist," Helmholtz exclaims in 1878, "must always have something of the vision of an artist" ("Facts" 392).

Helmholtz's theory of perception provides a first cornerstone from which to explore the major poetic, philosophical, and artistic developments around 1900, among them Rilke's poetic ideal of "sehen lernen" (learning to see) and Bergson's concern with matter and memory, but also Husserl's phenomenology and Stefan George's celebration of a radical Aestheticism. Central to both scientific discourse and aesthetic practice at the time is not only the attempt to better "understand" the relationship between "I" and the world, inside and outside, but equally as important are some of the specific issues raised in Helmholtz's scientific experiments regarding the subjective nature of visual perception, the relationship between vision and language, and the crucial role of art for human knowledge.

The Disintegration of Matter and Meaning around 1900

Helmholtz's writings are paradigmatic for nineteenth-century scientists trying to come to terms with the self-contradictory tendencies of empiricist research. Given the ocularcentrism and intimate connection between "seeing" and "knowing" in Western culture, the destabilizing effects of the conventional nature of vision needed to be contained and the gap between mind and matter bridged, without, however, abandoning the ideal of a rigorous science able to mediate between them, as Kant's dictum of the "thing in itself" had done. Helmholtz's denunciation of language and his emphasis on the intuitive vision of the artist must be seen as one such attempt of reconciliation. The rise of psychophysics represented another, yet similar, effort. The solution, offered by psychophysics, to the dilemma was to determine the essence of things, not in opposition to, but in coordination with, the physical sensation of the human body, using language as a guiding metaphor. For Gustav Theodor Fechner, one of the leading psychophysicists at the time, "the physical is like a kind of writing, while the spiritual, psychical side represents its corresponding meaning" (*Zend-Avesta* II: 313). Meaning, it follows, is immanent in all things, the material body itself functioning like a language that silently reveals its own secrets to those able to look at things objectively.

Psychophysics thus testifies to the significant comeback of the Galilean metaphor of the "book of nature" and its concomitant idea of a speaking gaze as the foundation of modern science in the latter half of the nineteenth century. Once again, material things were regarded as both signifier and signified at once, speaking a language of their own clearly audible (and visible) to those initiated into the true speech of nature, that is, the purified system of scientific discourse. To be sure, positivism differed from Galileo's endeavors insofar as it strictly refrained from all metaphysical speculation regarding the transcendental order of things as such, turning its gaze exclusively toward the physical reality instead. It shifted perspective from the universal cosmos to the particular thing. Yet, within the clearly defined parameters of individual objects, it nonetheless rediscovered the presence of meaning inscribed upon their very surface. In psychophysical research during the second half of the nineteenth century, matter itself came to be seen as a language of its own.

Psychophysics' belief regarding the immanence of meaning is symptomatic for nineteenth-century efforts to "solve" the Cartesian mind-body dichotomy and its ensuing epistemological problems. Fechner's theory is but one of many typical attempts both to acknowledge the discrepancy between sensuous experience and transcendental matter on the one hand and yet to stipulate their mutual translatability or interdependency on the other.

Hermann Lotze, for example, in his monumental essay *Microcosmus* similarly renounces the simple identity of soul and body (i.e., mind and matter), insisting that physical bodies exist independently from each other. Yet he also holds that the human mind and external nature are essentially and necessarily oriented toward one another:

> Let us therefore cease to lament as if the reality of things escaped our apprehension; on the contrary, it consists in that as which they appear to us, and all that they are before they are made manifest to us is the mediating preparation for this final realization of their very being. The beauty of colors and tones, warmth and fragrance, are what Nature in itself strives to produce and express, but cannot do so by itself; for this it needs, as its last and noblest instrument, the sentient mind that alone can put into words its mute strivings, and in the glory of sentient intuition set forth in luminous actuality what all the motions and gestures of the external world were vainly endeavoring to express. (Lotze 353)

The quote shows Lotze's monistic belief in the fundamental coordination of mind and matter as well as his effort to both acknowledge and overcome the traditional mind-body dichotomy. Like Fechner, Lotze points to the ease with which the translation of scientific insights into language can be accomplished given this parallelism and interdependency between the physical and the psychical. One might even question if "translation" is at all the right term for what Lotze has in mind. For to let nature come into its own is to simply "express" its essence and to "put into words its mute strivings," meaning that "the sentient mind" literally lets all things speak for themselves. Without this help, nature is considered incomplete and deprived of its proper mode of being. For Lotze, scientific discourse is but the genuine voice of nature proper, and his analysis still depends upon the ideal notion of a speaking gaze I discussed above.

It is hardly surprising to find that Lotze's celebration of the ideal collaboration between the physical and the mental rarely succeeds in hiding the insecurity and defensiveness that informs it. Empiricism tried to solve an epistemological crisis in modern perception it had helped to instigate and continued to perpetuate by means of its own research. The advances in physics and biology in particular frustrated the positivist optimism of nineteenth-century science and its belief in linear scientific progress toward objectivity and truth. Instead, modern physics revealed a mysterious and irrational universe whose laws appeared ever more incomprehensible. The general erosion of meaning around 1900 included even the most basic of facts, leading to the "slow disintegration of matter" itself, as Christoph Asendorf phrases it. For once the materiality of things started to slip through scientists' fingers in the form of exceedingly small particles whose location and velocity could no longer be measured independently from the position of the observer, and once a fundamental relativity had to be granted to the seemingly most objective categories like space and time, the world was plunged into a sea of uncertainty and instability. Ludwig Wittgenstein aptly summarized the pervasive feeling of insecurity and arbitrariness that pervaded modern culture: "All we see could also be different. All that we can describe at all could also be different. There is no a priori order of things" (*Tractatus* 68; 5–634).

This lack of a necessary structure of the universe ultimately affected the individual self as well. According to Georg Simmel, many inhabitants of the metropolis developed a "mental nervousness" as the typical response to "the rapid crowding of changing images, the sharp discontinuity in the grasp of a single glance, and the unexpectedness of onrushing impressions" that distinguished modern life (Simmel 410). Sigmund Freud, too, discerned a particular defense mechanism called "preparedness for anxiety," which, he claimed, was meant to simulate and cope with the heightened level of stimulation caused by the modern age.[15] Around 1900, the human individual emerged as a site of conflict, a battleground of contradictory forces and uncontrollable powers originating from both inside and outside the human body. In a world of moving images, all stable boundaries and demarcation lines were undermined by the steady flow of visual stimuli. Henri Bergson, in his highly influential book *Matter and Memory* (1899), regards matter as nothing but an "aggregate of images" in relation to "one particular image, my body" (*MM* 22). Both subject and object are revealed as imaginary constructs rooted in the *élan vital*, that is, the incessant movement of interconnected particles lacking any consistent shape, order, or direction.

Similarly, Ernst Mach's *Analyse der Empfindungen* unveils the fundamentally fictional nature of all spatially demarcated bodies: "Thing, body, matter, are nothing apart from the combinations of the elements,—the colors, sounds, and so forth—nothing apart from their so-called attributes," which means "that spaces and times may just as appropriately be called sensations and sounds" (Mach 7, 8). The declared "scientist" Ernst Mach (47) explicitly dismissed earlier psychophysical theory regarding the parallelism between mind and matter as "metaphysical." In his eyes, there remains absolutely "no opposition of physical and psychical," no difference between appearance and reality, sensation and thing, ego and world. The reason for this amalgamation of the world is that "the elements given in experience, whose connexion we are investigating, are always the same, and are of only one nature, though they appear, according to the nature of the connexion, at one moment as physical and at another as psychical elements" (Mach 61). Not only is the ego "a poor thing," subjected to various internal and external threats, as Freud had argued ("Das Ich und das Es" 322). For Mach, it never existed to begin with, leading him to conclude that the "ego must be given up" (Das Ich ist unrettbar) (24), a slogan that echoed throughout a whole generation of writers and artists at the beginning of the twentieth century, among them Hofmannsthal, Rilke, Jünger, and Döblin, to name but a few: "We are one with all that is and all that ever was," Hofmannsthal noted in 1894 (RA; GW III: 376).

If all things were seen to be interconnected around 1900, this was due to the absence of any privileged point of view from which to survey the visual world. Given the relativity of various perspectives, individual observers had to come to terms with the contingency of their insights into things. For the purpose of this overview, the academic debate about when exactly the subjective model of vision began to gain popular appeal—whether it already started in the 1820s, as Jonathan Crary contends in his *Techniques of the Observer*, or rather began with French impressionist painting during the latter half of the century, as most art historians insist—appears less relevant than the overriding sense of epistemological uncertainty caused by the proliferation of heterogeneous perspectives toward the end of the century. At that time both the subjective and the objective model of vision existed side by side, and the increasing fascination with the supernatural and the occult represents but the uncanny flip side of modernity's belief in rationalism. The latter thus gives rise to its own undoing. Since the progress of the natural sciences encountered little, if any, resistance in a world subjected to rational analysis, it was finally slowed down by its interior contradictions and the normative vacuum that ensued from its reign. The "poetry of life" was simply missing in a positivist universe exclusively built upon scientific knowledge, as Lotze himself readily admitted.

This desire for mystery was the major reason for the popular preoccupation with mysterious and scientifically inexplicable phenomena at the end of the century. Telepathy and telekinetic experiments throughout the nineteenth century—exemplified in the enormous appeal of Blavatsky's "Theosophic Society" founded in 1875—betrayed the waning faith in rational models of explanation and the growing readiness to regard all "things" in life (and life itself) as mysterious entities that cannot simply be "known" or rationally understood. And yet, the paradoxical goal of nineteenth-century mysticism was to "prove" that nothing can be proven. During 1905 and 1908, for example, the famous medium Eusapia Paladino was observed during as many as forty-three séances under the supervision of the Institut Général Psychologique in Paris. Some of the members of the institute included Henri Bergson, Pierre and Marie Curie, and Jean-Baptiste Perrin. Although they used cameras as well as other technological instruments in order to observe and measure Eusapia's abilities, they were unable to provide any conclusive evidence or explanation in their final report of over 260 pages.[16]

The increasing renown of the phantasmagoria and the history of spirit-photography during the nineteenth century provides even more evidence for this strange entanglement of science and the occult during the nineteenth century. Originally invented as a spectacle for urban mass entertainment to verify that ghosts do not really exist, the translucent images projected by the magic lantern and similar protocinematic devices produced the exact opposite effect. They were widely regarded as empirical proof for the unreliability of visual perception, which failed to distinguish between the real presence of material substance and the ephemeral appearance of mere phantoms. As Terry Castle argues, the phantasmagoria came to be identified with the human mind itself, which similarly seemed to project hallucinatory pictures onto the real world. Reduced to a complex array of arbitrary images emanating from individual observers, reality itself degenerated into an optical illusion about which no objective facts could be ascertained anymore.[17] Nineteenth-century spirit-photography took this process one step further, merging the scientific objectivity of the apparatus with the supernatural event that defies it. Showing bodies of dead people, spirit-photography testified to the fact "that the photographic image has persistently occupied an uneasy space between the worlds of science and magic" (West 172). In other words, the new technology was being used to materialize the immaterial: "In its final stages," Nancy West concludes, "spirit photography's importance may have resided less in offering its members 'proof' of an afterlife, as in casting their frightful memories into a magical technology" (West 201).

Aestheticist poetry partakes of a similar ideal of magic as does spirit-photography. It tries to materialize the primordial vision of the ever-changing life that sustains matter. In so doing, it inherits a dual legacy from Romantic metaphysics and nineteenth-century positivism. The latter has left its mark on the Romantic imagination and forced it to come to terms with the illusory and specular nature of its visions of transcendence.[18] Aestheticist poets are skeptical, self-doubting Romanticists. They need verifiable proof in the form of physical evidence to authenticate their poetic efforts of world creation. Hence, the Romantic absolute is no longer projected into a transcendent realm of infinite expansion, but is being compressed back into the matter of every-thing we see: "Every thing can become God," one reads in one of Rilke's stories; "[i]t must only be told" (Ein jedes Ding kann der liebe Gott sein. Man muß es ihm nur sagen) ("Geschichten"; Werke IV: 355). The Absolute implodes into things and resides therein; this is why poetry around 1900 emphasizes the materiality of language. Words, like all things, literally carry a different world inside themselves. Looking at language, one sees the face of another universe.

As I shall argue at length in the fifth chapter, Rilke's poetry of the middle period both thematizes and rhetorically performs this search for the materiality of language in an effort to combat its increasing commodification. Trying to come to terms with the ephemeral quality of linguistic meaning (i.e., the constitutive gap of signifier and signified), Rilke's New Poems labor to enrich poetry with the palpable substance of the spatial arts. Drawing from the explicit analogy between poetry and sculpture, Rilke's effort participates in the ekphrastic tradition that extends from Horace's "Ut Pictura Poesis" to today's "visual poetics" (Mieke Bal). Notwithstanding the opacity of the term, the ekphrastic principle can most generally be defined as literature's attempt to *describe*, or, using a more narrow definition, actually to *imitate* visual imagery, be it a person, an object, or a place. Ekphrastic language tries to "freeze" its own temporality so that it can achieve corporal existence and "take on the still elements of plastic form" (Krieger 107). It is an attempt to paint or sculpt things with words. Indeed, some scholars, such as James A. W. Heffernan and W. J. T. Mitchell, argue that ekphrasis specifically refers to the verbal representation of graphic representation in order to distinguish it from iconicity and pictorialism encountered in almost every literary text. "What ekphrasis represents in words," Heffernan argues, "must itself be representational" (Heffernan 300), that is, it must be another referential work of art.

Many of Rilke's *New Poems* are ekphrastic in Heffernan's sense of the term since they focus on a linguistic process of assimilation meant to inscribe the differences of the spatial arts into the chronology of literary discourse. My point here is not simply to demonstrate that Rilke's *New Poems* never quite succeed in their attempt to freeze temporality, but rather to argue that they reflect their own failure, which is precisely part of their aesthetic appeal. Suspended somewhere between the transitoriness of Hofmannsthal's poetic performances and the rigid *Gestalt* of George's poetry, Rilke's *New Poems* are characterized by their effort to emulate the spatial coherence of the arts without, however, forsaking the temporal dimension of language. The resulting tension gives rise to a kind of interior vibration that both interrupts and sustains Rilke's poems. The prevalent use of the sonnet form in the *New Poems* is indicative of this ideal of dynamic stasis to which Rilke aspires. Critics have often pointed out that the sonnet mediates within its very structure the conflict between the dynamic movement it describes and the petrified or standardized form that contains it.[19] On a strictly formal level, Rilke's thing-poems are thus characterized by the same conflict between stasis and movement that he claimed to perceive in Rodin's sculptures and Cézanne's paintings.

However, if ekphrasis names the aesthetic process by which language imitates the spatial arts, then this imitation must be evident not only on the structural but also on the content level of the poems. Rilke's words must describe their subject of reference as "other," while, at the same time, they construct the poem in order to function as its surrogate. Rilke must reconcile the visual immediacy of images with the narrative unfolding of language such that one can be fused with the other. Since this fusion can never be completely successful — otherwise we would have a material object in front of us and not a written text — the poem instead self-reflectively comments upon the ideal itself. Poetic "failure," in other words, is built into the process, and this allows Rilke to state programmatically a specific poetic objective interlaced within the actual aesthetic effort to enact it. The former always accounts for and thus mitigates the failure of the latter such that Rilke's poems can nonetheless be said to successfully enact or embody the poetics they enunciate. This means that his poems leave it up to the reader to finish the aesthetic process of transformation they claim to have unleashed. For the reader can either focus on the "failure" or the "success" enabled by these poems, depending on whether or not she is willing to "play" along and complete the work or withdraw from it and let it stand unfinished on its own.

Written in the characteristic form of the sonnet, the first of the new poems, "Früher Apollo," is paradigmatic in this regard. It highlights the role of mediator played by the spatial arts as it attributes to poetic language a kind of material presence. At the same time, it also emphasizes the temporal dimension of art. Rilke's poem gives shape to an aesthetic development that mirrors the forces of life.

Früher Apollo

Wie manches Mal durch das noch unbelaubte
Gezweig ein Morgen durchsieht, der schon ganz
im Frühling ist: so ist in seinem Haupte
nichts was verhindern könnte, daß der Glanz

aller Gedichte uns fast tödlich träfe;
denn noch kein Schatten ist in seinem Schaun,
zu kühl für Lorbeer sind noch seine Schläfe
und später erst wird aus den Augenbraun

hochstämmig sich der Rosengarten heben,
aus welchem Blätter, einzeln, ausgelöst
hintreiben werden auf des Mundes Beben,

der jetzt noch still ist, niegebraucht und blinkend
und nur mit seinem Lächeln etwas trinkend
als würde ihm sein Singen eingeflößt.

(*Werke* I: 481)

Early Apollo

As when sometimes through branches, leafless still,
a morning bursts with all the force of spring,

so there is is nothing in his head that could
prevent the radiant power of all poems

to strike us almost deadly with its light.
For there is yet no shadow in his gaze,
too cool for laurel are his temples still,
and round the eyebrows only later will

come climbing long-stemmed roses from his garden,
and petals, separating from their blooms,
will drift and rest upon his trembling mouth

that yet is silent, sparkling and unused,
and only hinting with a smile as if
a song were soon to reach his open lips.[20]

The poem clearly possesses a programmatic character. It operates on two interrelated levels, describing a material object of art while simultaneously reflecting upon its own power of signification. The beginning of the second stanza reveals the interdependency between these levels as it suddenly shifts focus from the external object to poetry itself. The particular appeal of the statue is said to reside in its openness, which allows the "brilliance of all poetry" to break through to "us." This abrupt switch from art to language is baffling, particularly since "brilliance" attributes to poetry a spatial dimension that language commonly lacks. The major quality of poetry is not "brilliance," but sound, as Rilke's poem itself convincingly demonstrates if read out loud. Poetry primarily addresses the ear and not the eye—unless, of course, one were to focus on its visual appearance in the form of writing.

This, however, is precisely what "Früher Apollo" demands of its reader. For the fifth line only makes sense if we assume that poetry is as intimately connected to the marble figure as one season to the next. The first stanza explicitly likens the statue's susceptibility to the openness of a winter landscape unable to ward off the coming of a spring morning. Poetry, in other words, "shines forth" in and through the statue much like spring is already announced in winter. Hence, the surface of the statue and that of the poem must be seen as intertwined, meaning that the words on the page literally re-present the sculpted material of the statue. "We" are thus addressed as both the onlookers of the statue and the readers of Rilke's poem: looking at one, we cannot but see the other as well. And yet, this solidification of language is undermined as soon as it is stated. For the aesthetic achievement of the statue consists precisely not in its own impenetrable substance, but rather in the lack thereof since it poses hardly any resistance against the poetic description at work in Rilke's poem.

The metaphor of the seasons in the first stanza thus resonates on two opposite levels at once. It evokes both the reification of language into words as well as the statue's dissolution into the temporal flux of signification. The notion of poetry "looking through" (*durchsieht*) the sculpture first serves as a reminder about the physical attributes and the "body" of poetry in the form of writing. At the same time, however, the comparison also hints at the irreducible polyvalence of poetic language, which always already contains the seed for another world literally hidden behind its manifest presence — which is to say that poetry only breaks through and starts to "bloom" if we look behind the appearance of the written word. This relationship between matter and temporality is presented as the central theme of the statue and the poem alike. Their confluence seeks to endow each one with the inherent qualities of the other such that the sound of Rilke's poem is attributed to the singing Apollo at the end, while the statue's proper "brilliance" is ascribed to poetry. Put differently, one might say that the poem gains shape by means of describing the statue, while the statue comes to life during the temporal unfolding of poetic language.

Indeed, it is crucial to note the spatiotemporal unity of Rilke's "Früher Apollo," which links together past, present, and future. The poem describes an ancient sculpture, yet also emphasizes the early stage of artistic development it represents ("Morgen," "Frühling," etc.). The statue projects forth a time still to come (". . . noch kein"; ". . . sind noch"; ". . . und später erst") and yet already present in the form of a gaze that is "without shadow." The shadow, of course, would result from the laurels crowning the head of the statue, a symbol for artistic perfection that adorns most representations of Apollo, the god of the arts. Being without laurels is equivalent to being unfinished, much like the spring being not completely present in winter or the Greek sculpture "shining through" the words that evoke it. The present state of the statue is thus characterized as a passing stage in an ongoing process of incessant change that pertains to the historical development of Greek art and nature as well as to Rilke's poem itself. Read in the context of Nietzsche's *Birth of Tragedy* (1871), which Rilke had studied carefully,[21] one might say that the early Apollo cannot yet fully contain the destructive Dionysian forces of life lurking behind the protective shield of artistic form. The "almost lethal" power said to linger behind both the barren landscape and the unfinished Greek statue alludes to the dissolution of the individual within the universal forces of life, as Nietzsche had prophesied. Art is not only dangerous, but might be lethal, because its light of truth destroys the illusion of autonomous subjectivity upon which modern society is built.

Indeed, Rilke's use of the season metaphor not only echoes Nietzsche's notion of the eternal recurrence of the same, but also indicates the circular logic that sustains the poem as a whole. Behind the poem stands the statue, behind the statue lurks the primordial power of life, which in turn is revealed in and through the "brilliance" of poetry. Poetic language, therefore, must be endowed with a material presence of its own in order to protect "us" from the all consuming and deadly insights of art. The poem, like the statue, has solidified into physical elements (using words like marble) to allow the reader a glimpse of the mercurial power of life "shining through" behind it. For Rilke, this materialization of language is both indispensable and debilitating at the same time. It must be overcome precisely so that it can be repeated over and over again.

However, my claim that Rilke's poetry literally figures its own deconstruction does not simply defer to Paul de Man's well-known argument about the self-deconstructive nature of language. The difference lies in Rilke's and Aestheticism's deliberate attempt to recuperate this deconstructive dimension of poetry for the active construction of an aesthetic world whose strength resides in its ability to endure and maintain this interior tension that threatens to burst the poem apart. For Rilke, the authenticity of poetry hinges on this endurance. It opens up a space in between words and things that pictures the potentiality of language to transcend its own laws of signification toward the real.

Film and the "Language-Crisis"

In the fifth chapter, I shall discuss Rilke's poetics in greater detail. For now, I want to argue that the ambivalence regarding the nineteenth-century metaphysics of visual "proof" is most evident in the ultimate modern phantasmagoria, namely film. In fact, the cinematic apparatus functions according to a similar logic or aesthetic process as many of Rilke's poems. Although a film consists of distinct and isolated units, its visual effect relies upon the disavowal of that difference as it transforms static imagery into moving pictures. The aesthetics of film thus epitomizes the period's ambivalence between rationalism and spiritualism, the objective and the subjective model of vision. On the one hand, film, like photography, relies on monocular perspective and thus continues the Renaissance tradition that privileges a divine, disembodied, and thus seemingly objective, point of view. Strongly influenced by Lacanian psychoanalysis and the Althusserian critique of ideology, an entire period of film studies during the 1970s was mainly concerned with exposing the interpellative qualities of the cinematic apparatus and the ideological effects of cinematic suture (scholars like Christian Metz, Jean-Louis Baudry, Jean-Luc Comolli, and other contributors to the *Cahiers du Cinéma*). In their view, the major achievement of film, regardless of its particular content, was to produce a "subject-effect" among its audience as the viewers identified with the ubiquitous gaze of the camera in order to regain control over the plethora of moving images.[22] One might conclude that film's technological reinauguration of visual supremacy was one of the major reasons for the increasing popular appeal of cinema around 1900.

On the other hand, however, mainstream films soon began to develop the equally characteristic technique of cinematic montage that challenged the Cartesian ideal of centralized vision. While the historical beginnings of editing remains a matter of dispute—Edwin S. Potter's *Life of an American Fireman* from 1902 being the most prominent case in point[23]—there can be no doubt that within ten to fifteen years of its arrival, the new medium had developed a clear sense of what was soon to be regarded as its most distinctive trait, namely the successive arrangement of heterogeneous images known as montage. Given that film exerted a decisive influence on most avant-garde practices during the beginning of the twentieth century, it appears one-sided to consider cinema an ideological means to reinstall the Cartesian subject of vision, as argued by the proponents of cinematic suture. Rather, film emerges as a fundamentally ambiguous phenomenon around 1900, a technological invention that simultaneously strengthened and undermined the rationalist notion of visual objectivity and its efforts to adequately represent the world in the form of moving pictures.

The inherent ambivalence of film regarding its epistemological meaning is symptomatic for a time period itself suspended between the binary poles of science and metaphysics, technological progress and regressive traditionalism, and elitist versus mass culture, yet equally characterized by the concomitant and often desperate attempt to bridge the gaps and to reconcile these oppositions. "Sensation" or "life experience" was the appropriate name for what appeared to be this reuniting principle.[24] The various notions of monism, phenomenology, life philosophy, etc., in circulation around 1900 all lauded themselves for having shattered the reified doctrines of previous systems of knowledge and exorcised the specter of meaningless words that haunted them. Theirs, by contrast, was a theory beyond all theory, a philosophical nonphilosophy based on the simple and unmediated observation of life as such. John Ruskin's call for the "innocence of the eye; that is to say, of a sort of childish perception" (Ruskin; qtd. in Gombrich, *Art and Illusion* 296), not only anticipates the aesthetic ideal of French Impressionism, but also captures these contradictory impulses of the later nineteenth century. In the eyes of many artists at the time, truth and objective knowledge of the world gain shape only in and through a radical form of individual subjectivism that recognizes the self not as a superior subject, but as an integral part of the world surrounding it. He who wants to know and see all things for what they truly are must liberate himself from the urge to know and surrender instead to the mysterious play of different colors, forms, and movement that constitute both reality and one-self. He must be open to the world and must regard himself as a permeable surface that sees and is being seen all at once. A time witnessing a "perceptual revolution"[25] in the arts and sciences that fundamentally changed the face of the world, the turn of the century is mesmerized by this "look of things" and the organismic idea of ever-changing "life," seeking to unravel the interplay of deceiving appearances and revealing essences that constitute it.

And again, film might be said to be the aesthetic correlative to this mystified understanding of the world, not only because the "imaginary signifier" actually seems to present "life" itself on the screen, but also because the cinematic apparatus is built upon a mechanism that reunites separate images into a coherent whole. Owing its genesis to the scientific experiments of Marey and Muybridge, among others, while, at the same time, developing into one of the most popular entertainment media of the entire century, film both literally and figuratively epitomizes the fundamental problem of modernity: fragmentation and the utopian dream for a new totality. The cinema thus provided the opportunity for mass audiences to both rehearse modern shock sensations, as Benjamin argued, and to escape from the traumatic impact of a destabilized modern world into the imaginary realm of beautiful pictures. As Anton Kaes points out, film was simultaneously attacked and defended both as a symptom of and the remedy for the alienation and fragmentation of the modern world.

In retrospect, it seems questionable if there was any aspect of modern life that was not in some way affected by or reflected in the arrival of motion pictures, meaning that "modern culture was 'cinematic' before the fact" (Charney, *Cinema* 1). Language, on the other hand, was stigmatized by artists and intellectuals as the antiquated and dysfunctional system of signification unable to keep pace with modernity. The traditionally assumed meaning of words literally became blurred right in front of the reader's eyes: "Stop these words," Hofmannsthal's heroine Sobeide exclaims in one of his early plays. "I am dizzy and they glitter before my eyes" (Laß solche Worte, mir ist schwindlig und sie flimmern vor den Augen) (*Gedichte; GW* I: 442f.). "Truth" had became a highly relative "thing" in its own right, either located within the individual body or within life as such, but certainly not at home in an academic discourse ultimately consisting of nothing but "a mobile army of metaphors, metonomies, anthropomorphisms, in short: a sum of human relations" (Nietzsche III: 314), as Nietzsche's diagnostic gaze had already realized in 1873. Having lost currency as the universal medium of exchange between all other objects, this kind of language had become self-absorbed and was separated from the world surrounding it: "Because words have placed themselves in front of the things" (Denn die Worte haben sich vor die Dinge gestellt) (*RA; GW* I: 479), Hofmannsthal lamented in 1895, and Rilke similarly stated in 1902 that "language has nothing to do with the things anymore" ([D]ie Sprache [hat] nichts mehr mit den Dingen gemein) (*Werke* V: 20).

However, in spite of this seemingly universal denigration of language around 1900, it exhibited an array of ambivalent characteristics not unlike those of the new medium film and vision in general. Language, too, was judged both responsible for and victimized by the modern process of alienation and fragmentation. Poets and philosophers alike juxtaposed two different kinds of language, one which had succumbed to rationalist forms of exchange and (ab)used words like "gambling-chips" (Fritz Mauthner), whereas the other created "live words" whose intuitive power enabled them to speak some primordial truth that appeared out of sight at the time. Rilke's comments are typical in this regard: "Strange: the word. The very same word that proves itself useless to capture the Absolute during dialogue becomes truthful as soon as it is not directed toward anybody anymore" (Merkwürdig: das Wort. Ebendasselbe Wort, welches im Dialog sich unbrauchbar erweist, das Letzte zu umfassen, wird, sobald es sich an niemanden mehr wenden muß, aller Wahrheit mächtig) (*Werke* V: 435).

Like in German Romanticism one hundred years earlier, this exemplary language was said to be expressed in poetry since poetry transcends the narrow boundaries of philosophical and scientific knowledge. If the meaning of life is nothing but life itself, philosophy once again required the art of aesthetic mediation in order to intuit "life as it is." The reader's aesthetic experience is called upon as a kind of superior perception of the world that helps to solve the crisis caused by the self-destructive tendencies of empiricism and the philosophical problem of how to best approach "life." Poetry served as a training manual for consciously experiencing and interpreting our immediate physical sensations since it affords a more meaningful and intuitively "true" perception of everyday reality. Like Helmholtz, many scientists and philosophers regarded art not as the "other" of science, but as its proper vocation: "The true scientist must always have something of the vision of an artist," Helmholtz concluded ("Facts of Perception" 392). Likewise, Henri Bergson praises the visionary power of the artist, notably the poet, to "make us see what we do not naturally perceive" (*Introduction to Metaphysics* 135).

It follows that "true" speech in the form of poetry is of a visionary power that far exceeds that of technological instruments and scientific observation. This speechless speech still lives somewhere within the reified facade of everyday commodities and language alike, the task of poetry being to give voice to this silence and to provide insights into the truth of things. Adorno's comments are exemplary in this regard because they capture this aesthetic ideal of the silent language of art: "Etruscan vases in the Villa Giulia are eloquent in the highest degree and incommensurable with all communicative language. The true language of art is mute. . . ." (*Aesthetic Theory* 112) (Etruskische Krüge in der Villa Guilia sind sprechend im höchsten Maß und aller mitteilenden Sprache inkommensurabel. Die wahre Sprache der Kunst ist sprachlos. . . .) (*ÄT* 171). Just as medical research around 1800 relied on a speaking gaze to authenticate the objective knowledge encrypted upon the surface of material objects, modernist poetry one hundred years later called upon the same metaphysical concept in order to vanquish the scientific ideals this gaze had originally been claimed to represent. The obvious goal no longer is to know things, but to feel them and to become one with them. And yet, the definitive objectives of art and science are not that far apart, since both are concerned with a higher truth that escapes ordinary vision and common language alike. At the turn of the century, the conflict between art and science had finally reached its zenith and thus a point at which it converted into a total confluence. Ultimately, the utopian dream of modernism remained the same as that of positivist science: to look at things and let them speak for themselves.

Mass audiences at the beginning of the twentieth century, however, increasingly lacked both Adorno's aesthetic education and taste as well as the necessary leisure time to further explore and develop these elitist ideals of the speaking gaze at work in modernist art. But neither were they able to comprehend the scientific revolutions proclaimed by quantum physics and microbiology at the time. If modernist art is understood as nothing but a symptom of a severe "language-crisis," so should modern science since both pursued the same objective by different means. Poetry simply explored the same crisis and inherent ambivalence of meaning that affected the entire culture around 1900, including film. The latter, however, was able to redeem itself in the eyes of mass audiences as a form of entertainment whereas language was not. The rapid succession of individual photographs, originally conceived by Marey and Muybridge for the sake of scientific knowledge, was quickly transformed into a source for mass entertainment. Film's scientific value became virtually irrelevant; this, however, does not mean that film was not also a symptom of the very epistemological crisis it seemed to express and "solve" on the screen.

Hence, the exclusive emphasis of literary criticism on the so-called "language-crisis" at the turn of the century fundamentally distorts the picture. Intellectuals at the time simply singled out language because it had fallen prey to its own philosophical history. Throughout the modern era, it had made promises it was unable to keep. The same, of course, could be said about film and the visual media around 1900, except that they were not measured in these terms any more. Although language was widely regarded as the major, if not only, culprit for the erosion of truth it had hitherto been said to represent, scholars today must, therefore, be careful not simply to perpetuate the earlier misperception in their own research. The art historian Konrad Fiedler already anticipated this dilemma in 1887, claiming that the "erstwhile overestimation of the epistemological power inherent in the human spirit" and expressed in language "can easily appear transformed into contempt. At first one thought to possess everything through knowledge, now one believes to lose everything because of it" (*Schriften zur Kunst* I: 208). I believe that Kittler and other contemporary media theorists fortify this distorted view of things by overemphasizing the aesthetic opposition between art and modern media at the time. Modernist poetry is characterized not by a "language-crisis," but by the aesthetic ideal of merging language and vision into one, an ideal that also informed the rise of modern science and philosophy. It follows that in spite of its own insistence on total autonomy, Aestheticism is literally circumscribed within this multifaceted force field of cultural modernity. Like the photographic image of the wrecked locomotive at the Gare Montparnasse, poetry around 1900 tries to provide objective proof for its surreal visions of modern life. The alleged crisis of language actually testifies to its apotheosis.

Focusing on this potential of language to provide insight into the essence of things, the following chapter seeks to further undermine the traditionally emphasized opposition between art and science, between aesthetics and modern media, between language and vision around 1900. It explores the speaking gaze of modernity by contrasting Edmund Husserl's phenomenology with Henri Bergson's philosophy of life. This juxtaposition of two major philosophers epitomizes and brings to light many of the ambiguities and contradictory tendencies inherent in late nineteenth-century culture. First, their texts either implicitly or explicitly mobilize a variety of visual metaphors derived from the new media, testifying to the increasing influence of popular culture in the realm of philosophy. Second, reading their philosophies side by side reveals the stark competition between the objective and the subjective model of perception around 1900. Husserl's *Logical Investigations* (1899) and his subsequent *Ideas for a Pure Phenomenology* (1913) represent an important attempt to halt the erosion of philosophical knowledge and scientific certainty that characterizes the turn of the century. Husserl continues the Cartesian philosophical tradition to advance a unified theory of perception and modern science, whereas Bergson, like Helmholtz, relies strongly on physiological and biological evidence to support his theories. Moreover, Bergson severely criticizes the confinements of analytical philosophy since he deems the "intellect" responsible for our inability to grasp and come to terms with "life."

Finally, both philosophers acknowledge and seek to overcome the self-destructive tendencies evident in nineteenth-century empiricism. Their shared emphasis on intuition is meant to guide human knowledge beyond the frontiers of the positivist universe toward the realm of pure logic (Husserl) or pure metaphysics (Bergson). Although Husserl claims to turn his gaze to the things themselves (*Zu den Sachen*), his phenomenological method after 1907 operates by means of a complete withdrawal from the transcendental world into the secure immanence of the mind. His "transcendental reduction" categorically brackets the question of whether there even exists a material world outside the mind. In Husserl, the speaking gaze survives only as the explicit negation of what appeared to be the most basic positivist assumption: the unquestioned being-there of a real world untouched by those who look at it. And yet, in spite of his antiempiricist stance, Husserl's phenomenology nonetheless continues the scientific-philosophical tradition to read the essence of things and to provide insight into the universal grammar of absolute logic that sustains the world at large.

Bergson's highly influential intuitivism and "life philosophy" (*Lebensphilosophie*) represents another and fundamentally different response to the modern process of fragmentation. Bergson shares with Husserl a profound disinterest in the material world since, in his eyes, the very notion of matter is nothing but an artificial construct of the human mind. It follows that Bergson does not trust the power of logic to advance a more profound understanding of the world, but rather turns toward a metaphysical theory of intuition to unveil the truth allegedly hidden behind our highly subjective perception of things. For Bergson, this truth of life consists of an incessant stream of interconnected particles, the *élan vital*, of which every-thing partakes and which must not be intellectually analyzed lest it disappear from sight. Whereas Husserl logically dissects the human act of perception in order to understand what it means to see, Bergson regards this analysis itself as responsible for our inability to grasp the look of things. This important difference between the two philosophers is best conceptualized by their different notions of language. Life, for Bergson, exists in a realm far beyond the ability of words to capture it. The art of intuition remains the only means to catch a glimpse of the ever-fleeting presence of life, which cannot but appear distorted in the mirror of language. For Husserl, by contrast, language ultimately functions as an adequate expression of both mental activities and the world we perceive. Husserl's phenomenology can be described as a final effort to come to terms with the essence of things. Husserl and Bergson thus define the most extreme parameters of the early twentieth-century discussion regarding the representational power of language, and their views strongly influenced the poetry of German Aestheticism, as will become evident in the second part of this book.

2   Intuition and Language

> And the entire art consists in letting the seeing eye speak.
> —Husserl 1907

The Speaking Gaze in Husserl's Phenomenology

This section traces the relationship between language and vision in Husserl's Göttingen period from 1900 to 1916.[1] Husserl's philosophy is of particular relevance for this study because it centers on the subject-object dichotomy and provides one of the most sophisticated theories regarding the nature and use of linguistic signs at its time. Moreover, Husserl is widely regarded as a "seminal figure in the evolution of modern philosophy," as *The Cambridge Companion to Husserl* asserts, and represents, in Jacques Derrida's view, both the epitome and the eclipse of the history of Western metaphysics. It follows that Husserl's understanding of self-evident perception and its relation to language must not be relegated to just one perspective among many. Rather, his views are symptomatic for the traditional valorization of intuitive presence over linguistic difference, which his philosophy, much like poetry around 1900, explicitly espouses and unwittingly challenges at the same time.

My goal is to reveal the discursive strategies that sustain Husserl's analysis of pure perception as well as his valorization of intuitive presence over linguistic difference. Phenomenology is built upon the metaphysical ideal of a "speaking gaze" that seeks to capture sight in and through language. As Husserl himself stated in his lectures from 1907, the goal of the philosopher is to (ad)dress one's insights in a word: "And the entire art consists in letting the seeing eye speak . . ." (Und die ganze Kunst besteht darin, rein dem schauenden Auge das Wort zu lassen . . .) (*Idee der Phänomenologie* 62). Husserl's formulation is telling, for his ideal of a "speaking gaze" indeed requires a particular "art" of reading "the things themselves." This art conjures the ancient dream of a language that does not signify, but actually coincides, with the eidos of the phenomenological world, giving things a voice of their own literally awakened by the touch of the philosopher's gaze. The speaking gaze thus constitutes the fundamental principle of the phenomenological analysis. It allows Husserl to divide the world into inside and outside, us and them, meaning and nonsense: "Whoever does not see or will not see, who talks and argues, yet always remains at the place where he accepts all conflicting points of view and at the same time denies them all, there is nothing we can do with him" (*The Idea of Phenomenology* 49) (Wer nicht sieht oder nicht sehen mag, wer redet und selbst argumentiert, aber immerfort dabei bleibt, alle Widersprüche auf sich zu nehmen und zugleich alle Widersprüche zu leugnen, mit dem können wir nichts anfangen) (*Idee* 61). Phenomenology, according to Husserl, does not argue with the facts, but describes them exactly as they present themselves: the phenomenological gaze literally speaks for itself.

With the help of this gaze, Husserl seeks to transform philosophical concepts into the essence of things, a transformation that ultimately allows him to disregard the analysis of matter in favor of an analysis of signs. In his *Ideas toward a Pure Phenomenology and Phenomenological Philosophy* from 1913, Husserl redirects the gaze from external reality toward the inner sanctuary of the mind. The discovery and increasing significance of the *epoché* or "transcendental reduction" represents the necessary and inevitable consequence of Husserl's failure to bridge the abyss between inside and outside, mind and world. Yet, already in his lectures on *The Idea of Phenomenology* from 1907, Husserl explicitly "brackets" questions of empirical existence and thus at least deemphasizes if not abandons the transcendental realm outside consciousness. This crucial shift of focus enables him to fully equate inner and outer perception without affecting the nature of the phenomenological gaze: "Perception and imagination are of equal importance for an eidetic analysis. . . ." (Für die Wesensbetrachtung rangiert Wahrnehmung und Phantasievorstellung ganz gleich. . . .) (*Idee* 68).

In the following, I argue that Husserl does not so much shift attention from outer to inner perception as intermix the two realms, a conflation that haunts his entire phenomenological enterprise. I shall support this assertion by means of a close reading of selected passages of Husserl's texts. For only from within Husserl's phenomenological universe—the actual words themselves—will it become obvious what it means to look at things and intuit their essence. In the course of my discussion, I advance two more theses that can be stated as follows. First, I contend that Husserl's ideal of a speaking gaze is constituted by a contradictory definition of language as both analogous to and fundamentally different from perception. Second, I regard photography and the process of "development" as an apt metaphorical description of Husserl's concept of intentionality.

One of Husserl's major goals in the *Logische Untersuchungen* (hereafter cited as *LU*) and the later *Ideen* was to explain how objective knowledge is possible given the necessity to ground it in subjective experience. Phenomenology can be envisioned as a quest to reveal and identify the unshakable foundation on which to erect absolute truth, and this is why the *LU* concentrate on the question of meaning in linguistic statements. If phenomenology is to describe the essence of things themselves, linguistic meaning must be proven to be the adequate expression of truth. Based on the crucial distinction between expression and indication ("Ausdruck" and "Anzeige"),[2] Husserl, therefore, asserts that every statement expresses an absolute meaning that is irreducible to the mental act or the physical signs that constitute it. Meaning exists independently of the communicative aspect of language, as Husserl tries to prove by reference to internal soliloquy as meaningful by itself: "The word only ceases to be a word once our exclusive interest is directed toward the sensual part, that is, toward the word as a mere sound. However, wherever we live in its understanding, it expresses something that does not change whether or not it is directed toward somebody" (Nur da hört das Wort auf, Wort zu sein, wo sich unser ausschließliches Interesse auf das Sinnliche richtet, auf das Wort als bloßes Lautgebilde. Wo wir aber in seinem Verständnis leben, da drückt es aus und dasselbe aus, ob es an jemanden gerichtet ist oder nicht) (*LU* II/1, § 8, 41–42).

Husserl's project remains primarily concerned with this ideal and self-identical meaning of statements rather than the "mere expression" carrying it. In the first investigation, he distinguishes between the physical expression on the one hand and the mental acts that either bestow meaning upon this expression or intuitively fulfill that meaning on the other. In other words, Husserl transforms the traditional twofold distinction between expression and its intended meaning into a three-part structure that again splits the second part into two separate acts: a meaning-intention and a meaning-fulfillment. This further distinction allows him to "solve" the problem of intentionality he inherited from Brentano, who claimed that every mental act was "directed" toward, or "intended," an object, yet could not convincingly specify whether this intentional object was a real physical entity or a mere "something" in our mind.³ Husserl introduces "meaning" as a third, intermediary notion located in between subject and object. This ideal meaning or "sense" of statements—the *LU* do not distinguish between *Sinn* and *Bedeutung*—connects the physical expression (i.e., the word) with the physical object (i.e., the real thing) to which the sign refers. Meanings are act-essences or "species" instantiated by linguistic utterances, while at the same time, given their ideal nature, they remain independent of these acts. It follows that every expression intends a meaning that need not necessarily correspond to an external object that fulfills this meaning, since such fulfillment (i.e., the demonstrated correlation between meaning and its referent) constitutes a separate act distinct from the meaning-intention itself.

As most critics argue, Husserl's linguistic theory is not unique at the time and closely resembles Frege's differentiation between idea, sense, and referent in his essay "On Sense and Reference."[4] One could, however, also relate it to Saussure's much later distinction of signifier, signified, and referent of 1922, except, of course, that Saussure emphasizes the differential play of semiotic values that constitutes meaning.[5] According to Saussure, the signified, or meaning, of a linguistic signifier is defined negatively through a process of differentiation from all other signifiers. The temporal dimension at work in Saussure's theory is completely alien to Husserl's understanding of language, which insists on the ideal self-presence of linguistic meaning.

It follows that his concept of intentionality must somehow account for the relationship between acts of meaning-intention and acts of fulfillment. For although fulfillment does not need to be demonstrated for every single utterance, the meaningful use of language nonetheless depends upon successful fulfillment in at least some cases. Otherwise, language would become completely solipsistic and cease to function as a means of signification at all.[6] In other words, Husserl must explicate how meaning-fulfillment is possible at all within the context of his theory. According to the first investigation, meaning-intentions are fulfilled if the meaning of the two respective acts coincides.[7] This certainly seems plausible at first, but actually poses a central problem for Husserl throughout the *LU*. For if the meaning-intention of one act can only be fulfilled by means of another act whose expressed meaning in turn requires fulfillment through a third act and so on, Husserl is faced with an infinite regress as the inevitable consequence of his theory of intentionality.

The question of methodology thus becomes central to Husserl's project. On what grounds can this process of fulfillment take place? What principle allows phenomenology to perceive the self-identical origin of meaning it claims to unveil? Husserl's answer to these questions is "intuition." His entire philosophy rests on the philosopher's ability to "see" the self-evident, originally given truth. The *Ideen,* for example, specify intuition as the "principle of principles" and the "legal source of knowledge" (*Ideen* I/1, § 24, 51), and the *LU* had already defined intuitive evidence as "nothing else but the 'experience' of truth itself" (Evidenz ist vielmehr nichts anderes als das "Erlebnis" der Wahrheit) (*LU* I, § 51, 193).[8] Such evidence, in Husserl's view, grounds and enables phenomenology.

It is crucial to recognize the primary importance of the gaze in this context. Husserl's ideal of *Schauen* does not simply provide access to a field of knowledge outside itself, but remains inextricably linked to it and contains the very truth it reveals. Rather than accessing truth, Husserl's gaze is truth itself since his notion of evidence, understood as a certain, apodictic, and adequate form of intuition, cannot even be conceived in separation from the knowledge it engenders. In light of its self-evident nature, Husserl, particularly after 1907, repeatedly insists that the "art" of looking cannot be further explained or taught since it is simply absurd to try to provide proof for proof itself: "The possibility of eidetic insights cannot be proven, but must be intuited. It is itself an eidetic insight. To ask for proof would already amount to a contradiction, since the proof would have to presuppose what needs to be proven and so ad infinitum" (Die Möglichkeit einer Wesenserkenntnis kann nicht erwiesen, sie kann nur eingesehen werden. Sie ist selbst eine Wesenserkenntnis. Nach einem Beweis fragen, das hieße schon, einen Widersinn begehen, da der Beweis das zu Beweisende voraussetzen würde und so in infinitum) (*Ideen* I/2, "Beilage" 23, 572).[9] In other words, eidetic vision in the phenomenological sense is the proof we are looking for in order to ascertain the objectivity of what we perceive. Husserl's aspiration to focus on the things themselves (*Zu den Sachen*) insists on there being no higher form of truth than the intuitive evidence of how things present themselves in actual experience.

In the context of the *LU,* this means that Husserl must turn toward the realm of perception as the primordial act of fulfillment able to reveal and thus guarantee the self-identity of meaning. If intuitive acts, contrary to signitive acts, can be proven to actually present the real object itself rather than re-presenting it within consciousness, Husserl's analysis is once again anchored and reestablished on the firm ground of objective knowledge. It follows that Husserl needs to address two crucial issues to support his theory of self-identical meaning: first, he must provide further evidence for his claim that intuitive acts actually do present the object itself rather than re-present it within the mind. And second, he must distinguish carefully between inner and outer perception since only the former provides intuitive evidence in the strict sense of the term. Outer (empirical) perception, by contrast, possesses both a signifying and an intuitive component, both of which require fulfillment, leading his analysis back to the infinite regress already discussed above. For, as one critic notes, this regress could only be avoided if Husserl were to "introduce an incarnate meaning, a meaning which cannot be subtracted from the intuitive content which it informs" (Dreyfus 105). The *LU* do indeed recognize such an "incarnate" meaning, yet they locate it exclusively in acts of inner, as opposed to outer, perception: "But I cannot doubt the adequate, purely immanent form of perception, since there remains no trace of an intention that still seeks fulfillment . . . : in perception, the object is not merely believed to exist, but it is itself and really given therein exactly as that which it is believed to be" (An der adäquaten, rein immanenten Wahrnehmung kann ich andererseits nicht zweifeln, eben weil in ihr kein Rest von Intention übrig ist, der erst nach Erfüllung langen müßte. . . . : das Objekt ist in der Wahrnehmung nicht bloß als daseiend vermeint, sondern zugleich auch in ihr selbst und wirklich gegeben und genau als das, als was es vermeint ist) (*LU* II/2: "Beilage" 770). Inner perception is adequate because "its content is identical to its object" (ibid.), Husserl claims. The intentional object is fully given in its entire "physicality": inner perception both intends an object and fulfills this intention.[10] By contrast, external perception cannot fulfill the meaning-intentions of signitive acts because it is in dire need of such fulfillment itself.

Husserl's notion of *Schauen* or intuition must hence be understood not only in terms of actual sensory perception, but rather in the much broader and metaphorical sense of recognition (both *anschauen* and *einsehen*): to intellectually perceive or realize the logical coherence and validity of a certain state of affairs. This crucial distinction between inner and outer perception is continuously emphasized by today's commentators, who caution their readers against the fatal equation of phenomenological experience with the real perception of external objects.[11] These attempts of clarification, however, are themselves nothing but symptomatic of Husserl's own difficulty to clearly distinguish his phenomenological ideal of *Schauen* from empirical vision. For example, when Husserl argues in 1907 that "'seeing' does not lend itself to demonstration or deduction" (*Idee* 38), his assertion seems all the more convincing to readers precisely because it not only implicitly refers to the—highly complex—phenomenological analysis of mental acts, but also connotes the much more accessible realm of everyday visual experiences. In spite of Husserl's disavowal, the phenomenological gaze continues to exploit the abundance of "evidence" provided by both sensory and reflective intuition. Therefore, his later concepts of "intuitive evidence" or "intellectual intuition" both suffer and profit from the kind of linguistic uncertainty they allegedly rectify. Husserl's argument, in other words, is built upon and rhetorically exploits the very metaphorical quality of language it claims to have left behind.

I shall argue throughout this essay that this ambiguity of "intuitive evidence" and its dual citizenship to inner and outer perception constitutes and structures Husserl's phenomenology on several levels: First, on the argumentative level, it betrays the fundamental uncertainty as to phenomenology's primary field of study, which, at various times, seems to be either restricted to the realm of pure consciousness (particularly in the *Ideen* from 1913) or, quite the contrary, to the transcendental world and the "things themselves," or concerns the relationship between both realms. This uncertainty accounts for the continual debates among secondary critics as to whether Husserl was a Realist or an Idealist,[12] whether the perceptual noema discussed in the *Ideen* from 1913 is a concept or a percept,[13] and whether the transcendental reduction brackets only the factual existence of empirical objects or includes the entire relationship between consciousness and such objects.[14]

Second, Husserl's gaze rhetorically oscillates between the two poles of actual vision and mental introspection, combining the strength of both while eschewing their individual weaknesses. Once intellectual intuition has been declared as "original" and "physically given," as the real perception intimately known and continuously experienced by everybody, Husserl's description can safely ground adequate knowledge on the former and disregard the latter. Critical questions as to the transcendental applicability of the phenomenological analysis are implicitly referred to and answered by the "intuitive evidence" provided through sensory perception, whereas veridical concerns regarding the adequacy of "meaning-fulfillment" or the nature of intentionality are dealt with by means of the secure method of mental introspection.

Finally, the ambiguity of Husserl's concept of intuition is symptomatic for the irreducible difference inherent in language. Contrary to Husserl's assertion in both the *LU* and the *Ideen*, language does not merely reflect the pre-expressive meaning of a self-identical logos. The phenomenological ideal of an adequate description revealing the essence of all things (be they empirical objects or mental acts) must seek to repress the fundamental difference that constitutes language, an effort doomed to fail the very moment it is stated. Husserl's project is haunted by the return of the repressed, which strikes back from inside the original presence phenomenology claims to occupy. In Jacques Derrida's words: "Even while repressing difference by assigning it to the exteriority of the signifiers, Husserl could not fail to recognize its work at the origin of sense and presence" (*Speech and Phenomena* 82). For Derrida, phenomenology is an exercise in exorcism that denounces linguistic difference in favor of the alleged immediacy of intuitive evidence. To paraphrase Derrida, one might say that the absolute, objective ground upon which phenomenology claims to stand is groundless, a search for no reason beyond language.

Husserl's ideal of a "speaking gaze" is thus constituted upon two ambiguities: first, the conflation of inner and outer perception, and second, his paradoxical understanding of language as both fundamentally different from, yet adequately descriptive of, perception. On the one hand, linguistic signs are said to be derivative and nonparticipatory in the exegesis of a primordial meaning that precedes them. This meaning must, therefore, be intuited rather than signified since intuition directly presents the object itself, whereas language merely re-presents it. The sixth investigation dedicates some length to the decisive gap that separates signitive and intuitive intentions.[15] And the *Ideen*, too, continue to insist on this "irreducible, essential difference" (unüberbrückbarer Wesensunterschied) (*Ideen* I/1, § 43, 90) between self-giving perception and the signifying symbolism of words because this difference is absolutely crucial for the phenomenological description of "things as they are." On the other hand, however, Husserl entrusts language with the nondistortive translation or expression of a prelinguistic meaning, which is provided by a pure phenomenological description that renders explicit what has been or could be intuitively experienced. This ideal of a nondistortive language is explicitly stated throughout his writings of the Göttingen period.[16] It expresses Husserl's belief that language, by its very nature, does not add or subtract anything from the self-evident truth it seeks to describe. Rather, it is the intellectual carelessness of those who speak and have spoken in the past that causes language to undermine the scientific effort to picture the things themselves.

Phenomenology is literally an attempt to come to terms with how things truly are. This process, however, implicitly denies the fundamental difference that allegedly separates vision and language. Similar to the contrast between inner and outer perception, Husserl first stipulates a major distinction between language and perception and then undermines his own stipulation. The question remains as to how language could ever adequately express a primordial, self-identical presence defined precisely as that which escapes language. This can only be possible if this presence (i.e., meaning) were always already inherent in language, and this ultimately means that words define essences rather than express them. Husserl's theory of language is thus caught in a double bind. If linguistic signs are truly able to present intuitive evidence, the latter would lose its privileged status of objective self-presentation and succumb to the nonoriginary play of difference. Yet if they are not, then the phenomenological ideal of the speaking gaze breaks down and words cannot be said to provide a "pure," nondistortive description of intuitive insights.

It follows that Husserl's denunciation of linguistic re-presentation in favor of intuition is purely rhetorical since both the assertion of intuition and the denunciation of language necessarily refer back, and hence remain bound, to the very discourse intuition is said to transcend. The phenomenological enterprise begins and ends in discourse, an insight that simply eradicates the very possibility of a self-given intuitive evidence of absolute presence. Phenomenology does not stand on its own, but is constituted by the referential play of presence and absence inherent in language; this is the true and only "object" it ever analyzes. For Adorno, the self-evident truths phenomenology claims to see are either tautological by nature, and thus unworthy of critical analysis, or they are self-constructed "things" devoid of meaning altogether: "Phenomenology might be described as the paradoxical attempt of a theory without theory. That is why it becomes subject to the revenge: all the things it declares to be self-sufficient are only for itself; what it claims to perceive needed to be created first in order to prove that phenomenology perceives anything at all" (*Zur Metakritik der Erkenntnistheorie* 131). One might specify Adorno's claim by focusing on the central relationship between vision and language in Husserl's texts. The various "species," "ideas," "noemata," and "intentional objects" Husserl claims to intuit intellectually are but linguistic constructs inherent in and confined to the very text that claims to reveal them as autonomous entities. They are born and die in discourse. Intellectual intuition does not actually present eidetic entities and thus prove their ideal existence, but instead simply reveals the constitutive mechanism of language and the differential play of presence and absence that engenders meaning. There is no preexpressive meaning, no ahistorical pure grammar of logic.

Adorno's critique thus ultimately coincides with Derrida's in rejecting a purely logical understanding of language, which, in turn, could only be sustained in conjunction with Husserl's notion of self-evident intuition. In Husserl's view, vision and language stand and fall together since the identity of each is defined in collaboration with, yet also in opposition to, the other. If, as argued above, his ideal of self-given and adequate "intuitive evidence" is a rhetorical construct based on the phenomenologically inadmissible fusion of sensory perception and mental introspection (i.e., inner and outer perception), then the alleged juxtaposition between language and vision breaks down and each will reveal a primordial hybridity at its core. This problem is most apparent in the context of the "perceptual noema" Husserl discusses in his later phenomenology.

In the *Ideen* from 1913, Husserl introduces new ideas and a different terminology in order to enable a more poignant description of intentionality and the eidetic principle. Husserl now refers to intentional acts as "noeses" and calls the intentional correlate to such act (i.e., what was formerly called the intentional object) the "noema." Moreover, since real perception does not adequately present its object, he needs to account for the process of recognition that enables us to perceive an object as what it is. Therefore, he further distinguishes between the *hyle* that describes the content or raw material taken up in a sensation, and the *morphe* as the interpretative sense that bestows meaning upon this material and determines it.[17] The *morphe* informing the *hyle* is also called the noetic phase, and the two together denote the proper components of intentional experiences or "noeses." This distinction between *hyle* and *morphe* avoids the equivocation of "matter" as both the content and the interpretative sense of intentional acts in Husserl's earlier discussion of intentionality.[18]

Fortified with this new terminology, the *Ideen* directly state at the very beginning what hitherto had remained the focus of contention: the "existence" of intellectual intuition and its "not merely external, but fundamental relation" to the "physical" originality of empirical vision (*Ideen* I/1, § 3, 14). "Thus essential insight is intuition, and if it is an insight in the precise sense of the term and not merely a vague representation, it follows that it provides a primordial intuition, grasping the essence in its 'corporal' selfhood" (Wesenserschauung ist also Anschauung, und ist sie Erschauung im prägnanten Sinn und nicht eine bloße und vielleicht vage Vergegenwärtigung, so ist sie originär gebende Anschauung, das Wesen in seiner "leibhaften" Selbstheit erfassend) (*Ideen* I/1, § 1, 15). By endowing an eidetic entity with a "corporal reality, so to speak" (*Ideen* I/1, § 24, 51) that can literally be "grasped" in an act of intuition, Husserl (deliberately or unwittingly) exploits a rhetoric that implicitly denies what it explicitly affirms: the ideal, transcendental nature of pure species and essences that are fully evident only in virtual acts of perception, yet are also said to essentially coincide with actual visual experience.

Given Husserl's equivocal understanding of the perceptual noema, it is hardly surprising to find commentators strongly disagreeing on the subject as well. Of the many differing views,[19] two in particular are worth discussing at length: Anton Gurwitsch's understanding of the noema as a percept, that is, a perspectival aspect of a real object outside of consciousness, and the opposing view represented by members of the California school (Dagfinn Føllesdal, Hubert Dreyfus, et al.), who regard the noema as a concept completely severed from transcendental materiality. The controversy is located at the very heart of Husserl's phenomenology, for it concerns the relationship between "I" and the world, mind and reality.

Gurwitsch identifies the perceptual noema with the material object in its particular mode of sensual appearance.[20] It follows that the relationship between this material object (the thing itself) and the single noema is comparable to that of the entire group of possible noemata (the system as a whole) and one single element of that system. In other words: the thing itself outside consciousness is nothing but the combination of all possible modes of adumbration in which it appears. While the noema is thus not simply identical to the thing itself, it nonetheless grants a partial "look" at it. Transcendental reality, according to Gurwitsch's reading of Husserl, is not severed from consciousness because the noema provides a reliable bridge between them. For Føllesdal and Dreyfus, on the other hand, the noema is an abstract entity, a mental concept that, by definition, cannot be perceived through the senses.[21] Noemata are known exclusively through the mode of phenomenological reflection and not by means of actual sensory experience, which, in their view, would violate the principle of transcendental reduction that sustains Husserl's analysis. Similar to the ideal meaning expressed in linguistic utterances, the perceptual noema constitutes an abstract sense rather than a concrete object or even an aspect thereof.

Since both sides present abundant textual evidence to support their views, the following remarks are not intended to introduce yet more material in an attempt to settle the dispute. In fact, I believe any such effort to be fundamentally misguided since it disregards the more crucial insight that critics' opposing views are merely symptomatic of Husserl's own indeterminacy regarding this question. The conflict literally bespeaks the constitutive ambiguity of the phenomenological gaze oscillating between inner and outer perception. Gurwitsch's reading clearly emphasizes the latter, whereas the members of the California school focus on the former. Both must pay a price for dissolving the ambiguity that pervades Husserl's entire project: as his critics show, Gurwitsch cannot but at times explicitly argue against the stated meaning of Husserl's text in order to assimilate phenomenology to the ideals of later Gestalt theory. Given his understanding of the perceptual noema as an incarnate sense, which he justifies by reference to the self-givenness of objects in acts of perception, Gurwitsch violates Husserl's central exhortation that sensory perception never provides adequate, that is, full intuitive evidence of its object, meaning that acts of external perception still require a separate act of fulfillment.[22] Only inner perception (i.e., phenomenological reflection) can lay claim to fully and "physically" seize its object during an act in which intention and fulfillment coincide—an act, however, that also leaves the material object in the real world completely out of the picture.

Føllesdal and Dreyfus, on the other hand, certainly remain truthful to Husserl's understanding of mental reflection, yet in doing so are forced to abandon the idea that phenomenology could ever reach beyond the limits of human consciousness, as Dreyfus readily admits. In his opinion, Husserl "must treat perception as referentially opaque and confine himself to what we take there to be rather than what is given. He can study the conditions of the possibility of evidence, confirmation, etc., but never its actuality" (Dreyfus 108). This restriction, however, causes problems on the opposite end of Husserl's argument since it not only contradicts his overall concern for providing an absolute foundation for objective knowledge, but also disregards his claim that sensory perception does indeed provide immediate access to external objects, albeit in a mode of adumbration. In identifying the noema with a concept, the California school seems to reinstall the very picture- (or sign-) theory of perception Husserl so vehemently rejected throughout his career.[23] Explicitly building on the analogy between linguistic and perceptual acts espoused by Husserl himself,[24] these critics tend to identify noematic sense and linguistic meaning, and this slights the epistemological difference separating signitive and intuitive acts.

Like his understanding of language, Husserl's notion of the perceptual noema thus remains highly ambiguous since there is ample evidence for it being both a concept and a percept at once. Rejecting either option as insufficient, Jeffrey Bell recently argued that the perceptual noema represents Husserl's final attempt to solve the paradox of infinite regress and must hence be regarded as "the neutral and non-productive 'quasi-being' which is neither a proposition nor a thing" (Bell 85), yet it can be "understood" as both at once (Bell 78). Fully aware of the paradox himself, Bell identifies the noema as the unidentifiable fault line that both separates the sense of an act from, and connects it to, the real object intended by that sense: "As a boundary, it is not to be identified, or posited, with either side, yet it is the condition for differentiating and identifying each side" (Bell 86).

Bell's understanding of the perceptual noema indeed "solves" the paradox simply by embracing it. Whether or not this solution represents what Husserl himself intended is ultimately less interesting a question than the new possibilities of understanding opened up by this interpretation. One of them is to situate Husserl's perceptual noema within the context of the visual media at the time. The indexical nature of photography, for example, actually registers the "corporal reality" of its object by means of a physical process that imprints light upon a receptive surface, a surface, moreover, that can be said to both reflect and shape the data it receives. As Roland Barthes noted, the photograph is "somehow co-natural with its referent" (Barthes, *Camera Lucida* 76) and thus provides an appropriate model or discursive metaphor for the entire phenomenological enterprise. Like Husserl's "speaking gaze," the photograph is "a message without a code" whose meaning nonetheless hinges on a particular "art" of reading and writing. In Barthes's words, the "photographic paradox can . . . be seen as the co-existence of two messages, the one without a code (the photographic analogue), the other with a code (the 'art,' or the treatment, or the 'writing,' or the rhetoric, of the photograph)" (Barthes, *Image, Music, Text* 19).

As I have argued throughout this essay, this very paradox of an "unfulfilled fulfillment" (Jeffrey Bell) sustains Husserl's phenomenological project, meaning that the perceptual noema might best be conceptualized as the pure potential to develop a photographic image of external reality within the human mind. The phenomenological "art of looking" is to transform the human mind into a camera able to take pictures of the world. While the history of philosophy has painted life in various colors, Husserl sets out to shoot it once and for all. Regarding material things as transparent signs for themselves, phenomenology ultimately replaces one for the other. Similar to photography, which preserves the illusion of an ideal presence irredeemably lost, the language of phenomenology is the memento mori of philosophical thought—which is to say that the eidetic essence of things might be nothing but a word, a notion that leads directly to my discussion of Rilke's poetry in the fifth chapter. For now, let me turn to the other important philosophical impulse around 1900.

Bergson's Intuition of Life

In contrast to Husserl, Bergson categorically rejects language, and his charge that discourse kills rather than presents life is crucial to his "philosophy of life." Although today almost forgotten, Bergson's work was extremely popular not only in France, but all over Europe during the first two decades of the twentieth century. His two major books, *Matter and Memory* from 1899 and *Creative Evolution* from 1907, to a large extent shaped the popular vitalist movement in both academic and public circles. It not only gave rise to the organicist ideals of the surging nationalism in France, but also influenced much of European modernism and the historical avant-garde.[25] The following remarks are bifocal in their attempt to provide a coherent introduction into Bergson's major concepts as well as an analysis regarding the word-image relationship manifest in the unfolding of his own texts. Both aspects are inseparable, for *what* Bergson wants to say is inextricably linked to *how* he says it. Advocating the ability of philosophical intuition to present life "as it really is" without being able to do so himself in his own writing, Bergson is forced to denounce the linguistic foundation on which his own thought is built. Thus, his texts are sustained by an oscillatory process of affirmation and disavowal similar to modernism's reflections on poetry and language in general.

"[I]ntellectualized time is space" (*Introduction to Metaphysics* 31), asserts Bergson. His entire philosophy might be understood as the effort to disentangle these two concepts and to recognize the primordial importance of time. In Bergson's eyes, the utter disregard for the real duration of movement emerges as the central philosophical problem from which all others can be deduced. Operating under the auspices of modern science, the human intellect artificially dissects a continuous movement into a series of immobile sections so as to be able to measure, predict, and ultimately manipulate it. Real movement survives only in the truncated form of a meaningless abstraction posited retroactively after its completion. It is only after movement has ceased to be movement, that is, after it has come to an end, that its real temporal duration can be translated into and equated with the physical space it traversed. Knowledge thus attained is based on a partial acquaintance with its subject of reference, while "real," "pure" duration itself eludes science, which contents itself with the "phantom of duration, not [with] duration itself" (*Intro* 31).

In order to illustrate this spatialization of time affected by science, Bergson repeatedly refers to the working of the cinematic apparatus, which similarly provides the impression of movement based on the continuous succession of immobile pictures. In his later work *Creative Evolution*, Bergson contends that "[m]odern, like ancient, science, proceeds according to the cinematographical method" (*CE* 357). Science extracts all specific movement inherent within individual figures or things, thereby reducing them to mere abstract forms or static "snapshots" of reality. In a second step, science endows these lifeless forms with an abstract movement, a "movement in general," that no longer resides within the things themselves, but emanates from a thought process that operates like the cinematic apparatus: "Such is the contrivance of the cinematograph. And such is also that of our knowledge. ... We take snapshots, as it were, of the passing reality, and, as these are characteristic of the reality, we have only to string them on a becoming, abstract, uniform and invisible, situated at the back of the apparatus of knowledge, in order to imitate what there is that is characteristic in this becoming itself" (*CE* 332).[26]

Bergson's critique of modern science exemplified in the cinematic apparatus coincides with Hofmannsthal's rejection of the modern separation of art and life, body and meaning. Both thinkers charge modernity with dissecting a primordial Whole into distinct units that subsequently are reconnected again as if nothing had happened. However, instead of regaining access to the Whole as such, modern science merely recreates the artificial *impression* of life, much like language succumbs to a mere tool of signification once it has been severed from the breathing body that sustains it. The incessant movement of life, in other words, cannot retroactively be imitated either technologically or linguistically, but must be immediately experienced in and through a direct gesture of the body such as raising one's arm, which serves as one of Bergson's favorite examples in his texts.

For Bergson, the invention of the cinematic apparatus was further proof that modern science operates within a self-made phantom universe of abstract space that does not correspond to the real. Contrary to the assumptions of contemporary physics, Bergson argued that time does not constitute the fourth dimension of space, but, quite the opposite, that space is an illusion based upon the misunderstanding of time. Bergson's reversal rests upon what *Matter and Memory* calls the commonsense perception of the material world that appears as an infinite number of images since "[m]atter, in our view, is an aggregate of images" (*MM* 9). Images are inherent in the object and hence exist independently of the human eye: "the object is, in itself, pictorial, as we perceive it: image it is, but a self-existing image" (*MM* 10). Matter reveals itself in perception as what it is, even though this revelation is specific and not total because our vision does not significantly alter matter, but isolates it from its surroundings and looks at it with a particular interest in mind, that of action. Only those aspects of matter are perceived that are of interest to our ability to act upon them; the rest is literally overlooked and vanishes from sight. They are still "there," but not for us, only for themselves. Perception is an instrument for human action, Bergson maintained, and, hence, it is selective, subjective, and partial: "[B]etween this perception of matter and matter itself there is but a difference of degree and not of kind, pure perception standing toward matter in the relation of the part to the whole" (*MM* 71).[27]

Bergson again sought to clarify his theory of perception with reference to modern media, arguing that perception does not consist in taking a subjective photograph of things that subsequently is being developed in the brain. Rather, "the photograph, if photograph there be, is already taken, already developed in the very heart of things and at all the points of space" (*MM* 38). In other words, to perceive an object is to acknowledge the autonomous existence of an image that fully corresponds with the object itself. During the act of perception, matter indeed persists in the form of phenomena rather than material substances, a crucial distinction that underlines the strong phenomenological dimension of Bergson's philosophy. In Bergson's eyes, however, phenomenology as well as modern science distort the picture because both fail to distinguish between the pure virtuality of matter and its diverse manifestations that result from interacting with it. There is no absolute essence or Husserlian *eidos* inherent in matter except for its ability to take on a variety of different shapes, as, for example, that of a picture or a photograph during the moment of pure perception. Images are not extrinsic to matter, yet neither do they identify its essence. Matter has no proper essence, but consists of nothing but the continuous movement of interconnected particles.

Modern science, however, arbitrarily interrupts this movement and falsely identifies the various manifestations of matter with matter itself. The phantom truth derived through this spatialization of time also accounts for the apparent congruency between matter and intellectual ideas in the natural sciences. Since science has literally shaped the object it investigates, the latter naturally fits the categories provided by the mind, a circular relationship reminiscent of Kant's crucial insight in his *Critique of Pure Reason*. Space, in Bergson's view, is nothing but a useful construct invented by the mind to better manipulate and control the external world. It functions as a practical schematization of an otherwise chaotic and constantly changing universe of interconnected particles more or less expanded in time.[28] Bergson's analysis hence differs from the Kantian position in that he does not regard space as a transcendental category innate to human perception. Space is neither objectively given in nature nor constitutive of our ability to reason, but an ingenious construct aiming "above all at making us masters of matter" (*Intro* 38).

It follows that, according to Bergson, absolute or true knowledge is not at all unattainable, as Kant had argued. Truth remains beyond the reach of the human intellect in its normal mode of operation, but that does not mean it could not be provided by what exceeds science, that is, an intuitive method of inquiry called metaphysics that consciously resists the spatialization of time. "To philosophize means to reverse the normal direction of the working of thought" (*Intro* 190). Metaphysics thus appears in Bergson as an ally rather than an opponent of modern science. Its field of inquiry is the human mind itself, giving rise to a form of self-investigation that, according to Bergson, necessarily remains alien to the intellect since it is oriented toward interacting with the material world outside. Intuitive metaphysics, by contrast, provides a "direct vision of the mind by the mind" (*Intro* 42), and thus, by extension, a "direct vision of its object" as well as "a vision of life complete" (*CE* xxiii). True knowledge of the material world emerges once we are able to recognize and correct the spatiotemporal distortions of the intellect's perception of reality. Intuition defines Bergson's philosophical method, as Gilles Deleuze argues, because it renounces the primacy of action over contemplation and hence begins to see the Truth: "We must strive to see in order to see, and no longer to see in order to act. Then the Absolute is revealed very near us and, in a certain measure, in us" (*CE* 324). It is "in us" because we, too, participate in the incessant movement that constitutes the real.

In his later book *Creative Evolution* (1907), Bergson argued that literally everything in the world results from what he called a "vital impetus" (*élan vital*), a primordial movement of gigantic force thrusting itself forward. The release of its internal tension through movement has led to the extension of matter and the formation of life. Due to the expenditure of its power during the course of its expansion—for this "impetus is finite, and it has been given once for all" (*CE* 277)—the impetus is threatened by inertia as the natural result of the loss of energy it suffers. Those "parts"[29] of the original movement that lose velocity and tend toward an extended state of solid immobility—which, to be sure, will never be reached completely—is matter in the form of inorganic objects. Contrary to matter and opposed to it as a difference in kind, Bergson posits life. Life is the "part" of the impetus that seeks to prolong the freedom of its expansive movement by continuously dividing itself, giving rise to plants and animal life as contingent effects of this effort. It follows that, once properly looked at, all "[m]atter thus resolves itself into numberless vibrations, all linked together in uninterrupted continuity, all bound up with each other, and traveling in every direction like shivers through an immense body" (*MM* 208). Within this gigantic metabody called reality, our own body functions merely as "the place of passage of the movements received and thrown back, a hyphen, a connecting link between the things which act upon me and the things upon which I act — the seat, in a word, of the sensori-motor phenomena" (*MM* 151f.). In Bergson's universe, there is no space, only time; there are no solid, differentiated bodies, only a continuous flow of vibrating energy; and there is no "formless ego, indifferent and unchangeable," because an ego "which does not change does not endure" (*CE* 5, 6).[30]

Bergson's intuition of the human body as a "hyphen" that receives and passes on movement brings up the question of language in his philosophy. If the body is neither a subject nor an object in the grammatical sense, but a mere syntactical marker devoid of a proper meaning outside the flow of things, one must ask what kind of language would be adequate in representing this body, particularly since Bergson's entire philosophy obviously rests upon this translation of intuition into language. Trying to explain what the initial impulsion or vital impetus "really is" or originally must have looked like, Bergson encounters various problems, for "the comparison of life to an impetus . . . is only an image" (*CE* 280). In order to avoid the misperceptions inherent in his central metaphor, Bergson enlists the service of a whole army of metaphors that compare the *élan vital*, among others, to "a shell, which suddenly bursts into fragments" (*CE* 109) or to "a center from which worlds shoot out like rockets in a fire-works display" (*CE* 271). Seeking to present life "as it really is," metaphysical intuition must not only work its way back toward a disinterested vision of life not bent toward action, but it is also forced to express this vision indirectly, that is, symbolically, with the help of those artificial constructs called words.

Indeed, in Bergson's universe, language, and not rationality as such, emerges as the single, most dangerous enemy of a true philosophy of life. For contrary to Bergson's alleged "irrationalism" repeatedly denounced by his critics, Bergson regards thought as absolutely crucial to philosophical intuition and its vision of life.[31] The real problem consists in the reification of thought in and through language: "The most living thought becomes frigid in the formula that expresses it. The word turns against the idea. The letter kills the spirit" (*CE* 141).[32] According to Bergson, words distort meaning since they only describe the superficial look of things instead of their continuous change in the flow of time. The Bergsonian universe consists of movement and tendencies, whereas the words used to describe them, Bergson argued, are modeled after the intellect's preference for spatial abstraction.

In spite of his urge to get "into closer contact with life" (*Intro* 126), Bergson fully realized that one cannot escape the distortions engendered by language, which is bound up with ideas and the process of meaning.[33] His texts, it follows, are literally haunted from the inside by this evil spirit of language, a demon he seeks to outwit metaphorically, yet which, in doing so, entangles him deeper and deeper into the fabrics of discourse rather than providing access to a reality allegedly located behind language. Bergson's metaphors, scarcely born, are orphaned by their creator, denounced as imprecise and misleading appropriations for a movement that cannot be "shown" as it really is. Consider the following image that likens the process of life first to the mechanism of a steam engine and then to the movement of raising one's arm:

> Let us imagine a vessel full of steam at a high pressure, and here and there in its sides a crack through which the steam is escaping in a jet. . . . So, from an immense reservoir of life, jets must be gushing out unceasingly, of which each, falling back, is a world. . . . But let us not carry too far this comparison. It gives us but a feeble and even deceptive image of reality. . . . Let us think rather of an action like that of raising the arm; then let us suppose that the arm, left to itself, falls back, and yet that there subsists in it, striving to raise it up again, something of the will that animates it. In this image of a *creative action which unmakes itself* we have already a more exact representation of matter. In vital activity we see, then, that which subsists of the direct movement in the inverted movement, *a reality which is making itself in a reality which is unmaking itself.* (CE 269f.)

The paradox expressed in the last sentence lingers at the heart of Bergson's intuition of reality. The *élan vital* is never fully present as such, or, to put it differently: it presents itself only as that which it is not, because the "present" instantaneously falls prey to the passage of time. Presence slips into the past as soon as it is realized, and it is gone the very moment it becomes present. In the renunciatory tone typical for the period around 1900 and the philosophical self-understanding of modernity, Bergson declares that "[n]othing is less than the present moment, if you understand by that the indivisible limit which divides the past from the future" (*MM* 150). Pure presence is unattainable and untenable, a mere point in time that serves a speculative rather than practical purpose: "in truth, every perception is already memory. Practically, we perceive only the past, the pure present being the invisible progress of the past gnawing into the future" (*MM* 150). Paradoxically, then, it is the past that "is," because it remains identical to itself and survives precisely as what it is, whereas the present "is not" and cannot endure but as that which it is not, the past.[34]

Similarly, the Whole is given exclusively in the form of its own self-cancellation. The metabody of interconnected vibrations and movement that sustains everything never "is" except within various arbitrary manifestations of its infinite "states" with which it both coincides and from which it nonetheless, in its pure state as virtuality, remains distinct. For the Whole *is* its own virtuality that can only become actual by losing itself. As Deleuze comments in his book on Bergson: "In short, the characteristic of virtuality is to exist in such a way that it is actualized by being differentiated and is forced to differentiate itself, to create its lines of differentiation in order to be actualized" (*Bergsonism* 97). One might say that Bergson's Whole is everything and nothing at the same time, too full to be properly represented and too lacking to become actual in and for itself. Since the virtuality of the Whole cannot be expressed as such, it follows that intuition, too, "is fugitive and incomplete" and cannot be sustained. If it could, Bergson asserted, the "object of philosophy would be reached." However, since intuition, like life itself, can never, by definition, be rendered permanent, the "philosopher is obliged to abandon intuition, once he has received from it the impetus, and to rely on himself to carry on the movement by pushing the concepts one after another" (*CE* 260). In other words, the philosopher must surrender himself to language in spite of its obvious insufficiency, because once he has intuited the Whole, he can only try to speak after it in a desperate attempt to represent the unrepresentable.

Bergson's own analysis is thus forced to oscillate between the description of the manifest pluralism of reality and the underlying unity perceived by philosophical intuition alone. In his eyes, monism is the truth about pluralism, yet the latter needs to be fully developed before it enables any philosophical investigation to intuit the first in its pure virtuality. This aporia is symptomatic of a philosophy that claims to investigate the absolute, yet ultimately fails to present it outside of the very same mode of linguistic representation it deems responsible for its concealment in the first place. Firmly established *within* this monistic reality (a reality consisting of the incessant vibrations of interconnected "movement," "images," "matter," "memory," "life," "consciousness" — name it what you will — for, "in reality," they are all the same) rather than looking at it from the outside as does the human intellect, intuition reveals all distinctions between matter and memory, subject and object, between differences in degree and differences in kind to be obsolete since literally everything is united within a single Whole as the absolute of being and the real duration of time.

A fundamental criticism of Bergson's philosophy of life is as self-evident as it is, virtually, impossible. It consists in exposing the Whole allegedly revealed by metaphysical intuition as precisely that which Bergson denounced the most: a convenient linguistic symbol devoid of any substance whatsoever, an empty word that lacks the very life it claims to present. Bergson himself, in turn, implicitly argued that such criticism pertains not to his idea of the Whole as such, but merely to the intellectual perspective of life that, naturally, refuses to accept that which cannot be posited as a fixed concept to work with. As a philosophy, that is, an intellectual enterprise to positively *reflect* or *represent* the virtuality of the Whole as a given "thing" in the real world, Bergson must fail and knows he does. Yet, this failure, in Bergson's view, does not falsify his claims, but, on the contrary, functions as indirect proof for the validity of his philosophy, which, like the Whole it seeks to present, must contradict itself in order to remain true to its intuitive nature.

This is also the reason why Bergson explicitly rejected the attempt to solve the problem of intuition dialectically since even a negative dialectics in Adorno's sense presupposes a fundamental disjunction rather than an essential connection between things.[35] For Bergson, dissonance is not the truth about harmony, as Adorno claims, but the reverse: harmony is the truth about dissonance. In order to escape the aporias of philosophical thought, Bergson turned his gaze toward what he perceives as empirical evidence for his theory — physical action: "[I]n theory, there is a kind of absurdity in trying to know otherwise than by intelligence; but if the risk be frankly accepted, action will perhaps cut the knot that reasoning has tied and will not unloose" (*CE* 211). A simple movement in space, Bergson maintained, reveals the entire secret of life, and the simple experience of raising one's arm already contains all the wisdom and knowledge to which modern science still aspires. The most potent kind of action, however, is that of artistic creation, for the visionary power of the artist "make[s] us see what we do not naturally perceive" (*Intro* 135). A poem, for example, still harbors a trace of the pure intuition to which it owes its existence, in spite of the fact that during the process of its linguistic unfolding, the poem, too, suffers the same kind of extension and alienation that distinguishes the Whole of life: "Thus, a poetic sentiment, which bursts into distinct verses, lines and words, may be said to have already contained this multiplicity of individuated elements, and yet, in fact, it is the materiality of language that creates it. But through the words, lines and verses runs the simple inspiration which is the whole poem. So, among the dissociated individuals, one life goes on moving" (*CE* 282). As a consequence, Bergson is left with a kind of neo-Romantic belief in art as the only true allusion to the real, since for him the intuitive wisdom of art begins where philosophical and scientific knowledge ends.

This belief was radicalized in German Aestheticist poetry, in which poetic language appears not only to provide a direct access to life, but to sustain life itself. Aestheticism identifies Bergson's *élan vital* with the seamless flow of poetic words that constitute a material world of its own. Trying to bridge the objective and subjective perspective on reality, it simultaneously draws from both the metaphysical and the positivist legacy of the nineteenth century and thus represents a kind of fusion of phenomenological and life-philosophical impulses at the turn of the century. On the one hand, Aestheticism disavows Bergson's radical denunciation of language, yet embraces his metaphysical insights into the interconnectedness of life that cannot be rationally understood, but must be intuited in and through the senses. On the other hand, Aestheticism rejects Husserl's logical-analytical method of investigation, yet nonetheless draws from Husserl's phenomenological effort to merge language and vision. Like Husserl, the poet seeks to find the right word for the essence of things and the nature of language. A brief discussion of Hofmannsthal's early reflections on poetic language may help to elucidate this dual legacy of Aestheticism.

The Magic Potentiality of Language

For the young Hofmannsthal, the term "magic" defines the inherent power or potentiality of poetic words to transcend the limits of representation and to render present what ordinary language can merely signify. Poetry reunites signs and things, matter and meaning precisely by refusing to force an artificial connection between them. Once left alone and freed from the burden of signification, language is believed to miraculously perform on its own accord the very task to which it was forcefully subjected beforehand. Hofmannsthal's "Gespräch über Gedichte" (1903) is exemplary in this regard. It not only advocates the being of language as meaningful in itself, but also insists on the redemptive power inherent in poetry. Gabriel, one of the fictional protagonists in the dialogue, defines the symbol as the "magical power" of poetic words capable of "touching our body and transforming us continuously" (Um der magischen Kraft willen, welche die Worte haben, unseren Leib zu rühren, und uns unaufhörlich zu verwandeln) (503). The expression once again conjures a physical, indeed corporal, connection between language and body, meaning and flesh. Poetry does not signify a thing, but literally posits the thing itself, Gabriel argues, since poetry "sees every thing for the first time" and supplies it with "the miracle of its Being" ("Gespräch"; *Erzählungen; GW* 503).[36] The eucharistic context that surrounds this evocation of symbolic language is as obvious as the nagging doubt underlying it: asked about the "reality" of this ideal of symbolic substitution, Gabriel remains silent at first and then concedes that all depends on the enchanting power of the symbols themselves—a believer's concession to lack any positive proof whatsoever for his belief.[37]

Being uttered by one of the protagonists in a fictional context, this sentiment cannot simply be read as the author's personal perspective. Nonetheless, Gabriel's assertions in the "Gespräch" strikingly resemble similar assertions made by Hofmannsthal himself, for whom poetic language is neither representational nor exclusively self-referential by nature, but a "potentiality" able to call forth the things themselves as what they always already are. And yet, this potentiality cannot be redeemed without forfeiting its inherent power. This leads to a reverse formulation: successful poetry is impossible, a contradiction in terms. Successful poetry is doomed to fail, yet it succeeds by means of its necessary failure. This can only make sense if we recognize a dual function at work in poetry: language (i.e., poetic speech) dies the very moment it is born, itself giving birth to the things it says by means of words that have no meaning other than expressing their potential to name. After this originary moment of poetic self-expression has passed, both words and things alike are doomed to linger in a state of alienation devoid of the mythical realm they once shared. This is the crucial paradox inherent in Hofmannsthal's reflections on language: words present the things they signify only because and if they refuse to signify at all, by remaining pure symbols.

On the basis of this primordial interdependency of things and words, Hofmannsthal both demands and rejects the fundamental distinction between art and life. He argues that both realms are inextricably intertwined, but need to be separated from each other precisely in order to be once again perceived as one.[38] Poetic language must not be forced to create a bond between its own realm and the world of phenomena since words are not simply empty vessels charged with the mere transportation of referential meaning—this being, rather, the "modern" (i.e., scientific, positivist, etc.) disfiguration of language caused by the proliferation of quasi-mathematical concepts throughout the nineteenth century.[39] Rather, words are beings in their own right and things are meaningful in themselves since being and meaning are coextensive: "All that is, is, Being and Meaning are one, hence all beings are symbols" (Alles was ist, ist, Sein und Bedeuten ist eins, folglich ist alles Seiende Symbol) ("Nachlass"; *RA III:* 391).[40]

This understanding of the relationship between being and meaning is not only striking, it is at the philosophical forefront of its time. If all things really functioned as "symbols" (in Hofmannsthal's sense) for one another or for themselves, then there would be no need for symbols or language at all. Meaning would already be inherent or inscribed within the things as such. Being would be its own meaning, and that meaning would be the simple fact that things are the way they are. All things would be revealed as signs for themselves, and this, in fact, is a formulation that Edmund Husserl advanced in his *Ideen* from 1913: "The sensually appearing thing possessing the sensuous qualities of Gestalt, color, smell, and taste, is anything but a sign for something else; it is, rather, in a certain sense, a sign for itself" (Das sinnlich erscheinende Ding, das die sinnlichen Gestalten, Farben, Geruchs- und Geschmackseigenschaften hat, ist also nichts weniger als ein Zeichen für ein anderes, sondern gewissermaßen Zeichen für sich selbst) (*Ideen* I/1, § 52, 113). The logical absurdity of this formulation poignantly captures the constitutive paradox of Hofmannsthal's early poetics: the nonidentical identity of material things and linguistic signs. Obviously, a sign is, by definition, different from what it signifies, and for a material object to function as a sign for itself means that it is in fact alienated from its own self at the very moment that it is claimed to present itself. Husserl's formulation implies that the phenomenological gaze is able to identify difference as the difference of identity.

Hofmannsthal's own reflections on life and poetry center on precisely this paradox since the poetic word is said to present the transcendental thing as both other and same simultaneously. His comments, therefore, at different times concentrate on either side of an identity that really is not: "There is no direct path leading from poetry to life, and none from life to poetry," Hofmannsthal categorically declares in 1902 during a public lecture on life and poetry" (Es führt von der Poesie kein direkter Weg ins Leben, aus dem Leben keiner in die Poesie) ("Poesie und Leben," *Reden und Aufsätze* I: 16), whereas four years later he argues the exact opposite: "There is no antithesis between book and life, between poems and life" (Es gibt keine Antithese von Buch und Leben, von Gedichten und Leben) ("Dichter und Zeit"; *RA; GW* I: 79), and two years before he had already noted: "Wrong all defining; wrong: all cheap antitheses between 'art' and 'life' . . ." (Falsch das Definitive; falsch: alle billigen Antithesen wie 'Kunst' und 'Leben' . . .) ("Nachlaß"; *RA; GW* III: 451). It is precisely because word and thing (poetry and life) are said to be inextricably linked, yet fundamentally different nonetheless, that Hofmannsthal can play off one side against the other. If there "leads no direct path from life to poetry, from poetry into life," this can only mean that any attempt at mediation between them is fundamentally misguided. Poetry *is* life since words enable all things to come forward and present themselves in the purity of their proper name. Language can only matter once the meaning of words is simultaneously identified with and separated from their referents. As I have argued in the first chapter of this book, this nonidentical identity of sign and referent is at the core of the modern project and its inauguration of the speaking gaze. The goal is to decipher the inherent meaning and the look of things without recourse to the rationalist mode of signification.

Hence, what Hofmannsthal — and Aestheticism in general — envisions as the "potentiality" (Agamben) of language, Bergson discusses in terms of the "virtuality" of an ever-changing "Whole." Similar to the pure voice of poetry, this Whole must differentiate itself in order to pass into actuality and become "real," yet it paradoxically loses itself (i.e., its virtuality) precisely in and through this process of self-realization. The exploration of this paradox characterizes both the poetic and philosophical reflections on language around 1900. Hofmannsthal's contradictory "understanding" of poetic or symbolic language as calling forth the things themselves sounds less fantastic within a philosophical framework that rejects the idea of autonomous individuality in favor of an interrelated network of all things. If "we are nothing different in the world" (dass wir und die Welt nichts Verschiedenes sind) ("Gespräch," *Erzählungen* 503) such that "the universe is condensed within our body" (In unserem Leib ist das All dumpf zusammengedrückt) ("Gespräch," *Erzählungen* 504), then poetry emerges as the adequate medium to express this underlying interconnectedness of life.

Indeed, Bergson's intuition of the *élan vital* as an "immense body" (*MM* 208) and his metaphor of the individual as a "hyphen" or "connecting link" (*MM* 151f.) receiving and passing on movement within this body is crucial to the intellectual debate of life around 1900. Moreover, it directly links to Hofmannsthal's own visions about poetry and the human body. In a public lecture from 1906, Hofmannsthal likens the poet to a seismographic instrument recording the intricate vibrations of the *élan vital*:

> Er [der Dichter] ist der Ort, an dem die Kräfte der Zeit einander auszugleichen verlangen. Er gleicht dem Seismographen, den jedes Beben, und wäre es auf Tausende von Meilen, in Vibrationen versetzt. . . . Seine dumpfen Stunden selbst, seine Depressionen, seine Verworrenheiten sind unpersönliche Zustände, sie gleichen den Zuckungen des Seismographen, und ein Blick, der tief genug wäre, könnte in ihnen Geheimnisvolleres lesen als in seinen Gedichten. Seine Schmerzen sind innere Konstellationen, Konfigurationen der Dinge in ihm, die er nicht die Kraft hat zu entziffern. ("Der Dichter und diese Zeit"; *RA; GW* I: 72)

> He [the poet] is the place where the forces of time demand to be equalized. He resembles the seismograph whose vibrations register every tremor even if thousands of miles away. . . . Even his darker hours, his depression, his confusion and unpersonal states resemble the twitches of the seismograph, and a profound gaze could discover in them more secrets than in his poems. His pains are inner constellations and configurations of things within himself which he does not have the strength to decipher.

Once again, the poet is configured as the topographic locus of intersecting forces emanating from everything that exists. His body *is not* except in acting out the inner vibrations of the world at large, meaning that his actions and even his psychological mood could be read — by a "profound gaze," that is, the kind of gaze Bergson attributes to metaphysical intuition — as the immediate and unalienated self-expression of life. The poet's very existence is a kind of language spoken by the things themselves in which he functions as a mere punctuation sign — the hyphen — that literally embodies meaning. The words of the poet express a message whose meaning cannot be understood rationally, but must be experienced as a part of one's own body. And yet, Hofmannsthal's ideal of an organic language in the corporal sense(s) — the "language of the real," as Friedrich Kittler calls it with reference to Rilke's acoustic experiments with the gramophone (*Gramophone* 74f.) — is based on a common metaphor that died the moment it was conceived, for it cannot sustain the intuition it evokes. Acting out the vibrations of the *élan vital*, the poet's body has always already translated and hence distorted the fundamental truth of life it records. Like Bergson, Hofmannsthal's comparison of the poet to a seismograph mobilizes the scientific ideal of measurable accuracy only in order to reject and replace it with his own magical vision of things. But his metaphor nonetheless remains indebted to the very process of translation it seeks to overcome.

Trying to intuit life, the (scientific, philosophical, poetic) translation of movement into signs is inevitable since the primordial "language of the real" is nothing but gibberish noise, as Kittler rightly insists. The real has no language, no voice, no meaning because it is strictly opposed to the symbolic. "The real is the impossible," says Lacan, and unlike the never ending trace of signifiers, "the real is that which always comes back to the same place" (Lacan, *Four Fundamental Concepts* 49). It only makes sense to speak of an "embodied meaning" and to identify it with the real as the extreme and indeed ineffable limit of signification if one concomitantly recognizes that this notion itself is but a signified and projected ideal from within the symbolic realm of language. Linguistic difference has always already affected and distorted the language of the body Hofmannsthal envisions. But it shelters it as well since only in and through language can the body be said to speak at all. The simultaneous inevitability and impossibility of translation haunts Husserl's phenomenology as well as Bergson's philosophy of life and Hofmannsthal's reflections on poetic language alike. All of them seek to reveal a primordial truth that cannot be revealed without getting lost in the process. The contradictory nature of Bergson's Whole, which loses itself in the very moment it passes from virtuality into actuality, is similar to the pure voice of language getting lost in its own discourse. The crucial difference between Hofmannsthal and Bergson, however, consists in the latter's utter disregard for the performative power of language, which is explored and acknowledged in Hofmannsthal's aesthetic and metaphysical reflections. Whereas Bergson turns away from language toward intuition, the young Hofmannsthal turns from intuition toward language and hence embraces the paradox of merging meaning and materiality, art and life.

Still, the question remains what exactly distinguished the Aestheticist gaze around 1900 from its theological, scientific, or philosophical precursors throughout the modern era that similarly claimed to read God's (or Nature's or the Logos's) indecipherable writing within the human soul or in the Book of Nature? As Jacques Derrida points out, however, all rationalist models of reading were firmly anchored in an absolute logos that alone endowed them with meaning.[41] The speaking gaze before 1900 presupposed a tertium quid or a common ground (God, mathematics, grammar) that allowed for the translation of vision into language in order to make sense of the various signs encountered in the world. As I argued in this chapter, the chiastic relationship between vision and language around 1900 literally seeks to uproot this triangular scheme in an attempt to break through to the immediacy of life. All eyes at the time were focused on the things themselves, and all theories were built upon the explicit rejection of theory altogether. If nineteenth-century empiricism and psychophysics had still assumed a fundamental parallelism between the world of the mind and that of reality, the constitutive paradox of the speaking gaze around 1900 consisted in presupposing an utter lack of presuppositions.

Unlike science or philosophy at the time, however, modernist poetry does not advance verifiable truth claims about individual things or the world at large. Rather, it sought to create a new world *in* and *as* poetry whose purpose for being is to prove nothing beyond the possibility of its own existence. Solely based on the premise of its autopoietic originality, the speaking gaze of Aestheticism is born of the poetic ideal of poverty rather than the positivist objective of plenitude. Another paradox ensued, for it is on the basis of this self-sufficient gaze that the ultimate truth about life could be seen, read, felt: namely that there is no higher truth, no absolute spirit, which, in turn, liberates all things simply to be in and for themselves. Things are what they are and exist in an autonomous mode of self-sufficiency, much like the speaking gaze is its own cause and its own reason for being. What remains is the primal Nietzschean insight that recognizes no transcending qualities of life other than life itself. For the entire world is present at each and every moment in all of its parts, and to write a poem about this insight is to materialize all of its secrets at once. Modernist poetry thus replaces the representational model of truth (i.e., truth as correspondence) with one founded on artistic creation alone: "Prior to thought there must have been poetry" (Bevor "gedacht" wird, muß schon "gedichtet" worden sein), Nietzsche had argued in his *Will to Power*.[42] Aestheticism rehearses the paradox of a gaze that speaks an original truth for which no criteria of truthfulness are adequate anymore. The speaking gaze around 1900 reads a message without a code that cannot and must not be rationally "understood" in the mind, but literally experienced in and through the senses, because it emanates from no particular source and is directed toward no particular addressee. The opacity of these metaphorical exercises in (non)reading calls forth the poetic experience of a meaningful world liberated from the burden of identifiable meaning.

What, then, is the role of the reader during this process, and how are these poems to be read? Indeed, given the proclaimed self-sufficiency of Aestheticist poetry and the speaking gaze that informs it, the process of reception seems irrelevant and the reader utterly superfluous. And yet, all art implies and addresses an audience since its whole purpose consists in conveying an original message that must arrive somewhere for somebody lest it be irretrievably lost. In other words, it is precisely Aestheticism's enigmatic nature and its autopoietic stance that engenders the need for some form of validation from an outside agent. Although modernist poetry denounces this authentication process as trivial, it cannot but simultaneously call upon readers to acknowledge this triviality and hence concede their own superfluousness. Both on the level of production and on the level of reception, Aestheticist poetry is built upon this paradox of a contingent autonomy that simultaneously recognizes and disavows its dependency upon individual poets and readers alike.

The following excursus examines Aestheticism's inherent ambivalence vis-à-vis the reader in the context of contemporary methods of reading. Obviously, my remarks are not meant to provide a comprehensive overview, let alone an in-depth analysis of the different models of interpretation I discuss. Rather, I want to situate my own readings within an important debate that seems particularly pertinent with regard to Aestheticist poetry. More precisely, I contrast the recent rise of a posthermeneutic criticism with traditional methods of hermeneutic interpretation. Whereas the latter focused mostly on text-immanent readings of individual texts, the former examines modernism mainly with regard to the institutional and sociohistorical processes said to control the production of meaning around 1900. One focuses on language as matter, the other on language as meaning, yet neither method gives sufficient attention to the crucial interplay between both poles at work in high literary modernism, for Aestheticism reverses the Romantic perspective on poetic language. It continues the hermeneutic search for the essence of things not on the level of the signified and the power of poetic imagination, as Novalis and Schlegel had suggested, but on the level of the material presence of the signifier visualized in the form of a poem. This reversal of the Romantic paradigm requires the reader of Aestheticist texts to draw simultaneously from the hermeneutic and posthermeneutic approach toward literature since both perspectives are already operative within the poems themselves. The poem, in other words, opens up a material world of its own, and the reader, much like the modern poet, scientist, or philosopher, is charged with developing a kind of cross-eyed view of language as both matter and meaning. In the eyes of this ideal reader, modernist poetry not only signifies the embodiment of meaning, but literally *is* embodied meaning, and this superimposition of words and/as things epitomizes the scientific and philosophical ideal of a speaking gaze able to read the look of things in the modern world.

EXCURSUS

METHODS OF READING

> Those who lament the demise of criticism are fools. For its time has long since past.... "Sovereignty" and the "autonomous gaze" ... have become a lie.
> —Benjamin, 1928[1]

A Posthermeneutics?

Literary criticism has finally bid "A Farewell to Interpretation."[2] For some critics, the dismissal of hermeneutics has been long overdue. Susan Sontag spoke out "Against Interpretation" already in the sixties, arguing that "[i]n place of a hermeneutics we need an erotics of art" ("Against Interpretation" 104). Although today her visions might appear somewhat tainted by the overall spirit at the time, Sontag rightly anticipated the demise of hermeneutic methods of reading at the end of the twentieth century. In the wake of French poststructuralism and the waning hope to "learn from history" by thinking and representing it "as a narrative" (*In 1926* xi), Hans Ulrich Gumbrecht recently recognized the rise of a "nonhermeneutics" that dispenses with the confining paradigm of traditional interpretation. The latter is charged with an inherently idealist agenda unable—or unwilling—to pay attention to the "materialities of communication" that actually sustain the signifying process. In his foreword to Friedrich Kittler's *Aufschreibesysteme*, David Wellbery similarly argues "that a literary criticism informed by post-structuralism is, in fact, a post-hermeneutic criticism," which, "to put the matter briefly, stops making sense" ("Foreword" ix). Of course one is tempted to ask what exactly that is supposed to mean were it not for the obvious fact that this very question itself is precisely what is being questioned and put on trial in Wellbery's statement, namely the hermeneutic effort to give meaning to that which resists it, be it a simple text or the world in which we live (call it Being, life, the real).

To concede this much and to allow for the posthermeneutic questioning of meaning is not, I hasten to add, to embrace irrationalism and the end of communication, as some critics have argued. Sure, Wellbery's statement engages in a performative self-contradiction since his exhortation to stop making sense cannot but make sense nonetheless, and it thus implicitly relies on the same mechanism of interpretative understanding it calls into question. While such scholastic reasoning may be logically valid, it completely misses the powerful rhetorical dimension of this posthermeneutic stance, which is, after all, of crucial interest to literary critics. Wellbery's efforts are still directed toward the analysis of literary texts, yet he approaches the question of meaning from its opposite end, so to speak. His criticism focuses on those instances or elements generally overlooked as mere nonsense or, quite simply, "noise." Not only does noise pervade all systems of signification, Wellbery contends, but its existence must continuously be suppressed by means of an interpretative method whose only goal remains over and over again to "make sense." Both of these factors—the irreducible existence of nonsense and its continuous suppression—are, in Wellbery's view, constitutive for the production of (textual) meaning and the survival of hermeneutics. Since traditional forms of interpretation cannot but presuppose the very sense or meaning they purportedly find represented in language, hermeneutics describes a tautological practice at best, a narcissistic projection of its own methods and prejudices upon textual matters whose sole purpose becomes to valorize the applied method as such.

Kittler's work, for example his reading of E. T. A. Hoffmann's "Der Goldne Topf," tries to unveil this self-reflective mechanism at work within Romantic literary texts in which truth is said to reside in the interiority of the author as subject, while its revelation, in turn, depends upon the ingenious "divination" of the reader-subject to "understand" what the text really means to say.[3] Literature thus functions as a kind of mirror reflecting back to the interpreter his or her own self-ideal as a coherent, autonomous subject forever relishing the uncontestable truth of its own being. The hermeneutic method sanctions this specular relationship between mankind and language. It calls upon readers to become authors to become readers again and again until, finally, the spiraling effects of this universalizing process leave no space unaffected by the endless proliferation of meaning. Posthermeneutics, by contrast, seeks to expose the sociohistorical roots of this seemingly "natural" ideal of (self-)understanding: the dissemination of knowledge in the form of books and other learning material, the institutionalized methods of "correct" reading and writing, the instrumentalization of the mother's voice as the disembodied origin of pure meaning, etc. As soon as the reader recognizes and critically investigates the contingent effects of these various "apparati" instead of relying on their efficiency to "make sense," a whole array of interrelated metaphysical notions both derived from and constitutive of the hermeneutic enterprise — for example, "understanding," "subjectivity," "interpretation," etc. — are thrown into relief, breaking apart the apparently boundless universe of linguistic meaning.

According to Kittler, this is precisely what happened in the "discourse network" of 1900. Literary modernism at the turn of the century discovers the materiality of signification and thus leaves the hermeneutic universe and its emphasis on sense-production behind. Instead of focusing on the meaning potential of language, modernism zooms in on the obscurity of the signifier and the breakdown of communication. Aestheticist authors, in other words, literally write down and inscribe the death of Romanticism into their texts. Although I generally agree with this line of criticism, it is too unbalanced and generalized to be convincing overall. Posthermeneutics provides a trenchant critique of the history of modern signification, yet it fails to elucidate the provenance of the material letter on which it is based. Instead, it tends to promote a technological determinism that presupposes the givenness of media (print, analog, digital), much like earlier hermeneutics presupposed the existence of meaning. In other words, posthermeneutics differs from its predecessor in that the latter focused predominantly on the spiritual quality of language, whereas the former focuses predominantly on its material basis. From the perspective of literary criticism, posthermeneutics seems least interesting where it succumbs to the simplicity of this reversal and most productive where it resists it. In order to develop this argument and to understand what precisely is at stake in the recent shift of emphasis from sense to nonsense, from hermeneutic interpretation to the analysis of "meaning-production," I want to examine in greater detail both the theoretical and methodological implications of this shift.

Since posthermeneutics evolved out of French poststructuralism, a good place to start is the Derrida-Gadamer debate of the early eighties in which the philosophical similarities and differences between German hermeneutics and French deconstruction were already discussed at length. The most interesting question about this debate is to determine whether it has actually taken place at all. The Derrida-Gadamer encounter, as it was evasively phrased, certainly did not qualify as a dialogue as that term was understood by Gadamer, who expressed his disappointment and even some irritation with regard to the brief and, in his eyes, misguided questions posed to him by Derrida.[4] In light of this nondebate, some critics have charged Derrida with willfully sabotaging Gadamer's "goodwill" toward mutual understanding, while others have denounced Gadamer's condescending, even patriarchical, attitude and blamed his "closet essentialism" for the failure of communication.[5]

In more general terms, Manfred Frank has repeatedly lamented the lack of a "meaningful" exchange between the two schools. Contending that deconstruction is a mere variant of the hermeneutic enterprise that originated with Schleiermacher's philosophy, Frank relates both paradigms back to the Romantic tradition of interpreting the interplay between an abstract linguistic system and its subjective appropriation in individual speech acts. Language thus emerges as "Das Individuelle Allgemeine,"[6] a reservoir of potential meaning (*das Allgemeine*) whose instantiation into actual speech or text (*das Individuelle*) is tantamount to altering and affecting the very source from which it emanates. According to Frank's understanding of traditional hermeneutics, it never presupposed the idealist notion of pure, self-identical sense, because every form of linguistic utterance invariably expresses a sense that previously remained—quite literally—unspeakable. Every text, Frank argues, represents an innovative and individual performance in the form of a linguistic event that remains irreducible to the abstract system underlying it. Hermeneutics simply names the process by which the nascent meaning of a text is being understood as that which literally "makes a difference." Frank thus recognizes Derrida's insistence on "différance" as already "prefigured" in Schleiermacher's *Dialectics* and even regards some of Lacan's writings as paradigmatic examples for the hermeneutic interpretation of texts.[7]

Gadamer's and Frank's dogged efforts to elicit further negotiations regarding the similarities and differences between hermeneutics and deconstruction have remained unanswered or been dismissed by the other side as mere "attempts at ameliorative appropriation" (Wellbery, "Foreword" ix). Yet this refusal to enter into a hermeneutically charged dialogue is significant in and of itself. First, it bespeaks a certain weariness on the part of literary critics to have to continuously discuss the theoretical foundations of their work rather than being able to engage in reading literary texts. More important, however, this reluctance is also symptomatic of the intellectual distance or safety zone that posthermeneutics needs to establish between itself and its adversary for fear of contamination, since to engage hermeneutic theory on its own ground (i.e., by means of a close reading of some of its major proponents) would require a project similar to Frank's that might lead straight back to the interpretative paradigm posthermeneutics strictly opposes. It is, therefore, hardly accidental that in those rare cases where posthermeneutic scholars provide more precise references to what exactly hermeneutics "means," they either situate it in highly abstract terms within the larger context of the modern era since the Renaissance—the need for modern man to "interpret the world"—or they refer specifically to the works of Wilhelm Dilthey.[8]

Dilthey, however, represents an obvious and all too easy target: his ceaseless efforts to increase the scientific rigor of the humanities in general, his emphasis of the methodological rules and regulations that structure the process of interpretation along with the significance granted to the artistic genius (the subject par excellence) as the original source of meaningful interpretation, and, finally, his famous exhortation that the "last goal of the hermeneutic method is to understand the author better than he understood himself"[9]—all of this evokes idealist notions of subjectivity and indeed "presupposes that 'meanings' are always given—in the interiority of the subject's psyche," as Gumbrecht concludes ("Farewell to Interpretation" 396). Gumbrecht's criticism strikes to the core of Dilthey's idealization of artistic genius, which cannot be defended against the further objection, advanced by Wellbery, that the notion of genius "merely reproduces, tautologically, the discourse it seeks to interpret" (*Specular Moment* 121–22). The "genius" is indeed an ideal construction of poetic texts and not an anthropological fact existing in the real world—whoever claims the latter must come to terms with the transcendental problem of a self-originating subjectivity the genius is said to represent. In other words, if the hermeneutic method indeed rests on the original creativity of the ingenious reader, as Dilthey argues, then it cannot avoid being entangled in the self-reflective snares of idealist philosophy (i.e., Fichte's notion of a self-positing ego) that contemporary theory has successfully called into question. Dilthey's version of hermeneutics thus falls prey to the postmodern critique of metaphysics with which all hermeneutics is said to coincide. Precisely this latter assumption, however, is repeatedly challenged by Frank and Gadamer. They claim that deconstruction's critique of subjectivity slays a dead horse since hermeneutics, too, is built upon the "subject in crisis" and relies on a notion of "individuality" radically different from that of an idealist "subjectivity" ascribed to it by advocates of poststructuralism.[10]

My point here is not to come to some final judgment in the philosophical debate on subjectivity and meaning. Far from it, I want to argue that aside from its specifics, one can read the peculiar deadlock of the entire discussion itself as symptomatic not of the mere *improbability* of an encounter between hermeneutics and deconstruction, but of its structural *impossibility*. Any encounter requires a common ground upon which it can take place, and as long as deconstruction remains unable or unwilling to advance toward a new model of interpretation that accounts differently (meaningfully? — but how?) for the nonsense or blind spots it recognizes in literary texts, it cannot but avoid a hermeneutic dialogue in which the opponent enjoys a crucial "home advantage" to begin with. Let me briefly discuss the works of Jacques Derrida and Paul de Man as the two major paradigms that have emerged as a possible response to this dialogical impossibility.

De Man's own reading of literary texts often begins and ends with the startling confession that reading is, indeed, impossible, and this "impossibility of reading," de Man emphasizes, "should not be taken too lightly" (*Allegories of Reading* 245). This provocative statement does not declare the whole process of reading superfluous, but aims to reject its traditional concept, which holds the critic's genius to be responsible for giving meaning to a text. De Man reads texts to find an "essential disarticulation that was already there" to begin with (*Resistance to Theory* 84) and that reflects a linguistic necessity: any rhetorical figure posits its own deconstruction with it. It is not a subject that deconstructs the text, but "the text deconstructs itself, is self-deconstructive" (*RT* 118) since "the cognitive function [of literary language] resides in the language and not in the subject" ("Rhetoric of Blindness" 137).[11] Consequently, de Man denounces the critic's greatest insights regarding the meaning of texts as the unwittingly produced side effects of their greatest blindness. In other words, "the paradigm for all texts consists of a figure ... and its deconstruction" — a process that governs both the written text and its interpretation (*AR* 205). Hence, the important question for a reader is not to ask whether the author remained obtuse about what he meant to say, but "whether his language is blind or not to its own statement" ("RB" 137). The crucial insight for de Man is precisely that the terrain for the interpretation of literary texts never changes: everything takes place in language. This process, for de Man, remains independent of human agency and is controlled by the linguistic field and its chaotic openness: "[T]he inhuman is: linguistic structures, the play of linguistic tensions, linguistic events that occur, possibilities that are inherent in language—independently of any intent or drive or any wish or any desire we might have" (*RT* 96).

It remains questionable whether de Man's understanding of language does not grant linguistic structures the same kind of self-reflexive subjectivity he explicitly denied the human individual—"the return of the repressed," as Frank insists (*Was ist Neostrukturalismus?* 128). Be that as it may, what remains crucial in our context is the fact that de Man's theory of reading by no means transcends the hermeneutic model of interpretation. This need not diminish de Man's formidable exercises in reading literary texts, but it does problematize the sentiment that deconstruction has actually moved beyond hermeneutics. De Man himself was rather unconcerned about the popular charge that he practiced nothing but a particular form of "New Criticism,"[12] while Wellbery and others explicitly reject de Man's readings as "a negative theology of the literary work" ("Foreword" viii) unable to found a viable alternative to the traditional search for meaning in texts.[13]

Derrida, by contrast, has promised not only "the end of the book," but also "the beginning of a grammatology." His *Of Grammatology* from 1967 invoked a new practice of writing that follows the trace of "différance" as the constituent process that creates linguistic meaning. And yet, he also admits that any attempt to break out of the metaphysics of presence "is trapped in a kind of circle" which "describes the form of the relation between the history of metaphysics and the destruction of the history of metaphysics. . . . We can pronounce not a single destructive proposition that has not already had to slip into the form, the logic, and the implicit postulations of precisely what it seeks to contest" (Derrida, "Structure" 280–81). The circle Derrida evokes with regard to the impossibility of stepping outside of metaphysics is reminiscent of the "hermeneutic circle" that Heidegger embraced in *Being and Time*. If Derrida's grammatology thus signifies its own impossibility and remains an unkept promise, as some critics argue, then his own methods of reading are being reabsorbed into the same playful process of absence and presence, meaning and nonmeaning that sustains interpretation proper.[14] Hence, not only Frank and Gadamer consider Derrida "a hermeneutic thinker." The Italian philosopher Gianni Vattimo, for example, also regards Derrida's work as "a deconstructionist version of hermeneutics" that aims to suspend its traditional ideal of ultimate cogency "within a multiplicity of perspectives that render them possible (and also shows them to be *merely* possible)" (Vattimo, *Beyond Interpretation* 91–92, 100). It follows that deconstructive meditation "increasingly resembles a performance" (Vattimo, *Beyond* 101), providing Derrida's text with an Aestheticist appeal that, in Vattimo's eyes, takes precedence over its argumentative strand.

Made (in)famous by Habermas's (non)reading of Derrida in *The Philosophical Discourse of Modernity*, this reproach of blurring the generic difference between literature and philosophy is, of course, well known among advocates and adversaries of deconstruction alike. At first glance, it betrays a mere gesture of indignation that hardly advances any substantial criticism of the issues at hand other than a certain "provincialism" of those who feel the integrity of academic disciplines violated. But there is more at stake, for the literary tendency of deconstruction once again bespeaks the lack of a viable alternative to the hermeneutic principle it attacks yet continues to perpetuate nonetheless. If deconstruction cannot provide a theoretical alternative to the hermeneutic paradigm of reading and turns toward a peculiar kind of Aestheticism instead, does it not run the risk of succumbing to the "pleasure of the text" that founds the aesthetic enjoyment of the (hermeneutic) subject par excellence—the reader? Does the deconstructive message in the form of literature not implicitly rely upon and even call for the very methods of interpretation it seeks to replace? From this perspective, the literary "turn" of deconstruction involves a potentially self-destructive turning toward the very "origin" of meaning, which, and from which, it sought to split. Deconstruction prompts the question whether there really remains no-thing outside the "Fort-Da" game of language and the hermeneutic universe it constitutes.

The Materiality of Language

It is precisely at this point that posthermeneutics takes its leave from the deconstructive mode of reading by returning to Derrida's unkept promise of grammatology. "Writing" appears as the keyword in posthermeneutic criticism, not only in the Derridian sense of "différance," but particularly in its physical properties as the material basis for modern communication.

By focusing on the "exteriority of writing" (Wellbery), critics try to break the spell of universal meaning. Their goal is to move beyond the confinement of literary interpretation forever caught in the endless circle of presence and absence, signifier and signified, and meaning and nonmeaning that sustains both deconstruction and traditional hermeneutics. Breaking free — but where to? — to the letter proper, that black mark on a white surface traditionally charged with obscuring the self-identical presence of the truth it signifies. The letter emerges as the privileged site of reading since it makes a difference simply by being there. Posthermeneutics encourages the reader's gaze to seize upon the letter not as a transparent sign, but as a material object in its own right, with its own history and its own properties. Under the auspices of this gaze, a different universe unfolds, one in which hermeneutics is exposed as a historical construct based upon particular institutional and social apparati, one in which the production of sense is recognized as an anonymous and contingent process rather than the controlled result of individual action, and one in which the (technological) media literally inscribe their message onto the human body, which is subject to, rather than the subject of, the letter. As it focuses on this universe, posthermeneutics literally begins to speak a different language. It operates from the outside rather than the inside of signification and hence is able to recognize the nonbenevolent power of signs: "The object of study is not what is said or written but the fact — the brute and often brutal fact — that it is said, that this and not rather something else is inscribed" (Wellbery, "Foreword" xii).

Meaning, in the posthermeneutic sense, is the coerced effect of a violent contortion of a (linguistic) universe bent out of shape so as to appear forever meaningful by itself, ready to validate and tend to all subjects able to read and write. Nonhermeneutic readers, like Kittler, who attempt to leave this universe behind and look beyond, must, in Wellbery's words, "suffer through the difference that post-structuralism makes" ("Foreword" viii). Given the posthermeneutic emphasis on the letter, I am inclined to read this statement literally: the suffering, it seems, bespeaks the level of difficulty and the pain endured by any form of reading — and writing — that seeks to wrest itself from the hermeneutic grip of circulatory meaning. Such pain distorts the physical body of those bearing it as well as the textual body of those recording it. Kittler's own readings indeed exhibit the particular marks of this suffering, evident, for example, in his unorthodox style of writing or the deliberate lack of a proper introduction or overall thesis statement.[15] Claiming that reading and writing around 1900 became a physiological study of autonomous codes guided by the laws of psychophysics, yet severed from the subject's own (un)conscious, Kittler implicitly validates his argument by performing it: his analysis cuts into pieces the structural coherence of the literary examples to which he refers. Quoting unsystematically from various texts at a time, he often reads passages with reference to the various technological and scientific inventions that allegedly shaped them, and not with regard to their interior meaning—for his own thesis, of course, forbids that they should have one to begin with. Rather than trying to understand them, Kittler's readings "spell out for the first time" the texts he engages (*Discourse Networks* 317). Kittler's method perfectly "makes sense," for if writing around 1900 indeed mirrored the fragmentation of the senses and the mechanical mode of operation of human consciousness, it literally makes no sense—now as well as then—to try to analyze these texts according to the hermeneutic principle they deliberately undermine.

As I argued in the first chapter, I believe Kittler's readings are partly based upon the same exaggerated notion of a profound "language-crisis" around 1900 that also informs more traditional scholarship. Although arguing from a decidedly hermeneutic perspective, Gotthard Wunberg, for example, similarly regards the "incomprehensibility" of literary modernism as its most characteristic trait, which he defines as the "impossibility to paraphrase the text" such that it "leads to a meaningful, consistent result" ("Unverständlichkeit" 313f.). For Wunberg, as for Kittler, the increasing autonomy and isolation of single aesthetic particles in literary modernism represents the logical conclusion of sociohistorical developments. More precisely, it reflects the triumphal success of scientific positivism and the concomitant rise of the visual media: "Ever since there is film, it has become possible for literature to delegate its traditional task. Now it can explore its own modernity, that is, the aesthetic autonomy of its signifiers" ("Unverständlichkeit" 350). Wunberg thus rephrases Kittler's basic argument, yet their joined efforts also give rise to some fundamental problems in literary criticism. Under the auspices of this theoretically sanctioned thesis of overall incomprehensibility, the often difficult and challenging poetic language around 1900 can legitimately be relegated to the side as little more than "pure metaphors," or "absolute ciphers," or a musical "Gebilde" that defies coherent meaning—especially since authors like George and Hofmannsthal explicitly endorsed this perspective as their own.[16]

The mere fact that hermeneutic and posthermeneutic criticism peacefully shake hands over the lack of sense allegedly encountered in literary modernism should suffice to make any reader suspicious. Both sides operate within a somewhat static framework of binary oppositions that juxtaposes "sense" and "nonsense" without examining in detail the ways in which the interdependency of both actually shapes individual texts. Thus, the alleged incomprehensibility of the discourse network around 1900 can be said to reintroduce, on a metatheoretical level, the hermeneutic mirror theory of literature it allegedly overcame. Instead of allowing the poetic subject to recognize its idealized self-image in the text it reads or writes, modern texts, according to Kittler, reveal the emptiness of the entire concept of bourgeois interiority and thus, once again, adequately reflect the (this time nonsensical) nature of the human self. Both times, the signifier has no story to tell of its own. Literature simply functions as the indispensable mirror in order to validate whatever notion of (hyper)reality and (non)subjectivity seems culturally en vogue at the time: once, around 1800, literature operated from inside the hermeneutic universe, while around 1900 it is used to observe and record the demise of this mechanism from the outside.

To be sure, there is little doubt that Kittler's work and posthermeneutic studies in general rank among the most productive and innovative in recent literary scholarship. Less obvious, however, is the methodological price to pay for opening one's eyes to the materiality of the letter. What epistemological terrain remains once the critic has abandoned the language game and come to see the sociocultural mechanisms responsible for the fabrication of meaning? What guarantees or enables (in the double sense of "begründen" as both to explain and to ground) the various "presuppositions" (exteriority, mediality, corporeality) Wellbery emphasizes in his discussion of Kittler's work? What is the significance of the posthermeneutic emphasis on external observation that replaces the imaginary inside of linguistic meaning? And who — or what — is responsible for the pain posthermeneutic texts both record and are made to bear?

These questions do not simply lead back into the twisted universe of traditional hermeneutics. Rather, they seek to locate both the posthermeneutic position and those who claim to inhabit it within the realm of exterior materiality thus disclosed. If the media are said to shape the production of meaning and give rise to those cultural phenomena known as literature, cinema, or cyberspace, one might ask who or what shaped them in the first place. Obviously film, for example, was not simply "born" that day in December 1895 during the Lumière showing at the Grand Café in Paris. Media do not suddenly emerge out of the blue, as Kittler's own work has convincingly demonstrated, nor can a mere descriptive account of their internal history—the various technological "inventions" succeeding and reinforcing each other—suffice theoretically to provide an answer to the question of origin. On the contrary, the history of cinema points toward a dialectical process of "overdetermined" sociopolitical changes caused, among others, by modern industrialization and urbanization in the nineteenth century. This process involves an interconnected array of macro- and microcosmic developments taking place within "the complex structured whole" of society, as the French Marxist Louis Althusser described it.[17]

Kittler's notion of "Aufschreibesysteme" seems to imply a similar structure at work on behalf of the letter, yet his own analysis remains ambiguously suspended between a broad Marxist critique of social materiality in general and the materiality of modern media in particular. Since Kittler emphasizes the latter over the former, the scope of his analysis remains too limited to support his major claim according to which "media determine our situation" and define the reality in which we live. What then is reality, one might ask, and how exactly does it take shape? Are media really the primary or even the only force at work here? Since Kittler does not explicitly engage these questions, Wellbery addresses them for him. According to him, posthermeneutics rejects the common notion of "Ideologiekritik" since Marx's own definition of ideology as "false consciousness" presupposes its opposite in the form of a "right" consciousness buried underneath and waiting to be revealed. In a phenomenological gesture, posthermeneutics abandons this notion of hidden truths and embraces the "surface materiality of the texts themselves," which "is the site of their historical efficacy" (Wellbery, "Foreword" xvii).

Let me note in passing that Wellbery's critique of "Ideologiekritik" stands as a red herring in the context of Marxist criticism, particularly in light of Althusser's radical redefinition of ideology as a necessary and irreducible precondition for the sustenance of any human society, even a communist one.[18] Strongly influenced by Lacanian psychoanalysis and its emphasis on linguistic structures, Althusser, contrary to Marx, abandoned the hope of ever completely stepping outside of ideology. This concession brings structuralist Marxism in much closer alliance with the posthermeneutic enterprise than Wellbery seems ready to admit. Generally speaking, though, Marxism remains far too concerned with objective reasoning and the determination of historical truths (i.e., Marx's "historical materialism" or Althusser's continued emphasis, inherited from Engels and Lenin, on the "last instance" analysis) to be of any assistance to a literary critique that set out to question the validity of precisely these concepts. Although posthermeneutics seeks to fold the hermeneutic universe of signification back upon the material basis that constitutes it, it nonetheless refuses to identify with a traditional Marxist perspective, for the latter does not allow for historical contingency or for giving methodological preference to surface appearances in the form of literary texts and the materiality of writing. Marxism is an obvious, yet dangerous, ally for posthermeneutics and ultimately needs to be avoided, and this accounts for the tension between traditional leftist academic circles and Kittler's media studies in Germany during the last decade.[19]

This posthermeneutic effort to sever the materialities of communication from their broader materialist framework remains problematic because it avoids coming to terms with the question of origin or grounding both of the letter and the entire mediated reality it evokes. Having forsaken both the (hermeneutic and deconstructive) language game of (non)meaning as well as the basic principles of Marxist dialectics, posthermeneutics needs to rely on a genealogical account of history exemplified in the works of Michel Foucault and New Historicism on the one hand and Niklas Luhmann's systems theory on the other.[20] Yet in doing so, it inherits their theoretical and methodological baggage as well. Gumbrecht himself acknowledges a precarious tendency in New Historicism to supplant the traditional paradigm of "learning from history" with that of discursively "making history" as text, in which case the notion of autopoietic subjectivity threatens to be reintroduced under the guise of New Historicist authors expressing themselves in and through the stories they write.[21] Similarly, Foucault's genealogical approach posits a contingent and discontinuous series of historical events and epistemic changes that can be studied merely by means of the complex network of interrelating discourses. He does not, however, determine the epistemological position of the "archaeologist of knowledge" who surveys this historical field. Althusser, who faced the same problem of accounting for the validity of his own insights into the all-comprehensive mechanism of ideological interpellation, tried to address and solve the dilemma as a true

Marxist: he simply claimed to inhabit a space outside of the ideology he scrutinized—a hardly convincing argument.[22] Explicitly rejecting the scientific objectivity allegedly commanded by Marxism as yet another discursive effect, Foucault's texts ultimately remain obscure with regard to their own location within the discursive history they describe, as Frank argues.[23] One wonders where Foucault's archaeologist comes from and how he knows what he knows. If it is neither the human subject nor language itself that produces knowledge, who or what does?

Precisely this question is at the very basis of Luhmann's cybernetic model of systems theory. It operates under the paradoxical premise that the observation of the contingent effects that govern modern society as a whole requires systems theory to posit itself as necessary and thus to occupy the very privileged position Luhmann himself declares impossible.[24] Modernity, for Luhmann, is but the name for an amorphous locus or structure inhabited by a variety of what he calls "autopoietic" subsystems, that is, self-reflective systems able to reproduce themselves independently from their environment. Since the task of modern society as a whole is to enable pluralism and the peaceful resolution of social conflict, it follows that the law of contingency that enables this process to unfold must itself be posited as necessary. Any efforts to break out of this paradox, Luhmann argues, are either doomed to fail, that is, to lead to new and different dichotomies that merely extend rather than overcome modernity, or, if they truly were successful, would obliterate modernity as such without any possible clue to imagine what follows it since we cannot think that which exceeds the operational mode of thought itself, namely difference. Hence, the paradox of necessary contingency—the fact that one must start somewhere by means of an arbitrary distinction that "cut[s] into the unmarked state of the world" (*Art* 42)—is constitutive of our thought. This, in turn, liberates the critic from having to account for the paradoxical position he occupies as long as his "analysis reclaims for itself the characteristics of its object of study: modernity" (*Beobachtungen der Moderne* 12). In other words, since nobody can observe himself observing things, it makes little sense to fret about an epistemological dilemma that cannot be avoided: "The unobservability of paradox," Luhmann concludes, "legitimates the arbitrariness of beginning" (*Art* 42).

While Luhmann's cybernetic model of modern society sounds theoretically convincing by virtue of acknowledging its fundamental paradox, it provides little insight with regard to the realm of aesthetics other than a generalized, if intriguing, description of the social subsystem called "art." In *Art as a Social System,* Luhmann spends over 400 pages discussing "art" without specific reference to—let alone an in-depth analysis of—an individual work of art. Instead, he argues that art cannot possibly "make a difference" in modern society since this would contradict his basic contention regarding the closed and self-referential nature of all systems. According to Luhmann, nobody is able to observe the totality of the world, not even by means of the work of art: "Focusing one's observation on the means of observation—on artistic means (such as twelve-tone technique)—excludes a total view of the world. No further reflection can get around that. . . . Transparency is paid for with opacity . . ." (*Art* 61). Although Luhmann acknowledges that the goal of art is to provide viable alternatives to the "way things are" and thus to "expose reality" in some way, he also insists that the means and inspiration for these aesthetic counter-paradigms are created within the system itself rather than provided by the real environment surrounding it. Like any autopoietic subsystem, art cannot, by definition, provide an adequate space for the intersection of conflicting perspectives on modern society at large since it remains obtuse to what exactly these perspectives are. Art can certainly *imagine* how other systems understand themselves, yet there is no hope whatsoever that such an aesthetic interpretation will ever fully *coincide* with the actual self-understanding of those systems to whom it refers. All works of art necessarily envision the other in ways prescribed by their own identity as art. Even if it claims to speak for and with the other, art only refers to itself, and aesthetic difference is just more of the same.

According to Luhmann, the unfolding of this paradox is what distinguishes art from other "things" in the world. Luhmann himself, however, is not interested in following the particular "ins" and "outs" of this process with reference to individual works of art. Rather, he provides an outside perspective of this operation as such, which is precisely what art itself cannot afford to do: "Whatever can be observed in art is thus the unfolding of a paradox that, for its part, escapes observation. . . . The only option is to observe forms instead of the unobservable, while knowing that this happens by unfolding a paradox" (*Art* 42). It follows that Luhmann is "not offering a helpful theory of art," as he himself concedes, but instead presents "a theoretical endeavor intended to clarify the context and contingency of art from a sociotheoretical perspective" (*Art* 3). No doubt, Luhmann is as clear-sighted about his own perspective as he can possibly be. He has managed to discuss art from the outside without being seduced by its charm, its beauty, or its paradoxical nature. Luhmann has nothing specific to say about any work in particular because, in his eyes, they are all more or less alike.

My point is that one need not disagree with Luhmann's overall theory regarding modern society to express some dissatisfaction and even disappointment about the insights it yields into the world of art. His comments are meant to elucidate the overarching idea of his systems theory rather than individual artworks. Although his critique of the institution of art is very informed, it remains too generic overall and hence ultimately serves to silence rather than enliven aesthetic objects. In order to resist this tendency, this study will give more credence to the Aestheticist perspective, according to which art is more than merely one system among many. Ideally speaking, one might say that the survival of art paradoxically hinges on its complete self-annihilation. There literally is no art except as other, for art *is* the other. The goal of art is to create an epistemological rupture that enables difference as such to emerge. Art is believed to be able to reflect and transform society at large precisely because it only exists in the form of its own negation. It cannot but keep alive the dream of a world "in which things would be different," as Adorno claimed, that is, a world in which things would be as they truly are by being different from what they have been made to be.

One may certainly disqualify this vision of art as an illusory construct contrived by artists and intellectuals who try to ensure the survival of their own subsystem, as Luhmann's theory implies. Yet the paradoxical "double character of art as both fait social and autonomous" (Adorno), that is, its ability to provide a space in which social contingency and difference are revealed as such, oddly mirrors that of system theory itself—which is to say that by disqualifying the self-understanding of autonomous art, Luhmann simultaneously jeopardizes the self-understanding of his own system theory since both are seen (or see themselves) as second-order observers, surveying the sociohistorical mechanisms that regulate modern society. Luhmann, of course, cannot admit this similarity and therefore charges the ideal of aesthetic autonomy pronounced by the *l'art pour l'art* movement with a fundamental misunderstanding of autopoiesis, a reproach worth quoting at length: "'L'art pour l'art' wants to thematize the essence of the system within the system itself and hence misses the crucial fact that autonomy does not abort the connections to the outside, but indeed presupposes them. It would lead to the end of aesthetic autopoiesis if dependency would be understood as the negation of dependency. Luckily, this program fails—for obvious reasons" ("Kunstwerk" 626; my translation).

Although he sounds as if he wanted to reprimand art for challenging the founding principles of his theory, Luhmann nonetheless formulates a crucial insight regarding the primary goal of art around 1900, which many of its critics have failed to notice. For the aesthetic autonomy of art was indeed supposed to end the autopoiesis of art by consciously subscribing to it. Aestheticism regards the autonomy of art as the paradoxical prerequisite for its transcendence *into* life and not, as is generally claimed, as an end in and for itself. However, instead of discrediting this vision, as Luhmann aims to do, his expressed relief about the historical failure of Aestheticism testifies to the very possibility of its success. In fact, I want to argue that art and aesthetic self-reflexivity can reasonably lay claim to the same epistemological clarity as does systems theory itself.

What does all of this mean for the discussion of posthermeneutic literary criticism? The previous analysis was intended to show: first, that the scholarly emphasis on the materiality of the letter opens up new dimensions for the reading of literary texts, while at the same time remaining trapped in the epistemological aporias of the poststructuralist perspective from which it emerged; and second, that Luhmann's recognition of contingency as a constitutive force of modern society does not categorically disqualify the revolutionary potential of art to thematize and disrupt the necessity of contingency. Quite the contrary, art might be understood as that paradoxical element of necessity that enables contingency to actually take place and become recognizable. Art *is* different and figures as the irreducible "supplement" within the postmodern thinking of difference itself. It literally embodies the difference it signifies. Wellbery himself acknowledges this ideal of self-cancellation at work in modern art: "Art is the subdomain of semiosis in which the random element intrinsic to all signification is elevated to a constitutive principle. . . . In art, I want to say, semiosis exposes itself to randomness, at once gives itself and withdraws itself within the singularity of its occurrence" ("Exteriority of Writing" 22). One can easily agree with Wellbery's statement without, however, subscribing to the entire agenda of posthermeneutics. Rather, Wellbery's own formulations bring to mind the hermeneutic wanderings of the later Heidegger and his notion of aletheia. Wellbery's comments are thus primarily directed against the Romantic ideal of the hermeneutic project and not against its twentieth-century variation.

It cannot be otherwise, for if posthermeneutics were truly to abandon the language game that sustains hermeneutics and deconstruction alike, there literally would be no space left for an analysis of the signifying process, and posthermeneutics would be forced to advocate and reinscribe the reign of absolute "nonsense" instead of analyzing the means of meaning-production.

Literary criticism ends in a cul-de-sac if it aligns itself too closely with media studies. The latter celebrate the arrival of the technological media as the irrevocable death sentence of art in general, and often "hail the conquering engineer"[25] as the replacement of the traditional artist. These days, Kittler himself is interested primarily in the social effects of digitalization and computer software and not in art—a distinction he, of course, would reject as immaterial and ideological, but one that I believe to be crucial. It follows that the methodological problems I have tried to point out are somewhat peripheral to his work, yet they are relevant for art and poetry around 1900. While that need not bother him or media studies in general, it should bother literary critics and those still interested in some kind of interpretative reading. By the same token, Foucault, New Historicism, and Luhmann can only offer limited insights into the single work of art because they do not share its basic premise of aesthetic autonomy. This indifference toward aesthetic difference also explains why Kittler readily adopts the overall incomprehensibility theory with regard to high literary modernism. If the work of art does not call forth a world of its own, but merely reflects the operative mechanism of media technology, it loses its privileged status and ultimately falls silent since it has nothing left to say.

I realize that posthermeneutic critics welcome this silence as a long-overdue repose from the idle chatter of hermeneutic sense-production, and although I value much of their basic critique, I fail to see how posthermeneutics can possibly lead literary analysis back toward the materiality of the letter as if that were the absolute and incontestable ground upon which its own analysis could positively take place. I want to argue the exact opposite, namely that posthermeneutic criticism, paradoxically, "misunderstands" both its history and its own trajectory by failing to distinguish between the various models of hermeneutic reading available today. To the degree that posthermeneutics in fact does examine the contingent effects of the primordial encounter between meaning and its other within the text—an encounter that constitutes and takes place within language—these readings remain, I argue, indebted to hermeneutics, albeit not in a Romantic, but in a Heideggerian sense. If the material ground for literary analysis cannot be identified or presupposed as something given without foreclosing the fundamental questions it seeks to answer, the appropriate critical practice is one that reflects its own unfoundedness. Wellbery himself concludes as follows: "The methodological consequence of my claim, then, would seem to be that the science of art, if you will, would develop its discourse as a reading of the unreadable, a reading that adheres to the moment of accidentality and non-sense that marks the work in its singularity and in the singularity of its history. But it is unclear whether such a reading could codify itself as a method, as a protocol, without obliterating the very thing it seeks to account for" ("Exteriority" 23).

"A reading of the unreadable" — is this not exactly what (a deconstructive, non- or post-) hermeneutics is all about, a nonmethodical method aimed at honoring aesthetic difference by means of a Heideggerian "Andenken" that tries to remember the different *as different*? Does, therefore, this literary practice not lead back to a particular tradition of hermeneutic reading exemplified in the later Heidegger's reflections on language and the work of art? I mean this not in the sense of rediscovering a primordial origin or presenting the common ground from which emerged both Gadamer's dialecto-dialogical method and Derrida's sense of "écriture," but in the sense of going back to a corpus of texts that problematize this notion of grounding itself. The task would be to try to unveil the difference within the identificatory power of language and the poetic notion of truth it enables.

Heidegger's understanding of *Dasein* and its relationship to Being can also be helpful with regard to the methodological concerns raised by post-hermeneutic criticism. According to Heidegger, *Dasein* must not be understood in the enlightened sense as an independent subject facing a world of objects, but needs to be determined in relation to Being as such, of which *Dasein* partakes. *Dasein* is turned toward Being and corresponds to it: "Man actually *is* the relation of this equivalence, and he is only that" (Der Mensch ist eigentlich dieser Bezug der Entsprechung, und er ist nur dies) (*Identität und Differenz* 22). The circulatory reasoning involved in the discernment of both Being and *Dasein* is deliberate: *Dasein is* its relationship to Being, a relationship that nonetheless already presupposes *Dasein* as one of its constitutive poles.[26] *Dasein* can only be itself by entering into a fundamental relationship with Being as the unconcealment of every-thing in the world: "The open harbors as its proper self the essential space of man, while he, and only he, is the form of being to whom Being reveals itself" (Das Offene birgt als es selbst die Wesensstätte des Menschen, wenn anders der Mensch, und nur er, dasjenige Seiende ist, dem das Sein sich lichtet) (*Gesamtausgabe* 54: 224). This logical circle involves a temporal paradox as well since *Dasein* alone may recognize Being as such and create the opening within which it will enable *Dasein* to become itself. *Dasein* thus emerges both as the cause and the effect of the primordial event of Being. It is called upon to properly open up the world into which it finds itself always already thrown.

Let me emphasize that one need not endorse Heidegger's entire philosophical project to appreciate its methodological insights for the study of literary texts. If one replaces "*Dasein*" with "the critic" and "Being" with "the text" in the quotes above, one can read Heidegger's comments as the outlines of an approach toward literary texts based upon the insight that text and critic are turned to and influence each other. In this sense, the scholar is not radically severed from his object of study, as Althusser and modern science contend, nor does he emerge as a mere effect of discursive epistemes (Foucault) or media systems (Kittler). Rather, the critic's gaze is retrospectively enabled by the world he engenders in his own critique. This is not a matter of simple dialectics between a subject and its own personal version of history, as criticized in Gumbrecht's reassessment of New Historicism. Instead, it demands a recognition of our passive inheritance of a history that nonetheless requires its active reconstruction in order to become realized: "[H]ermeneutics," Vattimo recently argued, "is legitimated as a narrative of modernity, that is, of its own provenance," and "it argues for its own validity by proposing a reconstruction of the destiny-tradition from which it arises" (*Beyond Interpretation* 12, 108). That reconstruction, or what Vattimo elsewhere calls the "hermeneutical return in infinitum,"[27] is absolutely necessary and cannot be circumvented. Yet it should not be mythologized either, as Heidegger often does. Rather, it must be performed self-critically and in full awareness of its inevitability.

In order to justify one's own reading of a text, one must provide an interpretation that accounts not only for its latent meaning, but also for the active reshaping of a hermeneutic world that enables both text and critic to relate to each other in the first place. This world need not be Heidegger's mythical reconstruction of ancient Greece—it might as well be Kittler's discursive network around 1900. In any case, however, one's analysis cannot simply be based upon some positive ground, such as the materiality of a letter whose provenance remains obscurely relegated to the domain of the governing media, presupposed as simply being there. Otherwise, the one "sense" that remains in posthermeneutics—the sense of getting it right by observing the mechanisms of meaning-production from the outside—must get it wrong if it refuses to account theoretically for the very "outside" it claims to inhabit. This, it seems, posthermeneutics cannot do since it would lead straight back to the very inside from which it allegedly took leave. I wonder if this tendency of language to give and lose itself in the web of its own being is not the actual cause for the physical pain posthermeneutics both suffers and records? Indeed, this pain has no proper place since it does not emanate from a self-identical origin that could be named without further proliferating and prolonging the agony it hopes to end. Posthermeneutics, too, must "suffer through" the difference language makes because its gesture of revealing the hidden grounds of writing and sense-production still remains caught therein. The materialistic critique of language is being reappropriated by the very mechanism it criticizes because the signifier cannot be set free to tell its story without being lost in the story it tells. Not only is this aporia always at stake during the process of reading and writing, but it also leads right to the core of the Aestheticist paradigm.

Modernist poetry around 1900 remains highly conscious of this predicament. In response, it tries to operate simultaneously from inside and outside the hermeneutic universe. Aestheticism linguistically deconstructs its own epistemological base, that is, the Romantic paradigm from which it emerges and upon which it depends for its own survival. This ambivalence gives rise to a high level of complexity in modernist poetry, which recognizes that there is no outside of language that has not always already been infiltrated by its mechanism of internal differentiation. In terms of contemporary media or systems theory, one might say that Aestheticism recognizes the ubiquity of the linguistic code that permeates and sustains society at large, at which point it sees the entire metaphysical history of binary oppositions breaking down. There remains no difference between art and life because the linguistic code constitutes both, and concepts such as identity and difference, inside and outside, subject and object, are nothing but the self-expression of the code underlying them.

The various chapters in this book try to remain mindful of this constitutive ambivalence of modernist poetry. If poetry around 1900 seeks to voice the ineffable and professes the death of the author, that demise should give rise, in the words of Roland Barthes, to "the birth of the reader" ("Death"; *Image, Music, Text* 148). Therefore, this study repeats the constitutive movement of the texts themselves in the process of reading them, which is why I operate from the inside out rather than, in a posthermeneutic manner, situating myself firmly outside of and in opposition to the text from the very beginning. Nor, however, do I presume to find an authorial and prior meaning in the text waiting to be restored, for either practice cannot but miss the intriguing self-performativity of language that is characteristic of Aestheticist poetry. What remains is for readers to follow the letter of the text, simultaneously looking forward toward the hermeneutic horizon and backward upon the trail of signification left behind. Unlike the gory locomotive at the Gare Montparnasse, readers cannot simply break through the interior realm of aesthetics onto the other side lest they are ready to accept the same disastrous consequences that distinguished the accident in Paris. Indeed, the surface of the literary text can be likened to the window at the train station: it allows us a glimpse of the other world that surrounds and sustains the inside. As the borderline that connects and separates two heterogeneous realms, the window of the text must be approached with caution rather than at high velocity. Even the posthermeneutic reference to the brutality of fact and the material aspects of communication does not liberate the critic from the grips of hermeneutics, but merely recognizes the constraints under which it—and all of us—are forced to operate. Otherwise, literary criticism is forced to destroy what it seeks to elucidate, namely the intricate play of materiality and meaning, sound and sense at work in literary texts. The ensuing ambivalence of a critique suspended between the material plane of isolated signifiers and the transcendental vision of their signified meaning not only is inevitable, but constitutes the very essence of literary criticism: "Like all authentic quests, the quest of criticism consists not in discovering its object but in assuring the conditions of its inaccessibility" (*Stanzas* xvi), the Italian philosopher Giorgio Agamben contends. Every reader must endure the impossibility of reading.

Adorno and Heidegger

My readings of works by Hofmannsthal, Rilke, and George presented in the second part of this study draw not only from Heidegger's philosophy, but also from another major reader of high literary modernism, Theodor W. Adorno. My choice of these two thinkers is determined by various factors, the most obvious being their shared emphasis and incisive commentaries on both phenomenology and life philosophy on the one hand and the three poets on the other. Their particular modes of reading, however, differ distinctly. Adorno shuns close readings and comments on fragmented passages exclusively, whereas Heidegger spends dozens of pages translating a single poem into his own idiosyncratic language, often losing sight of the original text. The two approaches are symptomatic of the larger philosophical framework within which they operate. For Adorno, the aesthetic fragment functions as a crucial reminder of the catastrophic impact of Western capitalism in modern culture. The process of commodification and mindless homogenization is best resisted in the nonsystematic form of the essay, whereas any effort to restore the imaginary wholeness of either poetic or critical texts silences the only remaining voice of criticism still alive in art today: the determinate negation of the untrue. For Heidegger, by contrast, poetry carries a more positive, yet far less specific, message regarding the primordial intertwinement of Being and truth. In order to understand what language means to say, the critic needs to circle the text and revisit every word over and over again until finally the presencing of truth (aletheia) is recognized in and through the work of art. "On the path towards language," however, Heidegger never experiences the Benjaminian "shock" of sudden awareness or the "flash of lightning" caused by the aesthetic "constellation" of highly charged particles left over and spurned by capitalist society. Rather, a critic inspired by Heidegger engages in a slow and tedious process of literally reinventing the originary moments of truth he claims to perceive in the text.

This leads to a second reason for consulting Adorno in the context of this study. Seeking to protect the "particular" or "nonidentical" from its appropriation into the capitalist mode of exchange, Adorno's sociopolitical mode of reading emerges as the necessary corrective to the mythological idealization of language recognizable in both Aestheticism and the later Heidegger "after the turn."[28] Adorno, whose own deconstructive "force" has repeatedly been acknowledged by critics,[29] still insists on the "social nature of poetry" that allows the philosopher to think the possibility of "a world where things would be different" ("Rede" 52). History sediments into language, he claims, meaning that Heidegger's search for the original meaning of single words is as misguided as his entire effort to name the essence of Being. Heidegger implicitly counters Adorno's dialectical investigation of language with an oracle-like affirmation of its obscure essence: "Saying and Being, word and thing belong together in a concealed, rarely contemplated, and unthinkable way" (Sage und Sein, Wort und Ding gehören in einer verhüllten, kaum bedachten und unausdenkbaren Weise zueinander) (Heidegger, "Das Wort"; *UzS* 237). His reflections on language literally silence any sociopolitical critique, a silence Adorno reads as the confession of its own complicity with the authoritarian violence governing the outside.[30] One of the most fundamental differences between Heidegger and Adorno thus lies in the latter's emphasis of negativity, his unwillingness to ever identify aesthetic truth with the primordial power of "worlding" recognized by Heidegger, who takes comfort in the idea that "truth is at work within art." This self-sufficiency of art as well as its (imaginary) rootedness in the lost origin of Greek philosophy stands in stark contrast to Adorno's emphasis on the fate of modern art as a *fait social* determined by capitalism. One might conceptualize this difference as that between history and historicity, between a dialectical effort of recuperating that which, for Adorno, has been irrevocably lost in the course of history (namely freedom from domination) and Heidegger's nondialectical effort to "unconceal" the presencing of an ahistorical truth at work in art.

In spite of these differences, however, the two thinkers also share some characteristic traits. Both insist on philosophical thought moving in and through language and thus endorse what Heidegger calls the "neighborly relations" between "Dichten und Denken," that is, the interdependency of art and philosophy. If Heidegger deliberately moves in circles, Adorno's thought moves in a dialectical spiral that seeks to reintegrate that which it was forced to exclude without ever coming to a final conclusion. And yet, Adorno pursuing a "negative dialectics" is not fundamentally at odds with Heidegger's effort to account for the "Gleichursprünglichkeit" of life and *Dasein*, of Being and language. Although their methods differ, the ultimate goal remains similar, namely to salvage, via art, a utopian moment in the history of modernity that cannot be assimilated into the prevalent mode of instrumental rationality. Of course, the complexity of the engagement between these two thinkers far exceeds the scope of this study. But I still want to suggest that Adorno's often problematic (mis)readings of Heidegger's "Jargon of Authenticity," his polemics against the "tautological" and "antidialectical" nature of Heidegger's philosophy, and his charge that ontology fortifies, instead of dismantles, modern myths and thus succumbs to a totalitarian form of pure "irrationalism"—all these attacks might indeed be read as therapeutic mechanisms of purification meant to exorcise what appeared "uncanny" in Heidegger, namely the sometimes striking similarities with regard to the meaning and essence of art in modern society, which Adorno desperately seeks to disavow yet implicitly acknowledges by means of the disavowal itself.[31]

This brings up the last reason for juxtaposing Heidegger and Adorno, which concerns the political implications of their work. Heidegger's enthusiastic cooperation during the early years of National Socialist power in Germany defines one possible response to the challenge of modernity. Adorno's critical theory inherited from Marx and Freud designates the other. I am aware that my attempt to draw from both thinkers may strike some readers as problematic in light of the ethical implications of their work. While I do not want to minimize the personal and theoretical differences between the two philosophers—differences that shall become more apparent in the subsequent chapters of this book—I similarly resist the tendency to disavow the complexity of their engagement by creating the juxtaposition of a "good" and a "bad" object of reference meant to serve as searchlights guiding the uncharted course of academic criticism. If Heidegger's poetics at times surfaces as the "return of the repressed" in Adorno's own *Aesthetic Theory*, it seems not only legitimate, but crucial, to read them in the context of each other in order to understand the ethicopolitical dimension of art and philosophy around the turn of the twentieth century.

Thus, a three-part structure emerges as the guiding theoretical framework for this entire study. While Kittler tries to situate himself completely outside the imaginary performance of the letter, whose historical modes of (ab)use he records, and Heidegger's metaphysical readings of modern poetry aim at precisely the opposite by literally following the path of language from inside the text, occasionally getting lost therein, Adorno's *Aesthetic Theory* might be said to occupy the middle ground between the two poles. He explicitly rejects the radical Marxist position exemplified in the works of the later Lukács, who more or less identifies all art and thought at the beginning of the twentieth century as a particular form of irrationalism leading straight to fascism.[32] On the other hand, however, Adorno similarly refuses to follow the hermeneutic paradigm of immanent reading, situating his critique in the force field between autonomous and socially determined art instead. What remains is a vast corpus of difficult readings that are often as idiosyncratic as they are insightful, for example when Adorno condemns jazz as the epitome of the capitalist culture industry, or unambiguously pits "Schönberg and progression" against "Strawinsky and reactionism" in his *Philosophy of New Music*, or denounces Rilke's "words of consolation" (*Trostsprüche*) as well as Hofmannsthal's "theater for children" (*Kindertheater*) as paling variants of high literary modernism in comparison to the lyrical works of Eichendorff and Mörike.

I emphasize what I consider to be some of the problematic aspects of Adorno's work from the very beginning, not only because this study tries to resist being appropriated by either one of the three theoretical sources informing it. More important, Adorno's critical comments about Aestheticism are symptomatic of a particular bias that pervades his readings, namely his adherence to some notion of a self-determining, nonalienated subject as the only basis for an active resistance against the totalitarian politics of capitalism. Adorno's critique consistently favors Romanticism (as well as modernist texts by Kafka, Proust, and Beckett) over Aestheticism because the former anticipated or mourned the loss of subjectivity, whereas the latter deliberately dissolved the human subject within the presymbolic realm opened up by the look of things, and indeed celebrated this dissolution as the regained freedom of mankind.

As recent critics have noted, Adorno thus develops an ambiguous, if not self-contradictory, notion of modern subjectivity: On the one hand, he regards the unified subject as the coerced effect of the pervasive social constraints inherent in capitalism and thus as a sign of domination. On the other hand, however, he equally rejects the dissolution of subjectivity and instead holds fast to the notion of a "liberated" or "free" subject able to preserve the integrity of its own "inner nature."[33] The latter, it seems, only serves as the necessary specter for his critique of the former, particularly in light of Adorno's refusal to flesh out the details of this utopian *promesse de bonheur* that characterized, for example, much of Herbert Marcuse's philosophy. Indeed, Adorno's harsh critique of Benjamin's arcades project and his (somewhat more nuanced) discussion of surrealism, as a kind of object fetishism that abandons theoretical mediation and thus fortifies the already existing reification of the real, stem precisely from Adorno's reluctance to allow for the kind of messianic redemption to which Benjamin aspired.[34] "Were one to speak forcefully, one might say that the work [Benjamin's arcades project] is located at the crossroads of magic and positivism. This spot is bewitched. Only theory is able to break the spell" (Wollte man drastisch reden, so könnte man sagen, die Arbeit [Benjamins Passagenwerk] sei am Kreuzweg von Magie und Positivismus angesiedelt. Diese Stelle ist verhext. Nur die Theorie vermöchte den Bann zu brechen) (Benjamin, *Schriften* I/3: 1096).

Adorno's critique of modernist poetry repeats this charge regarding the mystification of the commodity form over and over again: "The modernist poet is vanquished by the power of things like the outsider is subdued by force of the cartel" (Der Dichter der Moderne läßt von der Macht der Dinge sich überwältigen wie der Outsider vom Kartel) ("George und Hofmannsthal" 235). In other words, Adorno strongly resists what he elsewhere calls the "dissolution of all self-posited human existence" ("Charakteristik Walter Benjamins"; *GS* 10/1: 246). However, Adorno's apodictic rhetoric as well as his strong critique of Benjamin's project forestalls the question it implicitly poses, namely whether a radical Aestheticism is inherently uncritical, repressive, or even totalitarian by default. If "theory is able to break the spell," as Adorno put it in his letter to Benjamin, I do not see any aesthetic ground or reason to impose such a strict hierarchy between Romanticism and Aestheticism as long as one does not uncritically hypostatize either one. For Aestheticism's attempt to redeem subject and object alike in the form of poetic language pays the price of a potentially reified aesthetics, much like Romanticism often fell prey to a purely speculative or idealist notion of freedom devoid of material substance. The space between these two visions can only be bridged during the process of critical reading as discussed in my previous comments. Hence, the following chapter outlines what I consider the major differences between the "discourse networks" of 1800 and 1900.

PART II

3 Aestheticism, Romanticism, and the Body of Language

Given the complexity of their engagement, the relationship between Romanticism and Aestheticism, or what Kittler calls the discourse networks around 1800 and 1900, is still a matter of debate among literary scholars. According to Kittler, the Romantic ideal of intuiting the meaning of literary texts was seriously undermined by its competition with the visual media around 1900. The "moving pictures" actually presented the very images that both philosophy and poetry were merely able to suggest. Hence, literary modernism was forced to abandon the hermeneutic paradigm that relied upon the power of poetic imagination as a means to translate the author's original vision into language and back again. Around 1900, Kittler maintains, "transposition necessarily takes the place of translation" (*Discourse Networks* 265), meaning that writing no longer presupposed the Romantic "author" or any message at all beyond the factual event of writing as such. Confined to the symbolic, writing "realizes, materially, manifestly, the impossible sentence *I am writing*" (*Discourse* 334). Similarly, Roland Barthes has linked "The Death of the Author" to the writings of Mallarmé and French symbolism in particular, and thus implicitly supports Kittler's analysis: "Linguistically, the author is never more than the instance writing, just as I is nothing other than the instance saying I" ("Death of the Author" 145).

Contrary to Kittler and Barthes, however, most critics still focus on the fundamental "Epochenverwandtschaft" (Walter Müller-Seidel) between the two time periods.[1] They identify the birth of the modern episteme, to use Foucault's terminology, with the rise of Romanticism and thus tend to emphasize its similarities rather than its differences with literary modernism around 1900. Foucault himself dates the beginning of what he calls "literature" proper at the beginning of the nineteenth century, at which time language ceases to function as the self-effacing mediator between everything else and "acquires a being of its own" (*Order of Things* 360). More drastic still, Lacoue-Labarthe and Nancy argue that "we still belong to the era it [Romanticism] opened up. The present period continues to deny precisely this belonging" and uses "romanticism [sic] as a foil, without ever recognizing—or in order not to recognize—that it has done little more than rehash romanticism's discoveries" (Lacoue-Labarthe and Nancy 15).

These different perspectives on literary history do not simply betray the terminological confusion surrounding the time period we nebulously refer to as "modern" (e.g., modernity, modernism, avant-garde), but rather are symptomatic of the essentially ambivalent relationship between Romanticism and Aestheticism. Aestheticism does not define the discourse network of 1900, as Kittler argues, but operates in between Romanticism and the radical avant-garde, for it participates in both paradigms at once. Aestheticism shares with the avant-garde its resistance to the continuous proliferation of what it perceives as meaningless words, yet it does so meaningfully from inside rather than outside the hermeneutic circle. Kittler virtually obliterates this decisive difference between the *l'art pour l'art* movement and the avant-garde because he situates both vis-à-vis the power of cinematic images: "Words as literal anti-nature, literature as word art, the relation between both as material equality—this is their constellation in the purest art for art's sake and in the most daring games of the avant-garde. Since December 28, 1895, there has been an infallible criterion for high literature: it cannot be filmed" (Kittler, *Discourse* 248). I believe it is crucial to augment Kittler's account and to distinguish between the radical avant-garde (e.g., Dadaism, surrealism, Russian constructivism) on the one hand and high literary modernism (e.g., Aestheticism, symbolism) on the other. While this distinction is hardly ever observed in Anglo-American literary theory, it is nonetheless highly instructive for the understanding of both movements, as some critics have rightly argued with reference to Peter Bürger's influential *Theory of the Avant-Garde.*[2]

Hence, although I generally agree with Kittler's overall assessment, I disagree with the implicit notion that Aestheticism's "art for art's sake" represented a complete and utter disinterest in life on all levels. Instead, it seems obvious that modernist poetry ultimately shared the same utopian goal as the avant-garde, except that it operated from the other side of the equation, so to speak. Whereas the avant-garde sought to aestheticize life, that is, to pull art into life, high modernism tried to enliven art, that is, to pull life into art. One hoped to abolish the institution of art; the other sought fully to realize its utopian potential *as art*. In other words, Aestheticism continues the Romantic project of world transcendence by reversing its trajectory. Instead of expanding outward, it folds back upon itself. Poetry around 1900 thus reflects the paradoxical nature of nineteenth-century culture and its dual focus on science and metaphysics, materiality and its dissolution. It embodies a positivist vision of Romanticism, a poetry engaged in the process of deconstruction that differs from both the Romantic ideal of aesthetic production and its avant-gardist counterpart of demolition. Rather, Aestheticism tries to dismantle the history of artistic production from within by pushing it toward the brink of self-annihilation. It certainly mobilizes the materiality of linguistic signifiers, as Kittler claims, yet it does so in order to provide a physical basis for the meaning-potential of language and not in order to eradicate this potential altogether, as did the avant-garde.

The following outline of four central theses may help to substantiate this claim. First, I argue that posthermeneutic criticism does not adequately reflect the ambivalence of "sense making" that informs modernist poetry. For example, Kittler's discussion of Hofmannsthal's "Ein Brief" in the context of Morgenstern's nonsense poem "Das Große Lalula" aptly highlights their common problematization of language, yet tends to disregard the different means by which they operate.[3] Morgenstern's poem consists of words like "Kroklokwafzi" and "Seiokrontro," and, in Kittler's eyes, represents a typical example of the avant-gardist attempt "to write writing" and "to inscribe more and different sorts of things than any voice has ever spoken" (*Discourse* 212). Instead of deconstructing hermeneutics on its own ground, Morgenstern's poem simply refuses to signify anything at all. Disobeying all semantic and syntactical rules of language, "The Great Lalula" defines the materiality of writing as the site of resistance against meaning.

Aestheticism, by contrast, radicalizes the hermeneutic process by taking its method of reading to its disastrous conclusion: Hofmannsthal's Chandos pursues the search for linguistic meaning until the imaginary-symbolic space between words and things finally collapses and language itself begins to matter and become "real." Rather than the promised apprehension of the text's ultimate meaning, however, Chandos experiences a vortex caused by words that "stop making sense" and stare right back at him instead: "The individual words swarmed around me; they transformed into eyes that looked at me and into which I had to look in return: they form vortexes that incessantly turn and through which one enters into nothingness. I get dizzy looking down into them" (Die einzelnen Worte schwammen um mich; sie gerannen zu Augen, die mich anstarrten und in die ich wieder hineinstarren muß: Wirbel sind sie, in die hinabzusehen mich schwindelt, die sich unaufhaltsam drehen und durch die hindurch man ins Leere kommt) ("Ein Brief" 466). The subject is being read by the text it tries to read. Aestheticist texts literally face the real emptiness that pervades the imaginary space of the hermeneutic universe, yet this confrontation takes place in the context of seemingly meaningful, rather than nonsensical, texts. If Kittler implies that, in literary modernism, "the medium is the message" — to use McLuhan's famous dictum — my readings of Hofmannsthal, Rilke, and George aim to prove that the reverse is more accurate: their "message is the medium." The reversal indicates a crucial shift of perspective and expresses Aestheticism's quasi-religious belief in language itself as the productive source for everything it talks about.

This also means that the aesthetic differences between literature and the visual media around 1900 are not as exclusive as Kittler suggests. The "look of things" is important to high literary modernism, which seeks to undermine the dichotomy between words and images. Some poems even employ a cinematographic technique to achieve their magical effect of transubstantiation. Rilke's thing-poems are exemplary in this regard. They force the reader's gaze to oscillate between words and things as the two interdependent poles that define the aesthetic parameters of the poem. Minimizing the spatiotemporal difference between these poles, the two are ultimately superimposed upon each other: words become things without losing their identity as "dark spots" on the page. For George, too, the *Gestalt* of language vouches for poetry's construction of a different world. Aestheticism tries to picture the weakness of language as its inherent strength, meaning that the materialist aspect of language is often celebrated as an advantage vis-à-vis the "imaginary signifier" in film because it is in and through writing that signification begins to matter again.

My second thesis argues that Aestheticism recognizes the self not in the Romantic ideal of poetic subjectivity, but in the look of things and the experience of life. German poetry around 1900 assimilates and subverts the Romantic notion of aesthetic experience in which the subject envisions the other mainly as a mirror reflecting back the subject's own self. As David Wellbery argues, the poetic gaze in early Romanticism functions to constitute male subjectivity: "the act of seeing folds back upon itself, *sees its own seeing,*" such that "male identity—his *ich*—is constituted within the mirroring *that allows him to see himself being seen*" (*Specular Moment* 40-41). By contrast, poetry at the turn of the century transforms the typical Romantic juxtaposition of male subject and female object into one of a nonidentifiable identity between self and other. Once again, the Chandos Letter is paradigmatic in this regard, for once words are said to develop eyes of their own that gaze back at the beholder, he becomes subjected to the gaze of an "other." The hermeneutic paradigm of artistic self-recognition in and through the text breaks down the moment the reader himself is being read by the words he tries to read, meaning that language ceases to function as the imaginary space for the formation of the self. This reciprocity of the Aestheticist gaze upsets the Romantic power hierarchy. It reveals the seeing subject as the always already seen object and opens up a whirling abyss that does not lead toward a final self-understanding or coherent meaning, but rather "into an emptiness." Chandos falls into the nonsignificant space of Being opened up by the look of things, that is, a decentered network of interconnected stares that no longer add up to a coherent whole.

Poetry around 1900 ceases to function as the imaginary mirror for reading and writing subjects and becomes a gateway to a different, life-philosophical experience of the "self" instead. To put it paradoxically, one might say that Aestheticism hopes to redeem the philosophical ideals of early Romanticism by negating them. While the Romantics envisioned themselves on the move toward the final unification of self and world—"Die Wunderblume stand vor ihm, und er sah nach Thüringen, welches er jetzt hinter sich ließ mit der seltsamen Ahnung hinüber, als werde er nach langen Wanderungen von der Weltgegend her, nach welcher sie jetzt reisten, in sein Vaterland zurückkommen, und als reiste er daher diesem eigentlich zu" (Novalis)—the poetic goal around 1900 was to realize that this journey was always already completed even before it had begun. Aestheticism eradicates the spatial and temporal distance necessary for subject and object to *become* identified with one another since the self is always already "at home" in the world. The Aestheticist subject encounters life both within and without the borders of its own body: "Within me the universe, the zap of all things dead or alive moving most individually like in this tree" (In mir der Kosmos, die Säfte aller lebendigen und toten Dinge höchst individuell schwingend, ebenso in dem Baum)—this is how Hofmannsthal described one of his magical moments in 1895 (*RA; GW* III: 401). Aestheticism simultaneously creates and redeems its own nostalgia for life the very instant it expresses itself, because life cannot transcend itself, but always remains present and indeed, at every instance, sustains my own presence, my own being. Life is envisioned as a multiperspectival field in which the Romantic subject figures as a topographic void because the self is exposed as nothing but a word among words, a look among looks, and a body among bodies.

Aestheticism's critique of the Cartesian subject and the poetics of early Romanticism anticipates the postmodern dissolution of subjectivity. In his reflections on the gaze, Jacques Lacan, for example, argues that the "preexisting gaze" undermines the self-centered field of human vision. Although the individual actively perceives the visual world, it simultaneously remains the object of a gaze emanating not necessarily from some other person, but rather from the symbolic "Other" that locates the subject within the invisible order of the real. "I see only from one point," Lacan observes, "but in my existence I am looked at from all sides" (*The Four Fundamental Concepts of Psychoanalysis* 72). Lacan explicitly refers to this objectification of the subject as a mode of representation, of taking pictures: "[I]n the scopic field, the gaze is outside, I am looked at, that is to say, I am a picture.... Hence it comes about that the gaze is the instrument through which ... I am photo-graphed" (*Concepts* 106). In modernist poetry around 1900, this "photo-graphic" gaze indeed reveals the subject's imaginary at work within the symbolic universe of written texts. The snapshot taken by the "Other"—or, in a more familiar terminology, the pivotal "Augenblick" constitutive of art at the turn of the century—exposes the rigidly fixed position of the hermeneutic reader caught in a specular mode of exchange determined by the letter. Aestheticism replaces the Romantic mirror with the look of things as the utopian freedom of self and other outside the traditional rules of signification and meaning.

This Aestheticist practice of deconstructing hermeneutic paradigms and poetic subjectivity fundamentally changes the status of language: this is my third thesis. Although Romanticism had already recognized and even programmatically endorsed the autonomy of language, it bestowed upon literature a metaphysical function beyond the exploration of linguistic self-referentiality. The time period around 1800 is characterized by a utopian optimism about the future possibilities of language in the form of a "transcendental poetry" (Schlegel) and its universal "Zauberwort" (Novalis). This transcendentalism, however, casts a dubious light on the material presence of the signifier. In Romantic poetry, language cannot be left standing on its own ground, but needs to be engaged in the continuous process of becoming that ensures the proliferation of meaningful discourse and allows for the narcissistic self-representation of the poet's (and reader's) subjectivity in and through language. German Aestheticism, by contrast, unveils the Romantic quest for the origin—the home, the voice of the mother, ultimately the womb, as Kittler and Wellbery argue[4]—as the continued realization of the (linguistic) difference constitutive of discourse. Whereas the Romantic period ultimately denounced poetic language as an inadequate representation of the absolute (e.g., God, nature, subjectivity) whose essence necessarily transcends its own manifestation, the culture around 1900, under the strong influence of "life philosophy," displays a tendency to collapse both poles into one: existence becomes essence and language is said to embody truth.

Seeking the embodiment of meaning, Aestheticism contributes to "the other discourse of modernity," as Georg Braungart characterizes an often overlooked critical and aesthetic tradition that sought to overcome the metaphysical opposition of mind and body, sign and referent.[5] Unlike in Romanticism, what is at stake in modernist poetry is neither the Freudian unconscious nor the body as the locus of our instincts and drives, but the body of language and the language of the body. Aestheticism deconstructs hermeneutics and rediscovers materiality in and through language. Around 1900, the Romantic *Zauberwort* is always already present and absent, familiar and unknown, because, once properly looked at, words reveal themselves not as abstract notions, but as material beings that resonate with the life they evoke. Poetic language carries life within: it consists of a potentiality for pure, embodied meaning that cannot become manifest without falling prey to the commodification it critiques. The look of things ceaselessly evoked in modernist poetry *is* language speaking with its own, unalienated voice, yet it is also, at the same time, nothing but a constructed metaphor already dead by the time it meets the eye of the reader. The only means to make this potentiality of language known is for poetry to fold language back upon itself so that its inner life shines through the very words that mask it. Aestheticism does not seek to transcend language, but to withdraw into it until the Romantic journey of eternal becoming finally implodes into the being of life.

Given this mythologization of life and language around 1900, the ethical dimension of the sociocultural critique proclaimed by the Aestheticist movement rings hollow: this is my last thesis. Protesting against the reification and commodification of modern life without offering any concise vision other than the metaphysical ideal of life itself, Aestheticism succumbs to just one more of the many metaphysical notions it originally had sought to render superfluous. Life, like nature, God, or the holy spirit, is envisioned both everywhere and nowhere and thus hardly distinct from earlier philosophical ideals or scientific theorems. Moreover, in spite of its antisubjective tone, modernist poetry still advocates a narcissistic ideal of the poetic self, this time founded on the alleged lack of subjectivity rather than the reflection of its imaginary wholeness. The aristocratic stance that distinguished all three authors regardless of their actual social background is symptomatic of the ideological distance separating the poet from the "mob" (George), the "poor" (Rilke), or the "peasants" (Hofmannsthal) who roam in a world beyond the magical circle of art. The elitism of the George circle reveals the social impotence of an aesthetics whose "success" hinges on its failed implementation into real life. In other words, the Aestheticist ideal of embodied meaning in the "Weltinnenraum" (Rilke) of art cannot but remain fundamentally at odds with the reality it claims to transform. It is precisely the interminable fear that poetic words might fall prey to the instrumental rationality governing the outside that accounts for the self-reflexivity of modernist poetry and the fortification of its borders. Although the poetic voice of a language literally "speaking itself" promises to alleviate the pain caused by the alienation of modern life, it cannot do anything but commemorate its own failure to succeed. This ambiguity alone authenticates the sense of truth palpable in poetry around 1900.

Once Aestheticism stops reflecting upon its inevitable failure and becomes mesmerized by its own rhetoric and materiality instead of deconstructing it again and again, that interior space of extreme tension necessary to sustain the poem's magical vision of life collapses. The end of poetic ambiguity and the lack of self-reflexivity signals the beginning of a totalitarian politics that regards the external world as nothing but a blank screen for the aesthetic projection of the inspired artist. Fascism defines the moment at which aesthetics turns into politics in order to overcome its lack of influence upon social reality. "Only a God can save us," Heidegger still proclaimed in his *Spiegel* interview in 1966, fully aware of the disaster brought about by the false prophets of National Socialism and the alleged reincarnation of divine power in the *Gestalt* of the failed artist reborn as a national leader. For many critics, Heidegger's stubborn insistence on metaphysical redemption and his unwillingness to come to terms with his own contribution to the barbarism of the Nazi regime are the most disappointing and problematic aspects of his life and work. In spite of the persistent denial of hard-core Heideggerians, there can indeed be little doubt that Heidegger's political involvement was by no means accidental or an arbitrary personal choice that needs to be evaluated independently from his philosophical legacy. On the contrary, Heidegger's rectorship in Freiburg and his enthusiastic Nazi participation present the necessary and logical conclusion of his own call for a metaphysical revolution, for the crucial "Entschlossenheit" of *Dasein* and its "Sprung" into Being, as Rüdiger Safranski's biography clearly documents.[6] Heidegger's unyielding silence after the war hence indicates his refusal to think through the philosophical and ethical implications of his failed attempt of trying to help philosophy break out of its cave and take control of the sociopolitical reality of Being.

And yet, without trying to exonerate Heidegger, one might read his *Spiegel* interview as the quiet renunciation of his own political engagement in favor of a God who does not exist and divine ideals that will never come true. Having struggled his entire life with the Catholic faith, Heidegger's confessed hope for redemption is not as passive and facile a stance as it might appear at first. It does require the constant renewal of personal faith in the face of its eternal frustration. This forever hopeless activity also constitutes the basic principle of Aestheticist poetry, which seems able to provide a corrective vision of life as long as its "God" presents a phantasmagoria whose power relies on it being severed from the world it criticizes and seeks to change. Once this autonomy is abandoned in an effort to implement these ideals within the sociopolitical world, however, modernism ultimately destroys rather than protects the "true" reality it claims to have always already created aesthetically. This indeed seems to be the silent message of the look of things around 1900: "There is hope," Adorno quotes Kafka, "but not for us."

4 Hofmannsthal and the Voice of Language

Verstehen, Gestalten, Künstler sein, wozu?
Wozu denn Leben, und wozu die Kunst?
— Hofmannsthal

Poetry, Freedom, and Subjectivity

"[O]ur voices demand language and at the same time enjoy an almost perfect freedom of use vis-à-vis language" (Zumthor 4). Paul Zumthor's broad ethnographic and literary investigations into the history of oral poetry, ranging from antiquity to the present, from Africa to South America and Europe, lead him to unveil this "paradox of voice" (Zumthor 7) at the heart of language. Unlike the written sign, Zumthor argues, the voice "speaks itself at the very moment it speaks; in and of itself, it is pure exigency" (Zumthor 6). Although indebted primarily to anthropological research rather than literary studies, Zumthor's observations are particularly relevant for textual critics. Given the empirical rather than speculative basis of his study, his observations lend further credence to the literary and philosophical debate concerning the nature of signification and the relationship between spoken and written language, that is, what Jacques Derrida has termed the phonocentrism of Western philosophy. Western poetry, usually separated in the form of writing from this originary self-presence, seeks to regain its lost voice in an effort to speak of nothing but its own being: "From its initial outburst poetry aspires, like an ideal term, to purify itself from semantic constraints, to get outside language, ahead of a fullness where everything that is not simple presence would be abolished" (Zumthor 128). This venture of trying to utter the pure voice of language, Zumthor argues, "culminates in song" (Zumthor 4), and in the eyes and ears of literary criticism, poetry, indeed, is the music of literature. Giorgio Agamben affirmatively quotes Paul

Valéry's definition of the poem as a "prolonged hesitation between sound and sense" (Agamben, *The End of the Poem* 109), Hans-Georg Gadamer explicitly charges poetry with the exploration of the "tonality of language" (*Poetica* 21f.), and one of Adorno's favorite metaphors refers to the musical "murmur" of modern poetry ("Zum Gedächtnis Eichendorffs" 79f.).

Like music, lyric poetry can be said to commemorate a form of communication operating beyond the basic divide of signifier and signified. By liberating words from the burden of signification, poetic language reminds the critic that the essence of language does not consist in forging a bond between linguistic sense and extralinguistic reality, between word and thing. Twentieth-century hermeneutics argues that any such correspondence already presupposes a primordial ground upon which to take place, that is, a Heideggerian "clearing" that first allows to relate a linguistic utterance to the material world. This space of pure Being, Heidegger argues, is opened up in and through the work of art, most notably poetry, because "all art is, in essence, poetry" ("Der Ursprung des Kunstwerkes"; *Holzwege* 60). This metaphysical conception of (poetic) language is not unique to Heidegger or the hermeneutic-phenomenological tradition. In his book of the German drama, Walter Benjamin, for example, similarly states that "truth is not relational," but appears "in a primordial perception in which words possess their denominating nobility, which has not been lost to cognitive meaning" ("Ursprung des deutschen Trauerspiels"; *Gesammelte Schriften* 1/1: 216). Like Heidegger, Benjamin regards truth as a temporal occurrence rather than an empirical fact or a static relationship between words and things. Particularly in his early writings, truth is an uncontrollable event inherent in language. It erupts only for the flash of a moment and gives rise to those modern shock sensations that the later Benjamin believed had the power to shatter the reified relations that characterize capitalist society. "Language," he claims, "does not have a content," but literally "expresses itself" ("Sprache"; *GS* 2/1: 142, 145). The task of the philosopher, like that of the translator, consists in expressing a "pure language which does not mean anything or express anything" other than "the creative word" that names the essence of things ("Übersetzer"; *GS* IV/1: 19). The "language of truth" is but a "true language" ("Übersetzer"; *GS* IV/1: 16).

Given this potential of language, the ultimate goal of both author and critic is not simply to explore the meaning or the musical qualities of words. Rather, it consists in making audible the primordial voice of a pure language lost in the modern world. Benjamin's messianic belief in the "word of God" ("Sprache"; *GS* 2/1: 150) and the "self-expression" of language resonates throughout the history of twentieth-century literary criticism. In essays on Eichendorff, Mörike, George, among others,[1] Adorno again and again calls for the poet to submerge into language, to lose his sense of (estranged) subjectivity in order to reemerge as the poetic voice of language itself: "Hence the highest lyric works are those in which the subject, with no remaining trace of mere matter, sounds forth in language until language itself acquires a voice" (*Notes* I: 43) (Die höchsten lyrischen Gebilde sind darum die, in denen das Subjekt, ohne Rest von bloßem Stoff, in der Sprache tönt, bis die Sprache selbst laut wird) ("Rede"; *GS* 11: 56). Adorno's ideal of "language acquiring a voice" and "speaking itself" is echoed in the later Heidegger's formulation that "language speaks" (*Unterwegs zur Sprache* 19) and literally "comes to terms with itself through speech" (*Unterwegs* 161): "We leave speaking up to language," because "language is: language. Language speaks" (Der Sprache überlassen wir das Sprechen," because: "Die Sprache ist: Sprache. Die Sprache spricht) (*Unterwegs* 12, 13).

Both Adorno and Heidegger regard poetry as the privileged medium for the immediate and unalienated expression of an original truth that has been silenced in modern society. High literary modernism is exemplary in this regard since it claims that "true" language is saturated with a silence that vibrates throughout speech. The art of poetry, it follows, consists in the balancing act of giving voice to a speech on the brink of silence. At the end of the century, an "aesthetics of silence" ensues (Susan Sontag) by means of which modernist poetry quietly gestures toward the ineffable as that which informs all art. Aestheticism seeks to transcend the communicative purpose of language toward the evocation of a primordial sense that, paradoxically, is nonetheless said to reside within the very words that ostracize it. According to Heidegger, "[T]he essence of the word does not consist in its utterance, not in idle talk nor noise nor in its function to regulate the traffic of communication"; instead, the "essentially speaking word," the word of myth, is the "silent word" constitutive of all art ("Parmenides"; *GA* 54: 172f.). In Adorno's words: "The true language of art is beyond language" (Die wahre Sprache der Kunst ist sprachlos) (*Ästhetische Theorie* 171).

The following reading of Hofmannsthal's early works examines this relationship between speech and silence with regard to high literary modernism around 1900. The aesthetic self-referentiality characteristic of Aestheticist poetry is based on the paradoxical belief that language has a voice of its own that must be silenced in and through poetic speech before it can be heard. As a consequence, poetry around 1900 objectifies language and increasingly explores its own being as a linguistic artifact consisting of form and sound. The material substance and acoustic resonance of words takes precedence over the meaning expressed therein. Put differently, the voice of silence literally gains shape as an absence rendered present in and through the poetic constellation of words. The acoustic thus becomes intertwined with the visual since the dialectics of silence and speech is correlated to that of written and spoken language. Much like the written words of the poem seek to capture a pure meaning that ultimately escapes them, speech hopes to give voice to a silence it cannot express. The essence of poetry, in other words, is precisely that which transcends the poem, be it the silence of speech or the meaning of words. The chore of the artist is to express or literally give shape to this primordial "other" of poetry; the complimentary task of the critics is to follow its trace and mark its presence.

The task, needless to emphasize, is a formidable one. It requires a particular finesse or "technique" on both parts to understand what defies logical understanding, an ability to intuit what cannot be perceived. As a consequence, most scholars focus almost exclusively on the formal qualities (rhythm and rhyme, alliterations and assonances) of modernist poetry while disregarding or even dismissing its semantic content as secondary, enigmatic, or simply incomprehensible. As I argued in the previous chapters, I am suspicious of hermeneutics' good-natured retreat from the question of meaning. It rests on a quid pro quo, a sort of symbolic exchange in which the real text is replaced by the ideal meaning it is said to embody without being able fully to express it. This quantum leap of hermeneutics, if I may call it thus, is generally revered as the sign of a successful reading. Ironically, it is precisely this leap, the critic's sudden "eureka" uttered at the precise moment she perceives the ineffable, that distinguishes some of the best exegeses of art. The most important *Augenblick* in any reading, it is also the most idiosyncratic, a point strikingly illustrated in Roland Barthes's reflections on the nature of photography. Once he has found the one photograph that, in his eyes, captures the very essence of the medium — one in which the abstract "studium" of the image is entirely replaced by the personal "punctum" that pierces through the representation and reveals a "subtle *beyond*," as he says (*Camera Lucida* 59) — Barthes does not even bother to reproduce it, because "it exists only for me. For you, it would be nothing but an indifferent picture" (*Camera* 73).

My concern is not to question the authenticity of Barthes's, or anybody else's, epiphany in response to art, including my own. It would be a crude misunderstanding of deconstruction (both in its subjective and objective sense) to identify it(self) with such a denouncing gesture that simply aims at unveiling a primordial void at the center of the reader's aesthetic experience. Such a version of deconstruction merely corroborates the obvious fact that there is a void or silence inherent in art without which any effort of interpretation, including that of deconstruction itself, would be utterly superfluous. The purpose of art is the communication of the ineffable, and the fact that this effort can never succeed does not render it any less pleasurable or important for the critic to engage it nonetheless. I do want to suggest, however, that the collective retreat of literary critics from the "incomprehensibility" of modernist poetry might be indicative of a tendency to avoid something else that expresses itself therein, a somber noise distinctly different from the sweet melody of poetic language. We find a first indication for this presence when Roland Barthes, with reference to Mallarmé, speaks of "murder" as the most characteristic trait of modernist art (*Writing Degree Zero* 5), or in Agamben's claim that "art for art's sake" does not mean "the *enjoyment* of art for its own sake, but the *destruction* of art worked by art" (*Stanzas* 49). A tendency toward self-destruction inheres in the history of modern art and finds its most distinct expression in high modernism around 1900. The rumbling of physical violence is the basso continuo that accompanies the silent song of modernist poetry. Adorno's musical sensitivity, for one, perceives the "silent tremors" ("George und Hofmannsthal"; *GS* XI: 528) of this violence precisely in what he considers to be the most beautiful examples of lyric poetry.

The question emerges as to the meaning and origin of this violence: Where does it come from and what does it mean? Who or what exactly is being silenced in modern art and why? According to Heidegger, the silence emanates from Being itself. Being simultaneously appears and withdraws in the work of art, and poetry is foremost among the arts to commemorate this motion of *unconcealment* that defines Being. Put differently, the silence inherent in lyric poetry testifies to what Heidegger calls the "Seinsvergessenheit" of the modern era, the fact that in the eyes of modern man, the world has become reduced to a rigid and pregiven realm of objects confronted by a rationalist subject unaware of the ontological interdependency between itself and everything else. It is precisely the modern notion of subjectivity that poetry must overcome in order to speak of itself. Language is able to express its own voice only to the degree that it simultaneously silences the noisy *Gerede* of the "man" responsible for the proliferation of meaningless chatter. What Zumthor refers to as the "song of poetry" is the resonance of a poetic movement that vibrates from the suppression of subjectivity and the concomitant welcoming of Being. In the end, "true" language, for Heidegger, does not sing or speak, but falls silent and dissolves into the sacred moment of "worlding" it has opened and closed through speech.

Adorno sees things differently. He regards the disturbing "tremors" underlying poetic language as a symptom of the social reification caused by commodity fetishism. Capitalism oppresses the free expression of the human individual. The latter seeks refuge in the pure voice of language itself, yet it can never completely overcome the sociopolitical forces responsible for the silence it must endure and against which it tries to speak out—hence the inner dissonance characteristic of modern art. For Adorno, the fate of language and subjectivity is inextricably intertwined since language finds its own voice only in and through that of the human subject, while the subject is able to survive only by abandoning itself to a kind of "pure" language both autonomous and subservient, ubiquitous and self-effacing at the same time.[2] Adorno grants language a certain level of autonomy only to ascribe it immediately to the users of language. Poetic speech is freed from the serfdom of capitalism for the sole purpose of serving those who are said to acquire freedom through its voice.

The following reading of Hofmannsthal departs from Adorno at precisely this point. For Aestheticism implicitly challenges his notion that pure language, that is, the silent voice of poetry, is concerned primarily with providing a shelter for the alienated subject of modernity. Rather, poetry around 1900 speaks of the struggle to rid itself from the shackles of precisely the kind of humanist legacy Adorno upholds in his texts, meaning the (bourgeois/Marxist) ideal of free, self-expressive subjectivity. One might say that the violence in modernist poetry stems not from the sociopolitical restraints limiting the potential of human subjectivity, but rather from those that restrict the being of language itself. This interpretation, however, is also at odds with Heidegger, since he, too, subordinates language to a greater power that allegedly transcends it. For Adorno, language speaks of the human individual. For Heidegger, it bears the name of Being. Yet both thinkers limit the freedom of language to literally express itself. Poetry at the turn of the century, however, is far more self-reliant and self-absorbed than both Adorno and Heidegger were willing to concede. In Aestheticist poetry, language seeks to find its proper voice as a representation of its own "potentiality" (Agamben) to represent, which is to say that its efforts to express the "life" it carries within must always be understood as a genuine form of self-expression.

This is not to claim that words could ever become completely autonomous and independent from those who use them. If that were the case, language itself would acquire the status of self-sufficient subjectivity it denies to human agents. This problem haunts Paul de Man's radical conception of language as entirely "inhuman." Whereas he refers to "the fundamental non-human character of language" (*Resistance to Theory* 96), I argue that poetic language around 1900 aligns itself strictly with the human body rather than the mind. The poetic promise of freedom does not completely overcome the human, but rather shifts emphasis from spirit to matter, from subjectivity to the body of the individual. Hence, one need not completely renounce Adorno's and Heidegger's notion that poetry is concerned with human salvation or the unconcealment of Being in the world. For during the course of its attempted self-liberation, poetry—understood as a thing in its own right—might be able to liberate and present other things as well, and those certainly include the human body, but not the humanist construct of autonomous subjectivity growing on its back. Agamben phrases it most succinctly: "[T]he polemic of modern art is not directed against man, but against his ideological counterfeiting; it is not antihuman, but antihumanistic" (*Stanzas* 55).

Not only is this precisely the fundamental Aestheticist belief around 1900, but it also accounts for the alleged "incomprehensibility" of modernist poetry. The strategic retreat of traditional hermeneutics, its lack of curiosity when confronted with some of the most difficult texts in modernism, seeks to rescue humanism from the humiliation of being explicitly rejected in and through the very genre it had declared its most reliable ally. In poetry around 1900, it is the body that speaks, and not the subject. If a murder takes place in modernist poetry, the humanist notion of subjectivity is its first victim.[3] With it, however, dies the philosophical notion of extralinguistic meaning and that of the thing itself. Both are shown to take shape within the play of words hovering between silence and sound, written and spoken language. Aestheticism offers the materiality of the signifier as physical evidence of the demise of traditional humanism. The "body" of language is made to testify to the death of the subject.

The question remains as to the nature of this "body." It cannot be the written word because writing reifies rather than liberates language. But what else is there? How can we find a signifier that materializes the voice of language without suppressing it at the same time? Is there a sign that signifies the end of signification? Modernist poetry, I argue, identifies such paradoxical signs as the signs of punctuation that regulate the flow of language. Punctuation signs cannot be voiced outside of a specific context since they carry no meaning by themselves. Yet they are nonetheless crucial for linguistic meaning to emerge. Having no voice of their own, punctuation signs commemorate language itself. They materialize a pure potentiality for meaning without activating it, allowing language to find its proper voice in the body of a text.

The following reading of Hofmannsthal's "Vorfrühling" (1891) will serve to clarify this point. My argument is twofold, claiming, first, that "Vorfrühling" self-reflectively thematizes and performs its own production of linguistic meaning in the form of poetic speech. For Hofmannsthal in particular and modernist poetry in general, the world literally comes alive and dies in discourse. The purpose of poetry is to commemorate this paradoxical nature of language to both embody and disfigure the things to which it refers. Poetry around 1900 thus anticipates major insights of later poststructuralist theory: far from being "incomprehensible" itself, it merely promotes an overall incomprehensibility meant to deconstruct the Romantic tradition of universal sense. My second argument specifically concerns this relationship between Romanticism and Aestheticism. I contend that the latter abandons the Romantic ideal of transcendental consciousness and the power of poetic imagination in search of a prior, more meaningful, form of expression located beyond the traditional opposition of mind and body, sign and referent. A medium without a message other than the medium itself, the voice of language around 1900 is depersonalized and, unlike its Romantic predecessor, must not be "understood" in the mind, but literally experienced in and through the senses. The success of modernist poetry hinges on its sensibility to stop making sense and to explore the primordiality of language liberated from the burden of all identifiable meaning. Focusing in particular on the use of punctuation signs in Hofmannsthal's poem, I argue that it literally "makes the point" of identifying the pure voice of poetry with the body of language in its written form.

The Poetry of Breath: Hofmannsthal's "Vorfrühling"

Vorfrühling

Es läuft der Frühlingswind
Durch kahle Alleen,
Seltsame Dinge sind
In seinem Wehn.

Er hat sich gewiegt,
Wo Weinen war,
Und hat sich geschmiegt
In zerrüttetes Haar.

Er schüttelte nieder
Akazienblüten
Und kühlte die Glieder,
Die atmend glühten.

Lippen im Lachen
Hat er berührt,
Die weichen und wachen
Fluren durchspürt.

Er glitt durch die Flöte
Als schluchzender Schrei,
An dämmernder Röte
Flog er vorbei.

Er flog mit Scheigen
Durch flüsternde Zimmer
Und löschte im Neigen
Der Ampel Schimmer.

Es läuft der Frühlingswind
Durch kahle Allen,
Seltsame Dinge sind
In seinem Wehn.

Durch die glatten
Kahlen Alleen
Treibt sein Wehn
Blasse Schatten.

Und den Duft,
Den er gebracht,
Von wo er gekommen
Seit gestern Nacht.

("Gedichte" I: 17f.)

Early Spring

The spring wind is gliding
Mid boughs that are bare,
In his heart hiding
Strange things and rare.

His cradle hath swung
In sob-shaken air,
And oft hath he clung
In passion-loosed hair.

Acacia blossoms
Beneath him snowed,
His breath cooled the bosoms
That throbbing glowed.

Lips in their laughter
First he would claim,
Soft fields thereafter
Woke when he came.

The flute he passed through in
A sobbing cry,

The sunset's red ruin
He swiftly flew by.

In silence proceeding
Through whispering rooms,
And quenched with his speeding
The lamps' yellow blooms.

The spring wind is gliding
Mid boughs that are bare,
In his heart hiding
Strange things and rare.

Through the reviving
Alleys and meadows
His breath is driving
Wraith-like shadows.

A scent without name
He bears in his flight
From whence he came
Since yester-night.[4]

Although widely regarded as one of Hofmannsthal's most accomplished poems — Stefan George ranked it among his best — "Vorfrühling" has rarely been the object of a close reading. Adorno's brief remarks situate it mainly in the context of French Impressionist painting, while other critics revere its musical form of expression, yet nobody seems interested in paying attention to the performance of the letter in Hofmannsthal's text.[5] Instead, one usually encounters statements such as this from Michael Hamburger, who, referring to "Vorfrühling," professes that "to a very large degree, the German language itself has written this poem" (Michael Hamburger 28). Even Adorno concurs: "As if to enact a form of self-control, Hofmannsthal's poems recite themselves. Their talkative tone allows the verses to listen to themselves" (Wie zur eigenen Kontrolle rezitieren seine [Hofmannsthals] Gedichte sich selbst. Ihr Redendes gestattet es den Versen sich zuzuhören) ("George und Hofmannsthal"; *GS* 10/1: 211). A poem literally written and recited by and for language itself, "Vorfrühling" serves as an exemplary specimen for the analysis of modernism's ideal to give rise to the pure voice of speech and to "let language speak itself." Can we hear what it says?

Adorno's and Hamburger's comments offer a good starting point for exploring this question. Hofmannsthal's "Vorfrühling" (1891) is indeed exemplary for the musical qualities of poetic language. It is one of the few poems for which the *Blätter für die Kunst* chose to publish a musical score, written by Clemens Frankenstein.[6] And yet, the effort is somewhat redundant, because the poem, when read aloud, sings a kind of melody on its own accord. Moreover, its rhythmic structure mirrors the erratic nature of the "running" wind it describes. Although the meter consistently shows two stressed syllables, the verses begin and end irregularly as masculine or feminine, while their length varies between as few as three and as many as six syllables. The changing rhythm at work within the poem stands in contrast to its structural coherence, which features nine stanzas of four verses each. The external appearance of the poem suggests a formal regularity or stasis at odds with its internal emphasis on incessant flux, creating a latent conflict between discharge and containment that erupts in the last two strophes. In contrast to the rest of the poem, most lines in the eighth and the ninth stanza begin with a stressed rather than an unstressed syllable, while the rhyme pattern changes from the embracing pattern "abab" to "abba" in stanza eight and "abcb" in stanza nine, thus setting them apart as a coda from the rest of the poem. The repetition of the first stanza further corroborates this sense of conflict, for it literally encloses the first part of the poem and excludes the coda. This rupture of the poem's formal and structural coherence is significant and deliberate. Looking at its first publication in the *Blätter für die Kunst* in December 1892, one notices that the original version of the poem was indeed printed without the repetition of the first stanza and also featured the last two stanzas in the very center of the poem as stanzas four and five. Hofmannsthal's subsequent rearrangement of "Vorfrühling" highlights the importance he bestowed upon the last two stanzas and the aesthetic break they signify.

Although my reading will concentrate on the significance of the coda at the end of the poem, I shall briefly examine the first part of Hofmannsthal's poem (stanzas one through seven). It presents the history of the wind's travels within the repetition of the first and the seventh strophes, which function both as beginning and end of the narrative proper. Continuous movement is its central theme. Written in the past and perfect tense, these stanzas enumerate the multitude of "strange things" the wind not only witnessed, but literally "touched," or even brought to life by means of its ability to change and adapt to them. Shaking blossoming flowers from the tree or playing with human hair, the wind literally "runs through" and inhabits these things much like the flute whose sobbing cry *is* nothing but the metamorphosed wind itself caught in a different shape.

The fourth stanza provides a good example in this regard. Located at the structural core of the poem's first part, it accentuates the sensuous intimacy of the lips "it has touched" by breaking through the repetitive syntactical pattern that dominates the first line of stanzas two through six. Instead of beginning with the same pronoun "Er" followed by the finite verb form, the strophe begins with the object rather than the subject of the sentence. The rupture visually situates the immediate perception of things themselves at the (geographic and figurative) center of the poem, yet it also speaks to its cardinal theme of trying to overcome the inside/outside or subject/object dichotomy. The image of the laughing lips represents the kind of physical openness necessary for the wind to become alive inside every-thing it encounters. The wind enlivens these things much like our breath "running" through the human body sustains it as a whole, a parallelism anticipated and motivated by the immediately preceding line describing the "breathing" limbs touched by the wind.

The wind recalls the breath of life. It *is* life, a life that continuously needs to breathe while, simultaneously, in and through this breath all living things seem forever joined together in the shapeless body of ceaseless movement evoked in Hofmannsthal's poem. Although it never tarries in the presence of these things, the wind nonetheless connects with them physically and, in parting, takes part of them along on its journey. The transitoriness of life is both acknowledged and overcome in this peculiar memory of things past. The temporal change from past to present tense in stanzas one and seven signifies that all things "are" still alive within the "Wehn" of the wind itself. This fusion of wind and things is also expressed in the first line of these strophes, which, on a grammatical level, refuses to grant the wind the same amount of self-determining subjectivity it enjoyed in the narrative proper. Instead of "Der Frühlingswind läuft," a parallel construction to the other introductory lines of the first part, we read: "Es läuft der Frühlingswind," a phrase that indicates an essential change with regard to who or what "it" is that actually "runs." Once again, the wind has metamorphosed by virtue of the "things" that now are being carried along with "it." The wind literally *is* the presence of things past that are alive and still breathe therein.

The last two stanzas, however, speak a different language. Their tone is sharper, the verses grow shorter, and the rhythm becomes more pronounced. A kind of dramatic climax is palpable, introduced by the eighth stanza's rewording of the previous one in which the union of wind and things was still experienced as "sein Wehn." This "Wehn" connotes not only the blowing movement of the wind proper, but its pains of labor as well— "Wehn" understood as the spastic movement of one body giving birth to another. The poem's first part can thus be read as the story of the wind's impregnation by the things that he now carries along as part of its own self, while the eighth stanza describes the actual moment of delivery that once again (grammatically) separates the wind's "Wehn" from the strange things "it" was before: "Durch die glatten / Kahlen Alleen / Treibt sein Wehn / Blasse Schatten." The adjective "glatt" emphasizes the slickness of a world in which it has become difficult, if not impossible, to hold onto things, meaning that the erstwhile promising narrative pregnant with life literally "gives birth to" (Treibt sein Wehn) nothing but mere shadows of all those things it once bore within. What had originally seemed the long-awaited renewal of nature brought about by the winds of spring is revealed as mere reverie.

The coda thus rearranges "things" both literally and figuratively on the syntactical and semantic level alike. Adding several new words such as "shadows" while repeating others, the eighth stanza seemingly restates the previous one, yet completely alters its tone and meaning, creating a fundamental split within what appeared to be the impervious unity of life itself. In a self-reflective gesture, the text is being restructured so that it says different things than before. The presence of life is lost, a shift emphasized in the last stanza, which reverts back to the perfect tense and ends with a yet intensified image of darkness—"night." The coda tells a different story from the rest of the poem, for once the wind of life abides, things emerge as their own shadows until night comes and darkness reigns. The wind of spring can merely conjure, almost teasingly, the absence of a late life in the form of "pale shadows" without being able to enliven the scenery of the barren alleys.

If one were to give a provisional summary of Hofmannsthal's poem, one could particularly refer to its peculiar title—"Vorfrühling"—and regard the entire text as a clever deconstruction of a traditional literary topos (spring) that promises more than it can keep. The poem provides a chilling, if aesthetically pleasing, moment of disillusionment fairly typical for the young Hofmannsthal and representative of one of his most favorite themes, the transitoriness of life—(Wie kann das sein . . . ?). It seems that after all is said and done, what remains for both poet and readers alike is to acknowledge the transitoriness of life aesthetically by writing or reading about it. Although the wind can slacken and spring may never come, the poem *as art* prevails and outlasts the powers of death it both conjures and conquers. In this sense, Hofmannsthal's poem ultimately triumphs over the night with which it ends.

This fairly typical reading for Hofmannsthal studies in general is, in this particular case, based on an oversight, because it must come to terms with a particular and quite literary point—a syntactical marker, that is, a simple period in the most common linguistic sense. The last stanza is grammatically incomplete and hence difficult to "understand" unless the reader chooses to disregard the period that separates the last line of stanza eight from the first in stanza nine. The oversight of this period is significant. Along with the "Und" that starts the stanza, it allows one to align "the fragrance / it has brought" with the verb "treibt" that properly refers to the "pale shadows" mentioned earlier, in which case the last stanza can be read as the mere continuation of the previous one. The wind now drives along not only the shadows of things past, but also their smell. Only by means of this syntactical connection does the whole poem "make sense" again. However, if left standing alone by itself, the last stanza remains fragmentary and resists interpretation because of the complete lack of finite verb forms causing a semantic incoherence with regard to its proper meaning. To be sure, I do not refer to the missing auxiliary verbs needed to complete the lines "Den er gebracht *hat*" or "Von wo er gekommen *ist*," for they are unambiguously implied by the text itself. Rather, what remains uncertain is the semantic trajectory of the entire stanza and its connection to the poem at large. The reader is forced to guess what the poem means to say, and this is precisely the reason most might tend to disregard the point of separation and seek to reconnect the two last stanzas in spite of the grammatical rules they have to bend.

In light of this oversight, it becomes clear that if the above-mentioned interpretation and its emphasis on the eternal quality of art remains engaging at all, it is with regard to the further questions it raises rather than those it purports to have answered. At stake is not merely a specific topos of modern poetry, but the nature of language itself, particularly its ability to render present—via the power of signification—all those things that are, in fact, absent—which is to say that the motif of transitoriness not only applies to the proper theme and semantic content of the poem (i.e., the cyclical nature of life), but also pertains to the linguistic medium that sustains its aesthetic form as such. If we grant "Vorfrühling" this quality of poetic self-reflexivity and, at the same time, refuse to overlook the syntactical markers that structure the text, then two more oppositional readings of the poem can be put forward.

The first focuses on the transitory nature of both human memory and linguistic representation unable to present life as it really is. Let me call this the Romantic interpretation, in that it emphasizes the ideal of poetic transcendence and regards language as the failed and reified expression of the absolute. The "night" pictured at the end of the poem is an image not only for the darkness that ensues once the wind has blown over and individual things have passed away; rather, it self-consciously refers to the poem's own constitutive process as a mere constellation of words, and thus speaks, on a metalevel, to the semantic obscurity that ensues once the reader's gaze fails to "make sense" of the words it encounters. Such a gaze literally goes blind and ends up in the dark. With its final emphasis on "Nacht," the poem reveals the fragility of a hermeneutic sense utterly dependent upon the meaning it needs to engage. As it allows for multiple readings and refuses to privilege one in particular, the poem exposes its own failure to illuminate, indeed enliven, the dead signifiers that promised life, much as the wind ultimately failed to really bring about the spring it announced. The pale shadows mentioned in the poem can be regarded as its own literary images evoked by symbolic structures that have lost their power to call forth and present the meaning they signify. Since the poem ultimately remains a prisoner of language in the form of a written text, it inevitably succumbs to the very darkness and petrification it laments. Hofmannsthal's "Vorfrühling" has failed because language always fails, and it is that failure that it self-consciously acknowledges as unavoidable. The lack of a verb in the last line intensifies this morbid, lifeless atmosphere left behind both by the wind of spring and the poem alike. Language always signifies death. It is death itself.

The second reading, which I shall call the Aestheticist reading, also acknowledges the poem's emphasis on transitoriness and its ultimate failure to make sense. However, it seeks to redeem this inadequacy of language by focusing on its equally inherent power to call forth the life of which it speaks. From this perspective, the very life the poem seems unable to represent is nowhere to be found outside of the text either, since the entire theme of presence and absence is predicated upon, and hence illuminates, nothing but its inherent power to create the world in the first place. It is only because poetic language has always already called things by their proper name that it can subsequently be charged with the failure to adequately represent them once again. The textual evidence in support of this Aestheticist endorsement of the constitutive function of language can be found in the last stanza in general and the final line in particular. These might be read without intuitively adding the missing verb, in which case the poem remains unfinished, and the last sentence incomplete. The fragmentary character of the poem calls for a continuation of the narrative, the abrupt ending of which signifies the "night" as the lack of a wor(l)d that ensues were language simply to stop and fall silent. This "night" is not to be seen primarily as a symbol for the intuitive lack of referential language and its inability to render present what it signifies. Rather, it *is* the literal darkness resulting from the lack of language and the silencing of the poetic word.

The Aestheticist perspective on language is thus essentially ambiguous. Language not only enables the meaning it forestalls, but also calls forth the world that it simultaneously hides behind the symbolic bars of signification. Hence, it is impossible to decide which of the two readings I suggested is more accurate. No matter how they look at it, readers are forced to provide the missing links themselves. They must choose to disregard particular signs or invent others if their reading is to "make sense." It follows that the question of the "right" interpretation literally becomes one of *reading:* once read aloud the poem achieves meaning via a particular *intonation* of the text. The reader must become a speaker and give voice to the text. His task consists in deciding where and which words to accentuate so that the poem begins to speak beyond the limits of what it is able to say in its written form. The reading gaze gives way to the poetic ideal of spoken language. Hofmannsthal's poem deliberately calls for a corporeal voice since otherwise its meaning remains, quite literally, unheard or lost in the dark of the "night" with which the poem ends. "Vorfrühling" relies on spoken rather than written language to make its point—and this, incidentally, consists in granting priority to speech rather than writing. Being spoken, language itself speaks, since language finds its own voice the very moment it gets lost in speech.

The wind both described and poetically simulated within the erratic rhythm of Hofmannsthal's verses can be likened to the breath of the reader. Just as the wind, in the first part of the poem, functions as the invisible bond that physically connects and enlivens the various "things" it has "touched," poetic language needs to be spoken in order to express its own potentiality for creating meaning. Language and this potentiality for meaning lie at the heart of matter. Things *are* as long as they are one with the wind, that is, as long as they are nurtured, indeed embodied, in and through the breath of the speaker who sings their names by virtue of the poem's acoustic qualities continuously emphasized by Hofmannsthal's critics. Once these things are released and severed from the speech that sheltered them, they succumb to their own "pale shadows" in the form of empty signs. Such a language is alienated from itself and the things it signifies, and the (temporal and spatial) difference between sign and thing is responsible for the loss of their primordial unity and the lack of unequivocal meaning the poem signifies at the end.

This juxtaposition of speech and writing also accounts for the peculiar tension between the poetic rhythm that enlivens the poem and its static reification in the form of a written text that is but the corrupt derivative of speech. In contrast to the discourse network around 1800, which calls for the continuous perpetuation of the reading and writing processes in order to authenticate meaning, Hofmannsthal's poem calls for the deconstruction of writing and the reactivation of the primordial power of language. Those who "understand" the Aestheticist message of "Vorfrühling" must also turn it back against itself and reverse its genetic mode of operation. They must stop *making* sense of it and instead begin to *feel* the voice of language within the sense(s) of their body.

And yet, I want to argue that it would be simplistic and ultimately misleading to contend that Hofmannsthal's "Vorfrühling" merely reaffirms the traditional metaphysical distinction between oral and written language. Rather, Hofmannsthal's juxtaposition of vision versus acoustics, written versus spoken discourse serves to reveal a fundamental dilemma at the heart of language, whose self-expression is the cause of its own undoing as language. Pure speech does not exist since language can never find its proper voice. For in order to speak, language requires the presence of a body that is not its own. Readers must lend their voice to language and thus prevent it from gaining full autonomy and self-presence. This is not to imply that the reader is the true subject of Hofmannsthal's poem. The text does not call upon readers to express themselves in language, but, on the contrary, to help language express itself as that which unites the subject and object of speech. The real "subject" of "Vorfrühling" is not the interiority of the humanist individual or that of an ideal reader/speaker/writer, but the wind that sustains life, that is, the breath of a living being able to voice language.

In quite a literary sense, the poem renders this point visually evident. The period separating the last two stanzas functions as a material stumbling block for the reader's gaze and its visionary powers of imagination. Rather than spiraling outward toward a potentially infinite universe of signification, the reading process in Hofmannsthal's works spirals inward instead until it ends up in a realm without any spatiotemporal extension at all. The reader's gaze finally encounters the mute body of language in the form of a punctum that cannot quietly be dissolved into meaning—which is to say that the first obstacle on the way toward pronouncing the voice of language can be overcome only if the reader understands herself not as an individual subject, but as part of the omnipresent force of life, in which case her voice cannot but merge with the poem to the effect that reader and language complement each other. On the basis of this fusion, language indeed gains a means of self-expression that does not speak of itself, but of life as such. As soon as language finds its own voice, it gets lost therein, because this voice inevitably presents a world without ever being able to represent itself. This self-cancellation of language in the name of things is the second reason why there is no pure speech that gives voice to language. "Pure" speech is either nonsensical, and hence not related to language at all, or self-effacing in the sense that it calls forth a world in which it gains a presence only in the form of writing.

In order to reveal this constitutive paradox of language, Hofmannsthal's poem must somehow signify the ability of language to speak and create meaning without simultaneously activating that meaning. The crucial issue is to evoke language's potentiality to speak by means of a sign that is not meaningful by itself, since otherwise language itself immediately vanishes from sight. This is precisely the function of the period separating the eighth and the ninth stanza. It carries no immediate meaning and hence cannot be understood outside the context in which it appears, yet is nonetheless decisive for giving meaning to the poem. On the one hand, the poem recognizes the period as a sign of the reification of language that must be dissolved acoustically within the living voice of its reader to become meaningful; on the other hand, however, the ultimate goal of this liquidation of language is to make language "matter" again and to recognize the primordially "real" qualities of language as opposed to the hermeneutic focus on its imaginary effects. Words are not meant to evoke the mere visual illusion of things, nor do they signify their abstract meaning, but they are themselves constitutive of these things and such meaning. The period ultimately makes the point that language only matters in precisely those moments of its own undoing, for the potentiality of language to signify and to name its own ability to name must remain unsaid or suspended in order to preserve itself. And yet, the paradox is that this potentiality has always already been realized in and through this suspension, which signifies the being of language.

Adorno's critical stance toward modernist poetry is based upon precisely this antihumanist emphasis on life around 1900: "Subjectivity no longer knows itself as the soul-providing center of the cosmos" (Nicht länger weiß sich Subjektivität als das beseelende Zentrum des Kosmos) ("George und Hofmannsthal"; GS 10/1: 234), he laments with regard to Hofmannsthal's and George's poetry. However, Adorno's Romanticist bias for the traditional notion of subjectivity might also be indicative of a more fundamental fear haunting all art criticism: that of being superfluous. Whereas Romanticism called upon the poetic imagination of the reader to complement its utopian visions, Aestheticism proposes the exact opposite, namely the silencing of an endless commentary that suffocates the voice of a primordial language that has always already spoken and said what it means to say. Of course this is not to argue that modernist poetry has truly captured the "voice of silence," for this ideal itself remains forever bound to the very language it seeks to transcend. Nor does it mean that Aestheticist poetry could ever truly dispense with commentary, my own included. Quite the contrary, the enigmatic nature of modernist poetry deliberately solicits literary criticism, yet does so solely for the purpose of undoing it. The entire process of (critical) reading is called upon to self-destruct and give way to the mere sensation of being in the world. Poetry around 1900 self-consciously thematizes this paradox and regards the human body rather than the mind as the site and the origin of meaning. Its ultimate message is thus not simply to "stop making sense," as posthermeneutic critics have proposed, but to signify the meaning-potential of language and the primordial quality of life as meaningful in itself. At the same time, Aestheticism's destruction of the hermeneutic ideal of total understanding cannot but offend the ears of traditional literary critics and their search for identifiable meaning. This may not be the least of reasons for scholars to plead deaf to the "voice of silence" and to denounce the "incomprehensibility" of modernist poetry while revering its musical qualities instead. For it is still easier to sing along to an inaudible tune than to fall silent and simply listen to oneself breathe.

Gestures of Speech

The previous reading of Hofmannsthal's poem may serve as an introduction into his reflections about the process of linguistic signification. Hofmannsthal's early works are self-reflexive about their own constitutive mechanism as language. They thematize the play of presence and absence, identity and difference that enables textual meaning and allows for various interpretations of a given text. At the same time, they lament the concomitant loss of an unequivocal sense that allegedly remains preserved in spoken language alone. Speech is granted priority because it is said to preserve the undifferentiated origin of a corporeal meaning in which sign and referent, spirit and matter have not yet been divorced. The voice inaugurates the originary ground upon which the written sign can subsequently take place and establish itself. But yet again, the primordiality of speech finds its most adequate expression in a poetic text whose goal is to prove visually that language matters and enjoys a physical presence of its own. For Hofmannsthal, the voice and the body of language are intertwined and codependent, and "Vorfrühling" calls upon the material presence of signification as physical evidence of the inherent ability of language to speak itself. The task of the literary critic consists precisely in resisting the temptation to dissolve this paradox—the friction between spoken and written language—in either direction. A study of Hofmannsthal's works cannot simply privilege one of the poles, nor can it be anchored in a positive or identifiable ground outside the self-referential play of signifiers at work within the literary text. Any such efforts are themselves based upon the constitutive interplay of speech and writing they seek to explain. This, at least, is the early Hofmannsthal's

Aestheticist stance vis-à-vis poetic and critical language. In the following, I shall try to contextualize the above reading of Hofmannsthal's poem by reference to his other writings around 1900.

The most programmatic endorsement of this magical understanding of language expressed in "Vorfrühling" can be found in Hofmannsthal's brief comments in "Eine Monographie" (1895) about the actor Friedrich Mitterwurzer whose language, Hofmannsthal contends, is free of the reified speech patterns that dominate public discourse:

> Wenn wir den Mund aufmachen, reden immer zehntausend Tote mit. Der Mitterwurzer hat seine Beredsamkeit das Schweigen gelehrt. Er hat die zehntausend Toten totgetreten, und wenn er redet, redet nur er. In seinem Mund werden die Worte auf einmal wieder etwas ganz Elementares, der letzte eindringlichste Ausdruck des Leibes, Waffen wie die Zähne und die Nägel, Lockungen wie das Lächeln und die Blicke, reine sinnliche Offenbarungen des inneren Zustandes. ("Eine Monographie"; *RA; GW* I: 480)

> Whenever we open our mouth, ten thousand dead talk as well. Mitterwurzer has learned his eloquence through silence. He has trampled the ten thousand dead to death, and when he talks, he alone speaks. In his mouth the words once again become something elementary, the last intense expression of the body, weapons like the teeth and the nails, temptations like the smile and the looks, pure sensuous epiphanies of an inner condition.

The "ten thousand" dead that usually accompany human speech are the emissaries of the entire hermeneutic tradition that assigns meaning to words by situating them within the discursive network of previous and possible statements. Under the auspices of this traditional system of signification, life speech is impossible since every word always remains caught within an antiquated network of preestablished symbolic codes and anterior meanings. Conjuring up the dead, language, too, dies the very moment it is being spoken.

The endless network of interrelated discourse based on the continual deferral of pre-sense pronounces the speaker's loss of self as well. In a letter to his friend von Bebenburg, Hofmannsthal relates his not feeling well to the lack of immediate life experiences during times of travel: "I often do not feel well during a journey: I miss the immediacy of experience; I watch myself living life, and whatever I experience appears as if read in a book" (Ich fühle mich während einer Reise meist nicht recht wohl: mir fehlt die Unmittelbarkeit des Erlebens; ich sehe mir dann selbst leben zu, und was ich erlebe, ist mir wie in einem Buch gelesen) (6 Sept. 1892; Frankfurt 1966; 19). To encounter one's life written down or illustrated in a book is, of course, the definitive moment in the lifelong voyage of most Romantic heros, from Eichendorff's *Sternbald* and Brentano's *Godwi*, to Novalis's *Heinrich* and beyond. The "Romantic irony," as it is called, demarcates the realm of aesthetic self-reflection and signifies the hero's eventual return back home to the proper self. Hofmannsthal's rejection of this Romantic paradigm is based on his life-philosophical demand for sensual immediacy and the concomitant emphasis of the body. His arduous travels in real life are similar to the fictional hero's metaphorical journeys through the hermeneutic universe of reading and writing. They forestall the crucial experience of "the fullest, most sublime presence" that Hofmannsthal's Lord Chandos senses and seeks to express in "Ein Brief." The Romantic trail of the signifier allegedly guiding the fictional hero and his reader back to their own selves cannot but self-destruct since it perpetually postpones rather than actualizes the definitive moment of returning home. Aestheticist poetry around 1900 literally cannot afford the time to chase romantically after the ever-fleeting presence of discursive (self-)signification. Beyond all poetic reflection, being and meaning must physically coincide for language proper to find its voice.

It follows that Hofmannsthal's denunciation of reading and writing applies only to the reified linguistic system endorsed by modern rationality and not to language in general. On the contrary, the real experience of life still depends upon the "creation of new terms, powerful, all-conjuring incantatory words whose last, most simple one God knows, God is" (Und dann das Bilden neuer Begriffe, mächtiger, vielbeschwörender Zauberworte, deren letztes, einfachstes Gott weiß, Gott ist) (*RA; GW* III: 375). Although the religious dimension of these "last words" betrays the utopian nature of Hofmannsthal's search for pure speech, it also sanctions his call for radical aesthetic action. Around 1900, to speak is to kill the living dead in language once and for all since the necessary rejuvenation of speech depends upon the poet's violent act of liberation from the restrictive and life-threatening paradigms of hermeneutics. Although the Romantics had liberated language from its burden of referentiality, they had stopped short of renouncing the ideal of a transcendental absolute and thus were forced to forestall a self-presence they could only imagine but not literally enact. Romanticism unwittingly impedes, rather than provides, access to an original presence lost in signification, leading Hofmannsthal to proclaim that the name "Romanticism" itself should be "put out of use" (*RA; GW* III: 484). The voice of pure language, by contrast, pronounces a death sentence it has always already executed, since otherwise it could not be heard at all. The history of linguistic meaning needs to be silenced before true speech can reemerge, which is to say that the voice of language remains inextricably bound to its own self-negation in the form of silence.

For Hofmannsthal, silence is constitutive of speech. Yet it can only be evoked in and through speech, and the actor Mitterwurzer is praised for silencing the dead by literally talking them to death. "Only in true speech is it possible to remain silent" (Nur im echten Reden ist eigentliches Schweigen möglich) (*Sein und Zeit* 165), Heidegger asserts in *Being and Time* and thus captures the essence of Hofmannsthal's early reflections on language. Silence is the ultimate limit and (im)possible fulfillment of speech as well as its lost origin and necessary ground for rejuvenation. It is not opposed to speech, but rather entwined with it, nurturing its magical power to materialize the presence of life. This presence becomes visually manifest in the physical body that voices language. Unlike Romanticism, Aestheticism does not simply strive toward poetic silence or the absolute as an end in and of itself. Rather, it recognizes this originary silence always already at work in speech, which thus partakes of the being of language. Poetic words are born and come alive only in and through a living body that, in speaking their name, both dissolves them into thin air and grants them a material basis for being themselves. As physical properties of that body, words become transformed into "weapons like the teeth and the nails," whose function it is to ward off death and to embrace life. For Hofmannsthal, to speak is to give voice to a primordial silence that testifies to one's own physical presence and hence to the being of language.

It is crucial, for two reasons, to remember that Hofmannsthal's brief essay "Eine Monographie" refers to an actor rather than an arbitrary individual. First, because the celebrated self-expression evident in Mitterwurzer's speech—the "inner condition" he so accurately portrays—always pertains to an other (i.e., the fictional character he personifies) rather than to the actor's own proper self. This split between self and other adequately captures the powerful powerlessness of language, for although speech depends upon human agency, it controls it nonetheless: "It is not I who thinks; it thinks in me" (Mauthner 42), Fritz Mauthner declared categorically already in 1902. His formulation anticipates Jacques Lacan's later investigation into the linguistic structure of the unconscious, and the early Hofmannsthal conceives of language very much along the same lines. For him, too, language is not a human invention, "because all of its meaning language already carries within itself, and whoever descends down into its dark chambers will encounter such a knowledge blowing from its shafts that he will fall silent like a mute" ([D]enn: allen Sinn hat sie [die Sprache] schon in sich und wer in ihre Gewölbe hinabsteigt, dem weht aus ihren Schachten ein solches Wissen entgegen, daß er verstummt wie ein Stummer) ("Nachlass"; *RA; GW* III: 414). The being of language precedes the speaking subject, yet requires it nonetheless since the task of the poet consists in setting language free so that it can literally learn to speak itself: "The point is not to express ourselves in language, but to express language within us" (Es handelt sich nicht darum, uns in der Sprache, sondern die Sprache in uns auszuprägen) ("Nachlass"; *RA; GW* III: 309). The parallels to later twentieth-century philosophy of language are obvious and best exemplified in Heidegger's *Unterwegs zur Sprache*, where he states: "That of which we speak, language, is always already ahead of us. We only speak after it" ("Das Wesen der Sprache" 179).

Hofmannsthal's claim that "when he [Mitterwurzer] talks, he alone speaks," must thus not be understood as a celebration of bourgeois subjectivity. On the contrary, he applauds the actor's ability to extinguish his own self by giving voice to the performativity of his body. Language, for Hofmannsthal, always seeks to express itself and not the extralinguistic intentions of the speaker. Around 1900, "it is language which speaks, not the author," as Barthes formulates it with reference to Mallarmé ("Death of the Author"; *Image* 143). This notion of the "author" is the second reason for remembering Mitterwurzer's profession, for it is much easier to bring language to life through actual speech as compared to written poetry. Although Hofmannsthal will later turn his attention to opera and the performing arts, in his early years he still faces the dilemma of having to write rather than actually speak poetry. Writing is paradigmatic for the process of alienation Hofmannsthal tries to avoid since it visually represents the reification of a once embodied and living language into the fixed grid of static symbols. In any text, letters have to take their place once and for all before signification can possibly begin to occur.

It follows that the status of poetry remains ambivalent for Hofmannsthal: as a textual document, the poem acts as irrefutable evidence that it has always already died before meeting the eye of its reader. Since it cannot not solidify into writing—otherwise it could never traverse the spatiotemporal distance that separates it from the reader—the only option left for poetry is to try to undo the process of its own reification retrospectively during the act of being read. As I argued above, Hofmannsthal's "Vorfrühling" does precisely that: it thematizes and self-consciously exploits the breathing apparatus—the "Windes Wehn"—of its reader to enact its own being and become alive again as pure and original, that is, spoken language. At the same time, however, the poem is not simply being undone, but also reaffirmed as the material evidence for the being of language. Language must be liberated from writing and the reification of meaning, but it must also return to and reinhabit the text in order to rejuvenate it from within. The point is that both movements, the transcendence and the restoration of writing in and through poetry, must occur simultaneously, a process that, in the eyes of the young Hofmannsthal, can only be described as the work of magic.

Literary criticism, however, has generally tried to dissolve this magical paradox toward either of its constitutive poles. Commenting on the complex relationship between life and poetry, Adorno, for example, converts the paradox into a dialectics: "The alienation of art from life advocated by George and Hofmannsthal is meant to elevate art, yet it reverts to a limitless and submissive closeness to life" (Die von George und Hofmannsthal urgierte Entfremdung der Kunst vom Leben, die die Kunst zu erhöhen gedenkt, schlägt in grenzenlose und gefügige Nähe zum Leben um) ("George und Hofmannsthal"; GS 10/1: 234). Adorno establishes an either-or relationship between art and life. In doing so, he misses the crucial point that, according to the Aestheticist ideal, art is united with life precisely by remaining separated from it, just like words gain their proper meaning by refusing to signify. Due to this limited perspective, Adorno once again charges Aestheticism with sacrificing the human subject to the forces of capitalism: "Instead of the things surrendering as symbols of subjectivity, subjectivity gives in and becomes a symbol for things. Thus, subjectivity accepts its own reification into the thing to which society has already condemned it anyway" (Anstatt daß die Dinge als Symbole der Subjektivität nachgäben, gibt Subjektivität nach als Symbol der Dinge, bereit, in sich selber schließlich zu dem Ding zu erstarren, zu dem sie von der Gesellschaft ohnehin gemacht wird) (ibid.). Aestheticism, by contrast, takes pride in this loss of subjectivity, which it pictures as the sine qua non for the liberation of language, humans, and things alike, whereas for Adorno it is tantamount to the individual's inability to withstand the hegemony of capitalism and the culture industry. Although Adorno criticizes the authoritarian tendencies inherent in the bourgeois notion of subjectivity, he cannot renounce it altogether without also forfeiting the necessary basis for active resistance. The rationalist perspective informing his language—"Subjectivity no longer *knows* itself as the soul-giving center of the cosmos"—betrays his defensiveness toward a kind of poetry willing to abandon completely the humanist ideal of subjectivity. Instead, it ought merely to expose its false redemption in the guise of the capitalist consumer, as Adorno's critique aims to do.

For Hofmannsthal, however, the problem of modernity cannot be solved dialectically since dialectics tries to reconcile that which should have never been severed to begin with. From an Aestheticist perspective, the modern era first distinguishes between art and life (meaning and materiality) and subsequently tries to undo the very separation it inaugurated. Both attempts violate the integrity of the primordial ground constitutive of art and life alike. In a time characterized by the fundamental forgetting of Being, as Heidegger would later argue, language necessarily succumbs to a universe of empty signs that interject themselves in between *Dasein* and its world. The following quote from Heidegger's *Introduction to Metaphysics* discerns both aspects of Aestheticism's notion of language, that is, the primordial power (*Gewalttat*) to name and call forth the world as well as its corrupt subsistence in the form of material signs:

> Das Nennen versieht nicht nachträglich ein sonst schon offenbares Seiendes mit einer Bezeichnung und einem Merkzeichen, genannt Wort, sondern umgekehrt: das Wort sinkt aus der Höhe seiner urspünglichen Gewalt-tat als Eröffnung des Seins zum bloßen Zeichen herab, so zwar, daß dieses selbst sich dann vor das Seiende schiebt. (*Einführung in die Metaphysik* 131)

Naming does not come afterward, providing a being that is already otherwise revealed with a designation and a token called a word, but to the contrary: from the height of its originary act of violence as the opening-up of Being, the work sinks down to become a mere sign. It does so in such a way that this sign then thrusts itself before beings. (Heidegger, *Introduction to Metaphysics* 182)

For Heidegger and Hofmannsthal alike, to speak is to open up violently the realm of being, and this creative potential inheres in pure language. It follows that the problem of modern alienation needs to be approached not from its desolate result, but from its original cause. By strictly separating the realm of art and life, Hofmannsthal hopes to avoid the false attempts of reconciliation yet simultaneously opens, in his eyes, the path toward the primordial understanding of both as fundamentally related in and through the body of speech. As Hofmannsthal emphasizes repeatedly, poetry does not artificially create a new language, but merely unlocks the invisible beauty and magic already inherent in every single word itself. Common language harbors gems we often fail to appreciate: "So tritt des Bettlers Fuß den Kies, / Der eines Edelsteins Verlies" ("Weltgeheimnis"; *Gedichte* 20), or: "Wir gehen auf staubverhüllten Perlen" ("Nachlaß"; *RA; GW* III: 315).

Like Adorno, most scholars seeking to "grasp" Hofmannsthal's poetics miss this crucial point. They try to clarify the "matter" of modern poetry by dissolving its constitutive paradox, that is, the nonidentical identity of art and life, word and thing, toward one of its poles instead of keeping the tension as such alive. Critics in the 1950s and 1960s generally interpreted the *Augenblick*—those moments of "preexistence" or "magic" Hofmannsthal associates with early childhood[7]—as a "religious experience" (Wunberg, *Der Frühe Hofmannsthal* 106–7) or an "epiphany" (Ziolkowski) that leads the subject toward its own self. More recent studies, by contrast, read the *Augenblick* as an "aesthetics of flight" (Ästhetik des Flüchtigen) (Neumann) that calls for a new poetics "at the border of the body" (Brandstetter and Neumann). They argue that Hofmannsthal's poetics does not point toward some divine presence of absolute self-consciousness, but rather discovers the physical reality of the human body as a language in its own right.

Although I basically agree with the second kind of reading, it oddly coincides with the first in its predominantly negative view of poetic language, which is said to completely efface itself in order to conjure either the spirit or the body as the "real" world of poetry. Critics' focus on this "aesthetic transformation" allegedly affected by poetic language implicitly presupposes the very separation of art and life that Hofmannsthal himself called into question. For him, language cannot signify or re-present life because it always already inhabits life, grants it, lives it. Hofmannsthal's poetics indeed tries to speak from the "ground zero" (Barthes) of language, that is, from the spatio-temporal realm that underlies and sustains the dualistic universe of signification. In this sense, poetry *is* a primordial quality of life, and the function of speech is precisely to uncover the original, yet forgotten, ground—the being of language itself—that reveals this original unity of words and things. Once this revelation has occurred, art withdraws, and things linger in a state of disarray, while an alienated system of signification mediates between them: "The thing itself," Agamben notes, "is not a thing; it is the very sayability, the very openness at issue in language, which, in language, we always presuppose and forget, perhaps because it is at bottom its own oblivion and abandonment" (*Potentialities* 35). Poetry around 1900 refuses to forget this potentiality of language, and the "language-crisis" refers less to the lack of absolute meaning captured in words than to this effort of language to find its own voice and "speak itself."

For Hofmannsthal, there is no "I" expressing itself in art. Diametrically opposed to the Cartesian notion of cognitively assured self-presence or the Romanticist ideal of poetic genius, Hofmannsthal's poetic "subject" emerges as a hyphen between things. It is a locus of intersecting forces in the form of a living body that can be read as the originary signature of things—the "metaphor of the subject" (Wiethölter 17). For many recent critics, his topographic sense of subjectivity redeems language in Hofmannsthal's eyes—not in the form of writing, to be sure, but understood metaphorically as the imaginary text written by the gestures and movements of the human body. Hofmannsthal's increasing interest in the performing arts is said to reflect both his emphasis on physical presence and his disinfatuation with the lyrical genre. Contrary to written texts, the life arts present a precarious balance between acoustics, that is, the ephemeral presence of music and speech, on the one hand, and vision, that is, the corporeal presence of moving bodies metaphorically envisioned as text, on the other. This facile interplay of eye and ear is regarded as superior to the complicated rhetorical mechanisms necessary to make language speak poetically and overcome its false materialization in the form of written symbols.

This juxtaposition of language versus the body is yet another false dichotomy that haunts Hofmannsthal studies, most notably those focusing on his later contribution to the performing arts. Again, critics advance a dualistic perspective and juxtapose the "true" language of physical gestures to the "false" language of linguistic utterances. Neither, however, can exist in total isolation, meaning that for Hofmannsthal, word and gesture always belong together and are primordially related.[8] This is not to deny that Hofmannsthal's later turn away from poetic production and toward real-life performances was prompted by his search for a more direct expression of life in the physical movements of the body. His comments on pantomime, ballet, dance, and opera generally focus on the communicative power of the "gesture" and must be situated in the context of Wilhelm Wundt's "Gebärdensprache" and the entire "Lebensreform" cult around 1900.[9] For Hofmannsthal, as for Wundt, Fiedler, Bergson, and many other artists and scientists at the time, the gesture is an immediate articulation of an inner emotion or thought and hence superior to everyday language: "A pure gesture is like a pure thought" (Eine reine Gebärde ist wie ein reiner Gedanke) ("Über die Pantomime"; RA; GW I: 504).

However, my discussion in the first part concerning the monistic principle around 1900 has shown that such efforts to find an authentic expression of inner life are related to the modernist ideal to give voice to a speaking gaze able to merge materiality and meaning into one. A language beyond language, the speaking gaze remains nothing but a fantasy still chained to the process of signification it claims to transcend. The same holds true for Hofmannsthal. Although in his later life he sought to express the intimate connection between language and the body not poetically, but by means of gestures and physical movements in space, the two forms of expression still complement rather than contradict each other. Visual forms of communication are not simply superior to language, but instead approach the same ideal of embodied meaning from its opposite end.

Given the abundance of studies regarding Hofmannsthal's occupation with theater, opera, and dance, let me briefly comment upon Hofmannsthal's relationship to film for clarification of my point. Hofmannsthal was indeed very interested in the new medium and wrote several film scripts, some of which were actually realized, with moderate success.[10] In his short essay "Der Ersatz für die Träume" from 1921, Hofmannsthal regards the cinema as the "honorable" space where modern man can still conceive of a more immediate contact with the fleeting life surrounding him. Regular language, he reformulates his well-known objection, has ceased to function as a mediator to life because "there remains too much of algebra in language, every letter covers up a number" (Es ist zuviel von der Algebra in dieser Sprache, jeder Buchstabe bedeckt wieder eine Ziffer) ("Ersatz"; *RA; GW* II: 143). Film, by contrast, is reminiscent of humanity's long-forgotten dreams and hence emerges as a new kind of language of the soul that has moved "from digits to epiphany" ("Ersatz"; *RA; GW* II: 145). In the essay Hofmannsthal evokes the visionary power of film in a whole series of literary images that strikingly resemble the strange apparitions mentioned by Lord Chandos in his "Letter": the old smelly basement, the look of an animal, scattered objects lying in the sun. The two texts reveal a structural and thematic parallelism that aligns the new medium of film with the motif of the "language-crisis" evoked in 1902.[11]

Moreover, Hofmannsthal's various comments on pantomime and gesture actually anticipate and rival central ideas later expressed in film theories by Münsterberg, Balázs, or Kracauer, as recent critics have noted.[12] Since film, unlike photography, "captures" the fleeting presence of life only for the duration of a magical *Augenblick,* it exemplifies Hofmannsthal's aesthetic notion regarding the constant flux of life and functions as a cultural vehicle for his critique of common language. Similarly, Chandos's enchanted gaze might be understood as the recording and projecting lens of the camera, while his body can be reconfigured as the apparatus itself that harbors the intimate connection of all things. In other words, Chandos, the narrator of the "Letter," might be said to "pose as a forerunner of Münsterberg's film viewer, giving in to the perceptual intensity of his own creations" (Oksiloff 75).

In spite of such similarities between the aesthetics of cinema and Hofmannsthal's poetics, he ultimately remained ambiguous about the medium. This ambivalence stems less from his "archaic modernism," which allegedly forced him to reject film as a symptom of mass culture,[13] and is rather indicative of the same reservation that led Bergson to denounce the cinematographic method. Unlike life philosophy, which focused on the pure duration of time, film merely suggests continuity on the basis of difference. The structural analysis of the cinematic apparatus reveals the contradictory nature of film, which, in the words of Jean-Louis Baudry, "lives on the denial of difference: difference is necessary for it to live, but it lives on its negation" (Baudry 306).[14] Film represents the incessant movement of life by means of a technological apparatus that cannot but falsify it. The "imaginary signifier" (Christian Metz) of film is exclusively based on visual appearances and their psychological effect upon the spectators. The moving pictures lack materiality on screen and hence realize Hofmannsthal's poetic ideals exclusively in the realm of the imaginary. In so doing, cinema exposes its fetishistic nature as well as its complicity with the more traditional means of representation, including everyday language. Both present a mere illusion of life, an illusion that is based upon the spatialization of time typical for modernity at large. By contrast, Hofmannsthal is still caught up in the paradoxical effort to somehow signify the end of signification, which is to say that regardless of the various aesthetic media he engages over the years—be they poetry, film, or the performing arts—his goal remains to intuit the primordial unity of meaning and matter, language and body, rather than promoting the superiority of one over the other.

Silence in "A Letter"

In the final part of this chapter, I want to turn to one of Hofmannsthal's most famous texts to support this claim. "Ein Brief," published in 1902, has been celebrated as the quintessential modern text, a work that not only marks a decisive shift in Hofmannsthal's literary career, but signals the definitive break of modernism with traditional nineteenth-century aesthetics, as Walter Jens and Richard Brinkmann have argued. The discussion usually centers on the so-called "language-crisis" that functions as the constitutive paradox of Hofmannsthal's text. Chandos's tormented confession that the words "disintegrate in [his] mouth like rotten mushrooms" is belied by the eloquence and rhetorical power of the statement itself. According to earlier critics, the paradox can be explained by Hofmannsthal's ability to exploit it aesthetically. It is only because he himself suffered through the "language-crisis" that he was able to express and thus overcome it poetically.[15] By contrast, more recent studies have questioned the genesis of the Chandos Letter out of a "language-crisis" allegedly experienced by Hofmannsthal himself and thus have tried to disassociate the biographical from the fictional realm.[16]

This seemingly academic issue about the relationship between Hofmannsthal and his most famous text is far from irrelevant. It speaks, above all, to the question of artistic genius with which traditional scholarship tried to account for what is still conceived as the aesthetically enticing, yet nonetheless theoretically vexing, problem of "Ein Brief." The real "crisis," in other words, consists in the ambivalent or paradoxical nature of Hofmannsthal's text, which critics desperately try to disentangle. Chandos, the diegetic hero allegedly suffering from speech paralysis, had to be rehabilitated by reference to the mature poetic genius of Hofmannsthal himself. The latter supplied the creative power the former was said to lack, thus resolving the aesthetic tension that characterizes "Ein Brief." The major problem with this approach concerns not only the obvious methodological taboo to equate fictional characters with their authors. More important, the affirmation of creative genius completely inverts Hofmannsthal's poetological ideal, for the notion of modern subjectivity is precisely what needs to be undone before the liberation of words and things can be effected in the first place. The human subject, like any other "thing," comes into its own in conjunction with poetic or linguistic effects and not as their cause. Like Bergson's philosopher of life, the poet tries to express and "speak after" his original intuitions of life, only to discover that life itself inheres in speech much as in other movements of his body.

Hofmannsthal's deconstruction of modern subjectivity also exposes the problematic aspect of Daviau's and le Rider's interpretations, which fall prey to the same misperceptions they critique. Although they disentangle Hofmannsthal's texts from his private life, they, too, imply a sense of artistic mastery and subjective control that runs counter to Hofmannsthal's own poetic visions. For him, the poet is not he who speaks or manipulates words, but he who lets himself be spoken by a language that "grows into one's mouth" and is like a "chain in one's hand" (*Gedichte; GW* 189), that is, represents a physical part of one's own body.[17] Even if one were to agree with critics' claim that Hofmannsthal's own poetic practice contradicts his poetological critique of subjectivity insofar as he ultimately remains in total control of the texts he writes, the question still remains as to the aesthetic relevance of this contradiction. Why should one further investigate this alleged conflict between the real poet Hofmannsthal and the fictional poet Chandos unless one were interested in corroborating Hofmannsthal's canonical status as an exemplary, ingenious writer at the turn of the century? Since this is not my primary concern, it is more germane to resituate this tension between mastery and resignation within the text itself rather than between the artist and his creation, particularly since Aestheticism itself is defined precisely by this perspectival shift away from the external world toward the work of art.

An adequate way of reading "Ein Brief" must locate and trace this aesthetic movement within Hofmannsthal's own text until the reader encounters its outer limits. This approach allows one to articulate a critique of Hofmannsthal's poetic ideal that emanates from within the text's own parameters rather than from an "objective" viewpoint outside the text. By means of this technique, it also becomes apparent that the traditionally emphasized *Sonderstellung* of the Chandos Letter with regard to both Hofmannsthal's own literary career and the history of literary modernism cannot be sustained. "Ein Brief" does not fundamentally differ from Hofmannsthal's other texts around 1900, nor does its self-conscious exploration of linguistic difference distinguish it from similar poetic and philosophical experiments at the time. The constitutive paradox of "Ein Brief" is nothing but the paradoxical nature of language itself.

In the end, Chandos explicitly acknowledges this paradox as a kind of mythical or magical experience in which "the silent things themselves" begin to speak in a language "of which not even one word is known to me" ("Ein Brief" 472). Chandos's call for a new language that allows us to "think with the heart" ("Ein Brief" 469) represents an emphatic rejection of stereotypical and lifeless metaphorical constructs in favor of new and truly unthinkable ones, those that do not immediately—and ideally never should—"make sense" and therefore have the potential to "become" that which they are not: a pure symbol that literally is the thing itself—a language beyond language. However, one may also reverse this perspective: Chandos's impossible language has always already been spoken the same moment it was declared impossible. His ideal to "think with the heart" came alive and died within the very metaphors he used to express it. Hence, it remains unclear and ultimately irrelevant whether Chandos's future silence is to be seen as a fulfilled language finally coming into its own or as a broken language unable to speak with its own voice. What is important, however, is to see if there remains in the end some kind of material proof or physical imprint that might serve to consolidate and thus anchor the self-reflexive movement of the text.

Hofmannsthal's "Ein Brief" does not dismiss language as such, but criticizes primarily the use of abstract terms and reified concepts that have become self-referential and out of touch with the living "things" they are supposed to represent. Chandos describes the gradual disintegration of an entire linguistic system into its single components:

> Es gelang mir nicht mehr, sie [die Menschen und ihre Handlungen] mit dem *vereinfachenden Blick der Gewohnheit zu erfassen*. Es zerfiel mir alles in Teile, die Teile wieder in Teile, und nichts mehr ließ sich mit einem Begriff umspannen. Die einzelnen Worte schwammen um mich; sie gerannen zu Augen, die mich anstarrten und in die ich wieder hineinstarren muß: Wirbel sind sie, in die hinabzusehen mich schwindelt, die sich unaufhaltsam drehen und durch die hindurch man ins Leere kommt. ("Ein Brief" 466; my emphasis)

> I could no longer comprehend them [people and their actions] with the *simplifying glance of habit*. Everything fell into fragments for me, the fragments into further fragments, until it seemed impossible to contain anything at all within a single concept. Disjointed words swam about me, congealing into staring eyes whose gaze I was forced to return; whirlpools they were, and I could not look into them without dizziness, their incessant turning only drew me down into emptiness. (*Lord Chandos Letter* 21; my emphasis)

Since the quote above emphasizes the lost ability to execute common vision first, the ensuing disintegration of language pertains particularly to its visual aspects in the form of writing. The words staring back at Chandos are those reified symbols that have gained a material existence of their own, independent from the real life experiences they are supposed to convey. As in the poem "Vorfrühling," Chandos presents the undoing of a reified language system as the indispensable step toward metaphorically embracing that which lies at its core. In this regard, the Chandos Letter again repeats the typical metaphysical distinction between a live and a dead language, particularly since the disintegration of common, everyday words represents more to Chandos than simply a loss. Chandos's unlearning of an abstract language system is accompanied by his simultaneous visual appreciation of the life surrounding him, such that the pure presence of things is witnessed and experienced as part of his own self:

> Diese stummen und manchmal unbelebten Kreaturen *heben* sich mir mit einer solchen Fülle, einer solchen Gegenwart der Liebe *entgegen*, daß mein *beglücktes Auge auch ringsum auf keinen toten Fleck zu fallen vermag*. Es erscheint mir alles, alles, was es gibt, alles, dessen ich mich entsinne,

alles, was meine verworrensten Gedanken *berühren,* etwas zu sein. ("Ein Brief" 469; my emphasis)

These dumb, often inanimate creatures *lift themselves toward me* with such fullness, such an intensity of love that my *enraptured eye cannot light on any lifeless spot anywhere about me.* And it strikes me then that everything, everything in this world, everything I can remember, everything that my most wayward thoughts might *touch* upon, is something after all. (*Lord Chandos Letter* 27; my emphasis)

Chandos becomes mute in order *to see what he feels* and he *feels what he sees.* This distinction between language and vision is central to the Chandos Letter. It focuses on two central themes, the "Sprach-Spiel" and the "Augen-Blick" (Neumann, "Sprach-Spiel"). Hofmannsthal scholars have generally seen these concepts in competition with each other in the sense that the infinite play of linguistic difference is finally overcome in the momentary "lightning" of visual truth. The proper meaning of one paradigm is thus defined in opposition to the other, most obviously in Hofmannsthal's early plays, where we find the individual self situated in between the interdependent, yet adverse, forces of language and vision, spirit and body, absence and presence. In "Die Hochzeit der Sobeide," to give a specific example, words are judged responsible for inhibiting meaningful discourse: "Stop these words," Hofmannsthal's heroine Sobeide exclaims toward the end of the play, "I am dizzy and they glitter before my eyes" (Laß solche Worte, mir ist schwindlig und sie flimmern vor den Augen) (442f.).

The quote recalls the disintegration of language described by Chandos and points to a typical motif in the early Hofmannsthal: the look of things is literally obstructed by the linguistic universe interjected between self and other. Those who must see (or read) words cannot see the things themselves anymore and hence are unable to feel the touch of the reciprocal gaze that sustains life.[18] The "Augen-Blick," it follows, is one of those rare moments of a quasi-religious epiphany in which the self *feels* itself *being seen* by an other. Let me emphasize again that this reciprocity of the gaze is fundamentally different from its poetic counterpart around 1800. Unlike the Romantic subject, the seen seer around 1900 feels himself touched by a gaze he does not control. This, in turn, prevents him from constructing an idealist self-identity because the other's look has already pierced the realm of the imaginary and made contact with the corporeal reality that sustains it.

Around 1900, that which looks back is language, and Sobeide, much like Chandos, must come to terms with a reality that is constituted upon words and things alike. Throughout the "Letter," there appears no gaze purified from language, an observation that holds true both for the extradiegetic readers of Hofmannsthal's texts and the fictional characters they encounter therein. On both levels, the poetic "Augen-Blick" is exposed as a linguistic metaphor that summons language the very moment it overcomes it. Hofmannsthal depicts the relationship between language and vision not as a static opposition, but as an interdependent play of metaphors in which the two poles simultaneously constitute and eradicate each other both *as* and *within* the text. Instead of maintaining a strict dichotomy between language and vision, the Chandos Letter simultaneously advocates and breaks down the juxtaposition between "Sprach-Spiel" and "Augen-Blick."

Given this subversive performativity of "A Letter," it becomes exceedingly difficult for the reader to *see* the difference between the time before and after his "language-crisis" because the words used to describe this difference are literally the same. This is most apparent in the central metaphor of the spiraling abyss that relates both to Chandos's earlier "language-crisis" (i.e., the words staring back at him from the bottom of an abyss) and to his later states of apotheosis, which he depicts as follows:

> Und das Ganze ist eine Art fieberisches Denken, aber Denken in einem Material, das unmittelbarer, flüssiger, glühender ist als Worte. Es sind gleichfalls Wirbel, aber solche, die nicht wie die Wirbel der Sprache ins Bodenlose zu führen scheinen, sondern irgendwie in mich selber und in den tiefsten Schoß des Friedens. ("Ein Brief" 471)

> All of this is only a kind of feverish thought, but thought in a medium more direct, more fluid, more incandescent than words. Whirlpools there are in it too, yet of a kind that does not appear to lead to the abyss like the whirlpools of language, but rather into my inner self and into the deepest womb of peace. (*Lord Chandos Letter* 31)

The vortex metaphor thus creates a bridge between the time before and after the crisis. Although it is called upon to mark a difference, the metaphor connects rather than separates Chandos's earlier and later state of mind. This metaphorical ambiguity pervades the entire text. The Lord's early projects leading up to his ultimate oeuvre entitled "Nosce te ipsum," for example, are characterized as follows:

> Ich wollte die Fabeln und mythischen Erzählungen . . . aufschließen als die Hieroglyphen einer geheimen, unerschöpflichen Weisheit, deren Anhauch ich manchmal, wie hinter einem Schleier, zu spüren meinte. Ich entsinne mich dieses Plans. Es lag ihm ich weiß nicht welche sinnliche und geistige Lust zugrunde: Wie der gehetzte Hirsch im Wasser sehnte ich mich hinein in diese nackten, glänzenden Leiber, in diese Sirenen und Dryaden, diesen Narcissus und Proteus, Perseus und Aktäon: verschwinden wollte ich in ihnen und aus ihnen heraus mit Zungen reden. ("Ein Brief" 463)

> I wanted to elucidate the fables and mythological tales handed down to us by the ancients, those endless sources of naive delight for painters and sculptors, as hieroglyphs of an arcane, inexhaustible wisdom, a breath of which I had convinced myself I could feel at times as though through a veil. I remember the plan well, but I no longer know what sensual or intellectual urges lay behind it. As the hunted stag strains toward water, so did I yearn to cast myself into those naked, radiant bodies, those sirens and dryads, Narcissus and Proteus, Perseus and Actaeon; I wished to become one with them and to speak forth from them in tongues. (*Lord Chandos Letter* 16–17)

This project certainly does not describe a rationalist project of scientific empiricism, at least not in the sense that Francis Bacon, the addressee of Chandos's letter and the founder of British empiricism, could have possibly approved of it.[19] Instead of explaining the things in the world in rational terms, Chandos's original hope was to "speak in tongues" the primordial language spoken by the things themselves. This hope to dissolve himself within the world that surrounds him not only renders suspect the proposed title of the entire project,[20] but it also reveals human self-knowledge to be based not on a strong sense of Cartesian subjectivity, but rather on an intimate relation with and understanding of every-thing around us, a self-understanding that demands individual openness rather than closure, artistic fluidity rather than scientific rigor.

Given this latent world of identities described in Chandos's earlier experiences of "life," the change allegedly affected by the "language-crisis" becomes questionable, as does the opposition between "Sprach-spiel" and "Augen-blick." There seems to remain little, if any, difference between Chandos's previous aspirations to "be in the middle of everything," to "disappear" in signs and things alike in order "to speak in tongues" from out of them ("Ein Brief" 463f.), and his later sensations of an "incredible empathy, a flowing over into these beings" ("Ein Brief" 468) that allows him "to think with the heart" and to speak "a language in which the silent things speak" to him ("Ein Brief" 472). Twice his body is depicted as the locus where signs and things meet, an unalienated space "consisting of nothing but chiffres" (469) able to "open up one creature after the other" (464). Both before and after his "crisis," Chandos portrays the human body as the site where a new language is inscribed. Twice, the body is said to consist of nothing but signs literally in touch with their external referents, meaning that the very distinction between self and other, sign and referent becomes immaterial and breaks down.

Indeed, the "Letter" seems to mirror this breakdown on the textual level by means of literary images that fuse and undermine the linearity of Chandos's story. The text not only mobilizes similar metaphors at its beginning and end, but uses similar key words throughout: "aufsperren" and "aufschließen," "Hieroglyphe" and "Chiffre," a homology that culminates in the juxtaposition of two different kinds of "vortexes," one of which is said to lead into the abyss, while the other, we read, leads to Chandos's own self.[21] It appears that anyone trying to think through these (dis)connections will herself inevitably fall prey to that metaphor, that is, will be absorbed into the linguistic vortex Chandos depicts in his letter. This aesthetic self-performance is central to Hofmannsthal's text. His letter, one might argue, reaches its proper destination each time the nauseating nonpresence of meaning is being experienced by the reader during the act of reading.

Obviously, such a one-dimensional reading of the "Letter" completely disregards the performative quality of Hofmannsthal's text, which literally works through these metaphors. If the text indeed folds back upon itself, the point is to examine how the "Letter" accounts for this temporal movement in spatial terms within its own aesthetic structure—*not*, to be sure, on the diegetic level of the text, but rather on its stylistic and material plane. The problem, in other words, needs to be solved on the material level of the signifier, and not with reference to its signified meaning. This, however, is precisely what most recent studies have failed to do. Recognizing the difficulty to distinguish the time before and after the "language-crisis" in Hofmannsthal's "Letter" while, at the same time, refusing simply to accept this difficulty as the definitive characteristic or the founding paradox of the text, contemporary scholarship argued in favor of dissecting the text into three distinct phases with each one of them allegedly governed by different notions of subjectivity and its relationship to the world. In doing so, however, critics have reinscribed de facto the very notion of spatiotemporal polarity and abstraction the "Letter" itself deliberately tries to undermine.

Waltraud Wiethölter, for example, claims that Chandos's earlier attempts to conjure the presence of meaning were stilled marred by his narcissistic gaze "that did not want anything else but itself" (Wiethölter 62), whereas the Lord later adapts his own self to "a body-language whose laws, rules, and grammar are least determined by the subject itself" (68; my translation). Chandos, in other words, gives up his Romantic illusion of self-governed subjectivity in favor of a self governed by the (Lacanian) Other.[22] To be sure, Wiethölter and others aptly configure the crucial difference between the "discourse networks" of 1800 and 1900. The first encounters the self in literally every-thing it perceives, the second reduces the same self to a thing among things and a body among bodies. In the context of our previous discussion, one might rephrase these critics' position as follows: Hofmannsthal's "Letter" describes the history of modern poetics from its Romanticist beginnings to its Aestheticist dissolution as one of loosing the (conscious) self in favor of finding the (physical) body. The transition from one to the other necessitates an equally crucial shift from verbal to corporeal signification, from linguistic to embodied meaning. The young Chandos was still engaged in a hermeneutic project because it was through the process of reading and writing that he had sought to discover both the external world and his own inner self. The older Chandos, by contrast, experiences his own self as a contingent and arbitrary body within the flux of life. As he rejects the idea of a ubiquitous, disembodied subject of pure consciousness, Chandos comes to realize that the silent language of things he romantically envisioned elsewhere always already speaks through the actions and sensations of his own body. In the end, Chandos has learned to feel within himself the language of life.

If I nonetheless hesitate to embrace this by now canonical reading of Hofmannsthal's "Letter" and its focus on the juxtaposition of words and gestures or subjectivity and the body, I do so because it strikes me as unbalanced in its disregard for the performative dimension of the text that emphasizes the connection between these poles.[23] Contemporary critics read the text referentially and reduce it to its "message" about embodied meaning at the end. Hence, all stylistic consideration falls by the wayside: the striking metaphorical similarity between the first and the third phase of the "Letter" is only mentioned in order to be immediately dissolved again within the larger framework of Chandos's personal development. In this sense, the somehow warped structure of the "Letter" seems to be more or less accidental and not worthy of further analysis. This, in turn, allows critics to situate "Ein Brief" in the broader cultural context of the time, such as the popular cult of the (naked) body or Charcot's and Freud's studies on hysteria and physiological dysfunctionalities.[24] Kittler, for example, discerns the nonhermeneutic "meaning" of Hofmannsthal's text as if he himself had indeed witnessed, like Charcot and Freud, the actual body language of the "patient" Chandos rather than merely read about the behavior of a fictional character. This perspective, however, distorts the picture, because Hofmannsthal's new paradigm of embodied meaning only unfolds within the old system of linguistic signification and hence remains intertwined with it. Reading the "Letter," the reader must not in the end abstract from the difficulties inherent in the reading process as such since the text merely performs the signification of this new "body language," but does not actually present that language itself. To take the "Letter" at face value, that is, to read it referentially as if it were nothing but a scientific document describing the symptoms of alexia, is to disregard the self-conscious exploration of the very letter that constitutes the text.

Although I am wary of the common fallacy to identify Hofmannsthal himself with his fictional hero, the parallels established by the critical reception of both are striking. Twice, critics focus on the final message of the text and try to establish a linear narrative leading from one state of affairs to another. They read two life stories along the chronological lines of a time "before" (i.e., Hofmannsthal before the language-crisis exemplified in "Ein Brief" and Chandos before he lost his ability to "speak") and the time "after" (i.e., Hofmannsthal after he had forsaken poetry and turned toward the performing arts and Chandos after he experienced his quasi-religious epiphanies). As I argued throughout this chapter, it is precisely this Romanticist notion of becoming that Aestheticism seeks to overcome in favor of a Bergsonian *élan vital*, which cannot be intellectualized and dissected into different stages of a linear development. Rather, it needs to be intuited as a paradoxical whole, much as Chandos's epiphanies of a silent language spoken by the things themselves ultimately take shape in the form of a written text.

I want to suggest that there is no way out of the performative paradox that linguistically signifies a language beyond language except by *marking it as an impossibility in the structure of the text*. If "presence, then, is the trace of the trace, the trace of the erasure of trace" (Derrida, *Margins of Philosophy* 66), the "Letter" must somewhat recover its own tracks, that is, the trail of signification it leaves behind. This is why Hofmannsthal's text ultimately circles back to its own beginnings. The "Letter" signifies on two interdependent levels, telling the story of Chandos's changed relation to the world while simultaneously undermining that difference by means of the similar metaphors it employs. It reflects its own existence as text and relates it to the message evoked therein. Since Chandos's momentary experiences of "full, most solemn presence" are expressed in a medium itself defined by its "différance" (Derrida), the "Letter" must try to deconstruct the difference that constitutes it. At the same time, however, it must leave some form of physical residue (a trace, if you wish) to authenticate this process of self-erasure.

In the poem "Vorfrühling," this residue was pictured as a syntactical marker in the form of a period. In the "Letter," it takes the shape of stylistic and syntactic changes that both reiterate and disfigure earlier passages of the text. As Neil H. Donahue has argued, the "Letter" structurally culminates in the final image of the antique orator Crassus that haunts Chandos's thought:

> Das Bild dieses Crassus ist zuweilen nachts in meinem Hirn, wie ein Splitter, um den herum alles schwärt, pulst und kocht. Es ist mir dann, als geriete ich selber in Gärung, würfe Blasen auf, wallte und funkelte. Und das Ganze ist eine Art fieberisches Denken, aber Denken in einem Material, das unmittelbarer, flüssiger, glühender ist als Worte. Es sind gleichfalls Wirbel, aber solche, die nicht wie die Wirbel der Sprache ins Bodenlose zu führen scheinen, sondern irgendwie in mich selber und in den tiefsten Schoß des Friedens. ("Ein Brief" 471)

> At times the image of this Crassus lodges in my mind like a splinter that makes everything around it fester, throb, and burn. When that happens I could almost think that I myself am beginning to ferment, to send up bubbles, to boil and throw off sparks. All of this is only a kind of feverish thought, but thought in a medium more direct, more fluid, more incandescent than words. Whirlpools there are in it too, yet of a kind that does not appear to lead to the abyss like the whirlpools of language, but rather into my inner self and into the deepest womb of peace. (*Lord Chandos Letter* 31)

This image of an "irreducible fixation," Donahue argues in a detailed analysis, is the quintessential focus of the text and literally pictures, by means of the paratactical style used to describe it, Chandos's ideal of a spatialized or embodied language: "The stasis of hermetic self-containment in the splinter paragraph, based on reflexive reference, establishes the autonomy of the paragraph within the letter as a whole, which it nevertheless concludes and in form recapitulates. The paradox of autonomy within the letter is the formal execution of the paradox of immanent transcendence, a formal simulacrum of Chandos's described experience of 'secular revelation'" (Donahue 45). This crucial shift from abstract content to concrete form at the end of the "Letter" once again highlights the fact that language figures as culprit and liberator simultaneously. It is both the cause and the remedy for the separation of body and meaning. Hofmannsthal's view of language is neither entirely "negative" nor entirely "positive," but both at once. His text points to the fundamental interdependency of these binary oppositions that allegedly inform the entire culture around 1900, such as language versus intuition, mind versus matter, and meaning versus the body. Given Hofmannsthal's vision of language (for to call it his "understanding" of language would be to violate what he envisions), critics' emphasis on the "language-crisis" allegedly expressed in the "Letter" simply amounts to a tautology because language is always and necessarily "in crisis": it seeks to become what it is not by remaining true to what it already is. This aporia is the very essence of language.

Once we read the "Letter" as the self-conscious effort to highlight this aporia at the heart of language, the traditionally emphasized self-contradictory nature of Hofmannsthal's text is revealed as an integral part of its advocacy of embodied meaning. Since the latter cannot adequately be signified in ordinary, meaningful language, Hofmannsthal's text must create a geographical space for it to appear. Hence, the "Letter" tells the story of two different "moments" that nonetheless metaphorically blend together so that the narrative as a whole has nothing left to say (on the content level), but only to show (on the stylistic level). Seeking to erase itself, it becomes a medium without a message, or, put differently, its message consists in the transformative power of the linguistic medium itself, whose spatial reconfiguration visually presents the end of signification and the beginning of a body language still alive within the words that ostracize it. And yet, it is equally obvious that the "'stylistic revelation' of parataxis in the splinter paragraph" (Donahue 47) cannot picture this embodied language as poignantly as "Vorfrühling." The crucial period in the latter presents a more radicalized version of Hofmannsthal's ideal because it completely overcomes the temporal dimension of language and thus moves beyond signification without forsaking meaning altogether. In the following chapter, I will examine how Rilke tried to solve the same problem via reference to the spatial arts. My argument is that, once again, syntactical markers (periods, colons, ellipses, etc.) will be called upon to purify language from the vicissitudes of signification in order to create a material space—Rilke's *Weltinnenraum*—in which words and things can again be perceived as one.

5 Rilke's Stereoscopic Vision

Ja, alles, was wirklich geschaut wurde,
  muß Gedicht werden!
  —Rilke[1]

The Labor of Looking

Da neigt sich die Stunde und rührt mich an
mit klarem, metallenem Schlag:
mir zittern die Sinne. Ich fühle: ich kann—
und ich fasse den plastischen Tag.

Nichts war noch vollendet, eh ich es erschaut,
ein jedes Werden stand still.
Meine Blicke sind reif, und wie eine Braut
kommt jedem das Ding, das er will.

Nichts ist mir zu klein und ich lieb es trotzdem
und mal es auf Goldgrund und groß,
und halte es hoch, und ich weiß nicht wem
löst es die Seele los . . .

(*Werke* I: 253)[2]

Now the hour bows down, it touches me, throbs
metallic and lucid and bold:
my senses are trembling. I feel my own power—
on the plastic day I lay hold.

Until I perceived it, no thing was complete,
but waited, hushed, unfulfilled.

My vision is ripe, to each glance like a bride
comes softly the thing that was willed.

There is nothing too small, but my tenderness paints
it large on a background of gold,
and I prize it, not knowing whose soul at the sight,
released, may unfold . . .[3]

The introductory poem in Rilke's *Stundenbuch* (1899) describes the time of the poet's inspiration as a synaesthetic experience that literally makes the body tremble. Auditory, visual, and tactile senses all work together to produce an overwhelming feeling of creative power. It gives rise to a poetic subjectivity whose triumphant arrival is proclaimed by the threefold repetition of the "ich" in verses three and four. The "I" promises a kind of mythical redemption in which the human individual becomes reunited with the things surrounding him: ". . . und wie eine Braut / kommt jedem das Ding, das er will." The wedding signalizes the end of the modern dichotomy separating subject and object by means of an embrace mirrored not only in the rhyme pattern, but also in the structure of the poem. The poet stands not opposed to the world he perceives, but is part of it, engaged in an eternal process of receiving and giving that sustains all things. The "I" designates this power to seize and shape the surrounding world to the maturity of a gaze that not only perceives the things, but literally touches and completes them. Through the mere act of looking, the artist unlocks the reified forces of life. Under his auspices, things finally come into their own and fulfill the potential that had laid dormant inside them: "Nichts war noch vollendet, eh ich es erschaut, / ein jedes Werden stand still."

Located at its center, this "Werden" is the cardinal concept of Rilke's poem. The sixth verse describes the crucial moment of a "standstill," a rhythmic pause that results from the reversal of the *élan vital* running through the poem. This transformative shift from reception to production, from looking to writing defines Rilke's poetics. The poet, himself "touched" by, and hence but an object of, divine inspiration, returns the gift as he, now the sovereign subject of his own action, "seizes the corporeal day" and literally "paints" a new world in the guise of a poem. Indeed, the patron for Rilke's process of creative transformation is the spatial arts. He aims to paint a kind of poetry that is predicated upon, and hence authenticates, the gaze it describes. Just as the hands of the sculptor or painter give shape to the artwork, the gaze of the poet must materialize in the shape of words that express the essence of things. The poet's "I" becomes the "eye." It bequeaths a poem that appears to have written itself during the mere act of looking at the world.

Although this poetic transformation is said to affect all things, it is literally bracketed by the twofold repetition of "Nichts" at the beginning of stanzas two and three. The "Nichts" expresses an anxiety always present within Rilke's ideal of artistic creation, the fear that after all is said and done, "nothing" might remain to authenticate its success. In order to overcome this anxiety and convince aesthetically, the poem, therefore, must be conceived not only as an entire world of its own, but as a material work of art as well. Only then can the inherent flaw of language, that is, its inability to enter into a tactile relationship with the external world, be overcome. In the end, the painted poem is being lifted up like one of the many "things" it describes. This "thingness" of poetry and its material existence as a work of art allows the poet to liberate the soul of a person unknown—the reader.

The ellipsis in the end signifies an openness that is crucial for the magical transformation allegedly affected by the poem. It creates an outlet for the movement of creative energy passing from top to bottom through subject and object alike. This energy cannot remain confined to the fictional realm of the poem itself, but must be allowed to traverse the abyss separating its own world from the realm beyond. Poetic success hinges on the ever renewed ability of the artist to "touch" those outside of his reach by means of a poetic gaze that connects and intertwines everything it perceives. The fictional relationship between the lyrical "I" and its world is thus realized in the factual encounter between the reader and the poem itself, for it is on the receptive level that this poetic gaze gains shape. Due to the temporal nature of language, Rilke's poem not only describes the force of artistic creation, but self-referentially performs it in the act of being read. The reader's eyes traversing the letters on the page become synonymous with the poet's eyes scanning and rejuvenating the world he envisions. The artist animates the external world much like the reader enlivens the seemingly dead words of the poem itself, and the real activity of the latter serves to validate the imaginary performance of the former. To read is to realize the poetic gaze that gives life, meaning that the reader becomes a poet in his own right.

The identity between the two becomes more obvious in Rilke's later poetry, which, in contrast to the *Stundenbuch,* shifts focus from the "I" of the inspired artist toward the "you" of the reader. The introductory poem "Eingang" in his *Buch der Bilder* from 1902, for example, once again evokes the creative power of looking at things, yet also emphasizes the arbitrariness of the person looking:

Eingang

Wer du auch seist: am Abend tritt hinaus
aus deiner Stube, drin du alles weißt;
als letztes vor der Ferne liegt dein Haus:
wer du auch seist.
Mit deinen Augen, welche müde kaum
von der verbrauchten Schwelle sich befrein,
hebst du ganz langsam einen schwarzen Baum
und stellst ihn vor den Himmel: schlank, allein.
Und hast die Welt gemacht. Und sie ist groß
und wie ein Wort, das noch im Schweigen reift.
Und wie dein Wille ihren Sinn begreift,
lassen sie deine Augen zärtlich los . . .

(*Werke* I: 371)

Entrance

Whoever you are: in the evening step out
of your room, where you know everything;
yours is the last house before the far-off:
whoever you are.
With your eyes, which in their weariness
barely free themselves from the worn-out threshold,
you lift very slowly one black tree
and place it against the sky: slender, alone.
And you have made the world. And it is huge
and like a word which grows ripe in silence.
And as your will seizes on its meaning,
tenderly your eyes let it go . . .[4]

The poem indeed reads like an instruction manual for aspiring poets. While this programmatic character and its life-philosophical jargon can be judged to "undermine its aesthetic quality" (Willems 377f.), the poem also yields crucial insights regarding Rilke's poetic ambitions. The self-centered ideal of the inspired artist who passively receives the divine gift of creation has given way to a description outlining the various steps of a poetic practice allegedly open to everyone able to see for him- or herself. In order "to create the world," "you" merely need to leave behind the confinements of everyday life and step outside not only your familiar surroundings (die Stube), but the realm of the "known" in the factual sense (drin du alles *weißt*). Rilke's choice of "wissen" instead of the idiomatically more correct "kennen" locates artistic creation outside of and opposed to the intellectual sphere. It also alludes to the necessity of subverting existing linguistic idioms through innovative, poetic speech. Both "used" (commodified) language and the "known" room are part of the house "drin du alles weißt," the rationalized, modern world of everyday life Rilke rejects.

By contrast, the step over the exhausted threshold marks an entry into the unknown openness of life as such. This new world still lacks words and things alike, and the poem's challenge consists in the evocation of a powerful gaze able to fill the void and to recreate the world. This gaze is distinguished from common perception since the twilight implied by the poem (Abend) as well as your "tired" eyes impede a clear, enlightened vision of the world. If seeing things relates to reading poetry, the new gaze in question must take shape in the eyes of the reader. Hence, "Eingang" not only introduces the major themes of Rilke's entire collection of poems whose very title—*Das Buch der Bilder*—speaks to the relationship between vision and language. It also promotes the poem itself as the gateway for the reader to enter into the very "open" that remains one of Rilke's central themes. He who reads poetry experiences life itself, Rilke contends in an essay on Goethe: "The true and sublime art of the poet is to present the narrated events right in front of the reader's eye such that the present and its entire surroundings would seem to vanish. Given this naturalness of art, the reader should not merely feel the work of art, but actually experience the event itself" (Das ist des Dichters wahre, erhabene Kunst, dem Leser die Begebnisse, die er erzählt, so lebhaft vor Augen zu führen,—daß ihm die Gegenwart und seine ganze Umgebung zu entfliehen scheint, und daß er nicht nur ein Kunstwerk empfindet, sondern über dessen klarer Natürlichkeit die Kunst vergißt, und die Begebenheit—miterlebt) ("Der Wanderer"; *Werke* V: 283).

Although Novalis did not say it any different, I want to argue that Rilke's "neo-Romantic" (Käte Hamburger) stance nonetheless veils some fundamental differences between his own poetic ideals and those of German Romanticism. One of them concerns the peculiar nature of Rilke's gaze: whereas Romanticism specified the mind, or *Einbildungskraft*, of the reader as the locus where words are hermeneutically understood and transformed into the images they represent, Rilke endorses the physiological aspects of vision and thus grants full autonomy to the senses. For him, it is no longer the mind that sees, but the eye itself now operates in cooperation with the entire body. Similarly, "Eingang" calls for "you" not to stand in opposition to the world, but literally to enter into and physically engage with it. This movement is the prerequisite for both the liquidation of the old, reified universe and the creation of a new one through art. The two aspects are inextricably linked together since poetry is both the cause and the effect of a liberated world.

Being in this new world also necessitates being in a new language. Toward the end, the poem explicitly relates the making of the world to the power of a word "that still ripens in silence" (. . . wie ein Wort, das noch im Schweigen reift). The avowed similarity of world and word again emphasizes the self-referential nature of Rilke's poem, which transforms the visual world allegedly engendered by "your" look into the verses describing it and vice versa. Linguistic signs and external referents are declared interchangeable. The creation of the world takes place only in language so that language constitutes the world it evokes. Both realms converge at the very end of the poem in the empty, open space again signified by the three dots. Without naming it, the concluding ellipsis in "Eingang" specifies Rilke's aesthetic goals as the creation of a spatiotemporal "openness" that bridges inside and outside as well as "you" and the world.

"Through all beings works the *one* space: / interiorworldspace" (Durch alle Wesen reicht der *eine* Raum: / Weltinnenraum) (*Werke* II: 93). Rilke's later poem "Es winkt zu Fühlung . . ." seems to continue where "Eingang" breaks off, evoking the aesthetic ideal of *Weltinnenraum* or *Innenwelt* (*Rilke-Salome Briefwechsel* 325) as an expanding "void" filled by the ripening of a "silent word." Once again, Rilke's poetics resembles the Romantic ideal of language since this expression seems to call for a kind of speech that, if it could be voiced, would implode the subject-object dichotomy into one. In the eyes of Romanticism the "silent word" is the signifier of an impossible language able to speak the unspeakable, and poetry can succeed only by falling silent and effacing itself in light of what cannot be named. Like the previous poem from the *Stundenbuch*, "Eingang," too, appears to acknowledge its own impossibility, seeking redemption of its utopian claim in another realm elsewhere.

However, I believe this Romantic interpretation of Rilke's poem misses its more positive and positivist message. "Eingang" does not abandon the ideal of absolute poetry to the very words that, once written down, are declared responsible for its failure. Quite the contrary, the task of the poet consists in exploring our being in the world by daring to speak about it. Rilke's poetry entails both the realization to be always already within language and the willingness to abandon oneself to it. The "word that still ripens in silence," however, is not the spoken, but the written sign in the form of a comma, a period, or a colon, since it is "your look" that anchors poetic language and enables the comparison between world and word. Given the interdependence of vision and language that sustains Rilke's poems, the gaze of the reader emerges as a silent form of speech and the true expression of language. For Rilke, the obvious weakness of writing obscures its inherent strength, since it is the nature of writing to give existence to speech, to call things into the open and to make them seen, provided one is guided by the inner vision proclaimed in his poetry.

The reader's gaze leads to a final "begreif(en)," a term that connotes both a conceptual and a physical connection between "you" and your world. Poetic vision evokes a tactile intimacy that transcends the body-mind dichotomy and restores to sight a quality of touch that had been lost during the rationalist emphasis of the mind's eye scanning the geometrically structured universe of lifeless objects. Rilke's reader must see and feel his entry into language along a string of words that, much like "Eingang" itself, paradoxically dissolve and become manifest in(to) the three dots and the perceptual field they open up. At the end of the reading, "your" eyes have to both hold on to and "let go" of the poem and its language in order to enter into the *Weltinnenraum* it bespeaks. Rilke is a self-doubting Romanticist. He moves beyond Romanticism, not because he rejects hermeneutics or its poetic ideal of liberated language, but because he lacks verifiable proof that this poetics could ever be successful. His *Weltinnenraum* is but the hermeneutic ideal of an ever-expanding universality forced back into every single thing we see. These things are the cosmos *in nuce,* since "every thing can become God"

("Geschichten"; IV: 355). For Rilke, even a mere dot on the page literally contains a world.

Hence, the final ellipsis in "Eingang" is not a sign of poetic resignation, but actually delivers fulfillment. Contrary to Novalis's "geheimes Wort" or Tieck's "Zauberwort," Rilke fills the poetic silence with the matter of language. He envisions the voice of an unalienated language in the form of an ellipsis that marks its absent presence in the rationalized world of present absence. Reading the poem, "you" have already realized the world it bespeaks simply by resting your gaze on the words themselves. Rilke's "Eingang" demarcates the entry into a magical space of metamorphosis, a relay station that allows the artist's vision to materialize through language on its way toward a final embrace of the things perceived. The semantic ambiguity of the preposition "through" unveils the constitutive paradox of this poetic transformation. Rilke's gaze both moves beyond the realm of language and remains forever caught within. It splits into seeing the words that constitute the poem and the things called forth by overlooking them. Such poetry requires the presence of language only to deny and supplant it by vision, yet this vision nonetheless must hold on to language in order to materialize the things it sees.

This chapter examines the correlation between vision and language in Rilke's middle period. It is characterized by a peculiar work ethos inherited from the leading artists at the time. "I am learning to see" (Ich lerne sehen) (*Werke* VI: 710) — Rilke's *Malte* not only summarizes the primary task of the modern poet echoed throughout his entire oeuvre, but also unveils the paradox at the heart of Rilke's visual paradigm. The ability to see things as they really are, namely outside the bourgeois sphere of production and commodification, is itself based on a learning process that requires what it seeks to overcome: labor. Hence, Rilke's *Weltinnenraum* must not simply be understood as defining a utopian space located somewhere outside the material world or the realm of modern culture. The point is rather that such a space first needs to be recreated from within the present sociopolitical conditions that impede our immediate access to it. Although the *Weltinnenraum* cannot simply be presupposed or posited as a self-reliant "thing" in its own right, it must nonetheless take shape right in front of our eyes.

This is why Rilke is fascinated by modernist art. His admiration of Rodin continuously emphasizes the tremendous discipline and physical work on which hinges the liberation of human vision: "il faut toujours travailler!" Although itself the product of a free, liberated gaze, Rodin's work nonetheless forces the beholder "to shoulder the burden of looking," as Rilke states in one of his essays on Rodin ("Auguste Rodin. Zweiter Teil"; *Werke* V: 225).[5] For Rilke, Rodin's figures do not simply present a different look of things, but also document the process of how they came into being. They shelter the kind of gaze that, in Rilke's eyes, awakens life. Similarly, his praise of Cézanne and the French Impressionists centers on the openness of a visual field capable of bestowing upon things their natural way of being outside and beyond the confinements of the modern scopic regime. Modernist art does not concern itself with individual objects. It does not depict this or that particular thing, but instead teaches us a novel way of seeing things in general. Rilke explicitly attributes this achievement to Cézanne's lifelong commitment to artistic "work" and the labor of being "sur le motif." This work is preserved within the paintings themselves and must be repeated in the act of looking at them.

Rilke's *New Poems* are modeled after the spatial arts. They require the reader to "shoulder the burden of looking," as must the beholder of Rodin's sculptures and Cézanne's paintings. To see things is to read without reading and to unlearn "known" language in an effort to look at words differently without losing them from sight altogether. This labor of looking gives rise to a fundamental tension at the center of Rilke's poetics, which both undoes and upholds the ideal of material production. For Rilke, aesthetic destruction and creation are inextricably intertwined. A more immediate or less alienated relationship with the natural world can only be achieved by the arduous process of deconstructing the normative and ideologically deformed rules of perception that presently prohibit such a relationship. At the same time, however, the artistic goal of this liberation must itself be authenticated in and through a material product, and Rilke's new way of looking at things is deemed successful only if it allows him literally to present things. Put differently, one might say that Rilke's poetry tries to re-turn the reader's gaze in the twofold sense of reorienting and thus giving it back to him as a work of art. This re-turn of the gaze must take place in and through poetic language.

Like most intellectuals and artists around 1900, Rilke thus draws a sharp distinction between intellectual discourse and aesthetic language, that is, between secondary criticism and one's immediate self-expression through art. The latter is rooted in and returns to the body, while the former becomes severed from it. One makes you see, whereas the other forever ruins your vision. Critical discourse is perceived as yet another artificial obstacle preventing the direct communication between objects and the human eye. Art, by contrast, cannot but connect both poles. Hence, Rilke lauds Cézanne's inability to comment upon his own work, yet criticizes van Gogh's epistolary eloquence, because "all talk is misunderstanding. Insight is only within the work. No doubt about that" (*Letters about Cézanne* 78). In the same letter, he states: "[P]ainting is something that takes place among the colors, and how one has to leave them alone completely, so that they can settle the matter among themselves. Their intercourse: this is the whole of painting. Whoever meddles, arranges, injects his human deliberation, his wit, his advocacy, his intellectual agility in any way, is already disturbing and clouding their activity" (75). Cézanne's colors are Rilke's words. The free interplay of Cézanne's colors on the canvas, much like Rodin's creative use of sculpted fragments in ever-new artistic constellations, is likened to the rearrangement of words on a piece of paper.

Rilke, however, must come to terms with the particularities of language, for the poet has no things to show, merely words meant to represent things. Hofmannsthal "solved" the same problem by calling on language to dissolve within the living body as the silent origin of speech. He relied upon the magical power of language to call forth the world from which it must withdraw in order to be. Rilke's ideal of "sachliches Sagen" differs from Hofmannsthal with respect to his fascination with vision and the spatial arts. Whereas Hofmannsthal increasingly saw language as an aesthetic performance taking place in real time, Rilke is forced to grant language a stronger physical presence if his art is to compete with that of Rodin or Cézanne. Therefore, Rilke's effort to discover the body of language is more invested in the materiality of words and things than Hofmannsthal's, meaning that he ultimately favors written over spoken language. Words are posited as meaningful things in their own right, and Rilke wants to use the spatial arts as a mediator, a kind of transformation platform meant to facilitate this metamorphosis of words into things.

Words and Things

The *New Poems* advocate a kind of "sachliches Sagen" able to merge words and things, yet the question remains as to the specifics of this relationship between language and vision, word and world. Rilke's reader must determine what really are the "things" his poems describe: words, images, or objects? Trying to answer this question, literary criticism has focused on the tension between the self-referentiality of the *New Poems* and their goal of objective representation. The discussion centers on whether Rilke's *Dinggedichte* are primarily concerned with the adequate portrayal of external objects or, on the contrary, merely utilize the presence of "things" as a means to focus on the autopoietic qualities of language. The immediate answer that comes to mind is that they are essentially both since the *New Poems* try to renegotiate the relationship between inside and outside. Although literary critics somewhat acknowledge this ambiguity at work in Rilke's poetry, they ultimately privilege self-referentiality as its most characteristic feature. In their eyes, Rilke's "thing-poem" does not merely describe material things, but itself *becomes* the thing it describes: "The poem absorbs predicates of the thing," Engelhardt already claimed in the seventies (Engelhardt 34), and more recently, Peter Por argued that "his [Rilke's] single topic is poetry itself" (Por 25). In another recent study, we read that Rilke "emphasized the submerging of the subject in the self-representation of the object" so that "[t]he poem in itself comes more and more to take the place of the real thing in itself" (Lawrence Ryan 32, 35).

This argument regarding the autopoietic quality of Rilke's poems is made most eloquently by Paul de Man. For de Man, too, "[t]he referent of [Rilke's] poem is an attribute of [its] language, in itself devoid of semantic depth; the meaning of the poems is the conquest of the technical skills which they illustrate by their acoustic success" (*Allegories of Reading* 31). Rather than using language in order to describe things, de Man asserts, Rilke's poems evoke things merely in order to "play at language according to the rules of rhetoric as one plays ball according to the rules of the game" (38). Again, Rilke's text is granted an "awareness of its linguistic structure" (54) in which the "figure's truth turns out to be a lie at the very moment when it asserts itself in the plenitude of its promise" (55). What remains in the end is "a picturesque description" or "a picture postcard" (43) outlining a process of transformation that sometimes "actually occurs before our eyes" (35). Apart from the fallacy to ascribe self-awareness to linguistic structures, de Man's interpretation suffers from a kind of hyperbole paradigmatic of Rilke studies in general. Focusing on the creative transformation Rilke hoped to achieve in his poetry, critics often fall prey to the very rhetoric they seek to examine and hence claim to see a real metamorphosis "actually occurring before their eyes." Rilke himself contributed to this myth. In a letter from 1925, he states that "many of my *New Poems* have somewhat written themselves, in their final version, often times several in one day" (viele meiner "Neuen Gedichte" haben sich gewissermaßen selbst geschrieben, in endgültiger Form, oft mehrere an einem Tag) (qtd. in Lauster 284).

However, Rilke's self-stylization as an inspired writer turns his poems upside down. They simply work too hard to negotiate their autopoietic and their descriptive quality to appear to be self-authenticating. Rilke's "thing-poems" occasionally fail to convince because they are far too concerned with being convincing. On the diegetic level, the *New Poems* certainly evoke the "Umschlag" or "Verwandlung" of subject and object into one, as Judith Ryan argues. On the extradiegetic level, however, this transformation remains fictitious—a poetic ideal. While this point may seem trivial, it nonetheless applies to Ryan's reading, which at times insinuates that Rilke's poetic achievement transforms both language and reality such that the poet would truly become reconciled with words and things alike. Contrary to Ryan's perspective, which simply mirrors the utopian vision of Rilke himself, the following remarks insist that "the 'seeing' and the 'building' of things" are precisely *not* "participating in a single process of creation" (18), because the poet "sees" one thing and "builds" another, namely a poem—if one were to call it a thing at all.[6] This is not to deny the self-referentiality of Rilke's poetry, but to question the success of its poetic program.

Most of Rilke's thing-poems do not easily lend themselves to Ryan's conclusion about their "quasi-dialectical structure" (19) either. Nor can we refer to Rilke's poetic ideal as the "total equilibrium between thing and form" (Herman Meyers 263-64). Both perspectives adequately describe Rilke's poetic ideal, but not his actual practice, which consists of a particular kind of movement based not on the connection of different poles, but on their separation. This separation leads neither to Ryan's notion of "metamorphosis" or aesthetic transformation nor to Meyers's perfect "equilibrium" understood as a harmonized balance of powers because Rilke's poems must continuously labor to maintain, rather than overcome, the tension between inside and outside. Put differently, Rilke's poems focus on the simultaneity of word and world or the coexistence of materiality and meaning without there being an absolute balance or a dialectical process negotiating between them. If dialectics there is, it is a Benjaminian "dialectics at a standstill" or a version of "negative dialectics" (Adorno) that speaks to the "hovering" quality of language itself (Adorno, "Jargon der Eigentlichkeit" 495). It denotes a kind of creative energy trembling within Rilke's poetry, which works to prevent the possible implosion of materiality and meaning. What is at stake in the *New Poems* is the threat of an actual collapse between world and word that would annihilate both, and hence must be avoided.

Contrary to the rhetoric of the *New Poems,* the labor of looking they emphasize refers less to a "real" poetic transformation than to the lack thereof. Instead of something new, there emerges a void. This void, however, is not simply nothing, nor does it give rise to an aesthetic transformation. Rather, it carries a definitive function: it literally marks the empty spot where the poetic metamorphosis ought to take place. Thus, it creates an opening that both connects and separates inside and outside, self and other. Because of this void, the reader's gaze is forced to "shoulder the burden of looking." The gaze must oscillate between (reading the) word and (seeing the) thing without ever coming to rest at either one of the poles. A successful reading of Rilke's poems is one that switches back and forth at such high speed that the two realms seem to become one. World and word are thus being fused together as they appear to become superimposed one upon the other. The look of things, in other words, is nothing but an optical illusion in the eye of the reader.

Heidegger's critique calls attention to precisely this specular quality of Rilke's poetry. His reading focuses on the return of the gaze, which the eighth elegy associates with the look of the animal. He takes issue with Rilke's juxtaposition of mankind and openness, that is, the idea that "man is not admitted into the open. Man confronts the world" (Er [der Mensch] ist nicht eingelassen in das Offene. Der Mensch steht der Welt gegenüber) ("Wozu Dichter?"; *Holzwege* 286), as he paraphrases it. For Heidegger, Rilke's notion of "the open" remains oriented exclusively along the multitude of beings, rather than focusing on Being itself in the sense of "aletheia" or the unconcealment of the world. Although Rilke's thing-poems advocate an ideal equilibrium between word and thing, they fail to recognize, in Heidegger's eyes, that this balancing act itself has already been achieved the very moment *Dasein* realizes its "being in the world." Since "Rilke neither suspects nor knows anything about aletheia" (*GS* 54: 231), his poetry remains primarily concerned with the articulation of individual things and the harmonious reconciliation of inside and outside instead of the presentation of Being, which itself *is* this reconciliation. It follows that "Rilke's poetry is the last remnant of modern metaphysics" (*GS* 54: 235). It neglects to speak about man's or *Dasein*'s existential condition, which locates us always already beyond the subject-object dichotomy. Rilke, in other words, presupposes and thus perpetuates the modern problem of fragmentation he hopes to solve in his poetry. He works too hard to re-turn the human gaze instead of simply acknowledging the primordial openness given in and through the wor(l)d we perceive.

Adorno's scattered remarks about Rilke's "Dingkult" advance a critique from the exact opposite direction. Whereas Heidegger charges Rilke with the glorification of poetic subjectivity and specific beings rather than Being as such, Adorno focuses on the alleged lack of both subjectivity and specificity in Rilke's poetry. His comments concentrate on Rilke's disdain for the critical reflection of art. Aesthetic autonomy, in Adorno's eyes, by no means includes a prohibition to speak about its genesis or its meaning. On the contrary, it requires philosophical discourse to speak out the truth enigmatically contained within each work of art.[7] Rilke, however, advocates the very rupture between art and criticism that Adorno's *Aesthetic Theory* seeks to overcome. For Rilke, the liberation of language from its referential burden compels "a carefree letting-go of oneself" ("Über Kunst"; *Werke* V: 429), "a half-unconscious finding" as opposed to the deliberate "search" of the intellectual ("Moderne Lyrik"; *Werke* V: 378). Once the living body rather than the conscious mind governs the moment of artistic production, Rilke suggests, it cannot but lead to the rebirth of a "new, young, and non-alienated" language of art ("Max Bruns, Lenz"; *Werke* V: 464). Rilke's abandonment of subjectivity and his refusal to specify the function of art cause Adorno to dismiss his reflections on art and his poetry alike: "Because it remains stupefied vis-à-vis the truth and precision of its own words—even the most vague expression ought to be determined as vagueness and not treated as if it were determined—[Rilke's] lyric poetry is bad in spite of its virtuosity" (Dadurch, daß sie sich abstumpft gegen die Wahrheit und Genauigkeit ihrer

Worte—noch das Vageste müßte als Vages bestimmt, nicht als Bestimmtes eingeschmuggelt sein—ist sie auch als Lyrik schlecht trotz ihrer Virtuosität) ("Jargon" 470).[8]

The opposed perspectives of Adorno and Heidegger are indicative of the ambiguity in Rilke's work, which simultaneously espouses and undermines the objectivity of words and things alike. Indeed, his poetry is best where it does not repress, but emphasizes the aesthetic labor that negotiates between these poles. In so doing, the *New Poems* are closer to Adorno than Heidegger, in spite of the fact that the latter esteemed his art considerably more than the former. The uncertainty regarding the ontological status of Rilke's "things" recalls Adorno's dictum that the work of art never actually possesses the apparent unity it must proclaim in order to question the way things are: "Dissonance is the truth about harmony" (Dissonanz ist die Wahrheit über Harmonie) (*Ästhetische Theorie* 168). Such dissonance within the work of art, the inner disparity it tries to conceal and yet discloses unwittingly in the very act of concealment itself, defines the self-destructive character of modern art: "Works of art that are deliberately conceived as a tour de force are semblance because they must purport in essence to be what they in essence cannot be; they correct themselves by emphasizing their own impossibility" (*Aesthetic Theory* 106) (Als tour de force konzipierte Werke sind Schein, weil sie wesentlich als das sich geben müssen, was sie wesentlich nicht sein können; sie korrigieren sich, indem sie die eigene Unmöglichkeit hervorheben) (*ÄT* 163). Adorno's description fits Rilke's *New Poems*. They, too, acknowledge their "own impossibility" and thus undermine the aesthetic ideal of "sachliches Sagen" that informs them. Suspended between words and things, matter and meaning, they simultaneously proclaim and disavow their ability to liberate everything from the burden of instrumental rationality that governs the outside. The work of art is understood as "process and instant (*Augenblick*) combined" (*ÄT* 154), the paradoxical product of the sociopolitical conditions of capitalism and the utopian vision of its transcendence.

For both Rilke and Adorno, art cannot simply rely on its aesthetic autonomy without losing its critical potential and falling prey to the realm of pure illusion. And yet, without this autonomy, it lacks both the historical validity and material substance necessary to authenticate its different vision of the world. The work of art must therefore never abandon its traditional impulse to imitate reality, while at the same time trying to stay true only to itself, which is to say that poetry literally describes the impossible art of being self-identical by promising every-thing its own unique identity. It envisions the liberation of the world while itself remaining a prisoner of the utopian space it calls forth. Fraught with this interior contradiction, the poem pronounces an ideal of (self-)harmony it cannot enact. Its hypocrisy lies in judging the world from an imaginary space inside, as if that were not also determined by the outside it denounces. Poetry speaks the truth, however, as soon as it thematizes and thus unveils its own hypocrisy.

To be sure, this is not to claim that Rilke's notion of artistic labor can be reconciled with Adorno's Marxism. Undoubtedly, Rilke's "work" remains largely unconcerned with the sociopolitical dimension of the capitalist critique it implies, as Reinhold Grimm and others have argued. Things rather than people are the true subjects of Rilke's poetry. According to Rilke, the inner voice of the poet emerges as the objective language of material reality, which is to say that human subjectivity is called upon to liberate the things rather than the other way around. As if in response to Nietzsche's dictum that "God is dead," one reads in Rilke's "Geschichten vom Lieben Gott" that "every thing can become God. It must only be told" ("Geschichten"; *Werke* IV: 355).[9] This aesthetic deification of commodities, however, can hardly be the answer to the sociopolitical problems caused by the "disenchantment" (Max Weber) of the modern world. Rilke's expressed goal to "talk *to* the things rather than *about* them" ("Moderne Lyrik"; *Werke* V: 370)[10] betrays the very anthropomorphization of objects that Adorno denounces as the "aesthetic weakness" of Rilke's *Dingkult*.

In the following, I seek to specify and redeem Rilke's "aesthetic weakness" in the context of the spatial arts as well as Husserl's phenomenology. Unlike Adorno, I read the *New Poems* not primarily in the sociopolitical, but rather in the aesthetic and philosophical context of its time. Although Adorno would have undoubtedly rejected this distinction as ideological, I believe it is ultimately more productive to question Rilke's poetry on its own grounds than to denounce its inconsistencies as nothing but "reactionary" symptoms of capitalist reification. On the contrary, it is precisely by "bracketing," in a Husserlian sense, the sociopolitical background of his poetry that one might discover its philosophical dimension. Without disavowing Adorno's disapproval of Rilke's "thing-cult," his emphasis on the "thingness" of art can also be regarded as a critique of the idealist impulses at the time. My major thesis contends that Rilke's paradoxical work ethos of an unburdened vision is symptomatic for a failed phenomenological perspective around 1900 that claims to "see" and adequately describe the essence of things.

In contrast to most critics who discuss the relationship between Rilke's middle period and Husserl's philosophy, I argue that Rilke implies a radical critique of phenomenology because he unveils the autopoietic dimension of language that Husserl refuses to acknowledge. It follows that Adorno's denunciation of Rilke's work as "irrational" misses the manifest materialist dimension at work therein, one that allows his poetry to expose the idealist and transcendental nature of Husserl's eidetic visions. In spite of Rilke's explicit rejection of art criticism, his poetry invites it nonetheless. The critique inheres in his ideal notion of artistic labor that structures the reading process effected by his poems. The reader's gaze is deliberately forced to oscillate between the ideal intuition of the "thing itself" to which Rilke's poetry seemingly refers and the recognition of mere letters on the page. "Seeing" thus becomes a process suspended between the Romantic ideal of poetic imagination and the Aestheticist turn toward the materiality of the letter, giving rise to a stereoscopic vision the reader cannot but acknowledge if she wants to make sense of Rilke's poetry.

The Blood of Language and the Art of Writing

I want to approach Rilke's middle period by way of a detour via the spatial arts that nonetheless leads right to the poetological center. It was in the realm of modern art where Rilke encountered the "realization" of those things he sought to express in his own poetry: "Somehow I too must find a way of making things: not plastic, written things, but realities that arise from the craft itself" (Irgendwie muß auch ich dazu kommen, Dinge zu machen, nicht plastische, geschriebene Dinge, — Wirklichkeiten, die aus dem Handwerk hervorgehen), he proclaims in a letter to his wife (*Briefe über Cézanne* 7). The sense of artistic inferiority palpable in this and similar statements throughout his middle period stems from the particular lack of "reality" attributed to linguistic signs as opposed to colors or marble. The former merely signify the physicality that the latter embody. Rilke's laments are, of course, fairly typical of the so-called "language-crisis" around 1900 and the concomitant valorization of vision as superior to language. Yet Rilke's poetic concerns must be contextualized within the contemporary art world at the time in order to gain full meaning.

In his popular essay regarding the "Origin of Artistic Production," published in 1887, the art historian Konrad Fiedler distinguishes vision from all other senses by its inherent ability to find its "own voice" and "express" itself aesthetically in the work of art. Fiedler regards the physical movements of the artist as the uncensored continuation and direct expression of the visual sense: "It is one and the same action that, beginning with sensations and perceptions, finally unfolds itself in expression movements" (*Schriften zur Kunst* I: 164; my translation). Fiedler's "expression movements" (*Ausdrucksbewegungen*) name the ideal of an uninterrupted creative process that organically lives and spreads through the body of the artist. It testifies to the unmediated connection between the eye and the hand. The self-expressive, yet silent, "language" of art stands in sharp contrast to everyday language since any effort to translate one's artistic insights into words inevitably goes astray, Fiedler argues. Language, in other words, is necessarily self-referential and hence unable to express anything else but its own being: "After all, the meaning possessed by the miracle of language is not that of signifying Being, but that it is itself a Being. And since that which emerges in linguistic form does not even exist outside that form, it follows that language can always only signify itself" (*Schriften* I: 123; my translation). In Fiedler's eyes, language deserts and ultimately confronts the human body as a distinct and autonomous entity, whereas the spatial work of art expresses the body and remains intimately connected to it. The hand of the artist is able to express what his eye has seen, whereas language is concerned only with itself. Of course one should question the basic assumption of Fiedler's juxtaposition of art and language. There is no reason to assume that the sculptor's hand is any more "expressive" or "authentic" than that of the writer. However, such a critique must also point to and acknowledge the widespread popularity of Fiedler's ideas among artists and intellectuals at the end of the century. Similar to Fiedler, Rilke acknowledges the superiority of the spatial arts as a form of artistic self-expression that involves the entire body as opposed to the fragmentation and autoreferentiality effected by language.

A brief and by no means exhaustive discussion of Rilke's *The Notebooks of Malte Laurids Brigge* may serve to elucidate this point. One of the central themes of *Malte* is the process of self-alienation affected by writing, which is contrasted with the ideal of self-expressive vision. Malte's effort to reassure himself of his own existence in and through the process of writing is depicted as an utter failure. Malte's "inability to protect himself against the chaos" (Huyssen 134) of modern life leads to a process of "Ent-Ichung" (Sokel) as he "is being written" by his own hand (*Malte; Werke* VI: 756). The "broken" author Malte thus emerges as the precise opposite of Fiedler's ideal artist. Whereas the latter is engaged in the self-authentic *Ausdrucksbewegung* of his entire body, Malte becomes increasingly separated even from his own hand: "For a while I can still write and say all of this. But a day will come when my hand will be far from me, and when I ask it to write, it will write words that do not belong to me" (Noch eine Weile kann ich das alles aufschreiben und sagen. Aber es wird ein Tag kommen, da meine Hand weit von mir sein wird, und wenn ich sie schreiben heißen werde, wird sie Worte schreiben, die ich nicht meine) (*Malte; Werke* VI: 756). The "phantom hand" Malte repeatedly evokes in his notebooks is symptomatic of a kind of writing that fails to render visible what the author claims to have seen. Writing independently on its own without interference from the "author," Malte's hand has broken free from the stifling rules of the mind and the oppressive regime of Romantic subjectivity. It engages in a self-governed activity that articulates the perspective of the body. The latter, of course, must no longer be understood as a clearly demarcated object in space, but as a mere vessel for a creative energy or an *élan vital* that transcends and transforms the individual. Malte's hand writes down the world as seen from the viewpoint of the body.

Rilke's *Malte* indeed exposes the purpose of writing, much like the purpose of painting, as an exercise in vision. The writer's goal is to learn how to see, and one of the central concerns of the novel is to specify this relationship between writing and seeing, as Graf Brahe illustrates to his daughter Abelone during their shared writing lessons: "'She cannot write it,' he said in a sharp tone, 'and others will not be able to read it. And will they even be able to see what I say?' he said wickedly as he continued to gaze at her" ("Sie kann es nicht schreiben," sagte er scharf, "und andere werden es nicht lesen können. Und werden sie es überhaupt sehen, was ich da sage?" fuhr er böse fort und ließ Abelone nicht aus den Augen) (*Malte; Werke* VI: 847). The paradox of a vision that needs to have been experienced before it can be written down, yet must be written down in order to be experienced, haunts the memoirs of the old Brahe. Since writing is both indispensable and yet "too slow for his recollections," he begins to see writing in a strictly metaphorical sense. The entire body is now envisioned as a kind of text: "'The books are empty,' yelled the Count with an angry gesture toward the walls, 'the blood, that's what counts, one must read in there'" ("Die Bücher sind leer," schrie der Graf mit einer wütenden Gebärde nach den Wänden hin, "das Blut, darauf kommt es an, da muß man drin lesen können") (*Malte; Werke* VI: 848). Blood, in this context, does not refer to family lineage or race, but rather to the living body as such. In order to see the world, Brahe suggests, one needs to be able to read the body—not, to be sure, in its solid form, but as the exterior of a pulsating energy that runs through it.

The flow of blood within the body relates to that of language within books. For Brahe, the body is like a book. If we look at them as material objects, they are empty, yet their insides are alive. Seeing things means to look through bodies and read their entrails as a kind of language that dissolves the gaze within its flow and carries the reader along. Brahe's comments elucidate this ideal kind of reading. He has no problems visualizing the body as text: "He took Abelone's hands and opened them like a book" (Er nahm Abelones Hände und schlug sie auf wie ein Buch), whereas Abelone, in an effort to remember the things she has seen, can only "look almost curiously into her empty hands" (*Malte; Werke* VI: 851). The episode is crucial because it insists on the subjective nature of vision, which cannot objectively be translated into language. As he moves beyond the writing exercises that still engulf Malte, Brahe experiences a freedom of vision that allows him to "read" the hands and eyes of those around him. Words and things alike take shape in the eye of the beholder and not in the mind of educated readers, as Brahe comments: "Me, I remembered his eyes. . . . I have seen a good many eyes, believe you me, but not that kind. For these eyes, nothing would have had to be there, they had it in them" (Ich aber merkte mir seine Augen. . . . Ich habe allerhand Augen gesehen, kannst du mir glauben: solche nicht wieder. Für diese Augen hätte nichts da sein müssen, die hatten es in sich) (*Werke* VI: 848). Taken literally, this expression, of course, refers to the retinal reflections visible on the surface of the living eye. In contrast to most Romantic heroes, however, Brahe does not recognize himself as he looks into the eye of the other. Rather, he sees things that seem to belong exclusively to the eye itself. The eyes that "have it in them" are eyes that carry within themselves every-thing they saw.

This visual autonomy upsets the rationalist perspective on things of which

Romanticism still partook. For Descartes and the discourse network around 1800, "[i]t is the mind, which sees, not the eye" ("Optics" 108), for the eye as well as any physical organ responding to a stimulating movement from the outside can be deceived, Descartes admits, but the mind cannot. For Brahe, however, vision takes place exclusively in the eye, meaning that, for him, disembodied perception does not exist anymore. The things one has seen become alive not through the power of poetic imagination or the memories of the "author," but are preserved within one's own blood, and the only successful kind of writing, the novel suggests, would be one nourished by these interior visions that sustain the human body as a whole: "Because the memories themselves are not yet it. Only when they become blood within us, and gaze and gesture, all of them nameless and not to be distinguished from our own self anymore, only then can it happen that in a very rare hour the first word of a verse arises out of their midst and springs forth from them" (Denn die Erinnerungen selbst sind es noch nicht. Erst wenn sie Blut werden in uns, Blick und Gebärde, namenlos und nicht mehr zu unterscheiden von uns selbst, erst dann kann es geschehen, daß in einer sehr seltenen Stunde das erste Wort eines Verses aufsteht in ihrer Mitte und aus ihnen ausgeht) (*Malte; Werke* VI: 724). This ideal of a poetic word literally "standing up" and "walking forth" from the midst of human memories again testifies to the physical attributes of language, which literally possesses a body of its own. Similar to the human body, this body of language shelters vision and carries our memories along with it. The gaze of the reader, like that of the writer, must bathe in the *élan vital* that runs through these bodies, for it connects and sustains them as what they are. Which is to say that any successful writer must simultaneously be a reader of the body—otherwise the essence of things is lost from sight. Unlike Brahe, Malte literally breaks apart because he wants to control rather than abandon himself to his own body and that of language. His writing exercises cannot but fail, for his efforts to master language will never capture the visual experiences contained therein.

Rilke's poetic goal of "sachliches Sagen," it follows, does not simply consist in speaking the name of things. Rather, language must once again become reconnected to the human body in order to express what it sees. Rilke's increasing interest in Rodin and Cézanne is mediated by this idealization of the spatial arts whose "language was the body," as he claims ("Rodin"; *Werke* V: 146). Indeed, Cézanne's paintings are said to gain expression only within Rilke's own blood: "my blood describes them to me, but my words pass them by somewhere out there and nothing is being called inside" (mein Blut beschreibt sie in mir, aber das Sagen geht irgendwo draußen vorbei und wird nicht hereingerufen) (*Briefe über Cézanne* 42). For speech to be meaningful, it must be invited to enter the body and then float through it. Poetry must reunite the language of the body and the body of language. Discussing Rilke's relationship to Cézanne, Anette Schwarz has convincingly demonstrated the corporeal process of signification at work in Rilke's poetic visions. To attain a *dingliche Wirklichkeit,* Schwarz argues, "the thing must first become an object of digestion and must be 'translated,' or decomposed, by the enzyme-colors into its irreducible, that is, indigestible 'color content.' ... 'Pure things,' in this thingly physiology, are only those that have been expelled by the process of metabolism" (Schwarz 197). In order to compete with the expressive quality—the *Ausdrucksbewegung*—of the artist, the poet needs to use his words as enzymes digesting and dissolving things within his own body before they can be reborn as poetic language.

Poems, in other words, are composed of the pulp of signification. Poetic writing originates from the organic rhythm that precedes coherent language, and the act of reading needs to *re-turn* the gaze to this original site—that is, to the studio of the artist where everything is being disassembled and re-arranged again—in order to understand what the reified text can no longer say. One must learn, like Brahe, "to read in the blood" although—or precisely because—it sweeps away all stable references and speaks a language beyond decipherable meaning. What remains for both writers and readers is to "blind" common vision in order to develop eyes that "have it in them" and look from the inside out: "'Do you see him?' he bellowed at her [Abelone]. And suddenly he took the silver candelabrum, lighting up her face, blinding her. Abelone remembered having seen him" ("Siehst du ihn?" herrschte er sie [Abelone] an. Und plötzlich ergriff er den einen silbernen Armleuchter und leuchtete ihr blendend ins Gesicht. Abelone erinnerte sich, daß sie ihn gesehen habe) (*Malte; Werke* VI: 850). Once Abelone is blinded and visually severed from the things outside, she is able to see them for the first time with her own eyes.

In light of the subjectivity of the artist's inner vision, Rilke, throughout his middle period, denounces art criticism not only as superfluous, but as dangerous. In his eyes, it serves to undermine rather than fortify the authenticity and ingenuity of those who see and express what has not been seen or expressed before. The task of the art critic, he argues, is not to analyze or critique a particular work. Rather, it consists in exercises of translation that serve to mobilize the inner vision of the body. The critic must be able to "see and speak the colors" of modern painting and "to repeat in words the smile of the Mona Lisa" or "the aging expression of Tizian's Karl V and the fragmented, lost look of Jan Six at the collection of Amsterdam" ("Worpswede"; *Werke* V: 9). Rilke's *New Poems* rest upon this conflation of poetry and the arts, and his essays about Worpswede insist from the very beginning on the translatability of word and image. An early painting by the painter Mackensen, we are told, "says with one word what he later repeated in long sentences" as he developed his "grammar and the sentence structure of his idiom" (Hier hat er mit einem Wort gesagt, was er später in längeren Sätzen wiederholt hat. Das soll kein Tadel sein; er hat uns zuerst ein wunderbar großes Wort seiner eigenen Sprache gezeigt und uns dann erst eingeführt in die Grammatik und den Satzbau seines Idioms) ("Worpswede"; *Werke* V: 48f.). Modersohn also developed "his own language" (*Werke* V: 66) in which he crafted "confessions in verses" (*Werke* V: 64): "So many powerful things — words for the almost ineffable — are present in this land, the language of Otto Modersohn. And it is clearly visible that he increasingly uses it as a poet" (So Mächtiges — Worte für fast Unsagbares — enthält dieses Land, die Sprache Otto Modersohns. Und es ist zu sehen, daß er sie immer mehr als Dichter gebraucht) (*Werke* V: 87).

The translatability of word and image works in the reverse as well, for Rilke discusses modern poetry also with reference to painting. About the poems of Hans Benzmann, he writes in 1896: "Benzmann has superb and brilliant colors on his pallet and he paints with a full brush. His pictures are saturated with hue and need to be looked at both with leisure and understanding. — These poems I call pictures in the true sense of the term. I have gazed at this book rather than read in it!" (Benzmann hat herrliche, leuchtende Farben auf seiner Palette und er nimmt den Pinsel sehr voll. Seine tonsatten Bilder wollen mit Muße und Verständnis geschaut sein. — Diese Gedichte nenne ich Bilder im eigentlichen Sinne des Wortes. Ich habe in diesem Buche geschaut, nicht gelesen!) ("Hans Benzmann"; *Werke* V: 302). About Hermine von Preuschen, Rilke exclaims: "She paints her magnificent poems. Their heavy flow of rhymeless rhythm flows like melted gold and she composes her colorful allegories on the canvas.... In front of these images, one asks oneself: is the poem a picture or the picture a poem?" (Sie malt ihre herrlichen Gedichte, deren schwerer reimloser Rhythmenfluß wie geschmolzenes Gold hinströmt, und sie dichtet in farbensatten Allegorien auf die Leinwand. . . . Vor diesen Bildern fragt man sich: Ist das Gedicht ein Bild, oder das Bild ein Gedicht?) ("Hermine von Preuschen"; *Werke* V: 310). Like the "I" of the introductory poem in the *Stundenbuch*, the inspired artist paints as he writes and writes as he paints because all art is nurtured by life itself. In order to express its essence, Rilke claims, art must invent a new language, as did Cézanne, whose "difficulties," according to Merleau-Ponty, "are those of the first word" ("Cézanne's Doubt" 69).

The ultimate goal of both poetry and art is to present life as such. Rodin's works, for example, simply "are" (*Werke* V: 169) and aspire to nothing else but the expression of "life itself, nameless life" ("Auguste Rodin. Erster Teil"; *Werke* V: 179). This lifelike character of Rodin's work held tremendous appeal for Rilke. Over and over again he describes how Rodin, who has mastered the art of looking, is surrounded by an abundance of life in the form of his own sculptures looking back at him. This reciprocal gaze gives rise to an essentially flat universe of perceiving and perceived images in which intellectual distinctions such as subject and object, inside and outside, become meaningless. Rilke's *Weltinnenraum* takes shape in the *élan vital* running through Rodin's sculptures: "There is only a single, thousand-fold, moving and modifying surface. For a moment, the whole world could be reflected in this thought. . . ." (Es giebt [*sic*] nur eine einzige, tausendfältig bewegte und abgewandelte Oberfläche. In diesem Gedanken konnte man einen Moment die ganze Welt denken. . . .) ("Auguste Rodin. Zweiter Teil"; *Werke* V: 213). This surface is but the reflection of the crucial "Werden" that sustains the matter of art and life alike.

According to Rilke, Rodin has exteriorized the interiority of things. He has turned them inside out and revealed their inner life to the eye of the beholder. Where there used to be only rigid forms separated from each other, there emerges in Rodin's studio a world of interconnected parts providing new insights into life. Looking at details from Rodin's *Gates to Hell* (figures 5 and 6), one gets a sense of this incessant movement that unites and enlivens his figures. The convoluted disarray of arms, legs, and entire bodies hopelessly entangled in one another testifies to their being part of a larger whole whose essence consists precisely in its lack of finite form. Rodin can reassemble his figures into ever-new aesthetic constellations, because what "matters" is not this or that particular shape, but the interior energy that sustains and connects them. Like Rilke's poem "Eingang" from the *Buch der*

Figure 5. Auguste Rodin, The Gates of Hell, *1880–1917. Bronze, S. 1304, Musée Rodin, Paris; photograph by Jean de Calan.*

Figure 6. Auguste Rodin, The Gates of Hell, 1880–1917, detail. Bronze, S. 1304, Musée Rodin, Paris; photograph by Jean de Calan.

Bilder, Rodin's work has opened the *Gates* to the primordial vision of life itself.

Rilke's characterization of Rodin's work as a "surface" anticipates his later description of Cézanne's paintings, which he similarly praises for expressing the creative power of seeing things anew and more truthfully. The history of art criticism has often pointed to the phenomenological dimension of Cézanne's work, which is situated between Realist and Impressionist painting, equally renouncing and endorsing both movements. His goal was to "'faire la chose,' i.e., to paint *the visual thing,* not the mere impression," and "critics almost universally agree upon the radically *objective* character of Cézanne's maturest works" (Forrest Williams 167). Rilke was fascinated by Cézanne's sense of objectivity, which did not eschew sensory perception, but embraced it as the sole path toward visual truth. For in spite of Cézanne's belief that there is a "right" picture for everything we see—what Husserl called the "eidos" of an object—he also insisted on this picture taking shape only in the sovereign eye of a seer unbound by the laws of common perception. Objectivity, in other words, is being attained entirely by subjective means. This paradox leads to the discernable demise of Euclidian space in Cézanne's paintings. Their visual coherence is undermined by a multiplicity of different perspectives guiding the viewer's gaze on the canvas. Oftentimes, the foreground recedes into the background and vice versa. Everything we see touches upon and becomes part of its surrounding. Cézanne merges the various outlines of the "things" he portrays such that they lose their physical autonomy as clearly demarcated bodies in space. And yet, he does not dissolve them entirely as did the Impressionists or pointillists. Rather, he mainly looks upon colors to give rise to form.

Still Life with Curtain and Flowered Pitcher (figure 7) exhibits this material-like substance of colors in Cézanne's work. The painting works to undermine the distinction of foreground and background, using the sinuous lines of curtain and napkin to mediate between them. The large bowl in the center appears slightly tilted and thus located on a different visual plane from the other objects on the table. In fact, the table itself seems somewhat elevated in the right back corner, giving the impression that things would have to start sliding toward the edge of the table. Overall, these deliberate spatial incongruities serve to undermine the presumed unified perspective of the painting. They create a slight rupture within the harmonious composition of the scene and the seemingly balanced view it bestows upon things.

Figure 7. Paul Cézanne, Still Life with Curtain and Flowered Pitcher, *ca. 1899. Oil on canvas; courtesy of the State Hermitage Museum, St. Petersburg.*

What is most striking about the painting, however, is the use of color as a means to let objects appear and present themselves to the viewer. The white cloth in the foreground to the left is distinguishable from the dark drapes in the background mainly on the basis of color since its shape and texture match that of the curtain perfectly. And yet, the other part of the napkin completely merges with the white bowl in the center in spite of their clear difference in shape. What matters in Cézanne's painting is not simply the givenness of any particular material form, but the visual impression of color that literally shapes these forms to begin with. The point, then, is not to deny the existence of matter and form, but to gain insight into their sensory composition.

This is most obvious with regard to the white cloth at the right, which has been left unfinished by the painter. Because of this lack of color, we "see" a part of the table behind the napkin without, however, there really being any particular "thing" shown at this precise spot. What appears instead is a rupture in color, a brown "looking through" and replacing the white that might have covered it. The table, in other words, can be seen without being seen. It is both present and absent at the same time, an object caught at the very moment that it presents itself to the gaze of the viewer. "The painter's vision is not a view upon the *outside*," comments Merleau-Ponty on Cézanne's paintings in general, and he continues: "The world no longer stands before him through representation; rather, it is the painter to whom the things of the world give birth by a sort of concentration or coming-to-itself of the visible. Ultimately the painting relates to nothing at all among experienced things unless it is first of all 'autofigurative.' It is a spectacle of something only by being a 'spectacle for nothing,' by breaking the 'skin of things' to show how the things become things, how the world becomes world" ("Eye and Mind" 141). Merleau-Ponty points to the moment of "presencing" as the central characteristic of Cézanne's paintings, and it is precisely this moment that mesmerized Rilke. For him, the plain "surface" in Cézanne's paintings, much like that of Rodin's sculptures, expresses life because it refuses to signify, and instead reveals, their essence and the inner bloodstream of things. In Rilke's view, both artists have found their own language and are now able to create the world from within by means of the *Ausdrucksbewegung* constitutive of their art. They have captured life like a genie in a transparent bottle, thus enabling us to see how everything is engaged in a process of incessant change right in front of our eyes. Rilke's claim that "all reality is on [Cézanne's] side" does not merely judge the "thing-like" character of his paintings, but again endorses the expressive "superficiality" of an art that "does not show it, but has it," as Rilke claims about van Gogh's work (*Letters about Cézanne* 50; footnote 3).

As soon as Rilke turns toward his own art, however, he does not "have" it, since he has not yet found the "first word" of his own craft. Trying to come to terms with this lack, his *New Poems* labor to fill it with the substance of art. However, Rilke's ideal of a perfect aesthetic balance between space and time by emphasizing the substantive quality of language takes revenge on him. Internally split to the core, the *New Poems* stumble over the materiality of their own words, because every one of them opens and closes itself at the same time that it attracts and rebuts the gaze of the reader. Although the thing-poem deliberately addresses words as autonomous objects in order to validate its implicit claim of wor(l)d constitution, it cannot help but suddenly encounter them in all their opacity as unequivocally foreign, a strange substance that undermines the transparency of the wor(l)d it creates. The "thing itself" is thus being reborn within the poem in the form of black letters on the page. Rilke's words are themselves unruly objects demanding to be seen and heard, like those in "Ein Prophet." The poem depicts a convulsive body that has lost control over the stone-like words it spouts forth:

> . . . . Und in seinem Innern richten
> sich schon wieder Worte auf,
>
> nicht die seinen (denn was wären seine
> und wie schonend wären sie vertan)
> andre, harte: Eisenstücke, Steine,
> die er schmelzen muß wie ein Vulkan,
>
> (*Werke* I: 566–67)
>
> . . . and words are being accumulated
> deep within him once again:
>
> not his own (for what could his words settle?
> And how temperedly would they be dealt!),
> other, harder: chunks of stone and metal,
> which, like a volcano, he must melt
>
> (*New Poems* 179)

Words are being born within the speaking subject, yet they are not the subject's own. They are literally "other," and their materiality needs to be "melted down" and digested before the subject can "throw them out" in the form of speech. The words of "Eine Sibylle" ("A Sibyl"), to provide another example, are like roaming bats leaving her hollow and burned out from a power she cannot master:

> . . . . Sie aber stand
>
> . . . .
>
> hoch und hohl und ausgebrannt;
>
> von den Worten, die sich unbewacht
> wider ihren Willen in ihr mehrten,
> immerfort umschrieen und umflogen,

während die schon wieder heimgekehrten
dunkel unter ihren Augenbogen
saßen, fertig für die Nacht.

(*Werke* I: 568)

. . . . But she returned
. . . .
high and hollow and outburned;

ever circled by the screaming flight
of words that, all unwatched for and unwilled,
lodged within her breast and propagated,

while the home-returningly fulfilled
sombrely beneath her eyebrows waited,
ready for the coming night.

(*New Poems* 181)

It is telling that these words "sit beneath her eyebrows," thus underlining not only the general connection between language and vision, but also their specific function as both mediator and barrier between the gaze and the outside world. To read is not simply to imagine things, as in Romanticism, but to encounter them as visions already contained within language. It is not the subjective mind of the imaginative reader that sees, but language itself. Vision inheres in language. In order to partake of it, one must not read the words, but see through them — not, to be sure, in the Romantic sense of eschewing their materiality in favor of the subjective hallucinations to which they give rise, but, quite the contrary, by getting into physical contact with them. Words are saturated with vision. They are the eyes of the reader.

And yet, although language enables vision, the words before us do not see the things the way we do who rely upon their help. Words, to be sure, stay in intimate contact with the things, yet their own vision forever remains inaccessible to us. We cannot witness the way language itself perceives the world. For as soon as words are placed before our eyes, their original insights immediately become obscured. Not only are they now physically in the way of our vision. Worse still, they only unveil dead images since they can no longer intuit things as they truly are. Rilke's words are things that used to have eyes of their own, but they lost them once and for all in the textual maze of signification. Exploited as signifiers that constitute discourse, they are condemned to tell dilapidated stories about what they once were able to see for themselves. It follows that neither by looking at words, as in the act of reading, nor by blinding one's regular vision, as suggested by the old Brahe, does the seer regain access to living things. Once called upon to surrender its vision, language obfuscates the images it provides and prepares the reign of darkness: "fertig für die Nacht."

The only possibility left for the reader of Rilke's poems is to both acknowledge the materiality of language and simultaneously liquify and digest this materiality within one's own body. The reader's gaze must merge with the text and dissolve it while standing opposed to it at the same time. Rilke's poetry gives rise to a stereoscopic vision of the reader. One eye must seize upon and hold fast to the physical being of language, whereas the other must intuit its liquified meaning as the language of being. A Münchhausen effect ensues in which language is charged with undoing the very process of instrumentalization to which it owes its own existence. Signifying their own deconstruction, words are now being reborn as meaningful things in their own right only to be immediately subjected to the same liquidation process all over again. The *New Poems* must self-destruct if they want to survive, and can survive only in and through this gesture of self-destruction. However, as in my previous readings, I argue that these poems leave a material imprint in the form of punctuation signs meant to authenticate this process of their own undoing.

Hence, my emphasis on the profound ambiguity at work in Rilke's poetry does not include a verdict with regard to its artistic "success" or "failure." I merely want to point to the specificity of his poetic vision, which could never be achieved through Dadaist wordplays or experiments in "visual" or "spatial" poetry conducted throughout the twentieth century (e.g., Schwitters, Morgenstern). Rilke does not just visualize some primordial nonsense by means of the idiosyncratic arrangement of words on paper, as Kittler's generalized account of the discourse network around 1900 at times suggests. Rather, he seeks to mediate the conflict between their exterior shell and the interior life that shell protects. Whether one regards the resulting tension within Rilke's poetry as symptomatic of his poetic success or his failure— whether, in other words, one reads Rilke's paradoxical gaze as a symptom or a critique of capitalist reification and commodity fetishism—is, in my eyes, a rather arbitrary and hence less relevant issue than the epistemological potential it yields. What remains crucial is to recognize that Rilke's poetic enterprise becomes undone — or undoes itself — because it desperately seeks a kind of empirical realization it cannot possibly achieve. Precisely the negotiation of this failure remains his major achievement.

Phenomenological Vision in the Face of Language: Reading Rilke's "Die Gazelle"

Let me examine the phenomenological dimension of Rilke's *New Poems* to clarify this point. In contrast to Husserl, Rilke fully acknowledged the structural ambiguity of language and made it the focus of his poetics. In the *New Poems,* words not only are regarded as the constituents of an autonomous meaning, as in Husserl, but are granted the freedom to become objects in their own right, freed from the intentionality usually ascribed to them. Although one may regard this difference as constitutive of that between poetry and philosophy in general, the juxtaposition of Husserl and Rilke is particularly instructive for the art of looking around 1900. As argued above, Rilke locates "truth" within the play of liberated, "superficial," nonsignifying linguistic elements. Language is said to be both every-thing and no-thing, a medium simultaneously identified with, and separate from, the appearances of modern life. This paradox reveals the intimate relation between Rilke's poetics and Husserl's phenomenology. For Husserl, words are but the contingent and dispensable signs of the self-identical essence of things. In his eyes, language testifies to the existence of pure meaning without, however, being identical to it. Similar to Husserl's convoluted apparatus of philosophical terms, Rilke's poems claim to describe the eidetic essence of things, but they cannot present it outside the very signifying process they so vehemently denounce. This, of course, was the reason why Rilke oriented his work along the "reality" of the visual arts in the first place, only to once again get caught in the same circle he wanted to escape.

Trying, unsuccessfully, to collapse materiality and meaning, Rilke's poetry, if unwittingly, deconstructs Husserl's entire premise of phenomenological intuition. Once words are simultaneously identified as both material things and transparent signs, they become riddled with an interior contradiction. As empirical objects in the real world, words cannot possibly "be" the ideal meanings they are said to represent. The speaking gaze in the *New Poems* remains chained to the words that pronounce what it sees. As a consequence, Rilke is forced to instrumentalize (as meaning) the very language he wants to set free, while Husserl, on the other hand, cannot but set free those terms he claims to instrumentalize. Contrary to Husserl's major argument, his phenomenological concepts do not simply describe or signify the ideal objects of intentionality, but, in some sense, literally *are* these object, whereas Rilke's poems never simply *are* the things themselves, but also signify them. This interior contradiction creates a "void" Rilke himself refers to as the *Weltinnenraum*, yet whatever term one chooses in order to describe this nonspace, Husserl's eidetic entities remain its prisoner. They are caught therein as time is arrested in a photograph.

This tension between Husserl's phenomenology and Rilke's *New Poems* is rarely recognized by critics. Käte Hamburger, for example, rightly claimed that Rilke develops "a lyric in lieu of an epistemology" (Käte Hamburger 84), yet her own readings of Rilke are often marred by the coerced attempt to prove the "uniqueness" of Rilke's poetry (Käte Hamburger 84, 152). Instead of giving equal attention to both the hermeneutic and deconstructive dimension at work in his texts, Hamburger stresses the former over the latter and thus fails to appreciate the interdependence of both. If poetry triumphs over philosophy, as Hamburger's analysis implies, it is not because it intends the things themselves more intimately or more directly than philosophy, but, quite the contrary, because it recognizes the futility of the entire project, yet performs it nonetheless.[11] At the center of Rilke's *Weltinnenraum* dwells this paradox that cannot be solved logically, but must be rehearsed over and over again in the act of reading. David Wellbery, therefore, focuses his critique on the semiotic overdetermination of Rilke's poetic language and, by way of a direct response to Hamburger's readings, concludes as follows: "[Rilke's] poems exemplify the dissolution of substantial things into a series of systematic partial values . . . which expose the illusory hope to ever achieve the final transformation of language into the presence of things. In this context of a 'general relativity of the world,' ideology consists in the pretense that the missing substantiality of things nonetheless exists, trying to fill the void left behind by this substantiality with the signifier of a full object, a fetish, a being" ("Gazelle" 132). Rilke's poetry, one might summarize Wellbery's position, is an antiphenomenology seeking to destroy the myth of the "essence of things" or the "thing itself." In its place, Wellbery argues,

Rilke pictures a primordial void. As soon as critical analysis approaches it, however, it gets caught in a paradox: on the one hand, poetic language seeks to fill this void by taking the place of the thing itself and covering up the lack, while, on the other hand, given the deferral of sense that characterizes discourse, poetry continuously perpetuates this void, unwittingly exposing its own failure to establish the absolute presence of things.

Hamburger's and Wellbery's perspectives, it follows, demarcate the extreme perimeters within which the scholarly debate of Rilke's middle period takes place, and critics usually argue in favor of either one of the two sides. The following analysis seeks to collapse this discursive field by reconnecting the seemingly oppositional poles that sustain it. At its center one finds Rilke's advocacy of a particular art of reading based upon a stereoscopic field of vision. It calls for an oscillating gaze that changes back and forth between words and images, signs and things. In other words, Rilke's best poems not only exhibit a "decompository tendency" to expose the ideological attempt of phenomenological fetishization, as Wellbery suggests (ibid.). More important, they simultaneously endeavor to account for the semblance of presence encountered in and through the oscillating gaze. The *New Poems* explore a stereoscopic vision at work during the process of reading and thus recognize both the fundamental difference as well as the intimate relation between words and things.

This stereoscopic vision is not dialectical in nature. It does not, as Judith Ryan argues, result in the "reversal of a negative 'void' into a positive presence." Nor is it "an emblem of an extreme negative aesthetics," as Erica Greber puts it (Greber 184). Rather, it labors to maintain the semblance of presence for the sole purpose of deconstructing it. Whereas Husserl conjures the imaginary ideal of a speaking gaze in which matter and meaning coincide, Rilke's poem advocates a mode of reading in which the gaze continuously oscillates between these two poles. The *New Poems* neither try to cover up the primordial void (i.e., the lack of an objective presence at the heart of matter) nor do they simply aim to expose it as such. Rather, they explore the interdependence of both attempts as constitutive of the process of reading, which is built upon the simultaneous acknowledgement and disavowal of its own impossibility. Rilke's poetry both exposes language as a fetish and idealizes it as the real thing the fetish seeks to replace. This paradox is the source of its aesthetic weakness as well as its strength.

Die Gazelle
Gazella Dorcas

Verzauberte: wie kann der Einklang zweier
erwählter Worte je den Reim erreichen,
der in dir kommt und geht, wie auf ein Zeichen.
Aus deiner Stirne steigen Laub und Leier,

und alles Deine geht schon im Vergleich
durch Liebeslieder, deren Worte, weich
wie Rosenblätter, dem, der nicht mehr liest,
sich auf die Augen legen, die er schließt:

um dich zu sehen: hingetragen, als
wäre mit Sprüngen jeder Lauf geladen
und schösse nur nicht ab, solang der Hals

das Haupt ins Horchen hält: wie wenn beim Baden
im Wald die Badende sich unterbricht:
den Waldsee im gewendeten Gesicht.

(*Werke* I: 506)

The Gazelle
Gazella Dorcas

Enchanted thing: however can the chime
of two selected words attain the true
rhyme that, as beckoned, comes and goes in you?
Out of your forehead leaf and lyre climb,

and all you are has been in simile
passing through those love-songs continually
whose words will cover, light as leaves of rose,
the no-more-reader's eyes, which he will close:

only to look upon you: so impelled
as though each limb of yours with leaps were laden,
and held its fire but while the neck upheld

the head in hearkening: as when a maiden
breaks off from bathing in some lonely place,
the forest-lake within her swift-turned face.

(*New Poems* 88)

In a self-referential gesture, the poem compares the gazelle to the power of language to conjure its essence. This essence is characterized as an inner rhyme, a movement that comes and goes not unlike the regular rhyme and pentameter at work in Rilke's poem. The gazelle, indeed, is a work of magic, and the first word we read simultaneously addresses both creatures, the poem and the animal, as one and the same. The "Gazella Dorcas" is born of the mere attempt to picture its referent via language, since due to its "enchanted" existence, the gazelle immediately converts into poetry any comparative statement made about it ("und alles Deine geht schon im Vergleich / durch Liebeslieder..."). To describe the gazelle is to enter the realm of lyrical language—this is the central premise of Rilke's poem. The premise is implemented as soon as it is stated: the gazelle's ears and antlers are addressed as laurel and lyre, the insignia of Apollo, the god of the arts.

Since everything happens "as if" controlled "by a sign," one might read both the gazelle and the poem describing it as mere signifiers for the wonders of presence and absence engendered by language. The gazelle not simply inspires poetry, but literally *is* poetry in its pristine form. This equation seems to render obsolete any attempt to elevate one side over the other. Contemplating the relationship between words and things, Rilke's poem refuses to concede ontological priority to either one of its constitutive poles. It appears that words do not imitate things, nor are things born out of words, but each is mirrored and takes shape in and through the other. And yet, the first stanza rhetorically refutes this reading, for it implies that language might *never* adequately describe or imitate the beauty of the gazelle. In other words, Rilke's "Gazelle" explicitly acknowledges the linguistic constructedness of an external object (the gazelle is but a poem and can only be referred to in the form of poetic verse) while at the same time questioning that any such linguistic reference be meaningful or possible at all. This hypothetical negation in turn serves to call into positive existence the verbal construct of the poem meant to defy it.

The "Gazelle" is pictured both within and beyond language. It is said to "walk through" the love songs it engenders much like the reader is called upon to "read through" the poem in order to "see" what she reads. Although this emphasis on movement serves to highlight the temporal dimension of language, Rilke's words are once again endowed with a physical quality that contradicts their status as transitory, ephemeral signs. The words inspired by the "Gazelle" (i.e., Rilke's poem) are like rose petals covering the closed eyes of those who do not read them anymore and thus truly begin to "see" (". . . deren Worte, weich / wie Rosenblätter, dem, der nicht mehr liest, / sich auf die Augen legen, die er schließt: // um dich zu sehen"). This is the defining moment of Rilke's poetics and its constitutive paradox: at precisely the moment in which words become objectified, that is, at the very moment they are freed from the burden of signification and become self-identical, material things in their own right, they enable a true and unrestricted kind of vision in the form of a gaze directed not outward toward the "real" object beyond language, but inward toward a transparent essence evoked by the very words that allegedly have ceased to signify anything at all.

This moment of transformation effected in the second half of the poem is, of course, facilitated by the incantatory quality of Rilke's language since words that can no longer be seen must be heard or felt instead. Hence, the regular and harmonic structure of the sonnet, the constancy of rhyme and meter as well as the skillful use of alliteration ("Laub und Leier"; "Worte, weich"; "Der Hals // das Haupt ins Horchen hält") and the repetition of vowels (such as the "ei" in the first part or the various umlauts in the second) all contribute to the "magic" described by the poem. Put differently, one might say that Rilke uses the sound of language in order to promote his ideal vision of things. This merging of eye and ear serves to reinforce the overall synaesthetic dimension of the poem. It calls upon the visual, auditory, and tactile senses in order to overcome the static equilibrium between the two interdependent, yet autonomous, realms of language and being by merging them into one. Instead of indeterminately oscillating between the two poles, the reader's gaze suddenly zooms in and seizes upon its object, "um dich zu sehen". The image sharpens, the picture takes shape, "The Gazelle" appears. This, indeed, is a typical example of the phenomenological dimension in Rilke's poetry so often noted by critics. Covering their eyes, the readers cannot possibly see any particular animal anymore, but rather must intuit *the* gazelle in its very essence, as the Latin title clearly indicates. What becomes visible in Rilke's poem is the intentional object itself, the eidos of its being.

Although Rilke thus appears to espouse the phenomenological ideal of eidetic intuition, he simultaneously undermines this notion, for the reader of Rilke's poem can only perceive a mental image of the animal; this, however, is precisely what Husserl so vehemently rejects throughout his writings. For him, the eidetic essence of things must never be pictured in the form of an image in human consciousness since the latter is contingent and empirical, whereas the former are necessary and ideal. Although the essence of things is implicit and hence evident within individual acts of consciousness, as Husserl argues, it is not "really" contained therein like a picture in a photo album. As I argued in the first part of this study, it remains unclear in Husserl how exactly ideal entities are to be intuited at all. Rilke's own efforts, for one, are constantly in danger of succumbing to a kind of neo-Romantic imagery sustained by the power of poetic imagination, a view at odds with Husserl's notion of objective, intuitive evidence as well as Rilke's own poetic ideal.

As a deliberate countermeasure, Rilke's poems emphasize the tactile materiality and ephemeral resonance of language simultaneously. He calls upon the reader to actually feel the words and listen to them rather than only reading them. Visual perception, for Rilke, once again must develop the tactile sense and the very physicality that had been lost during modernity. The goal is to stop reading and to close the semiotic gap between sign and referent by means of a language literally in touch with the body and with itself. Words become objects in their own right, covering the eyes of the reader and thus replacing them with the very words the reader originally tried to read. The ability to "see" the intentional object of the poem hinges on this crucial transformation of words into eyes that look for themselves and carry their immediate visions within.

The art of reading must leave ordinary perception behind and see things with words, through them and in spite of them. Because words are both obstacles and conduits in the path of poetic vision, they are self-asserting and self-effacing at the same time, necessary and ephemeral to the poetic process they inaugurate. Not only does "Rilke's poetics question the value of intuition to guarantee one's immediate awareness of a visible object," as Wellbery argues ("Gazelle" 131), Rilke also defines intuition itself as dependent upon language, thus undermining the popular distinction around 1900 between immediate perception and linguistic difference. For him, words are the eyes of every-thing, and intuition is but the poetic effect of coming into contact with the visions they carry within. This physical contact, for Rilke, defines the experience of reading, for example in "Der Leser" ("The Reader"), who looks up from the book,

> . . . .
> ... alles auf sich hebend,
> was unten in dem Buche sich verhielt,
> mit Augen, welche, statt zu nehmen, gebend
> anstießen an die fertig-volle Welt:
> . . . .
>
> (*Werke* I: 637)

> . . . .
> ... thereby upheaving
> all the book's deepness to the light of day,
> with eyes which, now outgiving, not receiving,
> impinged upon a filled environment:
> . . . .
>
> (*New Poems* 287)

Contrary to Romanticism, Rilke's notion of reading emphasizes the corporeal dimension of a gaze that literally lifts up what has been read and tries to "give" it to the external world with which it is said to "collide." The reader's eyes literally "have it in them," as the old Brahe used to say. By means of this tactile gaze, the *New Poems* attempt to solve the crisis of reading and writing discussed in *Malte*. Language figures as a material body that looks at things in its own way.

One might say that whereas the quartets of Rilke's "Gazelle" betray a certain stasis as they focus on the reader's gaze oscillating between words and things, the terzets stereoscopically blend both poles and let us see the ideal essence of the object intended. And yet, the poem also unveils the price to pay for this semblance of intuition and the heightened feeling of "real" presence. This price consists in the mortification of being since the phenomenological vision cannot but replace the "real" gazelle with a mere representation. The very moment Rilke's imaginary reader is said to intuit the ideal object itself, the moment she has replaced her eyes with the words that allow her to partake of the inherent vision of language itself, that is also the moment in which time stands still and life literally stops in midair:

"hingetragen," we see the "Lauf" of the gazelle, and while this image indeed implies movement, the remainder of the poem divulges the artificiality of this appearance, which culminates in the cessation of motion altogether. Rilke's formulation ("geladener Lauf") indeed evokes a loaded gun barrel as much as a galloping gazelle and thus speaks to the violence inherent in this ideal of purified vision. The reader becomes the hunter preying upon the eidos of the animal. The poem has "shot" a picture of life, so to speak, in the paradoxical effort to preserve things by killing them.

This paradox accounts for the tension palpable in the second part of Rilke's poem, which posits and immediately withdraws the defining moment of "pure" vision. Topographically located at the center of the poem, the phenomenological gaze—"um dich zu sehen"—itself is bracketed, so to speak, by two colons isolating it from the rest of the poem, with similar interruptions reappearing throughout the last two stanzas. Together, they provoke an atmosphere of suspended tension epitomized in the final image of the female bather "interrupting herself." The image itself exposes a motion in standstill. The moment of pure vision, that is, the stereoscopic impression that coerces two heterogeneous realms (i.e., time and space, language and being) into one gives rise to a kind of neutral space, a realm of pure mediation. Still vibrating within, time itself seems arrested in this space, as if something had passed by and is still passing by without, however, resulting in any movement at all.

A crucial "interruption" separates the quartets and the terzets, and the eidos of the gazelle takes shape within this ruptured space. What exactly is the nature of this "interruption" that harbors the essence of things? First of all, it is due to the many colons that fortify the generic caesura already inherent within the sonnet form itself. In his reading of Hölderlin, Lacoue-Labarthe contends that the caesura "prevents . . . the racing oscillation . . . and an orientation towards this or that pole. The disarticulation represents the active neutrality of the interval in between" (*Typology* 235). What appears in the caesura, according to Hölderlin himself, "is no longer the alternation of representation, but representation itself" (Hölderlin, qtd. in Lacoue-Labarthe, *Typography* 234). In other words, the caesura opens up a space of absolute neutrality that functions as the "interval in between" the two poles of word and world in Rilke's poem. The same can be said of the colon, which, in the words of Giorgio Agamben, possesses "an intermediary function": it is "a kind of crossing with neither distance nor identification, something like a passage without spatial movement" (*Potentialities* 222f.). The colon represents the fault line both separating and connecting inside and outside, word and thing. More precisely, it "represents the dislocation of immanence in itself, the opening to an alterity that nevertheless remains absolutely immanent" (*Potentialities* 223). The colon addresses whatever follows as always already enclosed within that which came before—it is the syntactical insignia of Rilke's *Weltinnenraum* and the "interstices of time." It is literally a placeholder that renders present the absence of the space "in between," the space where immanence and transcendence touch upon each other. In other words, the colon demarcates the poetically overdetermined realm of emptiness and plentitude, the phenomenological ideal of a spatial void inhabited by all those intentional objects of pure intuition.

Rilke's entire poem takes shape under the auspices of such a colon and the magic it yields. It begins with "Verzauberte:"—note the colon!—and everything that follows literally belongs to this enchanted beginning. The poem unfolds the colon's interior and makes visible the things it shelters, and the gazelle is pictured in the nonpictorial, poetic space opened and closed by the colon itself. Like Husserl's perceptual noema, the gazelle is a "quasi-being" that exists only in the moment of suspended tension between the I and the world. The "Gazella Dorcas" lives in the nonextended space and the imaginary visions afforded by the colon. The ability to "read" the colon is the prerequisite for seeing the gazelle and for entering Rilke's *Weltinnenraum*. And yet, the colon cannot be read since it carries no independent meaning that could be translated into language. Elements of punctuation, Adorno argues, are not signs of communication pertaining to the relationship between language and reader, but inhere within language itself. They regulate the traffic that occurs "within the interior of language, on its own paths" ("Satzzeichen"; *Noten* 106).

Rilke exposes this interior and the "incorporeal presence" (ibid.) of language that he expects his readers to perceive. If punctuation can be said to help regulate the heartbeat (i.e., the rhyme, rhythm, and meter of every text), then Rilke's reader, like the old Brahe, must learn to "read in the blood" of language. Closing the eyes, the reader must sense the rhythm of the poem and feel the pulse of language in order to "read" the colon and "see" the gazelle. The reader must experience the liquified meaning of words flowing through his own veins, as does the imaginary reader in Malte, who "closes his eyes over a verse he is rereading" so that "its meaning spreads throughout his blood" (*Malte; Werke* VI: 928). The reader of "The Gazelle" must literally feel his way alongside the string of words much like "The Blind Man" ("Der Blinde") in Rilke's poem fingers his way through the streets of Paris:

> Sieh, er geht und unterbricht die Stadt,
> die nicht ist auf seiner dunkeln Stelle,
> wie ein dunkler Sprung durch eine helle
> Tasse geht. Und wie auf einem Blatt
>
> ist auf ihm der Widerschein der Dinge
> aufgemalt; er nimmt ihn nicht hinein.
> . . . .
>
> (*Werke* I: 590)

> Look, his progress interrupts the scene,
> absent from his dark perambulation,
> like a dark crack's interpenetration
> of a bright cup. And, as on a screen,
>
> all reflections things around are making
> get depicted on him outwardly.
> . . . .
>
> (*New Poems* 217)

The visual ideal of the *New Poems* is embodied by the tactile vision of the blind man. Where he walks, the city cannot be, both because he does not see it and because he physically occupies the city's place. Yet he feels the space "he interrupts" as he himself becomes the fissure that reconnects the two halves of the city he has divided. "Sprung" in this context connotes both Heidegger's notion of "Riß" and *Dasein*'s decisive "Sprung" into Being by authentically "being in the world." The blind man dwells where all readers ought to be. "The reflection of things" painted upon the blind man's body "as if on a sheet of paper" are, indeed, nothing but the words that engage the reader's gaze in the form of the poem itself.

Like the protagonist in Rilke's "Der Blinde," the reader of Rilke's poetry needs to go blind in order to get in touch with the things surrounding him. Once the reader sees with words instead of eyes, once she uses words as eyes and feels the rhythm of language pulsating through her own body, she is able to become part of a scene she was merely able to imagine before. One might surmise that the tension palpable in the second part of the "Gazelle" results from the gazelle having been surprised by a reader who now perceives what otherwise would have remained literally out of sight. Taking notice of his sudden presence, the gazelle feels "interrupted," the poem suggests, much like the female bather who senses that she is being spied upon by an intruder.

The reader of Rilke's "Gazelle" is this intruder. Practicing the art of non-reading, she has interrupted and short-circuited the self-sufficient realms of being and language. The strained atmosphere of motionless tension captured in the image of the "loaded" animal's body bespeaks a moment of contact between human and animal, inside and outside, text and world. All boundaries seem to have collapsed for the flash of a moment, and the last stanza appears to inaugurate "a new level . . . insofar as the two poles of the poem [the realms of being and of poetry] are melted together into a single metaphor," as Judith Ryan contends (54; my translation). Ryan's reading, however, is problematic because Rilke's comparison serves precisely the opposite function. It explicitly links the gazelle to the bathing woman, without, however, merging them into one. Indeed, critics have often read Rilke's (in)famous "wie"-comparisons (i.e., "wie auf ein Zeichen," "wie wenn beim Baden," etc.) as evidence for "a weakness of the creative transformation," as Gottfried Benn contends ("Probleme der Lyrik" 1068). Instead of forging a convincing metaphor that merges the constitutive parts of the comparison into a new whole, the *wie* merely connects them without affecting an inner transformation in either. Adorno, to provide another example, equally directs his critique against a "poetry which allows itself every metaphor, even the plainly unmetaphorical as a comparison" ("Jargon" 470).

In disagreeing with Ryan, however, one need not necessarily sanction Benn's and Adorno's harsh criticism of Rilke either. Indeed, judged according to the poetic ideal of a seamless metaphorical assimilation that dissolves one element of the comparison into the other, Rilke's *wie*-constructions appear unpoetic and even clumsy at times. However, since Rilke's primary goal consists in undermining this seemingly "natural" ideal of poetic transformation, his style affords an aesthetic quality of its own. The *wie*-comparison both dissolves and preserves the integrity of the two terms compared. It recalls the complex relationship between language and being as two interdependent, yet nonetheless autonomous, realms. The poetic virtuosity of using "the plainly unmetaphorical as a comparison" thus accurately describes the oscillatory movement of Rilke's gaze in between the two poles of material reality and poetic utterance. Rilke's refusal to resolve the tension between sign and referent throughout the poem is indicative of his understanding of words as both matter and meaning. As for Hofmannsthal, poetic language here mediates the reconciliation of words and things by means of their separation from one another.

The suspended tension captured in Rilke's "as if" comparisons immediately undermines the seemingly harmonious reconciliation of being and language. The exemplary moment of phenomenological vision is unveiled as a highly precarious one, for it can disappear any time the gazelle decides to "shoot" away. The morbid atmosphere underlying the entire scene resembles that of a still life not painted but actually "shot" in a photograph. In a letter to Clara, Rilke narrates his "real" encounter with the "Gazella Dorcas" at the Jardin des Plantes and indeed mentions photography: "They [the gazelles] remained a few yards apart, ruminating, resting, looking. Like women look out of pictures, that's how they looked out of something with a quiet, irrevocable turn. . . . They were so beautiful that I could not walk away. And exactly as I felt in front of your tender photograph: as if they had just now been transformed into this shape" (Sie [die Gazellen] lagen ein paar Schritte voneinander, wiederkäuend, ruhend, schauend. Wie Frauen aus Bildern schauen, so schauen sie aus etwas heraus mit einer lautlosen, endgültigen Wendung. . . . Ich konnte gar nicht fortgehen, so schön waren sie, und ganz wie ich vor Deiner zarten Photographie fühlte: als ob sie eben erst in diese Gestalt verwandelt worden wären) (*Briefe aus Muzot* 161). The mention of the photograph in Rilke's letter points to the power of modern media to capture the look of things and to affect a momentary transformation from appearance to essence that informs Rilke's own ideal of "sachliches Sagen," *as if* Rilke, with the help of the photograph, could finally see and "feel" the magical moment of transformation that enables the primordial contact between the eye and the world.

Rilke's "[v]erzauberte" gazelle indeed reads *as if* it were itself based upon a photograph rather than life. The apparatus he used, however, is not the camera, but language, and Rilke's picture of the gazelle is like a photograph that inheres neither in external reality, nor in human consciousness, but only within the words that mediate between both realms. His poetic photograph denotes the ideal fault line between inside and outside, the imaginary and the real. The peculiar characteristic of Rilke's poetry, in contrast to Husserl's phenomenology, consists in relocating that ideal itself within the realm of the symbolic. Both, image and referent, are claimed to take shape exclusively within language. They are captured within the nonextended spaces represented by the multiplicity of colons that pervade the second half of the poem. Whereas Husserl claimed that language is a mere tool for the adequate expression of intuitive perception, Rilke's poem focuses on the photographic and mortifying ability of language itself. His failure to preserve the "Gazelle" in a more real, less mediated state unveils that of phenomenology itself. There is no "pure vision" in Husserl's sense except by doing violence to one's own insight since the speaking gaze must "shoot" a picture of the very life it seeks to preserve.

The last line of the "Gazelle" once again both acknowledges and disavows the possibility of the phenomenological perception it rehearses. Given the equivocality of the term, "Gesicht" refers both to the bather's face and to the ideal visions taking shape therein. Much like the bather literally "has" the lake in her face by turning away from it, the reader must turn away from the text in order truly to see what it says — an impossible task given the need to read the words in order to overlook them. Rilke's impossible art of reading thus consists in turning one's face into a projection screen for the inherent visions of language. The poetic text emerges as something to look at and something that informs and guides our vision toward the true look of things. And yet both, words and things, are chimeras. They are photographs of sorts that have already mortified the lifelike intuition they claim to render present. The gazelle is but a picture of life, preserved as the face of language.

In the last chapter, I reexamine this notion of the face of language once again with reference to Stefan George's poetry. I will argue that Rilke's admiration for the "reality" of the spatial arts and his ideal of "free" readers set him apart from the more ritualistically oriented work of Stefan George. Rilke's thing-poems cling to the very notion of irrecuperable materiality that George tries to transcend. In George's poetic vision, the body of language replaces and ultimately eradicates without a trace the reality it was supposed to render present. The dubious achievement of George and his circle thus consists in having pushed the reification of language to its limit. In order to ensure the purity of their aesthetic ideals, they shut out and abandon the external world without any immediate attempt to affect its necessary transformation. Social change is claimed to occur magically right in front of our eyes, provided that art has remained uncontaminated by the life surrounding it. However, once these ties between art and life are severed, such that there remains no interior trace (in the form of a signifier without signified) in the text that bears witness to the continued tension between these two realms, then poetry loses its potentiality for magical transformation and instead solidifies into its own death mask.

6 Other as Same
The Politics of the George Circle

Ich bin der Eine und bin Beide . . .
Ich bin ein end und ein beginn.
—Stefan George

Art, Religion, and the Gesamtkunstwerk of Life

"Can he who does not belong to the realm of art possibly claim to partake of life?" (Wer gar keiner kunst angehört darf sich der überhaupt rühmen dem leben anzugehören?) (*Briefwechsel George-Hofmannsthal* 87). Stefan George's rhetorical question highlights his belief in the inseparability of art and life. Those who are not situated within the aesthetic realm lose contact with real "life," because "life," for George, is precisely that which triumphs over the mundane reality of everyday existence. The self must withdraw from the outside world into the inner sanctuary of art in order to embrace "life." Given this premise, the *Blätter für die Kunst* insist from the very beginning on the radical separation of art and social reality: "The name of this publication partly already indicates what it is all about: to serve art and poetry in particular and to eschew everything that pertains to state and society" (Der name dieser veröffentlichung sagt schon zum teil was sie soll: der kunst besonders der dichtung und dem schrifttum dienen, alles staatliche und gesellschaftliche ausscheidend) (Landmann, *Einleitungen* 7).[1]

In spite of this and similar statements, it would be erroneous to interpret George's aesthetic stance as a total disinterest in life or material reality as such. Quite the contrary, his journal seeks to rescue modern society from the "false perception of reality" it deems responsible for the reification of life. George's poetry allegedly provides the only foundation for the possible rejuvenation of the world outside. The *Blätter für die Kunst* rehearse the same paradox that distinguished Hofmannsthal's and Rilke's reflections on art around 1900. Art needs to be freed from society in order to serve it, and the necessary transformation of the world can only be achieved by separating what ought to be united. Once art has been liberated from any kind of entanglement with reality—"an art freed from servitude"—it will inevitably affect and give rise to sociopolitical changes in modern life.

The social circle around Stefan George symbolizes the magical ring that protects arts against the disastrous intrusion of the profane outside. Friedrich Wolters's essay "Gestalt," published in 1911, extrapolates from inside the circle what the outsiders have yet to comprehend, namely the life-giving genius of "our spiritual leader" George ("Gestalt" 146), who was able to show the "Oneness of the world" (All-Eine der Welt) in his own *Gestalt*, understood as both his physical being in the world and the poetry it bequeaths: "[the One binds] eternal peace and eternal storm; it unites the infinite sphere which flows from center to periphery, from the periphery to the center ..., this complete, living world, this blessed god in whom everything can be found according to the measure of the reflected purity of his image" ([das Eine bildet] den ewigen frieden mit dem ewigen sturme einend die unendliche vom kern zum umkreis, vom umkreis zum kerne wallende kugel ..., diese ganze lebendige welt, den seligen gott in dem alles ist nach dem maasse der widergestrahlten reinheit seines bildes) ("Gestalt" 145). This god is George, and the dazzling redundancy of Wolters's praise reflects on a rhetorical level the paradoxical efforts to overcome the inside-outside dichotomy that defines it. The George-circle delineates the parameters of that paradoxical space—the mythical realm Hofmannsthal referred to as "pre-existence" and Rilke called the "Weltinnenraum"—in which the Aestheticist visions of life can finally take shape.

The resemblance between George, Rilke, and Hofmannsthal consists both in their shared hope for the rejuvenation of poetic language and in their explicit rejection of any art that seeks an immediate social effect. Poetry has literally nothing left to say but to confirm its own existence as art: "Anybody who is still tempted by the desire to 'say' or 'create' something in the realm of poetry or by other artistic means is unworthy even of entering the mere vestibule of art" (In der dichtung—wie in aller kunst-bethätigung—ist jeder der noch von der sucht ergriffen ist etwas "sagen" etwas "wirken" zu wollen nicht einmal wert in den vorhof der kunst einzutreten) (*Blätter für die Kunst*, zweite Folge, 4. Bd. Oct. 1894). The difference between George and the other two poets, however, lies in the way they dealt with the inevitable failure of their project. Once it became clear that the poetic rejuvenation of life remained an illusory hope at best, Hofmannsthal, for one, abandoned his earlier poetic ambitions and, after 1900, got increasingly involved in the public life and politics of the Habsburg monarchy. If Hofmannsthal had experienced the impossibility of writing authentic poetry, George's entire life was meant to prove the opposite. Although the relationship to George had already begun to deteriorate much earlier, Hofmannsthal's decision, in the first decade of the twentieth century, to leave the world of Aestheticism behind and turn toward the sociopolitical realm instead sealed the irrevocable end of their friendship. For Hofmannsthal, George indeed was "One who passes by" (Einer, der vorübergeht), as he put it in one of his early poems. More precisely, it was Hofmannsthal who "walked on" in life while George remained confined to the circle of Aestheticism.

Rilke's way of coping with the illusory nature of Aestheticist politics was less decisive and more ambiguous than Hofmannsthal's. He certainly did not abandon his ideal of world redemption in and through art, but instead chose to recuperate his doubts poetically as part of the project itself. Rilke's poetry skillfully oscillates between presence and absence, word and thing. Yet his vision of a world liberated from modern alienation and fragmentation, from instrumental reason and the commodity fetishism of capitalism remains phantasmic because it hinges on the reader's gaze to create the *Weltinnenraum* it promises. The paradox of a poetic vision that implicitly presupposes the sociopolitical revolution it claims to implement may not be the last reason for Rilke's repeated withdrawal from the world into the microcosm of the inner self. Unlike George and his circle, Rilke did not seek the communal realm necessary to implement his ideals into sociopolitical reality. In isolation from family, friends, and the world alike, the lonely poet Rilke relied instead on the contemplative reception of autonomous, disconnected readers in the whole of Europe—a phantom empire of "free" individuals pursuing the poetic *Auftrag* of speaking things into existence.

In the end, Rilke's poetic enterprise finds its last refuge in the exalted embrace of material presence as such. Mere being—including the "real" presence of actual letters on the page—appears as the solution to the problem it continues to perpetuate. Being is embraced as meaningful simply by virtue of its crude existence. Similarly, Rilke regards the creative act, by force of its mere facticity, as a guarantee for the social implementation of its poetic message—a truly messianic belief in the power of art to become real simply by being there: "But now it is. Is. Is. Amen" (Aber nun ists. Ist. Ist. Amen) (qtd. in Szondi 386), Rilke proclaims in a letter to the Countess Thurn und Taxis after he has finally finished his *Duino Elegies*. In spite of this and similar epiphanies, Rilke had wrestled with his religious belief in the emancipatory power of art throughout his life. It is precisely this sense of doubt that authenticates his faith.

A widespread phenomenon among many European poets around 1900, Rilke's celebration of aesthetic *Gestalt* or *Gebilde* as the revelation of a divine truth finds its most pronounced German expression in the George-circle. Contemporaries and scholars alike have pointed to George's "style," his self-aggrandizing "habitus," and the aesthetic "rituals" that function as important elements in a quasi-religious cult. George's poetry had "a mesmerizing, incantatory quality" (bannend wie Zaubersprüche), reports Edith Landmann (qtd. in Braungart, *Ästhetischer Katholizismus* 154), and Gottfried Benn declared that George's "will towards form, and this new feeling for form, was not simply Aestheticism, nor Intellectualism, nor Formalism, but the most exalted belief" ("Rede auf Stefan George" 1039).[2] Similar to the Eucharist, the source of the magical power ascribed to George's poetry ultimately relies on an act of faith. Those who claim to be worthy recipients of the *Blätter für die Kunst* must renounce their earlier beliefs and accept George as the divine prophet of a more spiritualized world. Thus, the reader of George's poetry is converted into his disciple. For only then can "the word become flesh and the flesh word, German language" (Gundolf 27), as Gundolf exalts.[3] George himself simply abstained from further commenting on the nature of this transformation, a gesture that reveals the inherent constraints of a radical belief forced to scorn all academic or critical investigation as dangerous heresy.

The alleged magic of George's poetry, however, depends upon the artificially created circle of ritual practice outside of which it loses its power: "Free within the necessary paths" (Frei in den bedingten Bahnen) (Wolfskehl 231; Gundolf 87). With this line from George's "Algabal," two of his disciples, Wolfskehl and Gundolf, summarize the essence of George's oeuvre, leaving it up to the reader to focus on the freedom or the coercion inherent in this poetic practice. Whoever chooses the former becomes a believer and hence "free" to join the aesthetic community, whereas all others—"the boisterous pack," "the mass," "the many" ("die laute horde," "das volk," "die vielen") — must remain outside of it and forever oblivious to the poetic wonders performed in George's poetry. Ludwig Klages clarifies the esoteric nature of George's circle, which preaches only to those "whose soul already participates" (Klages 3), and the journal *Blätter für die Kunst* repeatedly echoes the exclusivity of its sacred cause.[4]

Of course, George is not alone in promoting art as a surrogate for theology. Hofmannsthal's notion of "magic" and Rilke's glorification of the "angel" are no less idiosyncratic forms of secularized religion than is George's circle or his later Maximin cult. All three poets regarded aesthetic experiences as a sort of religious epiphany that allegedly spiritualizes and redeems external reality from the inside out. The major difference, however, consists in the radicality of George's approach and his willingness to put into practice the basic principles of his faith. To do so, he first needed to cut any remaining connection between his circle and the outside world: "We tried to initiate the reversal within art and leave it up to others to develop its continuation into life" (Wir suchten die umkehr in der *kunst* einzuleiten und überlassen es andren zu entwickeln wie sie aufs *leben* fortgesetzt werden müsse) (Landmann, *Einleitungen* 20),[5] the *Blätter für die Kunst* declares in 1896. Although this withdrawal signals the defeat of George's project on a strictly sociopolitical level, it is presented as a victory instead. Those who want to practice the Aestheticist faith must remain confined to the inside, since otherwise their efforts would dissolve within the overdetermined and chaotic structure of cultural modernity. Once within the circle, however, there simply remains no "outside": "The circle finally mutates into a 'nation-state' and its inner members become 'state-constituents'" (Braungart, *Ästhetischer Katholizismus* 82; my translation). The George-circle thus functions as the sociopolitical basis from which to launch the modern project of reconciliation and to which it always and inevitably must return given its phantasmic and narcissistic nature.

Although one might be tempted to equate Rilke's *Handwerk* with George's *Technik*, the formal rigidity and often noted coercion of language in George's poetry hardly coincides with the playful liberation of words and things to which Rilke (and Hofmannsthal) aspired. The main difference between Rilke and George hence does not consist in *what* they seek, but *how* they seek it. Rilke toils, George reigns. One doubts, the other knows. Whereas Rilke's gaze oscillates between poetic words and material things, George increasingly insists on the phantasmagoric quality of everything beyond his reach and that of poetic language. He tries to control and master language by breaking off the very connection to the material outside that Rilke had hoped to establish harmoniously. Rilke's gaze seeks to meet the actual referent of language, while George merely recognizes the signified of his own words. If Rilke still tries to convince both himself and his readers about the magical power of art, George preaches only to those already convinced to begin with. His self-assured style of writing implies that his poetry has always already said what it meant to say. If "you" fail to understand the "solution" it proclaims—see "Der Teppich" discussed in the introduction—it is because "you" are unworthy to share its secrets. George's clandestine language can be read and understood only by those who, like the "seher" below, have turned their gaze away from the mundane reality of everyday life toward the higher realm of art. Nothing could be further from Rilke's ideal of a commonly shared poetic vision—"Wer du auch seist"—than the esoteric nature of George's self-invented language:

> Des sehers wort ist wenigen gemeinsam:
> Schon als die ersten kühnen wünsche kamen
> In einem seltnen reiche ernst und einsam
> Erfand er für die dinge eigne namen—
> . . . .

(*Werke* I: 137)

> The word of seers is not for common sharing.
> In curious kingdoms, earnest and alone,
> When first his wishes roused him with their daring,
> He summoned things with names that were his own.
> . . . .

(*The Works of Stefan George* 136)

Ultimately, the politics and faith of George's circle are self-authenticating in the crudest sense of the term because he and his disciples simply refused to consider or even acknowledge anything that might serve to undermine the validity of their belief. The inherent danger of this self-congratulatory gesture celebrating the divine power of art consists in a radical form of aesthetic projection. It reduces the outside to a blank screen waiting to come alive through the utopian visions of the inspired master.

George's poetry violates language because it isolates it from life. He "chokes his words until they cannot escape him anymore" (Adorno, "George und Hofmannsthal"; X/1: 215), Adorno claims, and Gert Mattenklott similarly regards the major effect of George's language as the "petrification of life" (*Bilderdienst* 278).[6] This petrification of life is the *Gestalt* of the living word worshiped by the circle, which is to say that the "death" of material reality is the price to pay for the coming alive of language. George's poetry is able to redeem things only through a verbal embalmment that preserves their corpses in the mausoleum of poetic form. It follows that the scholarly discussion between George's advocates and adversaries, between those who cherish his "powerful words" (*Wort-Macht*) and those who denounce his "words of power" (*Macht-Wort* [Wolfgang Kämpfer]), is simplistic given that each paradigm remains inextricably linked to its own opposite. The reader cannot appreciate or discuss one without reference to the other. Let me support this claim with regard to another poem from the collection *Der Teppich des Lebens*, namely the one that immediately follows "Der Teppich" (see figure 3).

Urlandschaft

Aus dunklen fichten flog ins blau der aar
Und drunten aus der lichtung trat ein paar
Von wölfen · schlürften an der flachen flut
Bewachten starr und trieben ihre brut.

Drauf huschte aus der glatten nadeln streu
Die schar der hinde trank und kehrte scheu
Zur waldnacht · eines blieb nur das im ried
Sein end erwartend still den rudel mied.

Hier litt das fette gras noch nie die schur
Doch lagen stämme · starker arme spur·
Denn drunten dehnte der gefurchte bruch
Wo in der scholle zeugendem geruch

Und in der weissen sonnen scharfem glühn
Des ackers froh des segens neuer mühn
Erzvater grub erzmutter molk
Das schicksal nährend für ein ganzes volk.

(*Werke* I: 190f.)

Primeval Landscape

From brooding pines an eagle upward swept
Into the blue, and toward the clearing stepped
Two wolves. They lapped the shallow pool and swung
To stark attention, marshalling their young.

And then across the glossy needles whipped
A flock of hinds, and drank, and shyly slipped,
Back to the dusk of woods, but one remained
Alone among the reeds to wait his end.

Here the lush grass had never felt the blade,
But hands had been at work, for stems were laid
And further on a plough had ridged the sod,
Where in the fertile odour of the clod

And happy in the white and stinging sun
With fields and gains their novel toil had won,
Arch-father delved, arch-mother milked,
Shaping the fate of all this human ilk.

(*The Works of Stefan George* 185f.)

The first edition of *Der Teppich des Lebens* from 1900 pictured "Der Teppich" and "Urlandschaft" opposite each other on adjacent pages in the book. This placement is significant, for it designates the poems as two sides of the same coin. The life that originally took shape in the arabesque patterns and words of "Der Teppich" now appears as the "Urlandschaft" of a nascent world. My interpretation centers on the nature of this transformation from one poem to the next. What happens in the space that separates and connects the two?

Contrary to "Der Teppich," "Urlandschaft" is written not in the present, but in past tense. Whereas the first poem emphasizes a spatiotemporal immediacy and designates the act of reading as that which enlivens the meaning and being of the poem, "Urlandschaft" describes a past scenario independent from the reader's participation. It portrays a landscape observed from a distant and elevated perspective, thus situating the seer/reader in opposition to, rather than in conjunction with, the scene portrayed. The picturesque quality of the poem is most evident in its lack of lifelike impressions and the sense of solemn serenity it projects. The formal rigidity of the poem does not allow for a more animated depiction of the animals in the first two stanzas ("starr," "scheu," "still"), and the morbid atmosphere is adequately captured in the image of the dying creature isolated from the herd. The second part of the poem slightly alters this tone. It shifts focus from the picture of death to the fertility of the landscape itself evident in the unhampered growth of the "fat grass" and the "ripe" smell of the arable land that surrounds it. Although the harvested trees — "Doch lagen stämme" — are read as signs for the presence of a powerful force — "starker arme spur" — the people in charge of the "Urlandschaft" and hence responsible for the fecundity of the scene portrayed do not appear until the end of the poem. "Erzvater" and "Erzmutter" have left their mark on this primordial terrain, and their heroic work has prepared for the arrival of an entire nation: "Das schicksal nährend für ein ganzes volk."

Such lines as this may have prompted Gundolf to argue that "the content of [the collection] 'Teppich' is the emergence of human culture under the auspices of the Germans" (Gundolf, qtd. in Lauster 119). Be that as it may, what remains of George's "Urlandschaft" in the end is but mythological puffery, a rhetorical balloon that hides the obscurity of its utopian vision behind the bloated grandiosity of its stilted language. The usual awkwardness of George's poetry caused by his deliberate use of neologisms and antiquated, long-forgotten German vocabulary is amplified to the level of absurdity in lines such as "Erzvater grub erzmutter molk." Reading the last lines of the poem, I ask myself what it means to "nurture the fate for an entire people," as it should be translated more literally. Providing arable land certainly nurtures people, but how does it nurture "fate" as such? Similarly, the meaning of the two genitive constructions in the last stanza remains obscure. "Erzvater," one can surmise, is "pleased" about the "field" he "spurred," but it is unclear what exactly "erzmutter" was doing since the second half of the line cannot be reconciled with her "milking," unless one assumes that she indeed "milked" the "new distress of the blessings." The only reading possible in order to rescue the poem from nonsense is to apply the word "froh" to both genitives at once so that the lines read: "Des ackers froh [und froh] des segens neuer mühn / Erzvater grub erzmutter molk." This addition, of course, destroys the rhythm and highly formalized structure of the entire poem, which was probably the reason why George suppressed it in the first place. George's idiosyncratic contractions and idioms in "Urlandschaft" not only give rise to absurd syntactical structures, but are also symptomatic of the coercion of language that sustains his poetic visions.

Obviously, I regard "Der Teppich" as an excellent poem and "Urlandschaft" as a mediocre one at best. This estimate does not simply reflect my discomfort with the nationalist tone of the latter that many critics have seen as indicative of the protofascist sentiments of George and his circle. Rather, the poem's ideological fervor camouflages its aesthetic weakness. Or, conversely, "Urlandschaft" cannot convince aesthetically because it leaves the poetic realm behind and instead projects a mythologized vision of national renewal. In contrast to "Der Teppich," the reader's gaze no longer focuses on the poem itself, but is directed outward toward the fertile land of the ancestors and the utopian promise it allegedly holds. What is missing from George's "Urlandschaft" is the self-referentiality of the previous poem, its continuous movement between signifier and signified, word and thing. The reader of "Urlandschaft" contemplates a poetic picture of mythical landscape beyond the text rather than seeing the imaginary landscape of the carpet coming alive in the very words and texture of the poem itself. Playing with language, "Der Teppich" is provocative, seductive, and even teasing at times. It activates and challenges the reader to unveil its secret and loathes failure. Whether or not the secret truly exists is less important a question than the poem's daring and defiant gesture of revelation that requires and explicitly demands "your" help in order to be successful. In spite of its self-assured tone, the poem still acknowledges that its reader has a decisive choice about how to read.

This sense of choice is completely lost in "Urlandschaft." Due to its rigid structure and solemn tone, the poem mortifies rather than enlivens the scene it depicts. Since everything appears to be already finished and perfect the way it is, there remains no need for "Urlandschaft" to try to further animate this world or to invite the reader to enter into it. Instead, the poem increasingly slips away into a mythical and completely imaginary past. Unlike the animals witnessed in the first two stanzas, the heroic achievements of the parental figures are not presented directly, but are conjectured from certain clues and retroactively posited as the beginning of history. The "fate" emphasized in the last line of the poem further evinces a predetermined historical process independent of those individuals who are subjected to it. This denial of historical contingency and the suppression of individual agency are the main reasons why "Urlandschaft" is a weaker poem than "Der Teppich." The static image of a mythical accomplishment in the past replaces the procedural notion of history and truth at work in art, while the posited heroic act in "Urlandschaft" remains a pure conjecture on the diegetic level of the poem. It is stipulated rather than developed, enforced rather than enacted during the process of reading since the poem fails to convincingly unfold its poetic vision in front of the reader's eyes. Instead, it denies the reader any autonomy as well as the right to participate (or refusal to participate) in the creation of its primordial world. Unlike "Der Teppich," "Urlandschaft" neither concedes nor works through the dilemma of self-alienation, but simply represses it.

It follows that the seemingly insignificant step from one poem to the next indeed crosses a crucial boundary between aesthetic emancipation and aesthetic escapism, revelation and confinement, freedom and slavery. According to most critics, George's collection *Der Teppich des Lebens* is situated right at the cusp between his earlier Aestheticism and his later protofascism. Such generic demarcations are less significant than their negotiation within the single poems themselves. For every one of them is at risk of succumbing to the reification and absolutist vision prescribed in George's "Urlandschaft," and my inquiry into Aestheticist poetry around 1900 tried to scrutinize the different poetic strategies employed to ward off this danger. Metaphorically speaking, my entire discussion of Hofmannsthal, Rilke, and George took place within, and sought to elucidate, the fault line or imperceptible space that divides "Der Teppich" from "Urlandschaft." As in Rilke's "Die Gazelle," the interpretative goal must be to unfold the *Weltinnenraum* of poetic language and to examine the authenticity and legitimacy of the look of things it evokes. This look is mirrored in the eye of the reader, for the reader's agency and the poem's allowance for it determine the poetic success or failure of Aestheticism.

As I have argued in the previous chapters, the best poems around 1900 both acknowledge their inability to capture pure presence (i.e., truth, Being, life, etc.) and, at the same time, leave a textual imprint in the form of punctuation signs meant to authenticate this knowledge. George's poetry often fails in this regard because it mass-produces this imprint by means of an idiosyncratic language and the St-G print-type, rather than letting it emerge from within the specific context of each and every particular poem. A look at the table of contents in the first edition of the *Blätter für die Kunst* in 1892 corroborates this impression (figure 8). There are as many as ten different fonts or print patterns exhibited on a page of far less than one hundred words. The plethora of italic, boldface, and small and capitalized letters conspires to make the page itself appear as a work of art. All words seem unique and literally present a different perspective in light of their unusual "face" that distinguishes them from most others. And yet, the overall impression nonetheless is one of rigidity and petrification because the coming alive of language appears too coerced and strained to be convincing.

George's emphasis on *Gestalt* violates the delicate process of trying to negotiate the paradox of autopoietic language during the act of reading. Aestheticism, however, is justified to reject outside reality only if it remains conscious of the complex problematic arising from its dreams of transcendence. The true danger inherent in Aestheticism consists precisely in the self-promoting and static celebration of its poetic success. This danger is most evident in some of George's poetry, which succumbs to the very commodification it allegedly rejects. Wolters's uncritical praise elucidates the problem: "because their [George's poems'] being is also their meaning" (denn ihr [Georges Gedichte] sein ist auch ihr sinn) ("Gestalt" 150), he exclaims. This sentence unwittingly celebrates the final demise of both thought and poetry as their grandiose fulfillment. If true, Wolters's claim would amount to its own undoing and give rise to a truly reconciled world in which art and philosophy would indeed be superfluous.

Over and over again, Adorno evoked the ideal of such a world only to resist its false redemption in twentieth-century society. Confusing the real problematic with its imaginary solution, Wolters's statement also rings false in the context of Heidegger's reflections on modern art because it literally short-circuits his entire philosophical enterprise. *Sein und Zeit* attempted to answer the question as to the "meaning of being" (*Sein und Zeit* 2) by thinking through *Dasein*'s "being in the world." Heidegger's thought embarks on a journey that can never encounter a "solution" present at hand as if the goal of the entire quest were just to find a particular kind of being actually "out there." George's magical trick consists in abandoning the circuity of such efforts in favor of celebrating the *Gestalt* of poetry and the stylized rituals of his circle as the truth sought and found. The *path toward* truth is replaced by the *sight of* truth. The simultaneity of revelation and concealment that, according to Heidegger, distinguishes the work of art is being suppressed in favor of the static celebration of the poetic word as the literal incarnation of the absolute.

I. BAND

BLÄTTER
FÜR DIE KUNST

Oktober 1892

Blätter für die Kunst . . . . . . d. H.
Auszüge aus Hymnen Pilgerfahrten
    Algabal . . . . Stefan George
Der Tod des Tizian . . . . . . Hugo von Hofmannsthal
Die Kreuze . . . . Paul Gérardy
Eine Legende . . . . Edmund Lorm
Gedichte . . . . Carl Rouge
Nachrichten

Herausgegeben von **Carl August Klein** Berlin 9 Lothringerstrasse

Diese zeitschrift im verlag des herausgebers hat einen geschlossenen von den
mitgliedern geladenen leserkreis

Einzelne hefte liegen auf
Berlin: Behrs' buchhandlung Unter den Linden
Wien: Leopold Weiss Tuchlauben
Paris: Léon Vanier 19 Quai St. Michel

Figure 8. Table of contents of the first publication of the Blätter für die Kunst, *October 1892. Courtesy of the Stefan George-Archiv, Stuttgart.*

George's language is the *Gesamtkunstwerk* of life—it is life itself that speaks and looks back at the reader from out of the *Gestalt* of his poetry. George cannot and must not tolerate any doubt concerning the actual accomplishment of his divine mission, since to voice doubt is equal to blasphemy. Instead, George builds on an elitist cultural politics that represses dissent in any form. If this cult is to convince at all, it must eliminate any trace of a life beyond the circle. The more reality threatens to break through, the stricter the circle's politics, the tighter the poetic form, and the more rigid and severe George's gaze becomes in the many paintings and photographs that circulate among his disciples (see figure 9).[7] At the same time, however, the aesthetic cult of the circle literally seeks to breathe life into George's poetry. A critical activity that ought to activate an exchange between poem and reader, the process of reading for George becomes an act of faith and a sacred ceremony of the utmost importance, for to read well is to give life to what is being said. Hence, the *Blätter für die Kunst* continuously emphasize the importance of movement and rhythm in poetry.[8] Superior to all other artistic forms of expression, poetic verse is able to "say the ineffable" and "to achieve, in a word, the impossible" (Landmann, *Einleitungen* 38)—provided, of course, the reader reached the right timbre of his voice, found the adequate tempo of speech, and exhibited the correct body gestures during the act of reading. Applicants seeking admittance into the circle were required to prove their worthiness in private recitals of George's poems. Those who failed to read convincingly not only proved themselves unworthy; they were sinners and guilty of sacrilege because they had violated and thus spoiled the utopian world nascent in George's poetry.

The unsurmounted master of reading, however, was George himself, as Lou-Andreas Salomé commented on in one of his lectures: "Never before has a poem experienced such a victorious and overwhelming transformation for me as Stefan George's during his personal readings" (Für mich hat ein Gedicht noch niemals eine solche siegreiche und überwältigende Umwandlung erlebt, wie Stefan Georges Gedichte in seinem mündlichen Vortrag) (qtd. in Mason 14). Similarly, Rilke states in a letter to George: "Maestro Stephan [*sic!*] George, the immense impression left by your reading in the salon Lepsius urges me to pursue vigorously and with dedicated interest everything that pertains to your art" (Meister Stephan [*sic!*] George, der große Eindruck, den ihr Leseabend im Salon Lepsius auf mich gemacht hat, läßt den Wunsch nicht zur Ruhe gehen, Alles, was Ihrer Kunst gehört, mit ge-

Figure 9. Photograph of Stefan George by Theodor Hilsdorf, ca. 1928. Courtesy of the Stefan George-Archiv, Stuttgart.

treuem Interesse zu verfolgen) (qtd. in Mason 14). The George-circle literally orbited the voice of its master, and the aesthetic ritual of his private lectures performed in the semidarkened salons of friends and committed worshipers aspired to let language itself come into being. Overall, these efforts are reminiscent of Hofmannsthal's hope to breathe life into language by means of reconnecting speech to the human body from which it emanates. The famous last poem in *Das Neue Reich* (published 1928), "Du schlank und rein wie eine flamme," is exemplary in this regard. Not a single punctuation mark interrupts the rhythmic flow of words, and the repetitive structure as well as the rearrangement of the first stanza at the end clearly speak to the self-referentiality of George's verses. Indeed, if one identifies the "Du" with the poem itself, it begins to speak about the ephemeral body of poetic speech:

> Du schlank und rein wie eine flamme
> Du wie der morgen zart und licht
> Du blühend reis vom edlen stamme
> Du wie ein quell geheim und schlicht
>
> Begleitest mich auf sonnigen matten
> Umschauerst mich im abendrauch
> Erleuchtest meinen weg im schatten
> Du kühler wind du heisser hauch
>
> Du bist mein wunsch und mein gedanke
> Ich atme dich mit jeder luft
> Ich schlürfe dich mit jedem tranke
> Ich küsse dich mit jedem duft
>
> Du blühend reis vom edlen stamme
> Du wie ein quell geheim und schlicht
> Du schlank und rein wie eine flamme
> Du wie der morgen zart und licht.
>
> (*Werke* I: 469)
>
> You like a flame, unflawed and slender,
> You flower sprung from Crown and Spear,
> You like the morning, light and tender,
> You like a spring, withdrawn and clear,

Companion me in sunny meadows,
Encompass me in evening haze,
And where I go, you shine through shadows,
You cool of wind, you breath of blaze.

You are my thoughts and my desire,
The air I breathe with you is blent,
From every draught I drink your fire,
And you I kiss in every scent.

You like the morning, light and tender,
You flower sprung from Crown and Spear,
You like a flame, unflawed and slender,
You like a spring, withdrawn and clear.

(*The Works of Stefan George* 410)

Contrary to Hofmannsthal, the George-circle emphasized the static *Gebilde* rather than the performative gesture. It does not denounce writing as a sign for the reification of language and life alike, but instead embraces it uncritically and without hesitation. The development of a new font is offered as visual proof for the magical transformations allegedly affected by George's poetry. The *Gestalt* of his poetry *is* the *Gesamtkunstwerk* of life captured in language. This complete mythologization of poetic language literally petrifies the outside and forbids any reference to it. As George tells his readers in *Jahr der Seele* (1897), the "urbild" that inspires art must be forgotten, because it "has been transformed to such a degree that it became irrelevant even for the artist and hence rather confuses than solves anything" (*Werke* I: 119). As in the above poem, the "Du" is not an autonomous "other," but is literally incorporated into the "Ich" and becomes part of it. Any attempt to differentiate between the two is misguided because there simply *is no other* out there. Ultimately, "I and You [are] the same soul" as George maintained in 1897 ("Es [das urbild] hat durch die kunst solche umformung erfahren dass es dem schöpfer selber unbedeutend wurde und ein wissendarum für jeden andren eher verwirrt als löst. Namen gelten nur da wo sie als huldigung oder gabe verewigen sollen und selten sind sosehr wie in diesem buch ich und du die selbe seele") (ibid.). Nowhere in his entire oeuvre has George expressed his poetic vision more bluntly than in the following verses from *Der Stern des Bundes* (1914):

Ich bin der Eine und bin Beide
Ich bin der zeuger bin der schooss
Ich bin der degen und die scheide
Ich bin das opfer bin der stoss
Ich bin die sicht und bin der seher
Ich bin der bogen bin der bolz
Ich bin der altar und der fleher
Ich bin das feuer und das holz
Ich bin der reiche bin der bare
Ich bin das zeichen bin der sinn
Ich bin der schatten, bin der wahre
Ich bin ein end und ein beginn.

(*Werke* I: 359)

I am the One, I am the Two,
I am the womb, I am the sire,
I am the shadow and the true,
I am the faggot and the fire.
I am the bow, I am the shaft,
I am the seer and his prediction,
I am the sheath, I am the haft,
I am abundance and affliction,
I am the victim and the slayer,
I am the symbol and the meaning,
I am the altar and the prayer,
I am an end and a beginning.

(*The Works of Stefan George* 322)

The self-aggrandizing, totalitarian tone of the poem, its unabashedly narcissistic, almost child-like equation of "Ich" and world, beyond any attempt at their dialectical negotiation, as well as its disarming simplicity in form and content capture the grandiose aspirations of German Aestheticist poetry like none other. Both a promise and a threat, the poem keeps alive the dream of the utopian world it defiles.

Coda: A World of Images

Heidegger's and Adorno's postwar criticism of George's work not only helps elucidate the central aspects of Aestheticist poetry, but also speaks to broader cultural issues, such as the relationship between vision and language, which are at the center of cultural studies today, for George's ritualist aesthetics and the glorification of poetry reflect the zeal of many modernists to hold fast to the enlightening and redemptive power of language in the face of twentieth-century popular and mass culture. This notion was not only widespread around 1900, it also informed much of twentieth-century literary criticism, including that of Adorno and Heidegger. Both regard poetry in general as a privileged site for social reconciliation because such reconciliation is always already nascent in language itself. The demise of language in the twentieth century speaks the truth about a society unable or unwilling to heed its call. For truth and human freedom to (re)gain their proper voice, language must be enabled to speak for itself. In the work of both Heidegger and Adorno, this belief in modern poetry often leads to a strong criticism of visual and mass culture since they regard the proliferation of images as symptomatic of, and contributing to, the alienation and fragmentation of modern society. Poetry, by contrast, is said to carry its own true vision within, meaning that Adorno's and Heidegger's appreciation of poetic language often occurs in combination with a strong iconoclastic sentiment. I shall trace this iconoclasm in their readings of George's poetry and end this chapter with a discussion of this highly problematic juxtaposition of word and image, language and visual media in twentieth-century criticism.

One of the major concerns of Adorno's negative dialectics is not to destroy the modernist ideal as such, but to resist its false implementation or realization in sociopolitical terms. Although the George-circle did fall prey to this temptation, Adorno does not outright dismiss its aesthetic aspirations as mere signs of cultural decadence and "protofascist" sentiments, as other critics have done.[9] For Adorno, however, it would be equally as wrong simply to glorify their ritualist aesthetics as the redemptive solution to the modern dilemma of social fragmentation and alienation. Rather, George's legacy must be situated in a historical framework, which, according to Adorno, points back to the fate of art and subjective freedom under the rule of capitalism. In his "Rückblick auf Stefan George," Walter Benjamin focuses specifically on the influence of modern technology upon the bourgeois notion of art. Since George's poetry and his aestheticist "stance" regarded social antagonisms as the representation of cosmic or natural conditions independent of historical change, Benjamin argues, George remained obtuse to the contingent socioeconomic and technological forces that actually shaped and determined his art.

Aestheticism, in other words, is situated within a broad cultural shift from words to images, from autonomous art to popular culture. It reacts to this shift by trying to fuse language and vision in the form of a speaking gaze that focuses on the material aspects of language. The rise of visual and mass culture around 1900 led to a division among both artists and intellectuals at the time. Some embraced the new media and the concomitant destabilization of the modern world, while others tried to resist it, yet everybody was affected by it one way or another. George's poetry most forcefully celebrated the body and the being of language in response to this challenge. His work promises to redeem the modernist ideal of giving voice to language, while, at the same time, it perversely glorifies the petrification of truth as *Gestalt*. Although he and his circle withdrew from the increasingly destabilized world into the inner sanctuary of art, their work is nonetheless shaped by the exterior world it denounces: "All neo-romantic words are last ones" Adorno rightly concludes ("George-Hofmannsthal"; *GS* X/1: 235), emphasizing both the religious and defensive nature of Aestheticist poetry. Given the rise of modern media and the proliferation of moving pictures at the beginning of the twentieth century, George's emphasis on *Gestalt* seems an attempt to stabilize and anchor the flux of the modern world. It functioned as a psychological shield and a reliable guide to guarantee the individual's visual control over its environment. It also served to combat the disarray of multiperspectival images that rendered the world ever more complex and thus undermined the narcissistic ideals of modern subjectivity.[10] George expressed his efforts to "invent new names for things" most poignantly and programmatically in his famous poem "Das Wort," first published in 1919:

Das Wort

Wunder von ferne oder traum
Bracht ich an meines landes saum

Und harrte bis die graue norn
Den namen fand in ihrem born -

Drauf konnt ichs greifen dicht und stark
Nun blüht und glänzt es durch die mark . . .

Einst langt ich an nach guter fahrt
Mit einem kleinod reich und zart

Sie suchte lang und gab mir kund:
›So schläft hier nichts auf tiefem grund‹

Worauf es meiner hand entrann
Und nie mein land den schatz gewann . . .

So lernt ich traurig den verzicht:
Kein ding sei wo das wort gebricht.

(*Werke* I: 466f.)

The Word

I carried to my country's shore
Marvels and dreams, and waited for

The tall and twilit norn to tell
The names she found within the well.

Then I could grasp them, they were mine,
And here I see them bloom and shine . . .

Once I had made a happy haul
And won a rich and fragile jewel.

She peered and pondered: "Nothing lies
Below," she said, "to match your prize."

At this it glided from my hand
And never graced my native land.

And so I sadly came to see:
Without the word no thing can be.

(*The Works of Stefan George* 408)

The poem radicalizes the autonomy of art so as to declare its primacy over the real. The process of naming emerges as the genuine act of creation, which grants material existence not only to concrete objects, but to abstract notions as well. Dream worlds materialize and become real once they are called by their proper name; "wonders" and "dreams" gain actual physicality and can literally be "grabbed" as they start to "bloom." Without their name, however, all things are doomed to vanish as does the unsignifiable object at the end of the poem. The subjunctive "sei" in the last line, however, indicates a rhetorical distance between the lyrical I and its utterance. The statement can be read both as the expression of an illusory hope (i.e., "there *should* not be a thing independent of a word") or as a legal prohibition ("there *must* not be a thing independent of a word"). Both readings as well as the ambivalence itself highlight the precarious nature of the alleged symbiosis between word and thing. Their existence ought to be intertwined and codependent, but may not be so regardless of what the poem claims. In other words, the aesthetic perspective on life remains valid only within the borders of the mythical land to which the poem itself belongs—the realm of art—which brings the reading full circle back to the "George-Kreis" from which it started.

In *Unterwegs zur Sprache*, Heidegger comments on George's poem at length as he tries to assimilate it into his own philosophy of language. With a decisive and—from a literary critic's point of view—illegitimate "jump" into pure speculation, Heidegger identifies the "kleinod" in "Das Wort" as the word itself, for which another word, and hence existence as such, is lacking: "the word, the saying, has no being" ([D]as Wort, das Sagen, hat kein Sein) ("Das Wesen der Sprache"; *Unterwegs zur Sprache* 192), Heidegger summarizes his reading. Language cannot express its own essence, and its magical power can never be revealed or "begriffen" in the double sense of the German original: conceptually understood and physically grasped. There is no stepping behind language, no world beyond words. What remains is for the poet to articulate this moment of renunciation, which, paradoxically, enables him to find the very means of expression inaccessible to him before: "As self-denial, renunciation is a Saying which says to itself: 'Where words break off no thing may be'" (*Way to Language* 147) (Verzichten ist *als* Sichversagen ein Sagen, das sich sagt: "Kein ding sei, wo das wort gebricht") ("Das Wort"; *UzS* 228).

Heidegger's reading of the last stanza of George's poem rhetorically operates on two levels. It shifts focus from the prepositional *content of* the utterance to its factual *existence as* an utterance. The "kleinod" is preserved poetically by letting it go physically: "His renunciation having pledged itself to the word's mystery, the poet retains the treasure in remembrance by renunciation" (*Way to Language* 154) (Insofern der Verzicht sich dem Geheimnis des Wortes zugesagt hat, behält der Dichter das Kleinod durch den Verzicht im Andenken) ("Das Wort" 236). With the help of this "Andenken," the "secret" is both unveiled and forever locked away because the poet now knows he must renounce the knowledge he seeks in order to gain access to it. His inability to speak the essence of language now emerges as a poetic success. The creative power of language is preserved in the very moment that acknowledges its demise. Poetic truth is captured through the process of its renunciation.

Heidegger's reading of George is problematic not only because it is based upon the identification of the "kleinod" as the word itself, for which there is absolutely no hermeneutic basis, but more important, because it points to an ambiguity inherent in Heidegger's poetics, which at times overemphasizes the being of art, thereby reducing it to a mere object present at hand. The "Andenken" alive in poetry is identified with a simple message that acknowledges the mere facticity of being. The problem is most apparent in his artwork essay from 1935/1936, where Heidegger argued that the work of art opens up a space for truth to simultaneously reveal and withdraw itself. The artwork is characterized by an internal struggle (the "Geviert" of world and earth, humans and gods) similar to the movement of concealment and revelation in Heidegger's notion of "aletheia": "Im Werk ist das Geschehnis der Wahrheit am Werk" ("Der Ursprung des Kunstwerkes"; *Holzwege* 45), meaning that "art is the becoming and happening of truth" ("Der Ursprung des Kunstwerkes" 59). Contrary to the classical correspondence theory of truth, Heidegger insists on the "presencing" of truth in art, which denotes a temporal occurrence rather than a static fact.[11]

Precisely this notion of temporal movement gets lost during other passages in Heidegger's text, which refer to the "arrestment" of truth in art. Although the artwork essay acknowledges the presencing of truth as an event, it nonetheless distinguishes two separate moments, one concerned with the "creation," the other with the "preservation" of the work of art:

Demnach wurde im voraus das Wesen der Kunst als das Ins-Werk-Setzen der Wahrheit bestimmt. Doch diese Bestimmung ist bewußt zweideutig. Sie sagt einmal: Kunst ist das Feststellen der sich einrichtenden Wahrheit in die Gestalt. Das geschieht im Schaffen als dem Hervor-bringen der Unverborgenheit des Seienden. Ins-Werk-Setzen heißt aber zugleich: in Gang- und ins Geschehen-Bringen des Werkseins. Das geschieht als Bewahrung. Also ist die Kunst: die schaffende Bewahrung der Wahrheit im Werk. ("Der Ursprung des Kunstwerkes" 59)

Accordingly the nature of art was defined to begin with as the setting-into-work of truth. Yet this definition is intentionally ambiguous. It says on the one hand: art is the fixing in place of a self-establishing truth in the figure. This happens in creation as the bringing forth of the unconcealedness of what is. Setting-into-work, however, also means: the bringing of work-being into movement and happening. This happens as preservation. Thus art is: the creative preserving of truth in the work. ("The Origin of the Work of Art"; *Poetry* 71)

Heidegger's definition of what art "is" pictures truth as the property or even the prisoner of art waiting to be liberated during the act of reception. This liberation depends upon the "preservers," as Heidegger calls a particular class of people—the high priests of art? who are they?—whose task it is to mobilize the "arrested" truth contained within the artwork. Heidegger's sense of "fixedness" (Feststellen) or, worse still, in a passive construction, "truth's being fixed in place in the figure" ("Origin" 64) (Festgestelltsein der Wahrheit in die Gestalt) ("Der Ursprung des Kunstwerkes" 51), finally culminates in the mere existence of art: "And what is more commonplace than this, that a being is? In a work, by contrast, this fact, that it is as a work, is just what is unusual. In the bringing forth of the work there lies this offering 'that it be'" ("Origin" 65f.) ("Was aber ist gewöhnlicher als dieses, daß Seiendes ist? Im Werk dagegen ist dieses, daß es als solches *ist,* das Ungewöhnliche. Im Hervorbringen des Werkes liegt dieses Darbringen des "daß es sei") ("Der Ursprung des Kunstwerkes" 53). Similar formulations can be found in the later "Letter about Humanism" (1946), where Heidegger states: "But Being—what is Being? It is itself" (Doch das Sein—was ist das Sein? Es ist es selbst), and "there is Being" (es gibt das Sein) ("Über den Humanismus" 19, 22). Both, Being and art, are, and the purpose of art and philosophy is to circle within these tautologies in order to understand the meaning of their being.

To speak of an "arrestment" of truth in art, however, contradicts Heidegger's philosophical reflections on "aletheia" and his own poetic "travels toward language." The very notion that truth could ever be "arrested" violates the sense of mobility—the movement of revelation and concealment—that constitutes both critical thought and poetry alike. Contrary to the overall trajectory of his philosophy, the artwork essay at times suggests that the mere being of art guarantees the static presence of truth, in which case Heidegger's entire ontological difference would become undone since both truth and Being would be reduced to mere beings in the sense of modern science. Heidegger himself acknowledged this dilemma. In his *Zusatz* to the artwork essay written twenty years later, he dedicates several pages of etymological analysis to the word "fixed" (Feststellen), concluding that "the 'fix' in 'fix in place' can never have the sense of rigid, motionless, and secure" ("Origin" 83) (kann das "Fest-" im Feststellen niemals the Sinn von starr, unbeweglich und sicher haben) ("Kunstwerk" 71).

Whether his additional remarks are ultimately convincing seems less important than the fundamental problem they implicitly acknowledge. It consists partly in Heidegger's attempt to reflect upon the origins of art without distinguishing methodologically between literature and the spatial arts. Including painting and architecture while, at the same time, insisting on poetry as the essence of all art, Heidegger is at pains to reconcile the spatial and temporal dimensions of art. Much like Rilke, his generalizations inevitably lead him to embrace the notion of "Festgestelltsein" and that of aesthetic preservation. Yet both, the imprisonment of truth in the form of *Gestalt* and its continuous preservation during the process of reception, contradict the basic principles of his philosophical enterprise and situates him in close alliance to the ritualized aesthetic politics of the George-circle. George sought to apprehend and identify truth as present at hand and "arrested" in language, which was to be appreciated only by the chosen few. The members of the circle willingly abandoned the movement of revelation and concealment that Heidegger identified as the paradoxical essence at work in art.

Heidegger's own philosophy both resists and succumbs to Wolters's identification of being and meaning. It resists by way of traveling from one side of the equation to the other, thinking through the (linguistic) space that both connects and separates the two poles. However, once Heidegger emphasizes the being of art and stylizes the moment of poetic renunciation as one of final success, as he does in his reading of George's "Das Wort," he cannot defend his philosophy against the misguided attempt to short-circuit the constitutive movement of thought. To be sure, I am not concerned with defending the "good" against the "bad" Heidegger and leave it to others to determine who the "real" one is. My point is rather that any reflection on modernist poetry sooner or later gives in to the temptation of perceiving the voice of language and the *Gestalt* of truth. This moment of epiphany is inevitable, for it is the raison d'être of literary criticism. It marks the crucial *Augenblick* of reading in which the look of things takes shape and is finally apprehended in the gaze of the reader.

Adorno's reading of Heidegger and George is further evidence of this necessary epiphany during the act of reading. Adorno's critique centers precisely on these moments of reification I discerned in Heidegger's artwork essay. He repeatedly denounced Heidegger's "rhetorical moves" as the "empty essence" of his "jargon of authenticity." Heidegger, according to Adorno, fatally abandons human subjectivity in favor of the mystified call of language. He glorifies the ineffable as the truth precisely because it cannot be named. The falsity of his entire ontological system is identified in a mechanism of reified thought that hides what it claims to have found: the essence of Being (*Sein*): "The Absolute is supposed to be thought within Being, but only because it cannot be thought at all is it declared to be the Absolute" (Im Sein soll das Absolute gedacht werden, aber nur weil es nicht sich denken läßt, sei es das Absolute) (*Negative Dialektik* 111).[12] For Adorno, the asserted tautology of a "being" and an "art" that simply "is," is nothing but indicative of Heidegger's jargon that "turns in a circle" ("Jargon" 475) without ever moving beyond the "always already" acknowledged status quo of existence.[13]

Heidegger's belief in the evocative power of "authentic" words and the concomitant lack of human agency collides with Adorno's understanding of philosophical inquiry. In his view, the emphasis on single words is not the cure, but the major cause, for the reification of language. Words in isolation do not possess an inherent truth-content since they gain meaning solely as a part of the whole in which they function: "In truth all concepts are implicitly rendered concrete in and through the language in which they appear" (In Wahrheit sind alle Begriffe implizit schon konkretisiert durch die Sprache, in der sie stehen) ("Essay"; *Noten* 20). For Adorno, history sediments into language and resonates therein. The meaning of words cannot be freely determined, nor can it be restored to its original status with the help of etymological studies, as Heidegger attempts to do: "He [the philosopher] must neither conceive of words as already given nor must he invent a word" (Er [der Philosoph] darf so wenig ein Wort als vorgegeben denken wie ein Wort erfinden), he declares (Adorno, "Thesen über die Sprache des Philosophen"; GS I: 369). Language, for Adorno, necessarily reflects the influence of specific historical circumstances and the use to which it has been subjected. Given the increasing fragmentation and alienation in capitalist society, philosophy must seek to approach truth in a spiral movement, encompassing it from different sides. Critical thought reflects and undercuts social reification by reconfiguring the broken fragments of language into ever new word constellations that bear witness to the violence from which they emerge: "Only he who remains mindful of the relationship between language and individual words by means of their constellation measures up to what language as such insinuates.... Both elements are mediated in a language worthy of its name" (Nur der genügt dem, was Sprache erheischt, der ihres Verhältnisses zu den Einzelworten in deren Konfigurationen sich versichert.... In Sprache, die etwas taugt, vermittelt sich beides) (*Negative Dialektik* 452).[14] This "mobility of words" ("Jargon" 482) has been lost in Heidegger's "jargon," claims Adorno. Heidegger's etymological wanderings through language fail to examine the sociohistorical competence of language in favor of the original meaning he ascribes to it.

Given their similar philosophical ambitions to heed the voice and nature of language, however, these differences appear secondary in contrast to the continuous belief in the redemptive power of language, which Adorno and Heidegger both share with all three poets discussed in this book. Language literally calls forth or commemorates a different world of reconciliation between subject and object. If reified discourse is both the cause and the effect of a reified world, then liberated discourse cannot but be the cause and the effect of a liberated world. According to this utopian perspective on language, it is impossible to prioritize or even distinguish properly between the being and becoming of language since the striving of language to come into its own defines its very nature. The essence of language is its gradual development toward its own essence. Its becoming *is* its being, and this is why it cannot and never must "be" purely and immediately present as such, be it in the form of poetic *Gestalt* or philosophical thought. Such static "being" of language is a symptom of its death.

Both Heidegger and Adorno share this vision of language, and both at times cannot but violate it in their praise of George. Although highly ambivalent about George's legacy in general, Adorno nonetheless embraces some of his poems as the language of truth: "George is flawed where he tries to exercise a power he has usurped as though it were authentic. But this permits almost the reverse: it is the poems that appear inauthentic, without social context, that are authentic" (*Notes* II: 182) (Brüchig ist George, wo er als authentisch, ermächtigt Macht auszuüben trachtet. Das jedoch erlaubt beinahe die Umkehrung: authentisch sind die Gedichte, die als nichtauthentische auftreten, gesellschaftlich ungedeckt, isoliert) ("George" 527). The "almost" alone prevents Adorno's simplistic reversal of conventional judgment from falling prey to the very "authenticity" he so vehemently denounced. Still, to follow George is treacherous, not only for the reader of Adorno's essay, but also for Adorno himself, as his remarks on the following poem from George's "Jahr der Seele" will serve to demonstrate:

> Ihr tratet zu dem herde
> Wo alle glut verstarb ·
> Licht war nur an der erde
> Vom monde leichenfarb.
>
> Ihr tauchtet in die aschen
> Die bleichen finger ein
> Mit suchen tasten haschen —
> Wird es noch einmal schein!
>
> Seht was mit trostgebärde
> Der mond euch rät:
> Tretet weg vom herde ·
> Es ist worden spät.
>
> ("Werke" I: 165)

> You reached the hearth, but dwindled
> To cinders was the glow,
> The moon was all that kindled
> The earth with deadly hue.
>
> Your listless fingers crumble
> The ashes. If you strain,

And grope in them, and fumble,
Will light return again?

See, how the moon consoles you
With soothing gait,
Leave the hearth — she tells you —
It has gotten late.

(*The Works of Stefan George* 159)

The poem ranks among the most cited in George's oeuvre. Without fail, it serves those who invoke it as proof that George's poetry defies the reader's effort to understand its enigmatic essence. For example Klages writes in 1902: "Who could claim to know the meaning of the hearth whose glow has dwindled to cinders" (Wer wüßte ganz den Sinn des Herdes, auf dem die Glut verstarb?) (66). Or Gundolf in 1921, who regards it as "a completely incomprehensible poem" (eines in jedem "Sinn" unverständliche[s] Gedicht) and continues: "The secret is neither what one sees nor what one hears or is able to think, and yet, it is not hidden behind these sensations either. The secret is itself" (Weder was man hier sieht noch hört noch denken kann ist das Geheimnis und doch steckt es auch nicht dahinter. Es ist es selbst) (Gundolf, *George* 143) — a statement leading right back to Wolters's vision of George's *Gestalt* that simply equates being and meaning. As if a member of this circle himself, Adorno ardently joins the chorus: "This poem is fully and unallegorically absorbed in the sensory situation. No conceptual meaning is distilled from the situation" ("Stefan George"; *Notes* II: 185) (Unallegorisch geht das Gedicht in der sinnlichen Situation auf. Keine gedankliche Bedeutung wird abdestilliert) ("George" 529). What remains, for Adorno, is "the feeling of an era that prohibits the song that still sings of it" (ibid.).

A brief interpretation of the poem may suffice to cast doubt on Adorno's claim. Given the prevalent context of life philosophy around 1900, the poem appears as the allegorical presentation of a death scene. The "corpse-like" color of the moon recalls the mortality of human life, much like the "dying" coals that are being shuffled around to keep them burning. Yet mere *Schein* ensues from such efforts, a false source of light that recalls the derivatory glow of the moon illuminating the entire scene. George's "hearth" emerges as the glow of human life about to lose its fire.[15] The poem sanctions this triumph of death over life in the last strophe as it suggests accepting darkness and death as the inevitable effect of the passage of time. Asked to move away from what was sought to be kept alive, namely life itself, the "you" must step back into the gloom of brute existence it originally had hoped to enlighten. The poem suggests that to follow nature's advice is to accept the unintelligibility of a late world without light and without warmth. And yet, the incontestable beauty of the poem serves to mitigate the serenity of the scenario it describes. Like most modernist poems, this one, too, functions as a self-reflective exploration of its own being. Similar to George's "Der Teppich," it invites the reader to try to enlighten its obscure meaning and make it speak beyond what it has to say. The poem's final message, however, does not reward these interpretative efforts of the reader, but calls for their resignation. The conciliatory gesture ascribed to the moon bestows a glimpse into the secret of life only to renounce any attempt to solve it. The reader is left with a shimmer of hope granted by the mere being of the poem itself.

Adorno's thesis, according to which the poem remains entirely unallegorical, thus refers less to the poem as such than to his own reluctance to perform the very critique he declares obsolete. Instead of trying to enlighten the obscurity of the poem, Adorno himself endorses its refusal to shed light on the scene of life and death. In so doing, he specifically obeys George's poetic command to abstain from any further effort of interpretation. By contrast, Adorno might have commented on the imperative tone of the last strophe, which disguises its command in the form of conciliatory advice, allegedly uttered by nature itself. He could have questioned the origin of the poem's renunciatory message, which, in spite of its natural gesture, reflects the subtle, yet crucial transformation of vision into language: to "see" the moon is to "hear" its advice. The major question in this context is one of agency. Who speaks?—nature itself or the hidden voice of the lyrical "eye" that has mastered the art of looking? Does not the master himself issue a quiet mandate to his readers to simply let being and art be?

Adorno chose not to pursue the possibility of such a reading. Instead, he truly hears language come into its own, a quasi-religious experience not at all different from Klages's "Offenbarung" or Gundolf's celebration of George's "Zaubersprüche": "At times, however, language itself really speaks from George, as if for the last time, in a way that others have only feigned" ("Stefan George"; *Notes* II: 185) (Manchmal jedoch redet wirklich aus George, wie ein letztes Mal, und wie andere es nur vortäuschten, Sprache selber) (George

529), he concludes. Adorno's earlier use of the passive voice ("Keine gedankliche Bedeutung wird abdestilliert") ("George" 529) cleverly suggests a language that indeed speaks itself, but in fact merely highlights the author's own will to make it so. One is reminded of Clemens's unanswered question in Hofmannsthal's fictional "Conversation about poetry" ("Gespräch über Gedichte"): "You say *really*, Theodor?" (Du sagst *wirklich*, Theodor?) (503).[16] The question is not simply meant to promote the truism that language itself never speaks, neither in art, nor in philosophy. It rather points to the particular tension in Adorno's aesthetics, which calls for a negative dialectics guided by critical thought, yet at times must succumb to the temptation of what allegedly roams beyond it: pure and true language. To be sure, these rare moments of epiphany in Adorno's readings—inspired, no doubt, by the ghost of Benjamin and his messianic notion of history—do not invalidate them. Quite the contrary, they are indispensable for the utopian vision that Adorno wants to sustain vis-à-vis the reified world of Western capitalism. Rather, what I find peculiar is Adorno's insistence on language or music as the privileged medium that commemorates this utopian moment. Adorno's aesthetics clearly privileges sound over sight, leading him to take an uncompromising critical perspective on visual media such as film.

In spite of his explicit rejection of Heideggerian terminology, Adorno's comments thus demonstrate how dangerously close he comes at times to the "jargon of authenticity" in some of his own readings. Such is the tempting allure of the utopian hope to overcome the constitutive differences of modernity that Adorno at times takes a break from the "Sisyphus work" of philosophy (*Negative Dialektik* 114) to enjoy the fruits of his intellectual labor: to listen to the self-identical voice of a mute language he himself has enabled to speak. And while he generally acknowledges this utopian vision as what it is, he nonetheless claims it to be realized in some works by Eichendorff, Mörike, or George. "The act in which the human being becomes language, the flesh becomes word, incorporates the expression of nature into language and transfigures the movement of language so that it becomes life again" ("Zum Gedächtnis Eichendorffs"; *Notes* I: 69)—this is how Adorno summarized the acoustic effects of Eichendorff's poetry, a praise reminiscent of Gundolf's claim about the eucharistic power of George's words.

Given Adorno's bias for Romantic subjectivity, it is not surprising that he would reserve this praise for Eichendorff rather than George. But even the less radical notion that "language itself speaks" remains problematic in light of the circle's explicit attempt to arrest the flow of language and to regard the mere existence of art as meaningful in itself. The ritualistic cult of the George-circle (what Heidegger refers to as the "Festgestelltsein der Wahrheit in die Gestalt" of art) violates Adorno's dictum about the nonessential nature of truth. If ontology and phenomenology "hypostatize the insolubility of the problem as its solution" (*Zur Metakritik der Erkenntnistheorie* 191), as he claims in his comments on Husserl, so does George's poetry. And yet, Adorno favors George over Hofmannsthal and Rilke not because his poetry is less reified, but because it is more so. In a dialectical tour de force, the most coerced poetry suddenly emerges as the most liberated, while Rilke's verses are rejected as "unspecific" because they are concerned with the matter of things (Rilke's *Dingkult*). It seems that the utter self-sufficiency of George's poetry, which circles around a promise it fails to deliver, allows Adorno to fill the void with the meaningful presence of language itself. And although he knows all too well that the "stated secret itself does not exist" ("George und Hofmannsthal" 199) and that his own ideal of "language speaking itself" inevitably falls prey to the philosophical and sociopolitical abuse it sought to alleviate, he embraces some of George's poems precisely because they give voice to what he hopes to hear. These epiphanies are inevitable if one wants to keep alive the hope of redemption through language, as both Adorno and Heidegger aim to do.

However, by the time George first published "Das Wort" in 1919, this belief in the magical power of language was already anachronistic. The same is true of Adorno's hopes to salvage bourgeois subjectivity in the poetic voice of pure language or of Heidegger's ideal to "think after" (in the sense of *Andenken*) the "Sage" of language as the unconcealment of Being itself. Modern culture at the beginning of the twentieth century was already governed by the spec(tac)ular rather than the linguistic realm. Weimar cinema emerged as a respectable form of entertainment and aspired to be recognized as a sincere form of art. The moving images began to replace language as the locus where subjectivity celebrated its euphoric resurrection in the form of the camera's disembodied gaze with which the spectator identified. Even the conservative forces in Germany increasingly recognized the political potential of film for the purpose of nationalist propaganda, leading to the creation of the UFA in 1917. The visual media rather than poetic language shaped the face of the twentieth century.

Heidegger ranks among the most outspoken critics of this cultural shift from word to image during the twentieth century. For him, the entire humanist paradigm was based upon the letter and was being undermined by media technology. Heidegger lamented the ubiquity of visual stimuli bereft of any critical or analytical dimension whatsoever, which, he claimed, lead to the mere curiosity of seeing for the sake of having seen.[17] He relates the rise of visual imagery to the loss of true vision. Language, by contrast, is said to guarantee a deeper, less superficial way of looking at the world. Heidegger even traced the "ruining" of philosophy itself to the rise of visual metaphors that originated in Greek philosophy. Plato's ideas, Heidegger argued, are no longer connected to the notion of Being as the primordial event that lets things emerge into their own and creates an opening for the presencing of the world. Instead, Plato focused on the mere existence of things ("Anwesenheit") that are identified as always already being there. The world thus degenerated into an abstract space filled with material objects allegedly alienated from their proper essence (the Platonian ideas) whose immaterial purity they are said merely to re-present. This notion of representation, for Heidegger, was the beginning of the end of Western metaphysics. It culminated in the forgetting of Being itself and gave rise to the subject-object paradigm of the modern era as well as the reign of technology and instrumental reason in the twentieth century. In his *Introduction to Metaphysics*, Heidegger writes:

> Das Seiende wird Gegenstand. . . . Das ursprünglich Weltende . . . fällt jetzt herab zum Vorbild für das Abbilden und Nachmachen. . . . Das Auge, das Sehen, das ursprünglich schauend einstmals in das Walten erst den Entwurf hineinschaute, hineinsehend das Werk her-stellte, wird jetzt zum bloßen Ansehen und Besehen und Begaffen. Der Anblick ist nur noch das Optische. (*Einführung in die Metaphysik* 48)

> Beings become objects. . . . That which originarily holds sway . . . now degenerates into a prototype for reproduction and copying. . . . The eye, the seeing, which first viewed the project *into* the sway in an originary viewing, and pro-duced the work while seeing into the sway, has now been reduced to mere observing and inspecting and staring. The view is now only the optical. (*Introduction to Metaphysics* 66)

This is the "Time of the World-Picture," as Heidegger phrases it in his essay from 1938. Modernity itself must be understood, he claims, as the "conquest of the world as a picture" ("Weltbild" 94). The demise of language is tantamount to a growing inability to "see" things, a competence that originally had made visual forms of representation less relevant for premodern times.[18] Although Heidegger establishes a strong connection between "pure" language and "true" vision, he certainly does not speak in favor of the material letter in the sense that written language needs to be perceived visually.[19] On the contrary, language engenders the world only on the basis of its own self-withdrawal, which leaves no trace of its own presence. Like Being itself, language is not simply another thing among things because the word is that which gives, but is not given as such.[20] To conceive of language in the form of writing or grammatical structures would be to misperceive the nature of both language and Being as something present at hand. It would repeat the fundamental error that characterizes the history of Western metaphysics. True language, it follows, always already carries its own vision within.

Even Adorno concurs. He explicitly acknowledges that the original unity between word and image no longer exists, yet denounces the split itself as a historical contingency that needs to be resisted and rethought if truth is to emerge:

> Wie die Hieroglyphen bezeugen, hat das Wort ursprünglich auch die Funktion des Bildes erfüllt. . . . Die Trennung von Zeichen und Bild ist unabwendbar. Wird sie jedoch ahnungslos selbstzufrieden nochmals hypostasiert, so treibt jedes der beiden isolierten Prinzipien zur Zerstörung der Wahrheit hin. (*Dialektik der Aufklärung* 33f.)

> Hieroglyphs demonstrate that words originarily also fulfilled the function of images. . . . The separation of sign and image is irreversible. However, if it is unwittingly hypostatized once again, then each of the two isolated principles works toward the destruction of truth.

Adorno questions the entire juxtaposition of vision and language and acknowledges the efforts of poetic and philosophical language to reestablish the lost unity of word and image. And yet he also remains highly critical of the mimetic power of mere images in his discussions of modernity. As if to continue Husserl's phenomenological project, his *Negative Dialektik* unambiguously states the case against images:

Der Gedanke ist kein Abbild der Sache ... sondern geht auf die Sache selbst. Die aufklärende Intention des Gedankens, Entmythologisierung, tilgt den Bildcharakter des Bewußtseins. Was ans Bild sich klammert, bleibt mythisch befangen, Götzendienst. Der Inbegriff der Bilder fügt sich zum Wall vor der Realität. ... [N]ur bilderlos wäre das volle Objekt zu denken. (*ND* 205, 207)

The thought is not a copy of the thing ... but works on the thing itself. The enlightening intention of thought—demythologization—eradicates the image-like characteristics of consciousness. That which clutches to images remains confined to myth and idolatry. The essence of images coalesces into a wall in front of reality. ... The full object could only be thought in the absence of images.

In Adorno's eyes, images partake of the truth only to the degree that they remain linked to language: "Dialectics reveals every image as writing" (Dialektik offenbart vielmehr jedes Bild als Schrift) (*DA* 41), he argued in the *Dialectics of Enlightenment*, and the *Aesthetic Theory* states: "Artworks become images in that the processes that have congealed in them as objectivity become eloquent" (*Aesthetic Theory* 85) (Kunstwerke werden Bilder dadurch, daß die in ihnen zur Objektivität geronnen Prozesse selber reden) (*ÄT* 132f.). Adorno's predilection for words over images is equally evident in his praise for George, whose best poems allegedly resist their translation into painting and "find their specific intuition [*Anschaulichkeit*] in language, not in optical imaginations" ("Die Kunst und die Künste" 441). He ends his essay on "Die Kunst und die Künste" as follows: "For a reality devoid of images has become the perfect (and perverted) reflection of the imageless condition into which art would dissolve if the utopia that is enigmatically written into every artwork were to be realized" (Denn die bilderlose Realität ist das vollendete Widerspiel des bilderlosen Zustands geworden, in dem Kunst verschwände, weil die Utopie sich erfüllt hätte, die in jedem Kunstwerk sich chiffriert) ("Die Kunst und die Künste" 452f.).

It appears that Adorno's criticism, much like the subjectivity it sought to recover, withdraws into the inner sanctuary of language in the hope of remaining unaffected by the allegedly subversive visions proliferated by the mass media. His best readings, however, both endorsed and resisted the utopian notion of language as a refuge for the broken dreams of modernity, for Adorno remains true to what he himself said about Borchardt's work:

> Die Idee der Beschwörung einer nichtexistenten Sprache impliziert deren Unmöglichkeit.... Borchardts Klugheit hat, trotz des pathetischen Glaubens an den inspirierten Dichter, darüber keineswegs sich getäuscht. Wohl hegte er die Hybris.... Aber nicht minder wußte er, daß es Hybris war. ("Die beschworene Sprache" 540)

> The idea of conjuring a nonexistent language implies the impossibility of that language.... Borchardt's shrewdness had no illusions about that, despite his pathos-laden belief in the inspired poet. But there was hubris in him.... But he was no less aware that it was hubris. ("Charmed Language"; *Notes* II: 197)

Contrary to both Adorno and Heidegger, I believe that twentieth-century swan songs about the doom of literacy and language are not only exaggerated, but completely miss the point with regard to its sociocultural function. Regardless of its quasi-religious status around 1900, there is nothing inherently sacred about language as such. "In the beginning was the word," one reads in the book of books, yet this word, one must remember, was never conceived in terms of everyday communication, but imagined to carry its visionary powers within. In poetry and philosophy alike, language is claimed to be constitutive of reality if and only if it exceeds the mere use of linguistic signs. The true word, the word of God, says more than it signifies, for it speaks through silence and perceives the unperceivable essence of things.

It follows that Heidegger's and Adorno's critique regarding the (post)-modern proliferation of images misconstrues the symptom as the disease. They conflate the disarray and ideological abuse of images in twentieth-century society with their alleged deceptive nature, their essential "un-truth." Yet images per se are not more or less truthful than everyday language. The entire juxtaposition is ill conceived because it contrasts an idealized vision of pure, nonreferential language with the generic images governing contemporary culture. Once we fully acknowledge the metaphorical and utopian character of the poetic ideal of language, it becomes obvious that its alleged primordiality cannot be sustained since there remains no reason to assume that other media could not fulfill the same function. If modernist poetry around 1900 testifies to a certain historical need to mythologize language for the sake of truth, as one might argue with reference to all authors discussed in this book, could the same not apply to visual rather than linguistic paradigms? If Western philosophy still dreams of hearing the pure voice of language, why could we not hope for vision to develop its proper self-image? If the word speaks itself, why can the image not present itself? Why should truth reside only within the self-speaking word rather than the self-seeing image? It seems reasonable to allow contemporary society to further explore the possibility of a kind of "visual thinking" (Rudolf Arnheim) before dismissing images as inherently deceptive or inadequate for the presencing of truth. Since images have replaced words as the primary means of interacting with the world, the primary task for artists and intellectuals today does not consist in lamenting the fact or in simply fostering a new appreciation of visual culture, but in trying to make these images speak beyond their inherent mode of iconic reference. Is there a general theory of the visual "punctum" (Roland Barthes) for postmodern culture?

"What is at stake, then," Gumbrecht argues in *Making Sense in Life and Literature,* "is the invention of a new epistemology capable of theorizing and analyzing ways of sense making that perhaps no longer include effects of meaning and reference" (*Sense* 12). He is right, of course, except that this goal has been at stake throughout the history of modernity, and the effort of Aestheticism to capture the look of things in and through language can be understood precisely in these terms. Posthermeneutics, however, denounces the history of aesthetics in favor of "interfaces such as those between TV and psychic systems, or between computers and social systems" (ibid.). This juxtaposition between aesthetics and media is highly problematic, not only because it runs the danger of simply reversing the traditional value judgment espoused by Adorno and Heidegger, but also because its positivist stance implies that the search for something like primordial "truth" is superfluous or even dangerous. I, for one, think this search is inevitable, and the real challenge of the digital revolution governing contemporary society is to continue the quest to "make sense" of it, whereas any deliberate attempt to abort this process ultimately self-destructs or leads back to previous epistemological positions. This persistence in the search for truth might be the final lesson of modernist poetry and the look of things around 1900.

NOTES

INTRODUCTION

1. Wahr ist die Erkenntnistheorie, insofern sie der Unmöglichkeit des eigenen Ansatzes Rechnung trägt und in jedem ihrer Schritte von dem Ungenügen der Sache selbst sich treiben läßt. Unwahr aber ist sie durch die Prätention, es sei gelungen . . .

2. Jean-François Lyotard, "Ob man ohne Körper denken kann," in *Materialität der Kommunikation*, ed. Hans-Ulrich Gumbrecht and K. Ludwig Pfeiffer (Frankfurt: Suhrkamp, 1988), 813–29.

3. All translations from German into English are my own unless noted otherwise.

4. English translation: Walter Benjamin, *The Origin of German Tragic Drama*, trans. John Osborne (London: NLB, 1977), 30.

5. In the following, I will not explicitly distinguish between the various scholarly classifications for high literary modernism around 1900, such as "fin de siècle," "Aestheticism," "neo-Romanticism," and "decadence." In fact, I believe such classifications are both superfluous and misleading. Friedrich Gundolf, for example, regards Hofmannsthal as an "Aestheticist," whereas Peter Szondi classifies him as the "anti-Aesthete" he believed himself to be. Käte Hamburger believes it necessary to defend the "neo-Romanticist" Rilke from the accusation of being an "Expressionist," while Müller-Seidel emphatically argues to finally get rid of the term "Neu-Romantik" altogether: "Es ist ein gänzlich irreführender Begriff, ein Begriffsgespenst und nichts anderes!" See Walter Müller-Seidel, "Epochenverwandtschaft. Zum Verhältnis von Moderne und Romantik im deutschen Sprachgebiet," in *Geschichtlichkeit und Aktualität. Studien zur Literatur seit der Romantik*, ed. Klaus-Detlev Müller et al. (Tübingen: Niemeyer, 1988), 370–92: 390. Unlike Müller-Seidel, I believe none of the other terms to be any better; this is why I simply use "Aestheticism" or "literary modernism" throughout this book. I want to emphasize, however, that the rejection of such labels is not to deny aesthetic differences between various authors around 1900, but to claim that one can analyze them without recourse to the confusing disarray of academic categories.

6. Cf. Peter Bürger, *Theorie der Avantgarde* (Frankfurt: Suhrkamp, 1974). For a comprehensive critique of Bürger's approach, see Richard Murphy, *Theorizing the Avant-Garde: Modernism, Expressionism, and the Problem of Postmodernity* (Cam-

bridge: Cambridge University Press, 1999), 1–48. Murphy criticizes Bürger's approach for failing to acknowledge the indispensability and continued relevance of aesthetic autonomy, even for the avant-garde movement.

7. Andreas Huyssen, "Adorno in Reverse: From Hollywood to Richard Wagner," in *After the Great Divide: Modernism, Mass Culture, Postmodernism* (Bloomington: Indiana University Press, 1986), 16–43.

8. There is a tension in Jameson's later work regarding this point. On the one hand, his own analysis of postmodernist culture clearly resists the antihermeneutic and nontheoretical discourse of its object and instead advocates a continued critique of late capitalism, while, on the other hand, Jameson seems to accept the loss of critical distance as inevitable (*Postmodernism* 48) since the "status of art (and also of culture) has had to be irrevocably modified in order to secure the new productivities" in late capitalism, meaning that "it cannot be changed back at will" (*Postmodernism* 318).

9. Cf. Judith Ryan, *Rilke, Modernism, and Poetic Tradition* (Cambridge: Cambridge University Press, 1999).

10. For a detailed description of the first edition, see *Stefan George. Bilder und Bücher aus dem Nachlass*.

11. See also Heidegger, "Der Weg zur Sprache," in *Unterwegs zur Sprache*, 243.

12. Rainer Maria Rilke, *The Duino Elegies*, trans. Leslie Norris and Alan Keele (Columbia, S.C.: Camden House, 1993), 55.

13. Similar passages can be found in "Das Kleine Welttheater," vol. 1 of *Gesammelte Werke*, 373, 382–83.

14. Cf. Benjamin, "Motive," vol. 1/2 of *Gesammelte Schriften*, 646–47; Jacques Lacan, *The Four Fundamental Concepts of Psychoanalysis*, 106; Jean Paul Sartre, *Being and Nothingness*, trans. Hazel E. Barnes (New York: Simon & Schuster, 1992), 340–400; Maurice Merleau-Ponty, *The Visible and the Invisible*, 134–35.

15. Hans-Georg Gadamer, vol. 2 of *Gesammelte Werke*, 250; qtd. in Kai Hammermeister, *Hans Georg Gadamer* (München: Beck, 1999), 117.

CHAPTER 1

1. "Ich denke manchmal, es fehlt uns nicht an gelehrter Prosa, sondern an gelehrter Poesie." Niklas Luhmann, *Short Cuts*, ed. Peter Gente et al. (Frankfurt: Zweitausendeins, 2000), 5.

2. Given the long and intricate development of photography and animated pictures, the origin of film proper seems irretrievably lost, or rather: has never existed to begin with. Due to personal preferences, scholars have referred to different historical events or particular moments as the "birth" of motion pictures. See Jean-Louis Comolli, "Technique and Ideology," in *Narrative, Apparatus, Ideology: A Film Theory Reader*, ed. Philip Rosen (New York: Columbia University Press, 1986), 421–43. For a detailed description of cinema's historic predecessors,

see Georges Sadoul, vol. 1 of *Histoire Générale du Cinéma* (Paris: Editions Denoel, 1948).

3. Cf. Tom Gunning, "An Aesthetics of Astonishment: Early Film and the (In)Credulous Spectator," *Art and Text* 34 (1989): 31–45; and Dai Vaughan, "Let There Be Lumière," in *Early Cinema: Space, Frame, Narrative*, ed. Thomas Elsaesser (London: British Film Institute, 1990), 63–67: 63. I have personally checked the daily newspaper *Le Figaro* for the time of the first Lumière showing, but could not find any remarks lending credibility to the anecdote of the frightened spectators. Besides, it should be remembered that Lumière's premiere showed several less threatening films before *L'arrivée d'un train*, and this gave spectators sufficient time to adapt to the illusory power of the cinematic apparatus.

4. Kenneth S. Calhoon adds an interesting twist to this discussion as he relates Lumière's film to a painting by Magritte entitled "La Durée poignardée," which depicts a locomotive emerging from a fireplace into a living room (parlor). According to Calhoon, both "pictures" portray the threatening consequences of adequate representation (i.e., the demolition of the private interior through the invasion of dangerous images that became "real"), yet they simultaneously console the spectator by exposing such representation as illusory appearance—"a reminder that art never wanted the thing itself, only an imposter." Kenneth S. Calhoon, "Screen Memories: The Shadow of Technology in Early German Cinema," unpublished paper, presented at the Annual Conference of the German Studies Association in Los Angeles, 1991.

5. See, for example, Miles Orvell, *The Real Thing: Imitation and Authenticity in American Culture, 1880–1940* (Chapel Hill: University of North Carolina Press, 1989).

6. Anton Giulio Bragaglia, *Fotodinamismo futuristica*, ed. Anton Giulio Bragaglia et al. (Turin: Giulio Einaudi, 1970); qtd. in Bernd Hüppauf, "Experiences of Modern Warfare," *New German Critique* 59 (Spring/Summer 1993): 54, note 29.

7. Cf. Siegfried Kracauer, "Die Photographie," in *Das Ornament der Masse* (Frankfurt: Suhrkamp, 1977), 21–39.

8. Cf. Schivelbusch, *The Railway Journey*. Commenting on the psychological effect of the train ride, Wolfgang Schivelbusch alludes to the new cinematic medium as the artistic correlative to this cultural experience: "He [the traveler] perceives objects, landscape etc. through the apparatus with which he is moving through the world." The world outside was indeed converted into a tableau, a complex of "moving pictures" (Schivelbusch, *The Railway Journey* 61). See also Lynne Kirby, "Male Hysteria and Early Cinema," *Camera Obscura* 17 (1988): 113–14; and the collection of essays called *Cinema and the Invention of Modern Life*, ed. Leo Charney and Vanessa R. Schwartz (Berkeley: University of California Press, 1995).

9. In 1914, Kurt Pinthus publishes *Das Kinobuch*, a collection of several movie scripts that, alas, were never to appear on celluloid. Pinthus's own story is called "Die verrückte Lokomotive." It describes a train ride gone amok and literally

taking off into the air—an image reminiscent of the fatal accident at Gare Montparnasse. In 1935, Walter Benjamin implicitly mobilized the train metaphor by arguing that film had finally abolished the outdated and uncritical aesthetics of contemplation: "Then came the film and burst this prison-world asunder by the dynamite of the tenth of a second, so that now, in the midst of its far-flung ruins and debris, we calmly and adventurously go traveling" (*Illuminations* 236). A similar expression can be found in Adorno's *Aesthetic Theory*, which characterizes the relationship between the modern work of art and its spectator as follows: "The relation to art was not that of its physical devouring; on the contrary, the beholder disappeared into the material: this is even more so in modern works that shoot toward the viewer as on occasion a locomotive does in a film" (*Aesthetic Theory* 13) (Das Verhältnis zur Kunst war keines von Einverleibung, sondern umgekehrt verschwand der Betrachter in der Sache; erst recht ist das der Fall in modernen Gebilden, die auf jenen zufahren wie zuweilen Lokomotiven im Film) (*Ästhetische Theorie*, 27).

10. See, for example, W. J. T. Mitchell, *Iconology: Image, Text, Ideology* (Chicago: University of Chicago Press, 1986). Mitchell argues that Lessing's notion of a spatial versus a temporal art is misconceived since the hybridization between the arts is not a marginal practice, but rather at the very heart of art. Lessing's whole distinction relies not on differences in kind, but in degree, and is thus indicative of certain political and ideological biases.

11. Edmund Husserl, *The Crisis of European Sciences and Transcendental Phenomenology*, trans. David Carr (Evanston: Northwestern University Press, 1970), 89.

12. For a comprehensive exploration of Descartes's dilemma, see Margaret Atherton, "How to Write the History of Vision: Understanding the Relationship between Berkeley and Descartes," in *Sites of Vision*, ed. David Levin, 139-65.

13. See also Helmholtz's essay "The Origin and Meaning of Geometric Axioms (1)," in *Selected Writings*, 247-65, particularly 263-65, where Helmholtz treats this point at length.

14. Helmholtz, "Recent Progress in the Theory of Vision," 218; "Origin," 506f.

15. See Sigmund Freud, "Hemmung, Symptom, Angst," vol. 14 of *Gesammelte Werke*, 111-205; "Jenseits des Lustprinzips," vol. 13 of *Gesammelte Werke*, 1-69.

16. Eberhard Bauer, "Spiritismus und Okkultismus," in *Okkultismus und Avantgarde*, 60-80: 77-78.

17. Terry Castle, "Phantasmagoria: Spectral Technology and the Metaphorics of Modern Reverie," *Critical Inquiry* 15 (Autumn 1988): 26-61.

18. Adorno was among the first and most clear-sighted critics of this historical juncture between magic and positivism. For him, the allurement of a Dionysian flow of life is but the ideological guise of a capitalist society that ultimately serves to legitimize the reified world of commodity fetishism, as he argues in a famous letter to Benjamin in 1938: "the theological motif to call things by their name has a tendency to reverse into the wide-eyed presentation of its mere facticity" (das

theologische Motiv, die Dinge beim Namen zu nennen, schlägt tendenziell um in die staunende Darstellung der bloßen Faktizität) (Benjamin, vol. 1/3 of *Gesammelte Schriften*, 1096).

19. Lauster points to the sonnet as a poetic form whose genesis and historical use mirrors the struggle between stasis and mobility, space and time (288–311). In contrast to Lauster, who privileges the sonnet's formal stasis over its dynamic content, Ryan reverses the perspective and emphasizes the latter over the former (55–65). The different views literally bespeak the inherent ambivalence of the sonnet form itself.

20. Rainer Maria Rilke, *Selected Poems*, trans. Albert Ernest Flemming (New York: Methuen, 1986), 92.

21. Cf. Rilke's "Marginalien zu Friedrich Nietzsche," vol. 6 of *Werke*, 1163–77.

22. For a comprehensive critique of the ahistorical and ontological presumptions underlying theories of the cinematic apparatus, see Judith Mayne, *Cinema and Spectatorship* (London: Routledge, 1993).

23. Many of the essays in Thomas Elsaesser, ed., *Early Cinema: Space, Frame, Narrative* (London: British Film Institute, 1990), speak to this issue. See also Noel Burch, *Life to Those Shadows* (Berkeley: University of California Press, 1990), who distinguishes what he calls "primitive modes of representation" before 1909 from the "institutional mode of representation" and its spectator-oriented approach that controlled cinema thereafter.

24. Cf. Walter Gebhard, *Der Zusammenhang der Dinge. Weltgleichnis und Naturverklärung im Totatlitätsbewußtsein des 19. Jahrhunderts;* Monika Fick, *Sinnenwelt und Weltseele. Der psychophysische Monismus in der Literatur der Jahrhundertwende.*

25. The term is coined by Donald M. Lowe in his book *History of Bourgeois Perception* (Chicago: University of Chicago Press, 1982).

CHAPTER 2

1. All quotes by Husserl refer to the following edition and are cited in the body of the text: Edmund Husserl, *Husserliana. Gesammelte Werke*, ed. H. L. van Breda (The Hague: Nijhoff, 1958–). I shall use the following abbreviations: *LU* for *Logische Untersuchungen* (2 vols. Husserliana XVIII and XIX); *Idee* for *Die Idee der Phänomenologie. Fünf Vorlesungen* (Husserliana II); *Ideen* for *Ideen zu einer Reinen Phänomenologie und Phänomenologischen Philosophie* (2 vols. Husserliana III and IV). All translations are my own unless noted otherwise. For a historical account of Husserl's oeuvre, see J. N. Mohanty, "The Development of Husserl's Thought," in *The Cambridge Companion to Husserl*, ed. Barry Smith and David Woodruff Smith (Cambridge: Cambridge University Press, 1995), 45–77.

2. This distinction, of course, was the focal point for Derrida's critique of Husserl in *Speech and Phenomena*, which, however, shall not be repeated here.

3. Cf. Dagfinn Føllesdal, "Brentano and Husserl on Intentional Objects and Perception," in *Husserl, Intentionality, and Cognitive Science,* ed. Hubert L. Dreyfus (Cambridge: Massachusetts Institute of Technology, 1982), 31–41.

4. Cf. Gottlob Frege, "On Sense and Reference," in *Translations from the Philosophical Writings of Gottlob Frege,* ed. Peter Geach and Max Black (Oxford: Blackwell, 1960). Almost the entire collection of essays in *Husserl, Intentionality, and Cognitive Science,* ed. Hubert L. Dreyfus (Cambridge: Massachusetts Institute of Technology, 1982), points to this similarity.

5. Ferdinand de Saussure, *Course in General Linguistics,* ed. Charles Bally and Albert Sechehaye, trans. Roy Harris (LaSalle: Open Court, 1986).

6. See Peter Simons, "Meaning and Language," in *The Cambridge Companion to Husserl,* ed. Barry Smith and David Woodruff Smith (Cambridge: Cambridge University Press, 1995), 106–37: 110. Similarly Dallas Willard, "Knowledge," in *The Cambridge Companion to Husserl,* 138–67.

7. Cf. *LU* II/1, § 14, 56f.

8. Cf. *LU* II/1, § 21, 77.

9. See also *Ideen* I/1, § 19, 43, and *Ideen* I/2, "Beilage," 8, 534.

10. Dreyfus rightly claims that in the *LU,* "there is no mention of the intuitive sense," for Husserl did not coin such a term. Yet Dreyfus is mistaken, I believe, in claiming that Husserl at that time had "no way of generalizing his conception of a non-spatial, non-temporal, universal, abstract sense to cover a concrete form which is inseparable from the sensuous content it organizes" (Dreyfus, 106), for that is exactly how Husserl defines the "object" (*Gegenstand*) of inner perception, which he claims is "physically" (*leibhaft*) given in the act that constitutes it. Of course this object is not "really" physical, but that terminological ambiguity is precisely the foundation on which Husserl later erects his eidetic principle. The *Ideen,* in other words, merely continue the prioritizing of mental reflection already latent in the *LU.*

11. See, for example, Barry Smith and David Woodruff Smith, "Introduction," in *The Cambridge Companion to Husserl,* 1–44; 34–37 in particular; and Dallas Willard, "Knowledge," in *The Cambridge Companion to Husserl,* 138–67.

12. Harrison Hall, "Was Husserl a Realist or an Idealist?"; Herman Philipse, "Transcendental Idealism," in *The Cambridge Companion to Husserl,* 239–322.

13. Most essays in *Husserl, Intentionality, and Cognitive Science* discuss this question. See also Barry Smith and David Woodruff Smith, "Introduction," in *The Cambridge Companion to Husserl,* 1–44.

14. Cf. Jaakko Hintikka, "The Phenomenological Dimension," in *The Cambridge Companion to Husserl,* 78–105.

15. Cf. *LU* II/2, "Beilage," 14, 586–88.

16. In the introduction to the second volume of the *LU,* for example, we read: "Die in der Wesensintuition direkt erfaßten Wesen und rein in den Wesen gründenden Zusammenhänge bringt sie [die reine Phänomenologie der Erlebnisse]

deskriptiv in Wesensbegriffen und gesetzlichen Wesensaussagen zu reinem Ausdruck" (*LU* II/1: 6). In the *Idee* lectures from 1907, Husserl again asserts the possibility of "nestling" language against the clarity of vision: "[S]ie [Gegebenheiten] stehen anschaulich da, wir reden über sie nicht bloß in vager Andeutung, in leerer Meinung, wir schauen sie und sie schauend können wir ihr Wesen, ihre Konstitution, ihren immanenten Charakter herausschauen und unsere Rede in reiner Anmessung an die geschaute Fülle der Klarheit anschmiegen" (*Idee* 31). And again, in the *Ideen* from 1913: "Wir haben nicht philosophische Theorien aufgestellt, wir haben nicht von einem metaphysischen Standpunkt aus doziert, sondern selbstverständliche Folgen aus einigen prinzipiellen Feststellungen gezogen. Was diese aber anbelangt, so haben wir einfach beschrieben, was wir in der Intuition als direkt gegeben vorfanden, und haben es genau in dem Sinne beschrieben, in dem es sich gab, ohne jede interpretierende Hineindeutung, ohne Hinzuziehung von solchem, was uns durch gelehrte Traditionen, durch alte und neue Vorurteile zugemutet, statt eben am Gegeben selbst zu sehen war" (*Ideen* I/2, "Beilage," 15, 560). Similarly *Ideen* I/1, § 18, 39.

17. It is obvious that Husserl's concept of "hyle" as the unstructured matter of a sensation is problematic since such raw data, by definition, cannot be consciously registered as such, but is immediately interpreted and hence transformed into a meaningful form by the receiving consciousness. I shall not, however, pursue this issue any further in the context of my discussion.

18. Cf. Bell, 63.

19. For a comprehensive overview, see "Introduction," in *The Cambridge Companion to Husserl*, 1–44.

20. The following summary of Gurwitsch's interpretation refers to his *Studies in Phenomenology and Psychology* (Evanston: Northwestern University Press, 1966) and his essay on "Husserl's Theory of the Intentionality of Consciousness," in *Husserl, Intentionality, and Cognitive Science*, ed. Hubert L. Dreyfus (Cambridge: Massachusetts Institute of Technology, 1982), 59–71.

21. Cf. Dagfinn Føllesdal, "Husserl's Notion of Noema," in *Husserl, Intentionality, and Cognitive Science*, 73–80; and Hubert L. Dreyfus, "Husserl's Perceptual Noema," in *Husserl, Intentionality, and Cognitive Science*, 97–123.

22. Cf. Dreyfus, 108–10.

23. Jaakko Hintikka convincingly argues this point in his essay "The Phenomenological Dimension," in *The Cambridge Companion to Husserl*, 78–105: 81.

24. Cf. Føllesdal, 74.

25. For a detailed discussion of Bergson's influence on modern art such as fauvism, cubism, and futurism, see Mark Antliff, *Inventing Bergson: Cultural Politics and the Parisian Avant-Garde* (Princeton: Princeton University Press, 1993).

26. Similarly *CE*, 328, 343, 344f., 357, 361. Also *Intro*, 16, 18.

27. Bergson refers to "pure" rather than "real" perception because real perception always interacts with memory, that is, the history of previous perceptions

preserved in the mind. Incoming sensations emanating from the object are being mixed with the memory of previous sensations to propel the body into action. "Together, these two currents make up, at their point of confluence, the perception that is distinct and recognized" (*MM*, 127f.). Although a key issue throughout *Matter and Memory*, this aspect is less relevant in the context of this study and will not be developed further.

28. Deleuze rightly points to a development in Bergson's thought concerning the notion of space, which "seemed to him to be less and less reducible to a fiction separating us from this psychological reality" and rather "was itself grounded in being" (*Bergsonism*, 34). Unlike Deleuze, however, I want to argue that these qualifying shifts are symptomatic of a terminological uncertainty located at the very center of Bergson's philosophy.

29. It is, of course, inaccurate to speak of "parts" in this context since Bergson is at pains to avoid any term suggestive of solid states of immobility, which, in his eyes, do not exist and are a construct of the human mind. As I will argue in this chapter, however, this ambiguous terminology is difficult to avoid since it lies at the heart of Bergson's philosophy and haunts it from within.

30. Compare to Ernst Mach's famous formulation: "Das Ich ist nicht zu retten."

31. Georg Lukács's work is exemplary in this regard as he ranks among the most severe critics of such philosophical "irrationalism," which he sees leading straight *Von Nietzsche zu Hitler* (Frankfurt: Fischer, 1966). In the few pages Adorno dedicated to a critique of Bergson in his *Zur Metakritik der Erkenntnistheorie* published in 1956, a more balanced view of Bergson is palpable, for Adorno realizes the critical potential inherent in metaphysical intuition that indeed was directed against the very reification of thought to which it itself inadvertently fell victim: "In den Intuitionen besinnt sich die Ratio auf das, was sie vergaß. . . . Die Intuition ist kein einfacher Gegensatz zur Logik; sie gehört dieser an und mahnt sie zugleich an das Moment ihrer Unwahrheit. . . . In der unwillkürlichen Erinnerung versucht wie immer auch vergeblich der willkürliche Gedanke etwas von dem zu heilen, was er gleichwohl verüben muß. Das hat Bergson verkannt. Indem er die Intuitionen für die unmittelbare Stimme jenes Lebens ausgab, das doch nur als vermitteltes noch lebt, hat er sie selber zum abstrakten Prinzip verdünnt, das rasch mit der abstrakten Welt sich befreundet, gegen die er es ersann" (53f.). The brilliancy of Adorno's thought notwithstanding, his critique of Bergson not only culminates in the, for him, typical charge that those who seek to escape the restrictions of conceptual thought by (allegedly) avoiding it altogether end up perpetuating those same restrictions—a critique that strikes me as rather generic in essence, particularly since Adorno does not present a thorough textual analysis of Bergson's works. Moreover, Bergson presents intuition not as the "voice" of life, but as the "image" of life, an important misperception on Adorno's part that betrays his bias regarding the priority of language over vision, which will be elaborated upon further in the final chapter of this book.

32. Cf. *MM*, 56, 100, 102, 104. In *Creative Evolution*, he cautions his readers "to not be fooled by a metaphor" (*CE*, 64) because many a scientific explanation "is merely verbal," making us "again the dupes of words" (*CE*, 65), because practical life often "suggest[s] to us . . . a way of speaking that deceives us both as to what happens in things and as to what is present to our thought" (*CE*, 259). Words are "pseudo-ideas" (*CE*, 308) or mere "mirages of ideas" (*Intro*, 65) that mean nothing and are potentially dangerous as they give rise to misconceptions and false ideas of all kinds. Similarly *CE*, 20, 203, 233, 299, 305, 317.

33. In his later works, Bergson increasingly acknowledges the relationship between language and life as central to his entire enterprise: "Whether it be intellection or intuition, thought, of course, always utilizes language; and intuition, like all thought, finally becomes lodged in concepts" (*Intro*, 35). The true challenge hence consisted in questioning and ultimately overcoming language: "My investigation into the true philosophical method began the moment I threw overboard verbal solutions, having found in the inner life an important field of experiment," concludes Bergson (*Intro*, 89f.). Once philosophy decides "to cast aside ready-made ideas and to make contact with the thing" (*Intro*, 83), theoretical problems hitherto deemed insoluble will disappear without a trace since they were "unreal" to begin with and owed their existence merely to our tendency to substitute words for things, concepts for matter, models for life itself.

34. Cf. Gilles Deleuze, *Bergsonism*, 58–60.

35. "If metaphysics is possible," Bergson asserts, "it is through a vision and not through a dialectic" (*Intro*, 139). See also Deleuze, *Bergsonism*, 44.

36. "Poetry never substitutes one thing for another, because poetry strives feverishly to present the thing itself. . . . —So there are no comparisons? There are no symbols? — Oh no, there is rather nothing but that, nothing different" ([N]iemals setzt die Poesie eine Sache für eine andere, denn es ist gerade die Poesie, welche fieberhaft bestrebt ist, die Sache selbst zu setzen. . . . — Es gibt also keine Vergleiche? Es gibt keine Symbole? — Oh, vielmehr, es gibt nichts als das, nichts anderes) ("Das Gespräch über Gedichte," in *Erzählungen*, 498f.).

37. At the end of one of his public lectures entitled "Der Dichter und diese Zeit" from 1906, Hofmannsthal acknowledges that the quasi-religious experience he advocates in the form of poetic language presupposes his listener's belief in the existence and relevance of art: "I only address those who want to go with me, but not him who has promised himself to reject all of this. I can only speak for those who see that poetry is there. It is because of the existence of these people that poets are granted a life of their own" ([I]ch rede nur für die, die mit mir gehen wollen, und nicht für den, der sich sein Wort gegeben hat, dies alles von sich abzulehnen. Ich kann nur für die reden, für die Gedichtetes da ist. Die, durch deren Dasein die Dichter erst ein Leben bekommen) ("Dichter"; *RA*; *GW* I: 79).

38. The point is made explicit in his lecture on "Poesie und Leben," where Hofmannsthal first demands the strict separation of art and life and then concludes: "You are surprised by what I say. You are disappointed and think that I

drive life out of poetry.... But rest assured that I will give this life back to you" (Sie wundern sich über mich. Sie sind enttäuscht und finden, daß ich Ihnen das Leben aus der Poesie vertreibe.... Auch seien Sie unbesorgt: ich werde Ihnen das Leben wiedergeben) ("Poesie und Leben"; *RA; GW* I: 18f.).

39. See his public lecture from 1907 entitled "Vom Dichterischen Dasein" (*RA; GW* I: 82-87) in which he explicitly relates the time periods around 1800 and 1900 as poetic, while denouncing the nineteenth century as unpoetic.

40. See also "Nachlaß"; *RA; GW* III: 316, 400.

41. Jacques Derrida, *Grammatologie*, 30.

42. Friedrich Nietzsche, *The Will to Power*, ed. and trans. Walter Kaufmann (New York: Random House, 1967), 544; qtd. in Edward Jones, *Reading the Book of Nature* (Athens: Ohio University Press, 1989), 1.

EXCURSUS

1. "Narren, die den Verfall der Kritik beklagen. Denn deren Stunde ist längst abgelaufen. Die 'Unbefangenheit,' der 'freie Blick' sind Lüge... geworden." Walter Benjamin, "Einbahnstraße," vol. 4/1 of *Gesammelte Schriften*, 131.

2. Hans Ulrich Gumbrecht, "A Farewell to Interpretation," in *Materialities of Communication*, 389-402.

3. Cf. Friedrich A. Kittler, *Discourse Networks 1800/1900*, 70-123.

4. Diane P. Michelfelder and Richard E. Palmer, eds., *Dialogue and Deconstruction: The Gadamer-Derrida Encounter*, 52-57.

5. See, for example, G. B. Madison, "Gadamer/Derrida: The Hermeneutics of Irony and Power," in *Dialogue and Deconstruction*, 192-98; and John D. Caputo, "Gadamer's Closet Essentialism: A Derridian Critique," in *Dialogue and Deconstruction*, 258-64.

6. Cf. Manfred Frank, *Das Individuelle Allgemeine* (Frankfurt: Suhrkamp, 1977).

7. Manfred Frank, *Das Sagbare und das Unsagbare. Studien zur deutschfranzösischen Hermeneutik und Texttheorie* (Frankfurt: Suhrkamp, 1989), 20, 334, and throughout.

8. See Gumbrecht and Pfeiffer, *Schrift*, 390, as well as "A Farewell to Interpretation," 396.

9. Cf. Wilhelm Dilthey, "Die Entstehung der Hermeneutik," in vol. 5 of *Gesammelte Schriften* (Stuttgart: Teubner, 1964), 317-31: 331.

10. Cf. Gadamer, "Hermeneutics and Logocentrism," in *Dialogue and Deconstruction*, 119 and throughout. Similarly Manfred Frank, *Die Unhintergehbarkeit von Individualität—Reflexionen über Subjekt, Person und Individuum aus Anlaß ihrer 'Postmodernen' Toterklärung* (Frankfurt: Suhrkamp, 1986). Individuality, in Frank's view, describes a nonidentical, yet self-reflexive, mode of consciousness

that is not the cause of its own being, but the locus of a "continuous transformation of different statuses pertaining to one person at a time." Manfred Frank and Anselm Haverkamp, eds., *Individualität* (München: Fink, 1988), 19.

11. Almost the same wording can be found in Jacques Derrida, for whom "[i]t deconstructs it-self." Jacques Derrida, "Letter to a Japanese Friend," in *A Derrida Reader: Between the Blinds*, ed. Peggy Kamuf (New York: Columbia University Press, 1991), 274.

12. See his response in *RT*, 117.

13. In his recent book *The End of the Poem*, Giorgio Agamben appears among the most outspoken critics of the "deconstruction factory" he sees at work in literary criticism, which should not obscure the fact, however, that, in earlier years, he himself used to be on its board of directors, so to speak. More to the point, however, is the lack of a viable alternative evident in his critique as well. Charging deconstruction with a "theological foundation" that focuses on the "primacy of the signifier and the letter" in poetic works (77), he claims to detect the origins of modern European lyric poetry in twelfth-century poetry instead: "The razo, which lies at the foundation of poetry . . . is therefore neither a biographical nor a linguistic event. It is instead a zone of indifference, so to speak, between lived experience and what is poeticized [il poetato], an 'experience of speech' as an inexhaustible experience of love" (79). Although Agamben tries to flesh out this "zone of indifference" in several other essays, I fail to see how it differs from Heidegger's notion of "aletheia" or unconcealment that strongly influenced French deconstruction.

14. See, for example, Hans Hauge, "De la Grammatologie und die literarische Wende," in Gumbrecht and Pfeiffer, *Schrift*, 319–35.

15. Cf. Robert Holub, *Crossing Borders: Reception Theory, Poststructuralism, Deconstruction* (Madison: University of Wisconsin Press, 1992), 43. For a more comprehensive and well-balanced critique of Kittler's work in general, see the introduction to *Gramophone, Film, Typewriter* by Geoffrey Winthrop-Young and Michael Wutz, xi–xli.

16. Clemens Heselhaus, "Das metaphorische Gedicht von Georg Trakl," in *Deutsche Lyrik der Moderne von Nietzsche bis Ivan Goll* (Düsseldorf: Bagel, 1961), 228–57; Walter Killy, *Über Georg Trakl* (Göttingen: Vandenhoeck, 1967).

17. Cf. Louis Althusser, *For Marx*, trans. Ben Brewster (New York: Vintage, 1970).

18. Cf. Louis Althusser, *For Marx*, 232. For a more comprehensive account of Althusser's notion of ideology, see Louis Althusser, "Ideology and Ideological State Apparati: Notes towards an Investigation," in *Essays* (London: Verso, 1984), 1–60.

19. Cf. Winthrop-Young and Michael Wutz, "Introduction," xvi–xviii.

20. Cf. Wellbery, "Foreword," 17ff.; David Wellbery, "The Exteriority of Writing," *Stanford Literature Review* 9 (1): 11–24; Hans Ulrich Gumbrecht, "Interpret-

ing vs. Understanding Systems," *Cardozo Law Review* 13/5, special issue (March 1992): 1505–16.

21. Cf. Gumbrecht, *In 1926*, 411–20.

22. See Carsten Strathausen, "Althusser's Mirror," *Studies in Twentieth Century Literature* 24 (Winter 1994): 58–71.

23. For a comprehensive critique of Foucault's epistemological dilemma, see Manfred Frank, *Das Sagbare und das Unsagbare*, 362–426.

24. Cf. Niklas Luhmann, *Soziale Systeme. Grundriß einer Allgemeinen Theorie* (Frankfurt: Suhrkamp, 1987), 7–15 in particular. For an excellent discussion of the broader implications of Luhmann's work, see William Rasch, *Niklas Luhmann's Modernity: The Paradoxes of Differentiation* (Stanford: Stanford University Press, 2000).

25. Winthrop-Young and Wutz, "Introduction," xxxvii.

26. Cf. Heidegger, *Einführung in die Metaphysik*, 110: "Was der Spruch des Parmenides ausspricht, ist eine Bestimmung des Wesens des Menschen aus dem Wesen des Seins selbst" (What Parmenides' saying expresses is a determination of the human essence on the basis of the essence of Being itself) (*Introduction to Metaphysics* 153); also *Einführung in die Metaphysik*, 130: "Das Menschsein bestimmt sich aus dem Bezug zum Seienden als solches im Ganzen. Das Menschenwesen zeigt sich hier als der Bezug, der dem Menschen erst das Sein eröffnet" (Being-human is determined by the relation to beings as such and as a whole. The human *essence* shows itself here as the relation that first opens up Being to humanity) (*Introduction to Metaphysics* 181).

27. Gianni Vattimo, "An-denken: Thinking and the Foundation," in *The Adventure of Difference: Philosophy after Nietzsche and Heidegger*, trans. Cyprian Blamires and Thomas Harrison (Baltimore: Johns Hopkins University Press, 1993), 110–35: 128.

28. This period concerns Heidegger's thought after the publication of *Sein und Zeit* (1927), during which he increasingly shifted emphasis from the analysis of *Dasein* to that of "Being" proper and the "Seinsvergessenheit" of the modern age. On the notion of the turn in Heidegger's philosophy, see James Risser, "Introduction," in *Heidegger toward the Turn*, 1–16.

29. Cf. Terry Eagleton, *Walter Benjamin or Towards a Revolutionary Criticism* (London: Verso, 1981), 141; and Martin Jay, *Adorno* (Cambridge: Harvard University Press, 1984), 21ff.

30. For Adorno, Heidegger's "Ursprungsphilosophie" is directly related to social domination and the rise of fascism: "Fascism sought to realize a first philosophy.... The identity of fascism and originality amounted to the notion that he who had the power should be not merely the first one, but also the original one" (Der Faschismus suchte die Ursprungsphilosophie zu verwirklichen.... Die Identität von Ursprünglichkeit und Herrschaft lief darauf hinaus, daß wer die Macht hat, nicht bloß der Erste, sondern auch der Ursprüngliche sein sollte) (*Zur Metakritik*

der Erkenntnistheorie, 28). Similar comments are dispersed throughout Adorno's work. For a comprehensive discussion of the topic, see Mörchen, 364–90.

31. This is Hermann Mörchen's central thesis in his study on *Adorno und Heidegger*. Although Mörchen at times overstates the similarity between the two, he nonetheless provides ample and detailed evidence of Adorno's often misguided critique of Heidegger's work, particularly with regard to their shared views on language and the movement of philosophical thought. More recently, Rüdiger Safranski also comments on Adorno's "dangerous philosophical affinity with the person he attacked," Rüdiger Safranski, *Martin Heidegger: Between Good and Evil*.

32. George Lukács, *Von Nietzsche zu Hitler oder Der Irrationalismus und die Deutsche Politik*. For a specific critique of Lukács, see Adorno's essay "Erpreßte Versöhnung," in *Noten zur Literatur, GS* 11: 251–80.

33. See Joel Whitebook, *Perversion and Utopia: A Study in Psychoanalysis and Critical Theory* (Cambridge: Massachusetts Institute of Technology Press, 1995), 151–52 in particular, as well as Sabine Wilke and Heidi Schlipphacke, "Construction of a Gendered Subject: A Feminist Reading of Adorno's Aesthetic Theory," in *The Semblance of Subjectivity: Essays in Adorno's Aesthetic Theory*, ed. Tom Huhn and Lambert Zuidervaart (Cambridge: Massachusetts Institute of Technology Press, 1997), 287–308.

34. See Richard Wolin, "Benjamin, Adorno, Surrealism," in *The Semblance of Subjectivity*, 93–122.

CHAPTER 3

1. Walter Müller-Seidel, "Epochenverwandtschaft. Zum Verhältnis von Moderne und Romantik im deutschen Sprachgebiet," in *Geschichtlichkeit und Aktualität. Studien zur Literatur seit der Romantik*, ed. Klaus-Detlev Müller et al. (Tübingen: Niemeyer, 1988), 370–92.

2. Peter Bürger, *Theorie der Avantgarde* (Frankfurt: Suhrkamp, 1974); [English translation: Peter Bürger, *Theory of the Avant-Garde*, trans. Michael Shaw (Minneapolis: University of Minnesota Press, 1984)]. See Andreas Huyssen, "The Search for Tradition: Avant-Garde and Postmodernism in the 1970s," in *After the Great Divide: Modernism, Mass Culture, Postmodernism* (Bloomington: Indiana University Press, 1986), 160–77; Richard Murphy, *Theorizing the Avant-Garde: Modernism, Expressionism, and the Problem of Postmodernity* (Cambridge: Cambridge University Press, 1999), 26–48. Murphy in particular argues that Bürger's theory needs to be revised in order to provide a more nuanced understanding of aesthetic autonomy and aura at the beginning of the twentieth century.

3. Kittler, *Discourse Networks*, 217–18.

4. Cf. David E. Wellbery, *The Specular Moment: Goethe's Early Lyric and the Beginnings of Romanticism* (Stanford: Stanford University Press, 1996).

5. Georg Braungart, *Leibhafter Sinn. Der andere Diskurs der Moderne* (Tübingen: Niemeyer, 1995).

6. Safranski convincingly argues this point in *Martin Heidegger,* 225–306. See also Slavoj Zizek, *The Ticklish Subject: The Absent Centre of Political Ontology* (London: Verso, 1999), 10–11.

CHAPTER 4

1. About Borchardt: "It is as a speaking person that he becomes an organ of language. Rhetoric is concerned with its own conjuration. By imitating speech, his poetry makes itself resemble the potential of language, so that that potential can be manifested.... To Borchardt, the man who charmed language until it threatened to break into pieces with a clatter, language did not refuse its echo" (*Notes* II: 196, 210) (Als Redender wird er Organon der Sprache. Ihrer eigenen Beschwörung gilt die Rhetorik. Seine Dichtung macht durch Mimesis an die Rede dem Potential sich ähnlich, damit es erscheine.... Der die Sprache beschwor, bis sie klirrend zu zerspringen drohte, dem hat sie das Echo nicht versagt) ("Die beschworene Sprache"; *GS* 11: 539, 555). About George: "In George's poetry the technical work ... in an individual poem is almost always work on language as such at the same time.... For George, labeled as a *l'art pout l'art* artist, not the individual work, but language, in and through the work of art, was the highest ideal; he wanted nothing less than to change language" (*Notes* II: 187) (Stets fast ist die technische Arbeit der Georgeschen Lyrik ... im einzelnen Gedicht zugleich die an der Sprache als solcher.... Dem als l'art pour l'art-Künstler Abgestempelten war keineswegs das einzelne Kunstwerk oberstes Ideal sondern durch es hindurch die Sprache: nicht weniger wollte er, als sie verändern) ("George"; *GS* 11: 531). About Eichendorff: "The subject turns itself into *Rauschen,* the rushing, rustling, murmuring sound of nature: into language, living on only in the process of dying away, like language. The act in which the human being becomes language, the flesh becomes word, incorporates the expression of nature into language and transfigures the movement of language so that it becomes life again" (*Notes* I: 68–69) (Zum Rauschen macht sich das Subjekt selber: zur Sprache, überdauernd bloß im Verhallen wie diese. Der Akt der Versprachlichung des Menschen, ein Wortwerden des Fleisches, bildet der Sprache den Ausdruck von Natur ein und transfiguriert ihre Bewegung ins Leben noch einmal) ("Zum Gedächtnis Eichendorffs"; *GS* 11: 83–84).

2. In Adorno's words: "[L]anguage itself speaks only when it speaks not as something alien to the subject but as the subject's own voice" (*Notes* I: 44) ([E]rst dann redet Sprache selber, wenn sie nicht länger als ein dem Subjekt Fremdes redet sondern als dessen eigene Stimme) ("Rede"; *GS* 11: 57).

3. Gianni Vattimo's discussion of poetry provides an interesting context for this debate. See his "The Shattering of the Poetic Word," in *The End of Modernity,* 65–78.

4. *The Lyrical Poems of Hofmannsthal*, trans. Charles Wharton Stork (New Haven: Yale University Press, 1918), 23-24.

5. Adorno: "Images which express the true impulse of poems such as 'Frühlingswind' or those about the ice landscapes in [George's] 'Jahr der Seele' are taboo. . . . What is being misrecognized is nothing less than the formal principles that govern their own poetry" (Tabuisiert sind die Bilder, in denen die wahren Impulse des Gedichts vom Frühlingswind oder der Eislandschaften des 'Jahres der Seele' sich verwirklichen. . . . Verkannt wird nichts Geringeres als das Formgesetz, dem die eigene Dichtung untersteht) ("George und Hofmannsthal," 231). See also Klaus Weissenberger, "Rhythmische Grenzziehungen in Hofmannsthal's Lyrik," in *Wir sind aus solchem Zeug wie das zu träumen. . . . Kritische Beiträge zu Hofmannsthal's Werk*, ed. Joseph P. Strelka (Bern: Lang, 1992), 49-80: 78-80.

6. *Blätter für die Kunst*, dritte Folge, 3. Bd.

7. Cf. "Ad me ipsum" (1917) as well as "Ein Brief" (1902) and "Die Briefe des Zurückgekehrten" (1907). Concerning the poetic function of the *Augenblick* in Hofmannsthal's work, see Karl Pestalozzi, "Wandlungen des erhöhten Augenblicks bei Hofmannsthal," and Wiethölter, 23-46.

8. A recent study, aptly entitled *Leiblichkeit der Sprache, Sprachlichkeit des Leibes*, is among the first to explicitly oppose this dualism between verbal and physical language that allegedly characterizes Hofmannsthal's oeuvre: "The particular quality of Hofmannsthal's understanding of language, which the secondary literature so far has not yet sufficiently acknowledged, lies in his retreat to (or advancing toward) the psychic-physical origin of language as the place that unites body and word, world and language" (Vielmehr liegt der besondere, bisher von der Forschung noch kaum in ihrer Tragweite erkannte und gewürdigte Qualität der Sprachauffassung Hofmannsthals in seinem Rückgang (oder Vorstoß) zum psychisch-physischen Ausgangs- und Angelpunkt der Sprache als dem Ort einer Ursprungseinheit von Leib und Wort, und das heißt schließlich von Welt und Sprache) (Rutsch, 4-5). For a comprehensive overview of the critical literature, see Rutsch, 13-43.

9. Cf. Braungart, 230-35.

10. For a detailed discussion of Hofmannsthal's projects, see Oksiloff, 70ff.; and Elke C. Furthman-Durden, "Hugo von Hofmannsthal and Alfred Döblin: The Confluence of Film and Literature," *Monatshefte* 78/4 (1986).

11. The similarity between both texts spanning almost two decades further undermines the traditional view of a rupture in Hofmannsthal's life and work allegedly evident in the Chandos Letter. On the contrary, the language-crisis emerges as a literary theme open to readjustments and modifications over the time.

12. Cf. Oksiloff, 75-76; Steiner, 171-74.

13. Cf. Oksiloff, 80.

14. Similarly Christian Metz, who reformulates Baudry's thesis with regard to the dominance of the plot in narrative films: "The rule of the 'story' is so powerful

that the image, which is said to be the major constituent of film, vanished behind the plot it has woven . . . so that the cinema is only in theory the art of images. . . . The sequence does not string the individual shots; it suppresses them" (*Film Language*, 45).

15. Rudolf Borchardt's view is paradigmatic: "Since Goethe, he [Hofmannsthal] . . . is the first poet able to elevate his personal suffering to a status of general validity and total aesthetic value . . ." (Er [Hofmannsthal] . . . ist seit Goethe der erste Dichter, der einem selbstdurchlittenen problematischen Zustande durch den Ernst der Vertiefung, die Gewalt der Vision und die Verbindung mit allem höheren Dasein seiner Zeit Allgemeingültigkeit und völligen Kunstwert zu geben gewußt hat) (Borchardt, qtd. in Adorno, "George und Hofmannsthal," 210). More skeptical in this regard is Karl Pestalozzi, *Sprachskepsis und Sprachmagie*, 116-17. For a comprehensive summary of academic perspectives of the postwar generation up to the 1980s, see Koch, 131-34.

16. Donald G. Daviau, for example, reverses the commonly held belief about Hofmannsthal's "language-crisis" and concludes that "Hofmannsthal's view of language remains consistently positive throughout his life and contains no inconsistencies. His relationship to language was never negative and was by no means the problematic issue that the scholarship to date would have us believe" (Daviau, 302). Similarly, Jacques le Rider insists on disassociating Hofmannsthal himself from his fictional hero in "Ein Brief." He argues that Hofmannsthal's early work is characterized not by a "language-crisis," but by playful reference to normative historical traditions whose validity is continuously being challenged and redefined within the text. With regard to the "Chandos Letter," le Rider's reading is supported by a personal letter Hofmannsthal wrote to his friend Leopold von Andrian in 1902, which indicates that Hofmannsthal used the historical framework in the "Letter" mainly as a way to approach a particular linguistic tradition, while any personal reference to his own life was of secondary importance. On the basis of this letter—which contradicts another, more often quoted letter to Andrian a couple of months earlier, emphasizing the personal character of the "Chandos Letter"—le Rider rejects the commonly held belief that Hofmannsthal's "Letter" thematizes his own personal language-crisis. See also Riedel, 3.

17. See also Hofmannsthal's brief essay "Die Sprache" from 1896 ("Nachlaß"; *RA*; *GW* III: 413f.).

18. In many of Hofmannsthal's lyrical plays, nature looks back at the beholder. For example in "Das kleine Welttheater" when the poet contemplates nature: "Nun setz ich mich am Rand des Waldes hin, / Wo kleine Weiher lange noch den Glanz / Des Tages halten und mit feuchtem Funkeln / Die offnen Augen dieser Landschaft scheinen" ("Das kleine Welttheater"; *GW* I: 373). This gaze possesses the quality of touch: "Mit den Augen, den beseelten Fingern / Rührt ers an und nimmt sich ein Geheimnis . . ." (*GW* I: 382). Under the auspices of this gaze, being and meaning are revealed to be one, as Hofmannsthal notes in 1894: "Sein und

Bedeuten. Die Seele der Dinge, etwas das aus den Dingen uns mit Liebesblick anschaut, mit einem Ausdruck über allen Worten" ("Nachlaß"; *RA; GW* III: 387).

19. Cf. Wunberg, *Der Frühe Hofmannsthal*, 106–9.

20. That is Georg Braungart's perspective, 220–21.

21. The same metaphor also appears in other contexts such as "Die Briefe des Zurückgekehrten" (*Gespräche* 560–61) and the drama "Der Turm" (*Dramen; GW* III: 245).

22. Georg Braungart similarly distinguishes between what he calls the first and the third phase in Chandos's life: "Das Subjekt dieses ersten Zustandes glaubt, in einem Rausch der Sprachsouveränität sich der Welt bemächtigen zu können, und scheitert. Das Subjekt des dritten Zustandes, jener unverfügbaren Momente der Epiphanie und des mythischen Einsseins mit aller Kreatur, gibt sich selbst auf, geht einfühlend über in die einfachsten, niedrigsten Dinge: eine bei aller scheinbaren Parallelität genaue Kontrafaktur zu dem Drang des früheren Lords nach den letzten, höchsten Wahrheiten" (Braungart, 221). And Wolfgang Riedel summarizes his reading as follows: "Stellte sich ihm [Chandos] damals 'das Ich als Universum' dar, so heute das Universum als Ich. Oder zugespitzt: Legte er damals das im Selbstbewußtsein, als Geist, gegebene Ich in die Welt und das Leben hinaus, so gewahrt er die Welt und das Leben jetzt in sich selbst, freilich nicht im Bewußtsein, sondern in der Naturalität seines Leibes" (Riedel, 37–38). Riedel's comment echoes Adorno's formulation about Aestheticist poetry: "Anstatt daß Dinge als Symbole der Subjektivität nachgäben, gibt Subjektivität nach als Symbol der Dinge, bereit, in sich selber schließlich zu dem Ding zu erstarren, zu dem sie von der Gesellschaft ohnehin gemacht wird" ("George und Hofmannsthal," 234).

23. Gerhard Austin's *Phänomenologie der Gebärde* is typical in this regard. Austin juxtaposes bodily gestures and verbal forms of expression, claiming that the former cannot possibly be fully appreciated through language and must be physically enacted instead. Once he has postulated the "principle difference between immediate sensual and verbal experience" (47), he prioritizes the authentic "expression" of the former over the latter without recognizing the fundamental *petitio principi* of his approach, namely that a gesture expresses nothing at all outside its specific operative code, that is, its own "language."

24. Fick, 345–47; Georg Braungart, 219–29; Kittler, *Discourse Networks*, 217–18.

CHAPTER 5

1. Rainer Maria Rilke, qtd. in Käte Hamburger, 86.

2. All Rilke quotes given in the body of the text refer to the following edition: Rainer Maria Rilke, *Sämtliche Werke*, 6 vols., ed. Ruth Sieber-Rilke (Frankfurt: Insel, 1987).

3. Rainer Maria Rilke, *Poems from The Book of Hours*, trans. Babette Deutsch (Norfolk, Conn.: New Directions, 1941), 11.

4. Rainer Maria Rilke, *The Book of Images: A Bilingual Edition*, trans. Edward Snow (San Francisco: North Point Press, 1991), 5.

5. ". . . nur für die Arbeit eingerichtet, zwingen sie [Rodins Werkstätten] ihn [den Besucher], das Schauen als Arbeit auf sich zu nehmen."

6. Peter Por's recent analysis of the *New Poems* is haunted by the same dilemma. In contrast to Judith Ryan, Por argues that although his poems fail to rescue the real "outside" within the realm of poetic language, they are themselves conscious of this failure to become what they proclaim to be. Yet, for Por, it is precisely this failure that guarantees the poem's success: "The divine figure of art, which ultimately is nothing but the new poem itself, realizes and completes itself in the extreme transcendence of its own nonbeing" (Die göttliche Gestalt der Kunst, gemeint ist letztendlich das neue Gedicht selbst, verwirklicht und vollbringt sich in der äußersten Transzendenz ihres eigenen Nicht-Seins) (127). Although an adequate description of Rilke's poetic ideals, this practice of negative transcendence hardly warrants the predicate "realization" Por bestows upon it. For a more comprehensive overview regarding this debate, see Köhnen, 254–60.

7. "Der Wahrheitsgehalt der Kunstwerke ist die objektive Auflösung des Rätsels eines jeden einzelnen. Indem es die Lösung verlangt, verweist es auf den Wahrheitsgehalt. Der ist allein durch philosophische Reflexion zu gewinnen. Das, nichts anderes rechtfertigt Ästhetik" (*Ästhetische Theorie* 193) (The truth content of artworks is the objective solution of the enigma posed by each and every one. By demanding its solution, the enigma points to its truth content. It can only be achieved by philosophical reflection. This alone is the justification of aesthetics) (*Aesthetic Theory* 127f.).

8. This verdict notwithstanding, Adorno, in a typical dialectical move, at times salvages Rilke's aesthetic failure for a critique of the sociopolitical reality he claims responsible for it. Because of its involuntary revelation of the power of commodification in modern society, Rilke's reified poetry is said to "still stand on the verge" between simple irrationalism and the protest against it ("Jargon" 469): "The aesthetic weakness of this cult of the thing, its obscurantist demeanor and its blending of religion with arts and crafts, reveals the real power of reification, which can no longer be gilded with a lyrical halo and brought back within the sphere of meaning" (Adorno, *Notes* I, 40) ([D]ie ästhetische Schwäche dieses Dingkults, der geheimnistuerische Gestus, die Vermischung von Religion und Kunstgewerbe, verrät zugleich die reale Gewalt der Verdinglichung, die von keiner lyrischen Aura mehr sich vergolden, in den Sinn einholen läßt) ("Rede" 52).

9. "Ein jedes Ding kann der liebe Gott sein. Man muß es ihm nur sagen" (*Werke* IV: 355).

10. ". . . daß man leise begann, statt *von den* Dingen, *mit den* Dingen zu sprechen, also: 'subjektiv' zu werden" ("Moderne Lyrik"; *Werke* V: 370).

11. Ultimately, Hamburger's approach yields its own premise as the conclusion: Rilke wrote poetry in lieu of philosophy, and his oeuvre describes—in fact, it is—phenomenology at work, leading Hamburger to muse how much Husserl might have "envied" Rilke's philosophical insights (132) had he only known how to read poetry (97). Such aberrations aside, her analysis is problematic in several aspects. First, she implies that Rilke's poems fully transcend the metaphorical nature of language; at one point, she reads his reference to a tree not as literary image anymore, but "as the object itself" (143). Second, her attempt to "demonstrate" the central ideas of Husserl's philosophy (99) via Rilke leads to the simplification of some of Husserl's key terms such as "phenomenon," which Hamburger simply identifies with the perceptual appearance of things. For Husserl, however, phenomena originally referred to the "real immanence" of mental acts and only in his later works became identified with the intended object of such acts (the noema). Moreover, it remains unclear how exactly to envision the "phenomenological structure" that Hamburger sees realized in Rilke's poetry. For Husserl, phenomenology served as a basis for modern science. As Hamburger herself notes, it is characterized and employed as a method, a particular approach toward examining the structure of human consciousness and its relationship to the transcendental world. Hence, phenomenology itself is anything but a "structure," and Hamburger's entire essay culminates in the coerced effort to equate Rilke's poetic form with phenomenology's very own essence, as if the latter were but yet another of the many "things" the former seeks to describe. Another example of Hamburger's problematic reading of Husserl is her understanding of "intentionality," which she sees exemplified in the "Ich-Du" chiasm that structures Rilke's *Stundenbuch*. Husserl, however, did not face the philosophical problem of the "other" until the very end of his career, meaning that intentionality, for him, precisely did not denote the relationship between two subjects, but rather described the internal structure of intentional acts taking place in human consciousness. To regard the polar structure of the *Stundenbuch* as evidence or even the embodiment of "the problem of intentionality" is as misguided as the entire attempt to find direct correspondences between Husserl's philosophy and Rilke's poetry. This is not to deny the striking similarities between them, many of which are made evident in Hamburger's analysis, but to call for the critical investigation of both Husserl's and Rilke's vision of the world and the different means they sought to express it linguistically.

CHAPTER 6

1. *Blätter für die Kunst*, erste Folge, erstes Heft (1892).
2. Georges "Wille zur Form, dieses neue Formgefühl, das ist nicht Ästhetizismus, nicht Intellektualismus, nicht Formalismus, sondern höchster Glaube."

3. Even Thomas Mann characterized George's poetry as the "incarnation of spirit and the spiritualization of flesh" (Verleiblichung des Geistes und die Vergeistigung des Fleisches) (qtd. in Breuer, 227).

4. *Blätter für die Kunst,* dritte Folge, viertes Heft (1896); Landmann, 18f.

5. *Blätter für die Kunst,* dritte Folge, 5. Bd.

6. Numerous critics have echoed this verdict. In the eyes of Gottfried Benn, George's poetry is characterized by the "merciless harshness of formality" (unerbittliche Härte des Formalen) (Benn, "Stefan George," 1038), and Gundolf praises George's "infinite control over language" (schrankenlose Gewalt über die Sprache) (Gundolf, 78). This poetic "control" or "violence," however, cannot but kill the life it claims to have captured. The world as seen through George's poetry shrinks to a faint reflection or a mere shadow of the original "Urbild" it cannot represent. Benjamin rightly claimed that George's Aestheticist stance "removed life itself from the world" ("Rückblick"; *GS* III: 396). Claude David's reading of George's inaugural poem for the *Hymnen,* entitled "Die Weihe," gives a more explicit account of this poetic violence: "Die hier beschriebene Landschaft, . . . wird dermaßen stilisiert, man möchte sagen inszeniert, daß sie jede Realität verliert. Alle Sinneseindrücke sind abgestumpft oder werden verschwiegen; . . . Statt der freudigen Fülle eines impressionistischen Bildes, statt der malerischen Wirkung wird nur noch der Stil verlangt. Nur das Sinnvolle, das Symbolische wird beibehalten" (David, 216ff.).

7. See *Stefan George im Bildnis,* ed. Walther Greischel and Michael Stettler (Düsseldorf: Küpper, 1976).

8. Cf. *Blätter für die Kunst,* neunte Folge (1910); Landmann, 52.

9. According to Bertolt Brecht, George was "openly counterrevolutionary underneath his mask of despising politics, meaning he was not only reactionary, but was actually working for the counterrevolution" (unter der Maske der Verachtung der Politik ganz offen konterrevolutionär, d.h. nicht nur reaktionär sondern wirkend für die Konterrevolution) (qtd. in Klnucker 27). Similarly Georg Lukács, *Schriften zur Literatursoziologie,* ed. Peter Christian Lutz (Neuwied: Luchterhand, 1963), 474–75. A comprehensive overview regarding the prewar debate about George's relationship to National Socialism can be found in Martin A. Siemoneit, *Politische Interpretationen von Stefan Georges Dichtung* (Frankfurt: Lang, 1978), 13–19. Needless to say, the entire debate concerning George's relationship to German history was, and still is, mostly static, resembling a kind of trench warfare characterized by both sides continuously reiterating their own ideological concerns and personal beliefs without advancing new insights into either George's work or the aesthetics of fascism.

10. Volker Kapp, "Vom Bild als Übergegenwärtigung zum Bild als Simulation und Verrätzelung der Welt," in *Bilderwelten als Vergegenwärtigung und Verrätzelung der Welt,* ed. Volker Kapp et al. (Berlin: Duncker, 1997), 9–30; Klaus Schuhmacher, "Brüder der Schmerzen," in *Bilderwelten als Vergegenwärtigung und Verrätzelung der Welt,* 195–216: 195f.

11. Heidegger's description of art is reminiscent of Benjamin's understanding of aura since they both discuss the essence of art in a series of paradoxical formulations in which the furthest distance is revealed as the closest proximity. Cf. Martin Heidegger, "Andenken," in vol. 4 of *GA*, 147. See also McNeill's *The Glance of the Eye*, 292.

12. Similarly in *Jargon of Authenticity:* "The jargon is neither able nor willing to render concrete what it condemns to abstraction. . . . The unsalvageability of what this kind of thinking aims to rescue is being declared as its most unique element. It rejects any content against which one could argue at all" (Weder ist der Jargon fähig noch gesonnen, zu konkretisieren, was er zur Abstraktheit verdammt. . . . Die Unrettbarkeit dessen, was dies Denken retten will, wird weltklug zu dessen eigenem Element gemacht. Es weist jeden Inhalt von sich, gegen den zu argumentieren wäre) ("Jargon," 475).

13. Cf. Adorno's critique of the coppola "ist" in *Negative Dialektik*, 107–11.

14. Borrowing Benjamin's concept of "constellation," Adorno emphasizes the friction of colliding and interconnecting words: "There remains no other hope for him [the philosopher] but to arrange the words around the new truth such that their mere configuration engenders the new truth" (Es bleibt ihm [dem Philosophen] keine Hoffnung als die, die Worte so um die neue Wahrheit zu stellen, daß deren bloße Konfiguration die neue Wahrheit ergibt) ("Thesen," 369). The task of philosophy consists in "[liquefying] the reified movement of thought" rather than declaring it authentic or essential to language.

15. Heidegger, in some remarks on Greek philosophy and Hölderlin's poetry, indeed speaks of the "stove of being": "The stove, the place in the home that is homey [die Heimstatt des Heimischen], is being itself. In its light and sparkle, glow and warmth, all beings have always already gathered themselves" (Heidegger, qtd. in Krell, 5).

16. Although Adorno himself cites the exact passage in his essay on George and Hofmannsthal, he skips over some lines, including this particular sentence, and then continues the quote right after it. The omission "almost" speaks for itself. Cf. "George und Hofmannsthal," 234.

17. For an excellent discussion of Heidegger's various concepts of vision, see McNeill, *The Glance of the Eye*, 1–13.

18. For a comprehensive overview of relevant passages, see Mörchen, 543–60.

19. See Marc Froment-Meurice, *That Is to Say: Heidegger's Poetics* (Stanford: Stanford University Press, 1998), 43–59.

20. Cf. *Unterwegs zur Sprache*, 193.

WORKS CITED

Adorno, Theodor W. *Aesthetic Theory*. Edited by Gretel Adorno and Rolf Tiedemann. Translated by Robert Hullot-Kentor. Minneapolis: University of Minnesota Press, 1997.
———. *Against Epistemology. A Metacritique: Studies in Husserl and the Phenomenological Antinomies*. Cambridge: Massachusetts Institute of Technology Press, 1982.
———. "Die Aktualität der Philosophie." *Philosophische Frühschriften*. Vol. 1 of *Gesammelte Schriften*, 325–44.
———. *Ästhetische Theorie*. Vol. 7 of *Gesammelte Schriften*.
———. "Die Beschworene Sprache." *Noten zur Literatur*. Vol. 11 of *Gesammelte Schriften*, 536–55.
———. *Dialektik der Aufklärung*. Vol. 3 of *Gesammelte Schriften*.
———. "Erpreßte Versöhnung." *Noten zur Literatur*. Vol. 11 of *Gesammelte Schriften*, 251–80.
———. "Der Essay als Form." *Noten zur Literatur*. Vol. 11 of *Gesammelte Schriften*, 9–33.
———. "George." *Noten zur Literatur*. Vol. 11 of *Gesammelte Schriften*, 523–35.
———. "George und Hofmannsthal." *Kulturkritik und Gesellschaft*. Vol. 10/2 of *Gesammelte Schriften*, 195–217.
———. *Gesammelte Schriften*. Edited by Rolf Tiedemann. 20 vols. Frankfurt: Suhrkamp, 1973.
———. "Jargon der Eigentlichkeit." Vol. 6 of *Gesammelte Schriften*, 413–523.
———. "Die Kunst und die Künste." *Kulturkritik und Gesellschaft*. Vol. 10/1 of *Gesammelte Schriften*, 432–53.
———. *Minima Moralia: Reflexionen aus dem Beschädigten Leben*. Vol. 4 of *Gesammelte Schriften*.
———. *Negative Dialektik*. Vol. 6 of *Gesammelte Schriften*, 7–412.
———. *Noten zur Literatur*. Vol. 11 of *Gesammelte Schriften*.
———. *Notes to Literature*. 2 vols. Edited by Rolf Tiedemann. Translated by Shierry Weber Nicholsen. New York: Columbia University Press, 1991–92.
———. "Rede über Lyrik und Gesellschaft." *Noten zur Literatur*. Vol. 11 of *Gesammelte Schriften*, 48–68.
———. "Thesen über die Sprache des Philosophen." *Philosophische Frühschriften*. Vol. 1 of *Gesammelte Schriften*, 366–71.

———. "Zum Gedächtnis Eichendorffs." *Noten zur Literatur.* Vol. 11 of *Gesammelte Schriften,* 69–94.
———. *Zur Metakritik der Erkenntnistheorie.* Vol. 4 of *Gesammelte Schriften.*
———. "Zu Subjekt und Objekt." *Kulturkritik und Gesellschaft.* Vol. 10/2 of *Gesammelte Schriften,* 741–58.
Agamben, Giorgio. *The End of the Poem: Studies in Poetics.* Translated by Daniel Heller-Roazen. Stanford: Stanford University Press, 1999.
———. *Potentialities: Collected Essays in Philosophy.* Edited and translated by Daniel Heller-Roazen. Stanford: Stanford University Press, 1999.
———. *Stanzas: Word and Phantasm in Western Culture.* Translated by Ronald L. Martinez. Minneapolis: University of Minnesota Press, 1993.
Asendorf, Christoph. *Ströme und Strahlen. Das Langsame Verschwinden der Materie um 1900.* Berlin: Anabas, 1989.
Assmann, Aleida. "Die Sprache der Dinge. Der Lange Blick und die Wilde Semiose." In *Materialität der Kommunikation,* edited by Hans-Ulrich Gumbrecht and K. Ludwig Pfeiffer, 237–51. Frankfurt: Suhrkamp, 1988.
Austin, Gerhard. *Phänomenologie der Gebärde bei Hugo von Hofmannsthal.* Heidelberg: Winter, 1981.
Bal, Mieke. "Introduction: Visual Poetics." *Style* 22, 2 (Summer 1988): 177–82.
Barthes, Roland. *Camera Lucida: Reflections on Photography.* Translated by Richard Howard. New York: Hill, 1981.
———. *Image, Music, Text.* Translated by Stephen Heath. New York: Hill, 1977.
———. *Writing Degree Zero.* Translated by Annette Lavers. New York: Hill, 1968.
Baudry, Jean-Louis. "Ideological Effects of the Basic Cinematographic Apparatus." In *Film Theory and Criticism,* edited by Gerald Mast and Marshall Cohen, 302–12. 4th ed. New York: Oxford University Press, 1992.
Bell, Jeffrey A. *The Problem of Difference: Phenomenology and Poststructuralism.* Toronto: University of Toronto Press, 1998.
Benjamin, Walter. *Gesammelte Schriften.* 7 vols. Edited by Rolf Tiedeman. Frankfurt: Suhrkamp, 1991.
———. *Illuminationen. Ausgewählte Schriften.* Frankfurt: Suhrkamp, 1977.
———. *Illuminations.* Edited by Hannah Arendt. New York: Schocken, 1969.
———. "Das Kunstwerk im Zeitalter seiner technischen Reproduzierbarkeit." In *Illuminationen,* 136–69.
———. "Über einige Motive bei Baudelaire." In *Illuminationen,* 185–229.
Benn, Gottfried. *Gesammelte Werke in Acht Bänden.* Edited by Dieter Wellershoff. Wiesbaden: Limes, 1959–65.
Bergson, Henri. *Creative Evolution.* Translated by Arthur Mitchell. New York: Random House, 1944.
———. *An Introduction to Metaphysics: The Creative Mind.* Totowa: Rowman, 1989.

———. *Matter and Memory*. Translated by N. M. Paul and W. S. Palmer. New York: Zone, 1991.
Berkeley, George. "Essay towards a New Theory of Vision." In *A New Theory of Vision and Other Select Philosophical Writings*. London: Dent, 1914.
Blätter für die Kunst 1892–1919. Edited by Carl August Klein. Düsseldorf: Küppers, 1968.
Blumenberg, Hans. *Die Lesbarkeit der Welt*. Frankfurt: Suhrkamp, 1981.
Brandstetter, Gabriele, and Gerhard Neumann. "Hofmannsthal 1907. Schrift und Lektüre an der Grenze des Leibes." *Freiburger Universitätsblätter* 30 (1991): 33–75.
Braungart, Georg. *Leibhafter Sinn. Der andere Diskurs der Moderne*. Tübingen: Niemeyer, 1995.
Braungart, Wolfgang. *Ästhetischer Katholizismus. Stefan Georges Rituale der Literatur*. Tübingen: Niemeyer, 1997.
———. *Ritual und Literatur*. Tübingen: Niemeyer, 1996.
Breuer, Stefan. *Ästhetischer Fundamentalismus. Stefan George und der Deutsche Antimodernismus*. Darmstadt: Wissenschaftliche Buchgesellschaft, 1995.
Brinkmann, Richard. "Hofmannsthal und die Sprache." *Deutsche Vierteljahresschrift* 35 (1961): 69–95.
Bryson, Norman. "The Gaze in the Expanded Field." In *Vision and Visuality*, edited by Hal Foster, 87–114. Seattle: Bay Press, 1988.
———. *Vision and Painting: The Logic of the Gaze*. New Haven: Yale University Press, 1983.
Buck-Morss, Susan. *The Origins of Negative Dialectics*. New York: Free Press, 1977.
Burch, Noel. *Life to Those Shadows*. Berkeley: University of California Press, 1990.
Bürger, Peter. *Theorie der Avantgarde*. Frankfurt a.M.: Suhrkamp, 1974.
Burnett, Ron. *Cultures of Vision: Images, Media, and the Imaginary*. Bloomington: Indiana University Press, 1995.
Calhoon, Kenneth S. "Personal Effects: Rilke, Barthes, and the Matter of Photography." *Modern Language Notes* 113 (1998): 612–34.
Castle, Terry. "Phantasmagoria: Spectral Technology and the Metaphorics of Modern Reverie." *Critical Inquiry* 15 (Autumn 1988): 26–61.
Charney, Leo, and Vanessa R. Schwartz. *Cinema and the Invention of Modern Life*. Berkeley: University of California Press, 1995.
Crary, Jonathon. "Modernizing Vision." In *Vision and Visuality*, edited by Hal Foster, 29–50. Seattle: Bay Press, 1988.
———. *Techniques of the Observer: On Vision and Modernity in the Nineteenth Century*. Cambridge: Massachusetts Institute of Technology Press, 1990.
———. "Unbinding Vision: Manet and the Attentive Observer in the Late Nineteenth Century." In *Cinema and the Invention of Modern Life*, edited by

Leo Charney and Vanessa R. Schwartz, 46–71. Berkeley: University of California Press, 1995.

Daviau, Donald G. "Hofmannsthal and Language: A Positive View." In *Wir sind aus solchem Zeug wie das zu träumen. Kritische Beiträge zu Hofmannsthal's Werk*, edited by Joseph P. Strelka, 285–304. Bern: Lang, 1992.

David, Claude. "Stefan George und der Jugendstil." In *Formkräfte der Deutschen Dichtung vom Barock bis zur Gegenwart*, edited by Hans Steffen, 211–28. Göttingen: Vandenhoeck, 1963.

Deleuze, Gilles. *Bergsonism*. Translated by Hugh Tomlinson and Barbara Habberjam. New York: Zone, 1991.

De Man, Paul. *Allegories of Reading: Figural Language in Rousseau, Nietzsche, Rilke, and Proust*. New Haven: Yale University Press, 1979.

———. *The Resistance to Theory*. Minneapolis: University of Minnesota Press, 1986.

———. "The Rhetoric of Blindness." In *Blindness and Insight*, 102–41. Minneapolis: University of Minnesota Press, 1983.

Derrida, Jacques. *Margins of Philosophy*. Translated by Alan Bass. Chicago: University of Chicago Press, 1982.

———. *Of Grammatology*. Translated by Gayatri Chakravorty Spivak. Baltimore: Johns Hopkins University Press, 1998.

———. *Of Spirit: Heidegger and the Question*. Translated by Geoffrey Bennington and Rachel Bowlby. Chicago: University of Chicago Press, 1989.

———. *Speech and Phenomena*. Translated by David B. Allison. Evanston: Northwestern University Press, 1973.

———. "Structure, Sign, and Play in the Discourse of the Human Sciences." In *Writing and Difference*, translated by Alan Bass, 278–94. Chicago: University of Chicago Press, 1978.

Descartes, René. "Optics." In *Discourse on Method*, translated by Paul J. Olscamp, 63–173. Indianapolis: Bobbs-Merrill, 1965.

Dilthey, Wilhelm. *Gesammelte Schriften*. Stuttgart: Teubner, 1964.

Donahue, Neil H. *Forms of Disruption: Abstraction in Modern German Prose*. Ann Arbor: University of Michigan Press, 1993.

Dreyfus, Hubert L., ed. *Husserl, Intentionality, and Cognitive Science*. Cambridge: Massachusetts Institute of Technology Press, 1982.

Elsaesser, Thomas, ed. *Early Cinema: Space, Frame, Narrative*. London: British Film Institute, 1990.

Engelhardt, Hartmut. *Der Versuch, Wirklich zu Sein. Zu Rilke's Sachlichem Sagen*. Frankfurt: Suhrkamp, 1973.

Fechner, Gustav Theodor. *Elements of Psychophysics*. Edited by David H. Howes. Translated by Helmut E. Adler. New York: Holt, 1966.

———. *Zend-Avesta oder über die Dinge des Himmels und des Jenseits*. Leipzig: n.p., 1851.

Fick, Monika. *Sinnenwelt und Weltseele. Der Psychophysische Monismus in der Literatur der Jahrhundertwende*. Tübingen: Niemeyer, 1993.
Fiedler, Konrad. *Schriften zur Kunst*. 2 vols. Edited by Max Imdahl et al. München: Fink, 1971.
Føllesdal, Dagfinn. "Brentano and Husserl on Intentional Objects and Perception." In *Husserl, Intentionality, and Cognitive Science*, edited by Hubert L. Dreyfus, 31–41. Cambridge: Massachusetts Institute of Technology Press, 1982.
Foster, Hal, ed. *Vision and Visuality*. Seattle: Bay Press, 1988.
Foucault, Michel. *The Birth of the Clinic*. New York: Vintage, 1994.
———. *The Order of Things: An Archaeology of the Human Sciences*. New York: Vintage, 1970.
———. "The Subject and Power." In *Michel Foucault: Beyond Structuralism and Hermeneutics*, edited by Robert L. Dreyfus and Paul Rabinow, 208–26. Chicago: University of Chicago Press, 1983.
Frank, Manfred. *Einführung in die Frühromantische Ästhetik: Vorlesungen*. Frankfurt: Suhrkamp, 1989.
———. *Das Individuelle Allgemeine*. Frankfurt: Suhrkamp, 1977.
———. *Das Sagbare und das Unsagbare. Studien zur deutsch-französischen Hermeneutik und Texttheorie*. Frankfurt: Suhrkamp, 1989.
———. *Was ist Neostrukturalismus?* Frankfurt: Suhrkamp, 1983.
Freud, Sigmund. *Gesammelte Werke*. 23 vols. Edited by Anna Freud. Frankfurt: Fischer, 1961.
———. "Hemmung, Sympton, Angst." Vol. 14 of *Gesammelte Werke*, 111–205.
———. "Das Ich und das Es." Vol. 3 of *Studienausgabe*, edited by Alexander Mitscherlich et al., 275–330. Frankfurt: Fischer, 1975.
———. "Jenseits des Lustprinzips." Vol. 13 of *Gesammelte Werke*, 1–69.
Gadamer, Hans Georg. *Gesammelte Werke*. 10 vols. Tübingen: Mohr, 1985–94.
———. *Poetica*. Frankfurt: Insel, 1977.
Galileo Galilei. "The Assayer." In *Discoveries and Opinions of Galileo*, translated by Stillman Drake. New York: Anchor, 1957.
Gebhard, Walter. *Der Zusammenhang der Dinge. Weltgleichnis und Naturverklärung im Totalitätsbewußtsein des 19. Jahrhunderts*. Tübingen: Niemeyer, 1984.
George, Stefan. *Briefwechsel zwischen George und Hofmannsthal*. Edited by Robert Boehringer. München: Küpper, 1953.
———. *Werke*. 2 vols. Stuttgart: Klett-Cotta, 1984.
———. *The Works of Stefan George*. Translated by Olga Marx and Ernst Morwitz. 2nd, rev. ed. Chapel Hill: University of North Carolina Press, 1974.
Gombrich, E. H. *Art and Illusion: A Study in the Psychology of Pictorial Representation*. Princeton: Princeton University Press, 1960.
Greber, Erica. "Ikonen, entikonisierte Zeichen." *Poetica* 29, 1/2 (1997): 158–97.
Grimm, Reinhold. "Von der Armut und vom Regen: Rilke's 'Antwort auf die

soziale Frage.'" In *Gedichte und Interpretationen*, edited by Harald Hartung, 101–7. Stuttgart: Reclam, 1983.

Gumbrecht, Hans-Ulrich. "A Farewell to Interpretation." In *Materialities of Communication*, edited by Hans-Ulrich Gumbrecht and K. Ludwig Pfeiffer, 389–402. Stanford: Stanford University Press, 1994.

———. *In 1926: Living at the Edge of Time*. Cambridge: Harvard University Press, 1997.

———. *Making Sense in Life and Literature*. Translated by Wlad Godzich. Minneapolis: University of Minnesota Press, 1992.

Gumbrecht, Hans-Ulrich, and K. Ludwig Pfeiffer, eds. *Materialities of Communication*. Translated by William Whobrey. Stanford: Stanford University Press, 1994.

———. *Schrift*. München: Fink, 1993.

———. *Stil. Geschichten und Funktionen eines kulturwissenschaftlichen Diskurselements*. Frankfurt: Suhrkamp, 1986.

Gundolf, Friedrich. *George*. Berlin: Bondi, 1921.

Gunning, Tom. "An Aesthetics of Astonishment: Early Film and the (In)Credulous Spectator." *Art and Text* 34 (1989): 34–45.

———. "The Cinema of Attractions: Early Film, Its Spectator and the Avant-Garde." In *Early Cinema: Space, Frame, Narrative*, edited by Thomas Elsaesser, 56–62. London: British Film Institute, 1990.

Hake, Sabine. *Cinema's Third Machine: Writing on Film in Germany 1907–1933*. Lincoln: University of Nebraska Press, 1993.

Hamburger, Käte. "Die phänomenologische Struktur der Dichtung Rilke's." In *Rilke in neuer Sicht*, edited by Käte Hamburger, 83–158. Stuttgart: Kohlhammer, 1971.

Hamburger, Michael. *Hugo von Hofmannsthal. Zwei Studien*. Göttingen: Sachse, 1964.

Heffernan, James A. W. "Ekphrasis and Representation." *New Literary History* 22 (Spring 1991): 297–316.

Heidegger, Martin. "Andenken." Vol. 4 of *Gesamtausgabe*, 79–151.

———. *Einführung in die Metaphysik*. Tübingen: Niemeyer, 1998.

———. *Gesamtausgabe*. 65 vols. Edited by Friedrich-Wilhelm von Hermann. Frankfurt: Klostermann, 1981.

———. *Holzwege*. Edited by Friedrich-Wilhelm von Hermann. Frankfurt: Klostermann, 1994.

———. *Identität und Differenz*. Pfullingen: Neske, 1957.

———. *Introduction to Metaphysics*. Translated by Gregory Fried and Richard Polt. New Haven: Yale University Press, 2000.

———. *On the Way to Language*. Translated by Peter D. Hertz. New York: Harper, 1971.

———. *Parmenides*. Vol. 54 of *Gesamtausgabe*.

---. *Poetry, Language, Thought.* Translated by Albert Hofstadter. New York: Harper, 1971.
---. *Sein und Zeit.* Tübingen: Niemeyer, 1986.
---. *Unterwegs zur Sprache.* Stuttgart: Neske, 1959.
Helmholtz, Hermann von. "The Facts of Perception." In *Selected Writings,* 366–408.
---. "Recent Progress in the Theory of Vision." In *Selected Writings,* 144–222.
---. *Selected Writings of Hermann von Helmholtz.* Edited by Russell Kahl. Middletown, Conn.: Wesleyan University Press, 1971.
Hofmannsthal, Hugo von. "Ein Brief." *Erzählungen und Erfundene Gespräche.* Vol. 7 of *Gesammelte Werke,* 461–72.
---. *Gesammelte Werke.* 10 vols. Edited by Bernd Schoeller. Frankfurt: Fischer, 1979.
---. *The Lord Chandos Letter.* Translated by Russell Stockman. Marlboro, Vt.: Marlboro Press, 1986.
---. *The Lyrical Poems of Hugo von Hofmannsthal.* Translated by Charles Wharton Stork. New Haven: Yale University Press, 1918.
Horkheimer, Max, and Theodor W. Adorno. *Dialektik der Aufklärung.* Frankfurt: Fischer, 1985.
Husserl, Edmund. *Cartesianische Meditationen und Pariser Vorträge.* Vol. 1 of *Husserliana. Gesammelte Werke.*
---. *The Crisis of European Sciences and Transcendental Phenomenology.* Translated by David Carr. Evanston: Northwestern University Press, 1970.
---. *Husserliana. Gesammelte Werke.* Edited by H. L. van Breda. The Hague: Nijhoff, 1958–.
---. *The Idea of Phenomenology.* Translated by William P. Alston and George Nakhnikian. Dordrecht: Kluwer, 1990.
---. *Die Idee der Phänomenologie. Fünf Vorlesungen.* Vol. 2 of *Husserliana. Gesammelte Werke.*
---. *Ideen zu einer Reinen Phänomenologie und Phänomenologischen Philosophie.* Vols. 3 and 4 of *Husserliana. Gesammelte Werke.*
---. *Die Krisis der Europäischen Wissenschaften und die Tranzendentale Phänomenologie.* Vol. 6 of *Husserliana. Gesammelte Werke.*
---. *Logische Untersuchungen.* Vols. 18 and 19 of *Husserliana. Gesammelte Werke.*
---. *Die Phänomenologie des Inneren Zeitbewußtseins.* Vol. 10 of *Husserliana. Gesammelte Werke.*
Huyssen, Andreas. "Paris/Childhood: The Fragmented Body in Rilke's Notebooks of Malte Laurids Brigge." In *Modernity and the Text: Revisions of German Modernism,* edited by Andreas Huyssen and David Bathrick, 113–41. New York: Columbia University Press, 1989.

Jameson, Fredric. *The Political Unconscious: Narrative as a Socially Symbolic Act.* Ithaca, N.Y.: Cornell University Press, 1981.

———. *Postmodernism, or, The Cultural Logic of Late Capitalism.* Durham: Duke University Press, 1991.

———. "Reification and Utopia in Mass Culture." In *Signatures of the Visible,* 9–34. New York: Routledge, 1992.

Jay, Martin. *Adorno.* Cambridge: Harvard University Press, 1984.

———. *Downcast Eyes: The Denigration of Vision in Twentieth-Century French Thought.* Berkeley: University of California Press, 1993.

———. "Scopic Regimes of Modernity." In *Vision and Visuality,* edited by Hal Foster, 3–28. Seattle: Bay Press, 1988.

Jens, Walter. *Statt einer Literaturgeschichte.* Pfullingen: Neske, 1957.

Kaes, Anton. "The Debate about Cinema: Charting a Controversy (1909–1929)." *New German Critique* 40 (Winter 1987): 7–33.

———, ed. *Kino-Debatte. Texte zum Verhältnis von Literatur und Film 1909–1929.* Tübingen: Niemeyer, 1978.

Kämpfer, Wolfgang. "Wort-Macht oder Macht-Wort? Überlegungen zu Stefan George heute." *Recherches Germaniques* 15 (1985): 123–31.

Kittler, Friedrich. *Discourse Networks 1800/1900.* Translated by Michael Metteer. Stanford: Stanford University Press, 1990.

———. *Grammophon, Film, Typewriter.* Berlin: Brinkmann, 1986.

Klages, Ludwig. *Stefan George.* Berlin: G. Bondi, 1902.

Kluncker, Karlheinz. *Über Stefan George und seinen Kreis.* Bonn: Bouvier, 1985.

Koch, Hans-Albrecht. *Hugo von Hofmannsthal.* Darmstadt: Wissenschaftliche Buchgesellschaft, 1989.

Köhnen, Ralph. *Sehen als Textstruktur. Intermediale Beziehungen zwischen Rilke und Cézanne.* Bielefeld: Aisthesis, 1995.

Kracauer, Siegfried. "Kult der Zerstreuung." In *Das Ornament der Masse,* 311–20.

———. *Das Ornament der Masse.* Frankfurt: Suhrkamp, 1977.

———. "Die Photographie." In *Das Ornament der Masse,* 21–39.

Krell, David Farrell. *Daimon Life: Heidegger and Life-Philosophy.* Bloomington: Indiana University Press, 1992.

Krieger, Murray. *The Play and Place of Criticism.* Baltimore: Johns Hopkins Press, 1967.

Lacan, Jacques. *Écrits: A Selection.* Translated by Alan Sheridan. New York: Norton, 1977.

———. *The Four Fundamental Concepts of Psychoanalysis.* Translated by Alan Sheridan. New York: Norton, 1978.

Lacoue-Labarthe, Philippe. *Typography: Mimesis, Philosophy, Politics.* Edited and translated by Christopher Fynsk. Stanford: Stanford University Press, 1998.

Lacoue-Labarthe, Philippe, and Jean-Luc Nancy. *The Literary Absolute: The Theory of Literature in German Romanticism*. Translated by Philip Barnard and Cheryl Lester. Albany: State University of New York Press, 1988.
Landmann, Georg Peter. *Vorträge über Stefan George. Eine Biographische Einführung in sein Werk*. München: 1974.
———, ed. *Einleitungen und Merksprüche der Blätter für die Kunst*. Düsseldorf: Küpper, 1964.
Lauster, Martina. *Die Objektivität des Innenraums. Studien zur Lyrik Georges, Hofmannsthals und Rilkes*. Stuttgart: Heinz, 1982.
Le Rider, Jacques. *Hugo von Hofmannsthal. Historismus und Moderne in der Literatur der Jahrhundertwende*. Wien: Böhlau, 1997.
Levin, David Michael, ed. *Modernity and the Hegemony of Vision*. Berkeley: University of California Press, 1993.
———. *Sites of Vision: The Discursive Construction of Sight in the History of Philosophy*. Cambridge: Massachusetts Institute of Technology Press, 1997.
Lotze, Herrmann. *Microcosmus: An Essay Concerning Man and His Relations to the World*. Translated by Elizabeth Hamilton and E. E. Constance Jones. New York: Scribner, 1890.
Lowe, Donald M. *History of Bourgeois Perception*. Chicago: University of Chicago Press, 1982.
Luhmann, Niklas. *Art as a Social System*. Translated by Eva M. Knodt. Stanford: Stanford University Press, 2000.
———. *Beobachtungen der Moderne*. Opladen: Westdeutscher Verlag, 1992.
———. "Das Kunstwerk und die Selbstreproduktion der Kunst." In *Stil. Geschichten und Funktionen eines Kulturwissenschaftlichen Diskurselements*, edited by Hans Ulrich Gumbrecht und K. Ludwig Pfeiffer, 620–72. Frankfurt: Suhrkamp, 1986.
———. *Soziale Systeme. Grundriß einer Allgemeinen Theorie*. Frankfurt: Suhrkamp, 1987.
Lukács, Georg. *Von Nietzsche zu Hitler oder Der Irrationalismus und die Deutsche Politik*. Frankfurt: Fischer, 1966.
Lyotard, Jean-François. *The Postmodern Condition: A Report on Knowledge*. Translated by Geoff Bennington et al. Minneapolis: University of Minnesota Press, 1984.
Mach, Ernst. *The Analysis of Sensation*. Translated by C. M. Williams. Chicago: Open Court, 1914.
Mason, Eudo C. "Rilke und Stefan George." In *Rilke in neuer Sicht*, edited by Käte Hamburger, 9–37. Stuttgart: Kohlhammer, 1971.
Mast, Gerald, et al., eds. *Film Theory and Criticism*. 4th ed. New York: Oxford University Press, 1992.
Mattenklott, Gert. *Bilderdienst. Ästhetische Opposition bei Beardsley und George*. Frankfurt: Syndikat, 1985.

———. "Der synthetische Habitus. Bemerkungen zu Stefan George und seinem Kreis." In *Stefan George Colloquium*, edited by Ralph-Rainer Wuthenow et al., 33–47. Pisa: 1985.

Mauthner, Fritz. *Beiträge zu einer Kritik der Sprache*. 2 vols. Frankfurt: Ullstein, 1984.

McLuhan, Marshall. *Essential McLuhan*. Edited by Eric McLuhan et al. New York: Basic, 1995.

McNeill, William. *The Glance of the Eye: Heidegger, Aristotle, and the Ends of Theory*. Albany: State University of New York Press, 1999.

Merleau-Ponty, Maurice. "Cézanne's Doubt." In *The Merleau-Ponty Aesthetics Reader*, edited by Galen A. Johnson, 59–75. Evanston: Northwestern University Press, 1993.

———. "Eye and Mind." In *The Merleau-Ponty Aesthetics Reader*, edited by Galen A. Johnson, 121–49. Evanston: Northwestern University Press, 1993.

———. *The Visible and the Invisible*. Edited by Claude Lefort. Translated by Alphonso Lingis. Evanston: Northwestern University Press, 1968.

Metz, Christian. *Film Language: A Semiotics of the Cinema*. New York: Oxford University Press, 1974.

———. *The Imaginary Signifier: Psychoanalysis and the Cinema*. Bloomington: Indiana University Press, 1982.

———. *Language and Cinema*. The Hague: Mouton, 1974.

Meyer, Theodor A. *Das Stilgesetz der Poesie*. Darmstadt: Wissenschaftliche Buchgesellschaft, 1968.

Meyers, Herman. "Rilke's Cézanne Erlebnis." In *Zarte Empirie. Studien zur Literaturgeschichte*. Stuttgart: Metzler, 1963.

Michelfelder, Diane P., and Richard E. Palmer, eds. *Dialogue and Deconstruction: The Gadamer-Derrida Encounter*. Albany: State University of New York Press, 1989.

Miller, J. Hillis. "'Reading' Part of a Paragraph in *Allegories of Reading*." In *Reading De Man Reading*, edited by Lindsay Waters and Wlad Godzich, 155–70. Minneapolis: University of Minnesota Press, 1989.

Mörchen, Hermann. *Adorno und Heidegger: Untersuchungen einer philosophischen Kommunikationsverweigerung*. Stuttgart: Klett-Cotta, 1981.

Münsterberg, Hugo. *The Film: A Psychological Study*. New York: Dover, 1970.

Neumann, Gerhard. "'Kunst des Nicht-Lesens.' Hofmannsthal's Ästhetik des Flüchtigen." *Hofmannsthal Jahrbuch* 4 (1996): 227–60.

———. "Proverb in Versen oder Schöpfungsmysterium? Hofmannsthal's Einakter zwischen Sprach-Spiel und Augen-Blick." *Hofmannsthal Jahrbuch* 1 (1993): 183–234.

Nietzsche, Friedrich. *Werke*. 3 vols. Edited by Karl Schlechta. München: Hanser, 1969.

Okkultismus und Avantgarde. Von Munch bis Mondrian 1900–1915. Edited by Schirn Kunsthalle Frankfurt. Ostfildern: Edition Tertium, 1995.

Oksiloff, Assenka. "Archaic Modernism: Hofmannsthal's Cinematic Aesthetics." *Germanic Review* 73/1 (Winter 1998): 70–85.
Pestalozzi, Karl. *Sprachskepsis und Sprachmagie im Werk des Jungen Hofmannsthal.* Zürich: Atlantis, 1958.
———. "Wandlungen des erhöhten Augenblicks bei Hofmannsthal." In *Basler Hofmannsthal-Beiträge,* edited by Karl Pestalozzi and Martin Stern, 129–38. Würzburg: Königshausen & Neumann, 1991.
Por, Peter. *Die Orphische Figur: Zur Poetik von Rilkes 'Neuen Gedichten.'* Heidelberg: Winter, 1997.
Quine, Willard van Orman. *Theories and Things.* Cambridge: Harvard University Press, 1981.
———. *Word and Object.* Cambridge: Massachusetts Institute of Technology Press, 1960.
Rainer Maria Rilke–Andreas Lou Salome: Briefwechsel. Edited by Ernst Pfeiffer. Insel: Frankfurt, 1975.
Rasch, Wolfdietrich. *Die Literarische Décadence um 1900.* München: Beck, 1986.
Riedel, Wolfgang. *Homo Natura. Literarische Anthropologie um 1900.* Berlin: De Gruyter, 1996.
Rilke, Rainer Maria. *Briefe aus Muzot 1921–1926.* Edited by Ruth Sieber-Rilke and Carl Sieber. Leipzig: Insel, 1935.
———. *Briefe über Cézanne.* Edited by Clara Rilke. Wiesbaden: Insel, 1952.
———. *Letters on Cézanne.* Edited by Clara Rilke. Translated by Joel Agee. New York: Fromm International, 1985.
———. *New Poems.* Translated by J. B. Leishman. New York: Hogarth Press, 1964.
———. *Werke.* 6 vols. Edited by Ruth-Sieber Rilke. Frankfurt: Insel, 1987.
Risser, James, ed. *Heidegger toward the Turn.* Albany: State University of New York Press, 1999.
Rorty, Richard. *Philosophy and the Mirror of Nature.* Princeton: Princeton University Press, 1979.
Rutsch, Bettina. *Leiblichkeit der Sprache, Sprachlichkeit des Leibes. Wort, Gebärde, Tanz bei Hugo von Hofmannsthal.* Frankfurt: Lang, 1998.
Ryan, Judith. *Umschlag und Verwandlung. Poetische Struktur und Dichtungstheorie in R. M. Rilkes Lyrik der Mittleren Periode (1907–1914).* München: Winkler, 1972.
Ryan, Lawrence. "Rilke's Dinggedichte: The 'Thing' as 'Poem in Itself.'" In *Rilke-Rezeptionen—Rilke Reconsidered,* edited by Sigrid Bauschinger and Susan L. Cocalis, 27–36. Tübingen: Francke, 1995.
Safranski, Rüdiger. *Martin Heidegger: Between Good and Evil.* Translated by Ewald Osers. Cambridge: Harvard University Press, 1998.
Schivelbusch, Wolfgang. *The Railway Journey: The Industrialization of Time and Space in the Nineteenth Century.* Berkeley: University of California Press, 1986.

Schnädelbach, Herbert. *Die Philosophie in Deutschland. 1831–1933.* Frankfurt: Suhrkamp, 1983.

Schwarz, Anette. "The Colors of Prose: Rilke's Program of Sachliches Sagen." *Germanic Review* 71/3 (Summer 1996): 195–210.

Simmel, Georg. "The Metropolis and Mental Life." In *The Sociology of Georg Simmel*, edited by Kurt Wolff and translated by H. H. Gerth. New York: Free Press, 1950.

Smith, Barry, and David Woodruff Smith, eds. *The Cambridge Companion to Husserl.* Cambridge: Cambridge University Press, 1995.

Sokal, Walter H. "'Zwischen Existenz und Weltinnenraum: Zum Prozeß der Ent-Ichung in Malte Laurids Brigge." In *Zu Rainer Maria Rilke*, edited by Egon Schwarz, 90–108. Stuttgart: Klett, 1983.

Sontag, Susan. "The Aesthetics of Silence." In *A Susan Sontag Reader*, 181–204. New York: Vintage, 1983.

———. "Against Interpretation." In *A Susan Sontag Reader*, 95–104. New York: Vintage, 1983.

———. "Fascinating Fascism." In *Under the Sign of Saturn.* New York: Farrar, 1976.

Stefan George. *Bilder und Bücher aus dem Nachlass.* 2 vols. Edited by Stefan-George-Gymnasium Bingen. Heidelberg: Lothar Stiehm Verlag, 1973 and 1987.

Steiner, Uwe C. *Die Zeit der Schrift: Die Krise der Schrift und die Vergänglichkeit der Gleichnisse bei Hofmannsthal und Rilke.* München: Fink, 1996.

Szondi, Peter. *Das lyrische Drama des Fin de Siècle.* Edited by Henriette Beese. Frankfurt: Suhrkamp, 1975.

Vattimo, Gianni. *Beyond Interpretation: The Meaning of Hermeneutics for Philosophy.* Translated by David Webb. Stanford: Stanford University Press, 1997.

———. *The End of Modernity.* Translated by Jon R. Snyder. Baltimore: Johns Hopkins University Press, 1988.

Weber, Samuel. *Mass Mediauras: Forms, Technics, Media.* Edited by Alan Cholodenko. Stanford: Stanford University Press, 1996.

Wellbery, David. "The Exteriority of Writing." *Stanford Literature Review* 9 (1): 11–24.

———. "Foreword." In *Discourse Networks 1800/1900*, by Friedrich Kittler, vii–xxxiii. Stanford: Stanford University Press, 1990.

———. *The Specular Moment: Goethe's Early Lyric and the Beginnings of Romanticism.* Stanford: Stanford University Press, 1996.

———."Zur Poetik der Figuration beim mittleren Rilke: 'Die Gazelle.'" In *Zu Rainer Maria Rilke*, edited by Egon Schwarz, 125–32. Stuttgart: Klett, 1983.

West, Nancy M. "Camera Fiends: Early Photography, Death, and the Supernatural." *Centennial Review* 40/1 (Winter 1996): 171–206.

Wiethölter, Waltraud. *Hofmannsthal oder die Geometrie des Subjekts.*

Psychostrukturelle und Ikonographische Studien zum Prosawerk. Tübingen: Niemeyer, 1990.

Willems, Gottfried. *Anschaulichkeit. Zu Theorie und Geschichte der Wort-Bild-Beziehungen und des literarischen Darstellungsstils.* Tübingen: Niemeyer, 1989.

Williams, Eric B. *The Mirror and the Word: Modernism, Literary Theory, and Georg Trakl.* Lincoln: University of Nebraska Press, 1993.

Williams, Forrest. "Cézanne, Phenomenology, and Merleau-Ponty." In *The Merleau-Ponty Aesthetics Reader: Philosophy and Painting,* edited by Galen A. Johnson and Michael B. Smith, 165–73. Evanston: Northwestern University Press, 1993.

Winthrop-Young, Geoffrey, and Michael Wutz. Translators' introduction to *Gramophone, Film, Typewriter,* by Friedrich A. Kittler. Stanford: Stanford University Press, 1999.

Wittgenstein, Ludwig. *Tractatus Logico-philosophicus.* Vol. 1 of *Werkausgabe.* Frankfurt: Suhrkamp, 1984.

Wolfskehl, Karl. "Stefan George." *Pan* (1898): 231–35.

Wolters, Friedrich. "Gestalt." *Jahrbuch für die geistige Bewegung* 2 (1911): 137–58.

———. *Stefan George und die Blätter für die Kunst. Deutsche Geistesgeschichte seit 1890.* Berlin: G. Bondi, 1930.

Wunberg, Gotthard. *Der Frühe Hofmannsthal. Schizophrenie als dichterische Struktur.* Stuttgart: Kohlhammer, 1965.

———. "Unverständlichkeit. Historismus und literarische Moderne." *Hofmannsthal Jahrbuch* 1 (1993): 309–52.

Ziolkowski, Theodor. "James Joyce Epiphanie und die Überwindung der empirischen Welt in der modernen deutschen Prosa." *Deutsche Vierteljahresschrift* 35 (1961): 594–616.

Zumthor, Paul. *Oral Poetry: An Introduction.* Translated by Kathryn Murphy-Judy. Minneapolis: University of Minnesota Press, 1990.

INDEX

Adorno, Theodor W., 1, 12, 22–23, 39, 68, 81; academic popularism and, 4; Aestheticist poetry and, 23, 171; *Aesthetic Theory*, 22–23, 131, 171, 203–4, 271, 278 (n. 9), 292 (n. 7); *Augenblick* (magic) and, 278 (n. 18); Beckett and, 132; Benjamin and, 132–33; "Charmed Language," 272; cinema and, 39; definition of art, 4, 22; *Dialectics of Enlightenment*, 271; "Die Kunst und die Künste," 271; George and, 243, 255; German modernist poetry and, 165; German Romanticism and, 165; goal of language for, 263–64; Heidegger and, 1, 23, 262–63; Husserl critique of, 82; Huyssen on, 276 (n. 7); *Jahr der Seele* (George) and, 264–65; "Jargon of Authenticity" and, 131; Kafka and, 132, 145; Marxism and, 131, 205; *Negative Dialektik*, 1, 130, 270–71; *New Poems* (Rilke) and, 204; phenomenology and, 81–82; *Philosophy of New Music*, 132; Proust and, 132; Rilke and, 203–5; rise of fascism and, 286–87 (n. 30); role of capitalism for, 129–30, 151; role of image for, 271; role of language for, 151–52, 263, 270–71; role of poetry for, 148, 255; Romantic subjectivity and, 267–68; "Vorfrühling" (Hofmannsthal) and, 156

Adorno und Heidegger (Mörchen), 287 (n. 31)

Aestheticist poetry, 1, 3, 5–7, 10–11, 23, 25–26, 30; Adorno on, 23; Braungart on, 143; deconstructive criticism of, 3, 5, 7; *Der Stern des Bundes* (George) and, 254; *élan vital* in, 95; emergence of, 7; George and, 1; German modernism and, 168; German Romanticism and, 42, 103, 109, 127, 133; hermeneutic method in, 139, 166; Hofmannsthal and, 1, 95; Husserl and, 95; *Introduction to Metaphysics* (Heidegger) and, 68, 172–73, 269–70, 286 (n. 26); "language-crisis" and, 11; *l'art pour l'art* movement and, 138; literary goals of, 10–11; Lukács on, 25; mediations on, 1, 6; Nietzsche and, 102; political dimensions of, 24; Rilke and, 1, 239; role of language in, 23, 151, 161–62; role of punctuation in, 30; "speaking gaze" in, 101; subjectivism in, 172; "the look of things" in, 26; "Vorfrühling" (Hofmannsthal) and, 161–62

Aesthetic Theory / Ästhetische Theorie (Adorno), 22–23, 131, 171, 203–4, 271, 278 (n. 9), 292 (n. 7)

"Against Interpretation" (Sontag), 107

Agamben, Giorgio, 8–9, 98, 128, 146–47, 174, 230; *End of the Poem*, 147, 285 (n. 13); "Gazelle Dorcas" (Rilke) and, 231; *l'art pour l'art* movement and, 150; *Potentialities*,

174, 231; role of language for, 9; *Stanzas*, 152; Valéry and, 146–47; Zumthor and, 146
"Aletheia" (concealment and revelation), 20, 123, 129
"Algabal" (George), 240
Allegories of Reading (de Man), 22, 112, 200
Althusser, Louis, 118–19
Analyse der Empfindungen (Mach), 56, 57
Andrian, Leopold von, 290 (n. 16)
"Archaïscher Torso Apollos" (Rilke), 27
Arnheim, Rudolf, 273
Art as a Social System (Luhmann), 121
Asendorf, Christoph, 56
Aufschreibesysteme (Kittler), 107, 118
Augenblick (magic), 173, 176; Adorno on, 278 (n. 18); Hofmannsthal on, 173; *Lord Chandos Letter* (Hofmannsthal) and, 181
Austin, Gerhard, 291 (n. 23)

Bacon, Francis, 183
Barthes, Roland, 42, 273; *Camera Lucida*, 85, 149–50; "Death of the Author," 137; *Image, Music, Text*, 128; Mallarmé and, 150; still photography and, 86; *Writing Degree Zero*, 42, 150
Baudrillard, Jean, 38
Baudry, Jean-Louis, 176; *Cahiers du Cinéma* and, 65; Metz and, 289–90 (n. 14)
Beckett, Samuel, 132
Being and Nothingness (Sartre), 276 (n. 14)
Being and Time / Sein und Zeit (Heidegger), 21, 113, 169, 286 (n. 28)
Bell, Jeffrey, 85–86
Benjamin, Walter, 29, 107, 147; Adorno critique of, 132–33, 267; cinema and, 39; messianic ideals of, 24, 148; modern technology and, 255–56; *Origin of German Tragic Drama*, 2, 147; "Rückblick auf Stefan George" and, 255; "speaking gaze" and, 47
Benn, Gottfried, 233, 240, 294 (n. 6)
Benzmann, Hans, 212
Bergson, Henri, 68, 70–71, 86–95, 175, 281–82 (n. 27); cinema and, 87–89; *Creative Evolution*, 86; élan vital and, 41, 90; Hofmannsthal and, 100–101; Institut Général Psychologique and, 58; *Introduction to Metaphysics*, 68, 172–73, 269–70, 286 (n. 26); life philosophy of, 71; Lukács and, 282 (n. 31); *Matter and Memory*, 56, 86; metaphysics and, 89–90; role of ego for, 91; role of intuition for, 90; role of language for, 71, 91–92, 283 (n. 33)
Beyond Interpretation (Vattimo), 114, 126
Bilderdienst (Mattenklott), 243
Birth of the Clinic (Foucault), 44–45
Birth of Tragedy (Nietzsche), 28, 63
Blätter für die Kunst (George), 25, 240–41, 247–48, 249 (ill.); Frankenstein and, 157; George and, 240; levels of "reality" within, 237; role of punctuation in, 248; "Vorfrühling" (Hofmannsthal) and, 157
Blumenberg, Hans, 38, 43
Borchardt, Rudolf, 288 (n. 1), 290 (n. 15)
Bragaglia, Anton Guilio, 37–38
Braungart, Georg, 143, 291 (n. 22)
Braungart, Wolfgang, 241
Brecht, Bertolt, 294 (n. 9)
Brinkmann, Richard, 177
Buch der Bilder (Rilke), 216
Bürger, Peter, 138, 275 (n. 6), 287 (n. 2)

Cahiers du Cinéma, 65
Calhoon, Kenneth S., 277 (n. 4)
California School, 83–85
Cambridge Companion to Husserl, 73
Camera Lucida (Barthes), 85, 149–50
Camera obscura, 48, 50
Capitalism, 129–30, 151
Castle, Terry, 58
Cézanne, Paul, 27–28, 60; *Letters about Cézanne* (Rilke) and, 199; Merleau-Ponty and, 218; *New Poems* (Rilke) and, 28; Rilke and, 198–99, 210–11; *Still Life with Curtain and Flowered Pitcher*, 216, 217 (ill.); Williams and, 216
"Cézanne's Doubt" (Merleau-Ponty), 213
"Charmed Language" (Adorno), 272
Cinema: Adorno and, 39; Benjamin and, 39; Calhoon on, 277 (n. 4); commodification of art and, 40; early importance of, 35–36, 65; Heidegger on, 269; Kracauer on, 38; "language-crisis" as a result of, 40–41, 64–65; *L'Arrivée d'un train à la Ciotat* (Lumière), 35, 37; *Life to Those Shadows* (Burch) and, 279 (n. 23); Magritte and, 39; media criticism and, 39; Pinthus and, 39; Schivelbusch on, 277 (n. 8); visual arts and, 38; Weimar School of, 268–69
Cinema and Spectatorship (Mayne), 279 (n. 22)
Comolli, Jean-Louis, 65, 276 (n. 2)
"Conversation about Poetry" (Hofmannsthal), 267
Crary, Jonathan, "speaking gaze" and, 50; *Techniques of the Observer*, 57
Creative Evolution (Bergson), 86, 90
Critique of Pure Reason (Kant), 51
Crossing Borders: Reception Theory, Poststructuralism, Deconstruction (Holub), 285 (n. 15)
Curie, Marie, 58
Curie, Pierre, 58

Darstellung (presentation), 2
Das Buch der Bilder (Rilke), 193, 194
Dasein, 203; "being" and, 125–26, 172; definition of, 125; Heidegger on, 125, 130, 248
Das Kinobuch (Pinthus), 277–78
"Das Kleine Welttheater" (Hofmannsthal), 290–91 (n. 18)
Das Neue Reich (George), 252–53
"Das Wort" (George), 130, 256–58, 261–62, 268
Daviau, Donald G., 178, 290 (n. 16)
David, Claude, 294 (n. 6)
"Death of the Author" (Barthes), 137, 170
Deleuze, Gilles, 90, 93, 282 (n. 28)
De Man, Paul, 22; *Allegories of Reading*, 112; "New Criticism" and, 113; *Resistance to Theory*, 112; Rilke and, 200; role of language for, 64, 152
"Der Blinde" (Rilke), 232
"Der Dichter und diese Zeit" (Hofmannsthal), 283 (n. 37)
"Der Ersatz für die Träume" (Hofmannsthal), 175
Der Frühe Hofmannsthal (Wunberg), 173
"Der Goldne Topf" (Hoffmann), 108
"Der Leser" (Rilke), 229
Derrida, Jacques: Frank and, 113; Gadamer and, 109–10, 113; Heidegger and, 8; hermeneutic method and, 112; Husserl and, 45, 73; *Margins of Philosophy*, 187; metaphysics and, 73; *Of Grammatology*, 113; phenomenology and, 80; "speaking gaze" and, 45, 101; *Speech and Phenomena*, 45; Vattimo and,

113–14; visual perception and, 45; Zumthor and, 146
Der Spiegel, 144–45
Der Stern des Bundes (George), 253–54
"Der Teppich" (George), 244, 246–47, 266
Der Teppich des Lebens (George), 14–19, 15–17 (ills.), 242–43, 247; Gundolf on, 245; punctuation and structure of, 18–20; "Urlandschaft" in, 243–44
Descartes, René, 44, 49, 210
Dialectics (Schleiermacher), 110
Dialectics of Enlightenment (Adorno), 271
"Die Kunst und die Künste" (Adorno), 271
Dilthey, Wilhelm, 111
"Dingkult" (Rilke), 203, 205, 268
Discourse Networks (Kittler), 46, 109, 116, 137
Donahue, Neil H., 187–89
Dreyfus, Hubert, 83–84, 280 (n. 10)
Duino Elegies (Rilke), 240
Durchsieht (looking through), 63

"Eine Monographie" (Hofmannsthal), 167, 169
"Eine Sibylle" (Rilke), 219–20
"Eingang" (Rilke), 190–96, 194, 213; *Das Buch der Bilder* and, 193; main themes in, 193–94; role of language in, 194–96; *Weltinnenraum* in, 196
Einleitungen (Landmann), 250
"Ein Prophet" (Rilke), 219
"Ein Wort" (George), 22, 23, 25
Ekphrasis, 59–60
Élan vital (vital impetus), 90–92, 187, 191, 210; Bergson and, 41, 99; definition of, 90; Hofmannsthal and, 99; *Stundenbuch* (Rilke) and, 191
Empiricism, 50, 74

End of the Poem (Agamben), 147, 285 (n. 13)
"Epochenverwandtschaft," 137

"Facts of Perception" (Helmholtz), 50
"Farewell to Interpretation" (Gumbrecht), 107, 111
Fechner, Gustav Theodor, 54–55
Fiedler, Konrad, 69, 175; "Origin of Artistic Production," 206
Føllesdal, Dagfinn, 83–84
Foucault, Michel, 124; *Birth of the Clinic,* 44–45; New Historicism and, 119; *Order of Things,* 137–38; "speaking gaze" and, 44
Four Fundamental Concepts of Psychoanalysis (Lacan), 100, 276 (n. 14)
Frank, Manfred, 110–11
Frankenstein, Clemens, 157
Frege, Gottlob, 76
French Impressionism, 66
Freud, Sigmund, 56–57, 131, 186
"Früher Apollo" (Rilke): interpretation of, 62–64; *New Poems* (Rilke) and, 61

Gadamer, Hans-Georg, 8, 31, 109, 113, 147
Galileo, 10, 43
Gare Montparnasse, 128; *L'Arrivée d'un train à la Ciotat* (Lumière) and, 35; *Le Figaro* and, 35; train accident at, 35, 36 (ill.), 39, 70
Gates of Hell (Rodin), 213, 214 (ill.), 215 (ill.)
"Gazelle Dorcas" (Rilke), 225–28, 231–32, 257; alliteration in, 227; Benn on, 233; phenomenology in, 227–28; role of language in, 227, 231; role of photography in, 235; role of punctuation in, 231; Ryan on, 233; structure of, 227; Wellbery on, 228; *Weltinnenraum* in, 247

Gebärdensprache (Wundt), 175
George, Stefan, 22, 28, 53, 129, 235, 251 (ill.); Adorno on, 243, 255; Aestheticist poetry of, 1; "Algabal," 240; Benn on, 240, 294 (n. 6); *Blätter für die Kunst*, 25, 157, 240–41, 247–48, 249 (ill.); Brecht on, 294 (n. 9); *Das Neue Reich*, 252–53; "Das Wort," 30, 256–58; David and, 294 (n. 6); *Der Stern des Bundes*, 253–54; "Der Teppich," 244, 246; *Der Teppich des Lebens*, 14–19, 15–17 (ills.); "Ein Wort," 22; German nationalism of, 246, 294 (n. 9); Gestalt and, 30, 60, 140; "Gestalt" (Wolters) and, 238; Heidegger and, 255, 258–59; Hofmannsthal and, 239; *Hymnen*, 294 (n. 6); *Jahr der Seele*, 253, 264–65; Kämpfer on, 243; Landmann on, 240; Mann on, 294 (n. 3); Mattenklott on, 243; messianic ideals of, 240, 242; *On the Way to Language* (Heidegger) and, 258; Rilke and, 250; "Rückblick auf Stefan George" (Benjamin) and, 255–56; Salomé and, 243; *Technik*, 241; "Urlandschaft," 243–46; "Vorfrühling" (Hofmannsthal) and, 156; Wolters on, 248; "Zaubersprüche," 266
German literary idealism, 12
German modernist poetry: Adorno critique of, 165; epistemological philosophy of, 2; George and, 2; Hofmannsthal and, 2; importance of language in, 26; literary criticism of, 165; Rilke and, 2, 28, 197; role of punctuation in, 153; "speaking gaze" in, 101–2
German nationalism: George and, 246, 294 (n. 9)
German Romanticism, 8, 12, 68; Adorno and, 165; Aestheticist poetry and, 42, 72, 103; Hofmannsthal and, 169; Rilke and, 196; "Vorfrühling" (Hofmannsthal) and, 161; Wellbery on, 140
"Gespräch über Gedichte" (Hofmannsthal), 96, 99
"Gestalt" (Wolters), 238
Gestalt theory, 13, 28, 30, 84; George and, 30, 60, 248
Geviert (Heidegger), 18
Goethe, Johann Wolfgang von, 194
Gogh, Vincent van, 218
Gombrich, E. H., 46
Goodman, Nelson, 38
Grammophon, Film, Typewriter (Kittler), 37
Greber, Erica, 224
Grimm, Reinhold, 205
Gumbrecht, Hans Ulrich: "Farewell to Interpretation," 107, 111; *Making Sense in Life and Literature*, 273; New Historicism and, 119
Gundolf, Friedrich: "Algabal" (George) and, 240; *Der Teppich des Lebens* (George) and, 245; George and, 240, 267; Hofmannsthal and, 275 (n. 5); *Jahr der Seele* (George) and, 265
Gunning, Tom, 277 (n. 3)
Gurwitsch, Anton, 83–84

Hake, Sabine, 39
Hamburger, Käte, 195, 223–24, 275 (n. 5), 293 (n. 11)
Hamburger, Michael, 156
Handwerk (Rilke), 241
Heffernan, A. W., 59
Heidegger, Martin, 29; Adorno and, 1, 23, 262–63; "aletheia" (concealment and revelation) and, 20, 123, 259; *Being and Time*, 21, 113, 169, 286 (n. 28); Catholicism and, 145; cinema and, 268–69; *Dasein* and,

125–26; definition of art for, 260; George and, 255, 258–59; *Geviert*, 18; goal of language for, 8–9, 21, 263–64, 270; hermeneutics and, 113, 147; *Introduction to Metaphysics*, 68, 172–73, 269–70, 286 (n. 26); "Jargon of Authenticity," 8, 131, 262; "Letter about Humanism," 260; metaphysical redemption and, 145; National Socialist Party and, 131; *On the Way to Laguage*, 20–21, 170, 258; "Origin of the Work of Art," 260; Plato and, 269; Rilke and, 202–3; rise of fascism and, 286–87 (n. 30); role of language for, 151; role of poetry for, 129, 148, 255; Safranski and, 145, 287 (n. 31); "Time of the World-Picture," 269–70; Wolters and, 248, 260

Heinrich (Novalis), 168

Helmholtz, Hermann von, 50–53, 68

Hermeneutic method, 139, 147; *Being and Time* (Heidegger) and, 113; Braungart on, 143; definition of, 111; de Man on, 112; Derrida on, 112; Dilthey on, 111; Frank on, 110; Hamburger and, 223; Heidegger on, 113; Kittler on, 108, 115; literary criticism and, 124; Luhmann on, 122–23; role of language in, 127; Sontag on, 107; "Vorfrühling" (Hofmannsthal) and, 161; Wellbery on, 108–9; *Weltinnenraum* in, 196; Wunberg on, 116

Hoffmann, E. T. A., 108

Hofmannsthal, Hugo von, 18, 28, 60, 67, 96–100, 129; Aestheticist poetry of, 1, 95, 239; *Augenblick* (magic) and, 173, 241; Bergson and, 100–101; Brinkmann on, 177; cinematic interests of, 12; "Conversation about Poetry," 267; Daviau and, 290 (n. 16); "Der Dichter und diese Zeit," 283 (n. 37); "Der Ersatz für die Träume," 175; early works of, 148–49; "Eine Monographie," 167; *élan vital* and, 99; George and, 239; German Romanticism and, 169; "Gespräch über Gedichte," 96; Habsburg monarchy and, 239; Hamburger on, 275 (n. 5); Jens on, 177; *Leiblichkeit der Sprache, Sprachlichkeit des Leibes* and, 289 (n. 8); le Rider and, 290 (n. 16); literary criticism of, 163; *Lord Chandos Letter*, 139, 141, 168, 176–79, 180–86, 188–89; Mitterwurzer and, 167, 169; Müller-Seidel on, 275 (n. 5); role of language for, 166, 252; Szondi on, 275 (n. 5); "Vorfrühling," 153

Holub, Robert, 285 (n. 15)

Husserl, Edmund, 7, 29, 53; Derrida and, 45; Hamburger on, 293 (n. 11); *Idea of Phenomenology*, 45, 73–74; *Ideas for a Pure Phenomenology and Phenomenological Philosophy* and, 70, 74, 75–82, 97; "intellectual intuition" and, 79; "intuitive evidence" and, 79; *Krisis*, 49; *Logical Investigations* and, 70, 75; "noemas" (intentional objects) and, 82; "noeses" (intentional acts) and, 82; role of language for, 71–72, 81; role of phenomenology for, 74, 205–6, 222–23, 293 (n. 11); *Schauen* (intuition) and, 78; "speaking gaze" and, 45, 74, 224; *Speech and Phenomena* (Derrida) and, 279 (n. 2)

Huyssen, Andreas, 4, 276 (n. 7)

Hymnen (George), 294 (n. 6)

Iconology: Image, Text, Ideology (Mitchell), 278 (n. 10)

Idea of Phenomenology / Idee der

Phänomenologie (Husserl), 45, 73–74
Ideas for a Pure Phenomenology and Phenomenological Philosophy / Ideen zu einer Reinen Phänomenologie und Phänomenologischen Philosophie (Husserl), 70, 74, 75–82, 97
"Ideologiekritik," 118
Image, Music, Text (Barthes), 128
Imaginary Signifier (Metz), 30
Institut Général Psychologique, 58
"Intellectual evidence," 79–80
Introduction to Metaphysics / Einführung in die Metaphysik (Heidegger), 68, 172–73, 269–70, 286 (n. 26)
"Intuitive evidence," 79–80

Jahr der Seele (George), 253, 264–65
Jameson, Fredric, 3, 4, 6, 8
"Jargon of Authenticity" (Heidegger), 8, 131, 262, 295 (n. 12)
Jay, Martin, 48
Jens, Walter, 177

Kämpfer, Wolfgang, 243
Kaes, Anton, 39–40, 67
Kafka, Franz, 132, 145
Kant, Immanuel, 49; *Critique of Pure Reason*, 51–52, 89
Kino-Debatte, 39–40
Kittler, Friedrich, 37, 39, 70, 186; *Aufschreibesysteme*, 107, 118; "Der Goldne Topf" (Hoffmann) and, 108; *Discourse Networks*, 46, 139; hermeneutic method and, 108, 115, 117, 126; "look of things" and, 140; *Lord Chandos Letter* (Hofmannsthal) and, 186; McLuhan and, 140; "media transposition" and, 46; Rilke and, 100; Romantic ideal and, 137; visual media and, 39; Wunberg and, 116

Klages, Ludwig, 241, 265, 266
Kracauer, Siegfried, 38
Krisis (Husserl), 49

Lacan, Jacques, 29, 38; *Four Fundamental Concepts of Psychoanalysis*, 100, 142, 276 (n. 14); role of language for, 170
Landmann, Edith, 240
"Language-crisis," 9–10, 40–42, 116, 174, 206; Aestheticist poetry and, 11; *Lord Chandos Letter* (Hofmannsthal) and, 177; cinema and, 40, 64–65; definition of, 40; German modernism and, 10; Helmholtz and, 52; literary criticism during, 69
Laokoon (Lessing), 46
L'Arrivée d'un train à la Ciotat (Lumière): 35, 37, 277–78 (n. 9)
L'art pour l'art movement, 27, 122, 138, 150
Lebensphilosophie (life philosophy), 71
"Lebensreform" movement, 175
Lechter, Melchior, 18
Le Figaro, 35, 37
Le Rider, Jacques, 178, 290 (n. 16)
Lessing, Gotthold Ephraim, 46
"Letter about Humanism" (Heidegger), 260
Letters about Cézanne (Rilke), 199, 218
Levin, David Michael, 47
Life of an American Fireman (Potter), 65
Life to Those Shadows (Burch), 279 (n. 23)
"Live words," 67
Logical Investigations / Logische Untersuchungen (Husserl), 70, 76–78
Lord Chandos Letter / "Ein Brief"

(Hofmannsthal), 139, 141, 168, 176–78, 180–86, 188–89; *Augenblick* (magic) in, 181; Bacon, Francis and, 183; Braungart on, 291 (n. 22); Daviau critique of, 178; Donahue on, 187; Kittler and, 186; "language-crisis" and, 177, 185; le Rider critique of, 178, 290 (n. 16); literary criticism of, 168, 177–79, 181–86, 188; *Margins of Philosophy* (Derrida) and, 187; role of language in, 179, 184; "Sprach-Spiel" in, 181; "Vorfrühling" (Hofmannsthal) and, 180, 187; Wiethölter, 185
Lotze, Hermann, 55, 57
Luhmann, Niklas, 35, 119–21, 124
Lukács, Georg, 25, 131–32, 282 (n. 31)
Lumière, Auguste-Marie-Louis-Nicolas and Louis-Jean, 118, 277 (n. 4); artistic importance of, 37; *L'Arrivée d'un train à la Ciotat*, 35, 39, 277 (n. 3)
Lyotard, Jean-François, 1

Mach, Ernst, 56–57
Magritte, René, 39
Making Sense in Life and Literature (Gumbrecht), 273
Mallarmé, Stéphane, 137, 150, 170
Mann, Thomas, 294 (n. 3)
Marcuse, Herbert, 132
Margins of Philosophy (Derrida), 187
Martin Heidegger: Between Good and Evil (Safranski), 287 (n. 31)
Marxism: Adorno and, 131; Althusser and, 118; *Aufschreibesysteme* and, 118; autonomy of art within, 6
Mattenklott, Gert, 243
Matter and Memory (Bergson), 56, 86, 88, 281–82 (n. 27)
Mauthner, Fritz, 67, 170
Mayne, Judith, 279 (n. 22)

McLuhan, Marshall, 140
Merleau-Ponty, Maurice, 29, 213, 218; *Visible and the Invisible*, 276 (n. 14)
Metz, Christian: Baudry and, 289–90 (n. 14); *Cahiers du Cinéma* and, 65; *Imaginary Signifier*, 31, 176
Meyers, Herman, 201
Microcosmus (Lotze), 55
Mitchell, W. J. T., 46, 59; *Iconology: Image, Text, Ideology*, 278 (n. 10)
Mitterwurzer, Friedrich, 167, 169
Modernism and Poetic Tradition (Ryan), 276 (n. 9)
Modersohn, Otto, 212
Mörchen, Hermann, 287 (n. 31)
Müller, Johannes, 50
Müller-Seidel, Walter, 137, 275 (n. 5)
Murphy, Richard, 275 (n. 6), 287 (n. 2)

National Socialist Party, 131, 144
Nazism, 11
Negative Dialektik (Adorno), 1, 130, 271, 1
"New Criticism," 113
New Historicism, 119, 124, 126
New Poems / Neue Gedichte (Rilke), 27–28, 59–60, 198, 200–202, 212, 218, 221; Adorno and, 204; aesthetic creation in, 198; "Archaïscher Torso Apollos" in, 27; Cézanne and, 28; "Der Blinde" in, 232; ekphrasis and, 60; "Früher Apollo" in, 61; "Gazelle Dorcas" in, 226; literary criticism of, 200; phenomenology within, 222–23
Nietzsche, Friedrich, 28, 63–64, 102
"Noemas" (intentional object), 82, 83
"Noeses" (intentional acts), 82
Notebooks of Malte Laurids Brigge (Rilke), 207–10, 229; "Graf Brahe" in, 208–9
Novalis, 103, 194, 197; *Heinrich*, 168; "Zauberwort," 142

"Offenbarung" (Klages), 266
Of Grammatology (Derrida), 113
"On Sense and Reference" (Frege), 76
On the Way to Language / Unterwegs zu Sprache (Heidegger), 20–21, 170, 248, 258–59
Order of Things (Foucault), 137–38
"Origin and Interpretation of Our Sense Impressions" (Helmholtz), 53
"Origin of Artistic Production" (Fiedler), 206
Origin of German Tragic Drama / Ursprung des deutschen Trauerspiels (Benjamin), 2, 147
"Origin of the Work of Art" (Heidegger), 260–61

Paladino, Eusapia, 58
Perrin, Jean-Baptiste, 58
Phänomenologie der Gebärde (Austin), 291 (n. 23)
Phenomenology, 129; definition of, 73, 81; Husserl and, 73–74, 206; Rilke and, 206, 222; "speaking gaze" in, 73; Wellbery and, 224
Philosophical Discourse of Modernity (Habermas), 114
Philosophy of New Music (Adorno), 132
Pinthus, Kurt, 39, 277 (n. 9)
Plato, 269
Por, Peter, 200, 292 (n. 6)
Potentialities (Agamben), 174, 231
Potter, Edwin S., 65
Preuschen, Hermine von, 212
Proust, Marcel, 132
Psychophysics, 54
Punctuation: Aestheticist poetry and, 30; *Blätter für die Kunst* (George) and, 248; *Das Neue Reich* (George) and, 252; *Der Teppich des Lebens* (George) and, 18; "Gazelle Dorcas" (Rilke) and, 231
"Pure speech," 164

Quine, W. V., 7–8

Railway Journey (Schivelbusch), 277 (n. 8)
Rasch, Wolfdietrich, 42
"Recent Progress" (Helmholtz), 51
Resistance to Theory (de Man), 112, 152
Rilke, Rainer Maria, 1, 3, 13, 26–28, 53, 60, 129, 239; Adorno on, 203–5; Aestheticist poetry of, 1, 239; "Archaïscher Torso Apollos," 27; art criticism and, 211–12; Benn critique of, 233; Benzmann and, 212; Cézanne and, 28, 198–99, 210; *Das Buch der Bilder*, 193, 216; "Der Blinde," 232; "Der Leser," 229; "Dingkult," 203; *Duino Elegies*, 240; "Ein Prophet," 219; "Eine Sibylle," 219–20; "Eingang," 193; ekphrasis and, 60; "Früher Apollo," 61–62; "Gazelle Dorcas," 225–26; George and, 250; German modernism and, 197; Goethe and, 194; van Gogh and, 218; Grimm and, 205; Hamburger on, 195, 223, 293 (n. 11); *Handwerk*, 241; Heidegger on, 202–3; Kittler and, 100; *Letters about Cézanne*, 199; messianic ideals of, 239–40; Meyers on, 201; *New Poems*, 27–28, 59–60, 198, 200–202, 212; Nietzsche and, 64; *Notebooks of Malte Laurids Brigge*, 207; Por on, 200, 292 (n. 6); Preuschen and, 212; Rodin and, 197–98, 210, 213; role of language for, 26, 67, 222; Judith Ryan and, 201; Lawrence Ryan on, 200; Schwarz on, 211; *Selected Poems*, 279 (n. 20); *Stundenbuch*, 190–91; technological interests of, 13; "thing-poems" of, 3, 200; visual perception and, 228; Wellbery on,

223; *Weltinnenraum* and, 144, 189; *Zwischenräume der Zeit*, 47
Rodin, Auguste, 28, 60; *Gates of Hell*, 213, 214 (ill.), 215 (ill.); Rilke and, 197–98, 213
Rousseau, Jean-Jacques, 22
"Rückblick auf Stefan George" (Benjamin), 255–56
Ruskin, John, 66
Ryan, Judith, 224; *Modernism and Poetic Tradition*, 276 (n. 9); Por and, 292 (n. 6); Rilke and, 201; "thing-poems" and, 201–2
Ryan, Lawrence, 200

Safranski, Rüdiger, 145, 287 (n. 31)
Salomé, Lou-Andreas, 250
Sartre, Jean Paul, 276 (n. 14)
Saussure, Ferdinand de, 76
Schauen (intuition), 78–79
Schiller, Johann Friedrich, 38
Schivelbusch, Wolfgang, 277 (n. 8)
Schleiermacher, Friedrich, 110
Schwarz, Anette, 211
Sehen lernen (learning to see), 53
Selected Poems (Rilke), 279 (n. 20)
Simmel, Georg, 56
Sites of Vision (Levin), 47
Six, Jan, 212
Sontag, Susan, 107, 148
"Speaking gaze," 44–45, 75, 164, 224
Specular Moment (Wellbery), 111, 141
Speech and Phenomena (Derrida), 45, 80, 279 (n. 2)
Spirit photography, 58–59
Stanzas (Agamben), 152
Sternbald (Eichendorff), 168
Still Life with Curtain and Flowered Pitcher (Cézanne), 216, 217 (ill.), 218
Stundenbuch (Rilke), 190–91, 196, 213, 292 (n. 11)
Szondi, Peter, 275 (n. 5)

Technik (George), 241
Techniques of the Observer (Crary), 57
Theories and Things (Quine), 8
Theorizing the Avant-Garde: Modernism, Expressionism, and the Problem of Postmodernity (Murphy), 275 (n. 6)
Theory of the Avant-Garde (Bürger), 138
Theosophic Society, 58
"Thing-poems," 3, 200–202, 235
"Time of the World-Picture" (Heidegger), 270

Unbinding Vision (Crary), 50
"Urlandschaft" (George), 243–44; "Der Teppich" and, 244, 246; description of, 244–45; German nationalism in, 246; role of language in, 245; structure of, 246

Valéry, Paul, 146–47
Vattimo, Gianni, 8, 113–14, 126
Vaughn, Dai, 277 (n. 3)
Visible and the Invisible (Merleau-Ponty), 276 (n. 14)
Visual arts: Blumenberg and, 38; *Discourse Networks* (Kittler) and, 46–47; importance of cinema for, 37–38; media criticism and, 39; role of language in, 38
"Vorfrühling" (Hofmannsthal), 153–60, 171, 180; Adorno on, 156; Aestheticist poetry and, 161–62; *Blätter für die Kunst* (George) and, 157; George on, 156; German Romanticism and, 161; Hamburger on, 156; hermeneutic method and, 161; interpretation of, 160–61; literary criticism of, 163; *Lord Chandos Letter* (Hofmannsthal) and, 180, 187; "pure speech" in, 164; rhythmic structure of, 157–60; role of lan-

guage in, 161; role of speech in, 166; "speaking gaze" within, 164
Wellbery, David, 110, 123; *Aufschreibe-systeme* and, 107; de Man and, 113; "Gazelle Dorcas" (Rilke) and, 228; German Romanticism and, 140; "Ideologiekritik" and, 118; Kittler and, 107; literary criticism of, 223; phenomenology and, 223–24; Rilke and, 223; *Specular Moment*, 111 *Weltinnenraum*: Rilke and, 144, 189, 196, 213, 223, 231; hermeneutic method and, 196
West, Nancy, 58–59
Wiethölter, Waltraud, 185
Williams, Eric B., 42
Williams, Forrest, 216
Will to Power (Nietzsche), 102
Wittgenstein, Ludwig, 56
Wolters, Friedrich, 238, 248, 260, 261–62
Writing Degree Zero (Barthes), 42
Wunberg, Gotthard, 116, 173
Wundt, Wilhelm, 50, 175

"Zaubersprüche" (George), 266
"Zauberwort" (Novalis), 142, 197
Zumthor, Paul, 146–47, 151
Zwischenräume der Zeit (Rilke), 47